# How to Start, Finance
# and Operate
# YOUR OWN BUSINESS

# How to Start, Finance and Operate YOUR OWN BUSINESS

by James L. Silvester

*Foreword by Senator Paul Trible*

Lyle Stuart Inc.     Secaucus, New Jersey

Published by Lyle Stuart, Inc.
120 Enterprise Ave., Secaucus, N.J. 07094
Published simultaneously in Canada by
Musson Book Company,
A division of General Publishing Co. Limited
Don Mills, Ontario

Address queries regarding rights and permissions
to Lyle Stuart, Inc., 120 Enterprise Ave.,
Secaucus, N.J. 07094

Manufactured in the United States of America

**Library of Congress Cataloging in Publication Data**

Silvester, James L.
    How to start, finance, and operate your own business.

    1. New business enterprises.   I. Title.
HD62.5.S56   1984        658.1′1       84-50
ISBN 0-8184-0347-0

# FOREWORD

Do you want to start your own business?

Then you need the information this book can provide. As someone who participates daily in the representative process which is the hallmark of our national government, I am keenly aware of the limits to what government can do. While we can in some cases encourage, and in other cases provide information, and in certain limited cases direct action, we cannot create.

Only you can do that. I fervently hope you do. We all know that it is so-called "small businesses" which create jobs, which provide services, which strengthen communities, which are a critical element of the mysterious condition called "prosperity."

Yet I think we need to go a step beyond the phrase "small business" and think in terms of a particular type of small business—what I would call "Infant Business." The moment an idea moves from the dream stage in your mind to the planning stage, then I think you are an infant business. Now the challenge is to bring you forth into a productive small business.

James Silvester gives you the tools to help move you from being an infant business to a small business. In our society, each of us has the opportunity to create a small business. If you've picked up this book, you no doubt have the motivation. This book will help provide the third element you need—the knowledge to do so.

The combination of the opportunity our society provides and your motivation and knowledge will be what determines if our nation prospers. As George Gilder said about the processes of our economy:

> This is a drama most essentially not of measurable money and machines, aggregates and distributions, but of mind and morale. Above the vast architecture of production, and surrounding it, is a statistically invisible

atmosphere of moods and ideas, a phantasmagoria of images and visions of the future, which either admit, or eclipse, the sustaining light and power of the sun: the life-giving faith in the possibility that free enterprises can prevail among the unpredictable forms of wealth in the unknown world to come.

Paul Trible
*United States Senator from Virginia*

# PREFACE

This book is designed as a guide for those individuals seeking to be in business for themselves and those existing enterprises searching for new opportunities. Chapter I specifically deals with people who have not yet started their own businesses. It attempts to convey to prospective entrepreneurs the characteristics needed to be successfully self-employed.

Chapter II shows how an individual or existing firm may evaluate business opportunities so as to avoid potentially dangerous mistakes commonly made because sufficient analysis is lacking.

Chapter III deals with different sources of managerial assistance available to the small business community.

Chapter IV explains the importance of proper legal structure in fulfilling the objectives of owners and managers.

The nature of business funding arrangements in different situations is described in Chapter V. It also outlines the use of capital relative to the profit-making function and shows how to determine funding needs.

Chapter VI specifically reviews the nature of business funding and the various types of capital involved. In addition, traditional and non-traditional financial outlets are broadly described.

The details concerning the construction of the "all important" business plan is discussed in Chapter VII. An inadequate plan will be rejected without question. There are standards that must be considered.

Chapter VIII reviews the particulars in dealing with funding sources. Producing an excellent business plan isn't enough. The plan must be presented verbally in a confident and convincing manner keeping in mind that hard give-and-take negotiations will occur.

Chapter IX explains the need for sound management practices when operating a business in today's tough environment. Certain managerial techniques are identified and reviewed.

Chapter X explains some of the important elements to consider when starting and funding a service, retail, wholesale, or manufacturing business.

The book ends with chapter XI, which magnifies the sources listed in chapter VI by homing in on specific government programs directed at small firms and the individual investment preferences of many private funding outlets.

NOTE: Neither the author nor the publisher will be held liable for any transactions with any person, proprietorship, partnership, corporation, or association listed in this book. It is believed that all names, addresses, and telephone numbers listed in this book are accurate as of the time of printing, although no guarantee can or will be made.

# ACKNOWLEDGMENTS

I dedicate this book to my wife, children, mother, sister, and deceased father. Without their support and encouragement, this project would not have been possible.

Acknowledgment must also be given to all those fine students and friends who helped in gathering the pertinent information contained herein.

*Research Directors:*
Roy Carper III
Lara Davis
Fredrick Koerner
Steven Orndoff
Leslie Watada
Elizabeth Wray

*Typist*
Janet Heishman
Diana Rytter

*Researchers:*
Gary Bageant
Kay Balcer
Pam Bell
Terry Bennett
Elaine Dawkins
Marjorie Edmondson
William Eyles
Cecelia Farland

Carol Frederiksen
James Freeman
Brad Funkhouser
Anne Goldstein
Tania Gomez
Robert Greatorex
Peggy Hess
Valerie Hubbard
Laura Johnson
Daphne Manuel
Shawn Martin
Carl Myers
Rosalia Petrosino
Eleni Peyser
Shirley Prosser
Sue Robinson
Myrna Shirley
Judith Slaughter
Karl Witsberger
Karin Zeek

# CONTENTS

# INTRODUCTION

## A New Emphasis

It's a relief to note that a large contingent of public and private economists, academicians, and journalists are currently acknowledging the vital role of small businesses in the total economy. Many of these experts believe that government should do more to foster small business vitality and growth. In fact, some call it our economic salvation. Recently, a futurist (trend analyst) appeared on the ABC late night television show "The Last Word" and proclaimed that small business entrepreneurs will lead us back to economic prosperity in the 80's. There is reason to believe this is true.

Recent studies conducted by major universities, think tanks, congressional committees, and the U.S. Small Business Administration have revealed that most of the economic growth over the last ten years can be traced to the small business community. The same studies concluded that small firms are accountable for about 50 percent of the country's output and most of the growth in employment over the same period. To illustrate this point, one can turn to a research study conducted by MIT Professor David Birch which concluded that between 1969 and 1976, approximately 82 percent of all the new jobs created in the U.S. were the result of small business activity. To top all this off is the fact that most new innovations over the last century have originated in the research departments of small businesses or by individual entrepreneurs. These facts have given reason to call the small business sector, which comprises nearly 95 percent of all private firms in the country, the "vital majority."

For too many years small firms were looked upon as an insignificant part of our economic life and largely ignored by representative governments. A decade ago the catchword was "Big Is Better" and much of the country's tax policies and resources were shifted in favor of giant corporations at the expense of small businesses and prospective entrepreneurs. Society has paid the price of this approach. It is safe to say that a strong correlation exists between the nation's emphasis on large corporate organizations and its general economic decline. Without a doubt, many giant firms are stagnate and drifting without focus or resolve. Most cannot compete in the international marketplace and are severe drags on the U.S. economy

Many of these large concerns are attempting to maintain the status quo against enlightened politicians who would emphasize free trade and shift the country's resources, either wholly or partially, back to the more productive small business sector. If they are successful in their lobbying efforts and reverse this new direction, it would condemn the United States to continued economic stagnation and compromise our standing as a world leader. In addition, it must never be forgotten that American political freedoms are directly linked to the survival of the entrepreneur as a vital force in society.

James L. Silvester
Shenandoah College
School of Business Administration
Winchester, Virginia 22601

Chapter I

# ARE YOU THE TYPE
## It's Important to Know

### The New Wave

The 1980's have been called the "Decade of the Entrepreneur" for good reason. Despite severe economic conditions and the highest level of business failure since the Great Depression, more people are pursuing self-employment than at any time in our country's history, as evidenced in Table 1. Self-satisfaction, desire for independence, limited job opportunities, and layoffs seem to be the main reasons why individuals are seeking to be their own bosses.

### Know Your Limitations

The lure of self-employment should be tempered with a keen sense of reality and facts. Most new businesses fail within the first three years of operation, according to numerous studies conducted by private groups and the Small Business Administration. Researchers have concluded that most of these failures were due to poor business practices on the part of the entrepreneur. In addition, the studies found that many individuals seeking the self-employment option are not cut out for the task. Some people think they can beat the odds by buying an established business that has been in operation for some time or by purchasing a franchise. True, it will increase your chances somewhat in the beginning, but if you fail to use sound business techniques, and/or lack the necessary personality traits, then the possibility of success in any business endeavor is greatly diminished.

Whether you are starting a new business or buying an existing operation, you must ask yourself the following question which could reveal potential problem areas: Do I have what it takes? Most small businesses are risky at best, but your chances of success are improved if you realistically understand the difficulties involved and work out as many of them as you can before jumping in with both feet.

TABLE 1

NEW BUSINESS INCORPORATIONS

| 1965 | 203,897 | 1983 | 600,400 |
|------|---------|------|---------|
| 1966 | 200,010 | 1984 | 634,991 |
| 1967 | 206,569 | 1985 | 668,904 |
| 1968 | 233,635 | 1986 | 702,101 |
| 1969 | 274,267 | | |
| 1970 | 264,209 | | |
| 1971 | 287,577 | | |
| 1972 | 316,601 | | |
| 1973 | 329,358 | | |
| 1974 | 319,149 | | |
| 1975 | 326,345 | | |
| 1976 | 357,766 | | |
| 1977 | 436,170 | | |
| 1978 | 478,019 | | |
| 1979 | 524,565 | | |
| 1980 | 533,520 | | |
| 1981 | 581,661 | | |
| 1982 | 566,942 | | |

NOTE: These figures do not include new businesses that were started as sole proprietorships or partnerships. If they were, the numbers would exceed 1 million.

SOURCE: By permission of Dun & Bradstreet Credit Services, a company of The Dun & Bradstreet Corporation.

Studies by the U.S. Small Business Administration have concluded that most successful entrepreneurs display common characteristics. They are as follows:

## DRIVE
...Responsibility—ability to make sure things get done
...Persistence—willingness to see things finalized
...Health—having physical and mental stamina
...Initiative—ability to take charge when necessary and be the first to act
...Vigor—having the limitless vitality needed to succeed

## THINKING ABILITY

...Originality—ability to create new ideas and approaches

...Creativity—ability to think and explore in unorthodox ways; also initiative

...Critical Sense—ability to make intelligent comparison and comment

...Analytical Sense—ability to reason in practical, theoretical and abstract terms

## HUMAN RELATIONS ABILITY

...Sociability—ability to get along with others, including peers, in a number of settings (home, work, politics, international relations, etc.)

...Cooperation—willingness to work with others in a constructive manner

...Tactfulness—ability to hold or water-down discomforting comments or actions

...Cheerfulness—willingness to laugh and smile even when the going gets rough

...Consideration—ability to appreciate the value of other people's time and money

...Personal Relations—ability to get along with people who are close

...Ascendency—ability to govern and control wisely without excessive ego involvement

...Emotional Stability—having appropriate maturity level for the task

...Cautiousness—ability to give serious evaluation before taking risk; successful entrepreneurs avoid gambling, they are moderate risk takers

## COMMUNICATIONS ABILITY

...Oral Communications—ability to speak in a clear, concise, and logical manner

...Verbal Comprehension—ability to listen, absorb, and understand others' conversation

...Written Communication—ability to write in a clear, concise, and logical way

## TECHNICAL KNOWLEDGE

...The information a manager possesses about the physical process of producing the goods or services.

...The ability to use the information in a useful manner.

If it can be determined that you possess most of the above-mentioned traits or can acquire them if deficiencies exist, then your chance of success in a small business is greatly enhanced. In your comparison, try to avoid overly optimistic estimates of yourself. Be candid about your personality traits and abilities. It is better to learn now that you are not suited for self-employment before investing time, money, and hard work in something that is doomed to fail from the beginning. Economic and emotional scares can be avoided if you heed the warning signals.

Additional insight into self-evaluation can be gained by answering the questions in Table 2. Again, honest appraisal is called for to insure accuracy in defining yourself. Remember, you are risking your time and hard-earned dollars.

If most of the checks are on the left-hand side of the table, then your chances of small business success are reasonable. Make sure that these positive answers were not a result of wishful thinking. Checks found in the center or on the right-hand side of the table should be carefully examined to determine if these weaknesses can be overcome. Perhaps, in the short term, you should hire associates and/or consultants whose strong points compensate your weak areas. Many of your weak traits can probably be corrected through education and training. But that is a long-term consideration. If you are weak in too many areas, it is in your best interest not to pursue self-employment any further.

TABLE 2

RATING SCALE FOR PERSONAL TRAITS IMPORTANT TO A BUSINESS PROPRIETOR

INSTRUCTIONS: After each question place a check mark on the line at the point closest to your answer. The check mark need not be placed directly over one of the suggested answers because your rating may lie somewhere between two answers. Be honest with yourself.

ARE YOU A SELF-STARTER? _____

| I do things my own way. Nobody needs to tell me to get going. | If someone gets me started, I keep going all right. | Easy does it. I don't put myself out until I have to. |

HOW DO YOU FEEL ABOUT OTHER PEOPLE? _____

| I like people. I can get along with just about anybody. | I have plenty of friends. I don't need anyone else. | Most people bug me. |

CAN YOU LEAD OTHERS? _____

| I can get most people to go along without much difficulty. | I can get people to do things if I drive them. | I let someone else get things moving. |

CAN YOU TAKE RESPONSIBILITY? _____

| I like to take charge of and see things through. | I'll take over if I have to, but I'd rather let someone else be responsible. | There's always some eager beaver around wanting to show off. I say let him. |

HOW GOOD AN ORGANIZER ARE YOU? _____

| I like to have a plan before I start. I'm usually the one to get things lined up. | I do all right unless things get too goofed up. Then I cop out. | I just take things as they come. |

HOW GOOD A WORKER ARE YOU? _____

| I can keep going as long as necessary. I don't mind working hard. | I'll work hard for a while, but when I've had enough, that's it! | I can't see that hard work gets you anywhere. |

CAN YOU MAKE DECISIONS? _____

| I can make up my mind in a hurry if necessary, and my decision is usually o.k. | I can if I have plenty of time. If I have to make up my mind fast, I usually regret it. | I don't like to be the one who decides things. I'd probably blow it. |

CAN PEOPLE TRUST WHAT YOU SAY? _____

| They sure can. I don't say things I don't mean. | I try to be on the level, but sometimes I just say what's easiest. | What's the sweat if the other fellow doesn't know the difference. |

CAN YOU STICK WITH IT? _____

| If I make up my mind to do something, I don't let anything stop me. | I usually finish what I start. | If a job doesn't go right, I turn off. Why beat your brains out? |

HOW GOOD IS YOUR HEALTH? _____

| I never run down. | I have enough energy for most things I want to do. | I run out of juice sooner than most of my friends seem to. |

SOURCE: U.S. Small Business Administration.

## Unorthodox Characteristics

A. David Silver, a noted venture capitalist and author, who manages a venture capital firm in New Mexico, contends in his new book, *The Entrepreneurial Life: How to Go for It and Get It* (John Wiley and Sons, New York), that many successful entrepreneurs experience a number of common difficulties in early life that may account for their later achievements. These difficulties include "educational arrest, lack of social interaction or motivation, sickly in nature, less wealth than peers, and small physical build." In addition, Silver suggests that venture capitalists prefer adult entrepreneurs who suffer from "guilt," especially the kind of guilt derived from "divorce." They feel it is a highly "motivating" factor. Also, individuals experiencing guilt in their "marriages" are considered good prospects. Silver also implied in an April 19, 1978, article published by the periodical *Chicago Business*, that successful entrepreneurs tended to be dominated by "achievement oriented mothers" and have "extraordinary sex drives."

It should not be implied that the aforementioned characteristics are necessary in order to be successful in your own business. It is obvious that many people have made a go of their businesses without having a single characteristic mentioned in this section. What should be remembered is that some who have made it through self-employment had experienced stumbling blocks in earlier years, thereby providing a foundation to face the difficult choices encountered in starting and managing a business.

In addition, keep in mind that Mr. Silver was referring to venture capitalists, who tend to be a unique breed unlike other funding sources. These financiers pursue people and opportunities quite different from the typical Joe or Jane running the average small business. Generally, venture capitalists will invest only in firms and entrepreneurs that are geared for fast growth. They want to make big bucks and feel it takes a certain type of individual to accomplish this task. Chapter VI provides more discussion about venture capitalists.

## Not All Peaches and Cream

Once it is determined that you possess most of the necessary traits to run a small business and can deal with deficiencies that exist, you must consider the pros and cons of self employment before committing time and energy beyond this point. There are some distinct negative aspects of running your own business. They are highlighted below:

— Constantly Changing Buying Motives of Potential Customers—Rapid inflation and disinflation, compressed economic cycles, unanticipated trends, etc., can have a significant impact on a small firm.

— Number of Business Failures—The failure rate for small businesses is at an all-time high, obviously reflecting the current severity of the recession.

— Possibility of Losing Money—Where you find potential reward the possibility of risk is always present. An individual can lose a considerable amount of money if the business is a losing proposition and he fails to bail out in time to cut large losses.

— Psychological Damage—Business failure can produce negative psychological effects that may haunt someone for a long time to come. Some will completely avoid a second try at self-employment.

— Long Hours—Contrary to popular belief, most successful entrepreneurs put in 12-hour days. Most work as hard as corporate executives.

— Medium Income—Successful small business people make, on the average, about the same as a mid-level manager in a large corporation.

— Income Variation—Income derived from your own business will be less regular than the receipt of a salary or wage from an employer. If you are starting a new business, the first six to twelve months might be bad because the operation is normally functioning at a loss. Even after business income is generated, variations in profits can be expected because of many factors (seasonal business, slow accounts receivables, heavy inventories, etc.).

Keep in mind that where you find disadvantages in any situation, positive aspects will also surface. In keeping with this notion, below are listed the advantages in pursuing self-employment.

— Independence—Self-employment provides a degree of personal and economic freedom not found when working for somebody else.

— Economic Security—Many individuals feel that economic security can be gained through self-employment. Given the high level of employee cutbacks in large and medium-sized firms, sometimes self-employment becomes the only alternative. Some see it as insulation against future layoffs. Consequently, many business executives and hourly workers are seriously pursuing small business opportunities. Many are already running sideline businesses hoping to someday generate a full-time operation.

— Potential Profit—Where you find the potential for risk, profit opportunities also exist.

— Quality of Life—Many individuals find a high degree of fulfillment in self-employment. Some successful entrepreneurs have reported an enhanced self-image and positive attitude along with other psychological rewards.

— Good Economic Environment—With the recession almost over and economic expansion underway, it is an ideal time to be starting a small business. This is even more true of service enterprises which comprise most of the nation's small firms. The service field is expected to be the fastest growing sector of the economy.

— Consumer and Business Confidence Is Up—Buyers and sellers are very positive about the country's economic prospects at this point. If it continues, economic growth will follow suit.

— Lower Inflationary Expectation—For the time being, inflation is under control and that is a positive note to investors, managers, and consumers. High inflation erodes confidence in the economy and recession normally follows in order to correct spiraling prices.

— New Emphasis on Small Firms—As mentioned in the introduction, governments are starting to realize the importance of the small business sector to the whole economy. Consequently, more governmental resources and favorable tax legislation will be directed to the small business community. Someday in the near future the entrepreneur will be seen, not as an enemy to be wiped out, but as our economic salvation.

Chapter II

# EVALUATING BUSINESS OPPORTUNITIES
## Protection Against Disaster

### Take Time and Investigate

When seeking to start a business or buy an existing operation, investigation and analysis should be given high priority. It is surprising to note the many well-intentioned opportunity seekers, both individuals and companies pursuing expansion, who fail to properly examine prospective investment possibilities. The consequence of this inadequate investigation is generally financial hardship. In some cases, horror would be a better term to use.

Many reasons can be given for the lack of proper evaluation before jumping in with both feet. The primary ones are quite obvious. Lack of knowledge to conduct proper investigation and analysis and/or the inability to pay for professional help to do the necessary work tend to be cited as the major stumbling blocks. Impulsiveness and lack of patience are also dangerous motivations that can stymie adequate examination. Inappropriate or insufficient investigation will lead to predictable circumstances that include but are not limited to the following situations:

— underestimation of capital needs
— overestimation of market potentials
— underestimation of competition
— inappropriate location
— acquisition of obsolete equipment

— acquisition of unanticipated business debts and claims
— questionable business reputation that may take years to correct

Spend the time to investigate and analyze all possible aspects of a business proposition. Failure to do so could result in financial disaster, not to mention the negative psychological effects that can leave an individual or organization scared for a long time to come.

## Which Way to Go

What business opportunity should I pursue? This is a question generally answered before you know your suitability for self-employment. It is something that should be carefully examined up to the very minute before committing yourself to any course of action.

A good starting point would be an evaluation of your experience and background. This would include your education, employment history, and hobbies. Compare your achievements with what you like to do. The more knowledge and experience you possess that can be used in operating a business, the greater are your chances of success.

So it is wise to pick a field that you know something about. Make sure you like operating in that area. Dislike and lack of enthusiasm for the business you choose will probably lead to failure. You might consider working for another small business, in your area of interest, in order to learn the ropes.

Your road to business ownership can lead in four directions, each having unique pros and cons. One can purchase a firm already in business or start from scratch. Acquiring a franchise is another possibility, which incorporates the features of a start-up and existing operation. For example, when purchasing a franchise you are basically paying for the right to market an already established product or service owned by somebody else (the franchisor). Under your franchise agreement, you (the franchisee) will be expected to market the product/service successfully. The fourth road to ownership is limited to a few individuals. Someday you might be lucky enough to inherit a business. Since this possibility is remote for most people, its advantages and disadvantages will not be discussed.

## Purchasing an Existing Operation

There are positive factors to consider in buying an existing business. Occasionally a going concern may be available at a bargain price because the owner is anxious to sell. Investigation by you and your attorney or accountant should determine the owner's exact reasons for selling. Even though the price seems low, other factors might make the deal a costly endeavor.

Buying an existing operation reduces the time and cost associated with establishing a new business. Your customer base is already established and much of the leg work associated with starting out is already completed. In addition, the previous owner might convey some helpful tips and experiences in operating the business, thereby reducing the time involved in the learning process. You might consider hiring the former owner full or part time. The most important advantage in buying an existing firm is longevity. Simply put, the longer a business has been around, the greater are its chances for continuance. Research has concluded that a business surviving past ten years stands a good possibility of being around for a long time. Table 3 illustrates this fact.

TABLE 3

AGE OF BUSINESS FAILURE

| Age In Years | Percentage Of Total Failures |
|---|---|
| Five Years Or Less | 49.1 |
| Six To Ten Years | 30.7 |
| Over Ten Years | 20.2 |

SOURCE: "The Business Failure Record." By permission of Dun & Bradstreet Credit Services, a company of The Dun & Bradstreet Corporation.

Where you find positive aspects in a given situation, negative ones will also surface. Buying an existing operation can provide pitfalls to potential entrepreneurs. You may pay too much for the business because of inflated estimates of worth. Current inventories and accounts receivables (customer accounts) may be dated. The firm's equipment might be in poor condition but overstated in value for selling purposes. Customer relations (goodwill) might be in bad shape and the firm's present location may not be the best. Refer to Table 4 for causes of business failure.

Your lawyer and accountant should assist you in identifying negative conditions that may exist before purchasing an existing enterprise. Conducting an independent financial audit by a CPA of your choice should be mandatory. After the audit is completed, ask the CPA to analyze the financial statements carefully. In addition, request that the

TABLE 4

| Apparent Causes 1981 | Percent | Manu-facturers | Whole-salers | Retail-ers | Con-struction | Com-mercial Ser-vices | All |
|---|---|---|---|---|---|---|---|
| NEGLECT Due to.......... | Bad Habits | 0.1 | 0.4 | 0.1 | 0.2 | 0.1 | 0.2 |
| | Poor Health | 0.1 | 0.4 | 0.2 | 0.2 | 0.2 | 0.2 |
| | Marital Difficulties | 0.1 | — | 0.1 | 0.1 | — | 0.1 |
| | Other | 0.1 | 0.1 | 0.3 | 0.1 | 0.1 | 0.2 |
| FRAUD On the part of the principals, reflected by......... | Misleading Name | — | 0.1 | 0.0 | — | 0.1 | 0.0 |
| | False Financial Statement | 0.1 | 0.3 | 0.1 | 0.0 | 0.1 | 0.1 |
| | Premediated Overbuy | 0.1 | 0.1 | 0.0 | — | — | 0.0 |
| | Irregular Disposal of Assets | 0.2 | 0.3 | 0.0 | 0.0 | 0.1 | 0.1 |
| | Other | — | — | 0.0 | 0.0 | 0.1 | 0.0 |
| LACK OF EXPERIENCE IN THE LINE | Inadequate Sales | 58.2 | 58.9 | 60.9 | 63.6 | 50.4 | 59.4 |
| LACK OF MANAGERIAL EXPERIENCE | Heavy Operating Expenses | 32.5 | 25.6 | 21.9 | 21.5 | 29.9 | 24.7 |
| | Receivables Difficulties | 11.9 | 12.1 | 2.4 | 9.1 | 5.0 | 6.4 |
| UNBALANCED EXPERIENCE | Inventory Difficulties | 5.4 | 10.9 | 11.6 | 1.0 | 0.8 | 6.9 |
| INCOMPETENCE | Excessive Fixed Assets | 4.7 | 1.9 | 2.7 | 1.9 | 5.6 | 3.1 |
| | Poor Location | 0.5 | 0.7 | 4.2 | 0.5 | 1.5 | 2.2 |
| Evidenced by inability to avoid conditions which resulted in ......... | Competitive Weakness | 14.7 | 16.9 | 17.9 | 14.7 | 15.7 | 16.3 |
| | Other | 3.6 | 2.3 | 1.8 | 8.0 | 2.4 | 3.5 |
| DISASTER Some of these occurences could have been provided against through insurance | Fire | 0.3 | 0.1 | 0.2 | 0.0 | 0.2 | 0.2 |
| | Flood | 0.1 | — | 0.0 | — | — | 0.0 |
| | Burglary | 0.1 | 0.1 | 0.0 | — | 0.1 | 0.0 |
| | Employees' Fraud | — | 0.1 | 0.0 | — | — | 0.0 |
| | Strike | 0.1 | 0.2 | 0.0 | 0.0 | 0.0 | 0.1 |
| | Other | 0.1 | 0.1 | 0.2 | 0.2 | 0.0 | 0.1 |
| REASON UNKNOWN | | 8.1 | 7.5 | 9.3 | 9.9 | 16.5 | 10.1 |
| | Percent Of Total Failures | 13.2 | 10.2 | 41.0 | 21.5 | 14.1 | 100.0 |

*Because some failures are attributed to a combination of apparent causes, the totals of these columns exceed the totals of the corresponding columns on the left.*

SOURCE: "The Business Failure Record." By permission of Dun & Bradstreet Credit Services, a company of The Dun & Bradstreet Corporation.

assets listed by the seller be verified to determine true worth. These services will cost you several hundred dollars, but the cost is minimal compared to what you could lose in a bad deal. Talking to former, present, and potential customers of the business in question might reveal some interesting insights. Table 5 outlines most of the pros and cons in buying an existing business.

TABLE 5

BUYING AN ESTABLISHED BUSINESS

ADVANTAGES
Suppliers already established
Existing community goodwill
Established customer base
Location known to be adequate
Facilities are existent
Regulatory requirements have already been met
Credit relationships have already been established
Some inventories and supplies may be on hand
Many growing pains have been overcome
Proven employees

DISADVANTAGES
Ownership changes can result in loss of community goodwill and customers
Current policies may be difficult to break because of precedents established by
    former owners
Existing employees may resist change
Equipment may be in poor condition and/or obsolete
Present location may not be the best and moving is or will be required

## Starting a New Business

The advantages in starting your own business from scratch are many. You can avoid unpleasant precedents that might be established by another owner relating to vendors, customers, bankers, and creditors. Starting anew will insure some discretion over the location of the new enterprise, product/services to be marketed, employees hired, accounting and tax procedures used, etc. A new firm, with a unique product or service, may be the first to exploit a market in an area, thereby gaining a strong foothold against potential competitors.

A start-up situation can prove to be equally discouraging for a number of reasons. A lot of ground work is involved in acquiring business licenses and permits, establishing relations with suppliers, buying equipment/supplies, etc. Also, new firms generally lack a customer base to support operations initially and confidence and goodwill take time to build. In addition, credit by suppliers and banks may be slow in coming until you become established and prove your ability to pay. Finally, most new enterprises fail within the first three years of operation due to business and managerial incompetence on the part of the entrepreneur (refer to Table 4). Also, Table 6 lists most of the advantages and disadvantages in starting a small business from scratch.

TABLE 6

STARTING A BUSINESS

Many entrepreneurs prefer to start a small business and build it themselves from the ground floor up. There are unique advantages to this approach, but pitfalls also exist. Careful examination is warranted before moving in this direction.

POSITIVE FACTORS

Suppliers can be evaluated and chosen fresh.

Credit connections are new and can be nurtured from the beginning.

The latest equipment, supplies, and inventories can be picked according to exact requirements and specifications.

Client contacts and relationships are new. Negative precedents can be avoided from the beginning.

The development of community goodwill is wide open, with the possibility of developing a unique image.

The optimum location can be identified and acquired or leased.

Financial records can be tailored to exact needs.

NEGATIVE FACTORS

Starting a business entails a greater risk than buying an existing operation.

Capital and credit may be more difficult to obtain, given the lack of operating histories and/or the inexperience of the people involved.

Starting and organizing will require time and energy.

Positive customer and community reaction may be slow in coming.

Supplemental income may be needed until the business begins to turn profits.

Needed employees may be difficult to lure initially, given financial constraints in the early years of operation.

## The Franchising Route

Franchising, another road to business ownership, has distinct pluses worth noting. The product/service is established and, in some cases, customer goodwill has already been achieved. Many franchise organizations will provide partial start-up funding and credit after operations begin as well as local, regional, and national promotion assistance. In addition, your limited experience and/or education can be supplemented with the franchisor's extensive knowledge in a product or service area if management training and follow-up assistance is provided. Also, affiliation with some franchisors will allow for cost savings in purchasing supplies and equipment due to combined buying power of the franchisees through the franchise organization. The more reputable franchisors will recommend or require certain layouts, displays, facilities, property, business techniques, etc. It is wise to adopt these since most have proven successful in actual operation by other franchisees.

Taking the franchise route can cause you some headaches. Freedom to set your own prices and change or alter the product/service line may be limited. The degree of limitation will depend upon the franchisor. You will have to split your sales revenues with the franchise organization and payments vary anywhere between one and 20 percent of gross sales, with four being the average. Also, many franchisors require a lot of paperwork from their franchisees. If the above-mentioned situations haven't scared you yet, the franchise contracts might. They tend to be long, complex, and, in some cases, vague. Many questionable points may be diluted or hidden in legal terminology. See that your attorney reads the contract document to insure that the franchisor cannot evade its promises and responsibilities under the terms of the franchise agreement. Make sure that the organization is not expecting unreasonable demands in the form of up-front fees, percentage paybacks, limiting controls, etc.

High front fees can be discouraging for anyone pursuing the franchise alternative. Many of the better-known franchisors require that you have a couple of hundred thousand dollars before getting the franchise. That's only half the cost. They will lend you the rest. But don't be fooled by low fees either. It may mean that the franchise organization is not providing adequate support functions after operations commence.

Once you have narrowed your choice down to a particular franchise, additional evaluation is needed. The federal government and many states require franchise organizations to provide detailed information about their operations to prospective franchisees. This data is provided to assist you in making your decision. Even though the federal government has gone to extreme lengths to insure credibility within the franchise industry through disclosure requirements, indiscretions still exist. Question the franchisor concerning costs, business policies, contract terms, etc. Verify the answers with current franchisees. Talking to individuals associated with the franchise organization (as franchisees) will provide a valuable source of information. Don't ask the franchisor for references. Seek out the franchisees yourself so as to insure unbiased comments.

Find out if the franchise organization is reputable and delivers what is promised. Make sure that the franchisor is really on your side. In addition, call or write the National Better Business Bureau, 230 Park Avenue, New York, New York 10017, and the Better Business Bureau in the city where the franchise headquarters is located. Ask for a report on the company.

It is wise to consider a few questions before spending countless hours on a serious franchise evaluation. Therefore, the following questions are designed to provide an initial insight into what constitutes a reputable franchise organization. The answers you receive may save you time, money, and grief.

1) Were promises made concerning enormous profits?
2) Were promises made concerning minimal effort?
3) Were promises made concerning getting rich quick?
4) Was the franchisor more interested in making a sale than making the franchisee successful?
5) Was pressure exerted to sign a purchase contract?
6) Was pressure exerted to sign a purchase contract based upon the franchisor's threat that the "so-called" opportunity would not be available tomorrow?
7) Does the franchisor constantly pursue in order to make a sale? (Telephone, mail, showing up without an appointment, etc.)
8) Did the franchisor refuse or evade any direct questions?
9) Were the franchisor's answers to questions stated in vague terms?
10) Did the franchisor refuse or evade questions relating to references (other franchisees that can be asked for their opinions)?
11) Did the franchisor hedge on questions concerning training and assistance programs made available to franchisees? Did the answers lack specifics in reference to dates, length of assistance, trainers, etc.?
12) Did the franchisor hesitate to agree on having the franchisee's attorney available to ask questions and/or review the franchise contract?

If the answer to any of the aforementioned questions is "yes," serious consideration should be given before doing business with the franchisor. Once the differences are resolved to your satisfaction, if possible, and the initial research facts are in order, proceed by conducting a comprehension evaluation of the franchise deal by answering the questions that appear on pages 34 through 37. This should assist you in determining whether the franchise organization and agreement is right for you. In addition, several good books have been published by private and government organizations on the subject of franchising. Drop a note and ask for information. Several of these provide extensive information on franchise organization:

*Franchise Opportunities Handbook*
Superintendent of Documents
U.S. Government Printing Office
Washington, D.C. 20402

*Franchise Index/Profile*
Superintendent of Documents
U.S. Government Printing Office
Washington, D.C. 20402

*Directory of Franchising Organization*
Pilot Books
347 Fifth Avenue
New York, New York 10016

*The Franchise Annual Handbook and Directory*
Info Press, Inc.
736 Center Street
Lewiston, New York 14092

*IFA Membership Directory*
International Franchise Association
1025 Connecticut Avenue, N.W.
Suite 1005
Washington, D.C. 20036

*Investigate Before Investing: Guidance For Prospective Franchisees*
International Franchise Association
1025 Connecticut Avenue, N.W.
Suite 1005
Washington, D.C. 20036

Franchise firms that you feel are not acting appropriately should be reported to a number of private and public organizations. They are:

National Franchise Association Coalition
P.O. Box 366
Fox Lake, Illinois 60020

International Franchise Association
1025 Connecticut Avenue, N.W.
Suite 1005
Washington, D.C. 20036

Franchise and Business Opportunities Program
Federal Trade Commission
Washington, D.C. 20580

National Better Business Bureau
230 Park Avenue
New York, New York 10017

Better Business Bureau in the city where the franchise headquarters is located.

In addition, many states maintain agencies that monitor franchise organizations. If you have problems, write to the State Corporation Commission in your state capital.

Questions to Answer Affirmatively
Before Going Into Franchising

*Check if
answer
is "yes"*

*The Franchisor*
1. Has the franchisor been in business long enough (5 years or more) to have established a good reputation? _____
2. Have you checked Better Business Bureaus, Chambers of Commerce, Dun and Bradstreet, or bankers to find out about the franchisor's business reputation and credit rating? _____
3. Did the above investigations reveal that the franchisor has a good reputation and credit rating? _____
4. Does the franchising firm appear to be financed adequately so that it can carry out its stated plan of financial assistance and expansion? _____
5. Have you found out how many franchisees are now operating? _____
6. Have you found out the "mortality" or failure rate among franchisees? _____
7. Is the failure rate small? _____
8. Have you checked with some franchisees and found that the franchisor has a reputation for honesty and fair dealing among those who currently hold franchises? _____
9. Has the franchisor shown you certified figures indicating exact net profits of one or more going operations which you have personally checked yourself? _____
10. Has the franchisor given you a specimen contract to study with the advice of your legal counsel? _____

*Check if*
*answer*
*is "yes"*

*The Franchisor*

11. Will the franchisor assist you with:
    a. A management training program?          _____
    b. An employee training program?           _____
    c. A public relations program?             _____
    d. Obtaining capital?                       _____
    e. Good credit terms?                       _____
    f. Merchandising ideas?                     _____
    g. Designing store layout and displays?     _____
    h. Inventory control methods?               _____
    i. Analyzing financial statements?          _____
12. Does the franchisor provide continuing assistance for franchisees through supervisors who visit regularly?          _____
13. Does the franchising firm have an experienced management trained in depth?          _____
14. Will the franchisor assist you in finding a good location for your business?          _____
15. Has the franchising company investigated you carefully enough to assure itself that you can successfully operate one of its franchises at a profit both to it and to you?          _____
16. Have you determined exactly what the franchisor can do for you that you cannot do for yourself?          _____

*The Product or Service*

17. Has the product or service been on the market long enough to gain good consumer acceptance?          _____
18. Is it priced competitively?          _____
19. Is it the type of item or service which the same consumer customarily buys more than once?          _____
20. Is it an all-year seller in contrast to a seasonal one?          _____
21. Is it a staple item, in contrast to a fad?          _____
22. Does it sell well elsewhere?          _____
23. Would you buy it on its merits?          _____
24. Will it be in greater demand five years from now?          _____
25. If it is a product rather than a service:
    a. Is it packaged attractively?             _____
    b. Does it stand up well in use?            _____
    c. Is it easy and safe to use?             _____
    d. Is it patented?                          _____
    e. Does it comply with all applicable laws?  _____
    f. Is it manufactured under certain quality standards?          _____
    g. Do these standards compare favorably with similar products on the market?          _____
    h. If the product must be purchased exclusively from the franchisor or a designated supplier, are the prices to you, as the franchisee, competitive?          _____

*The Franchise Contract*
26. Does the franchise fee seem reasonable? _____
27. Do continuing royalties or percent of gross sales payment appear reasonable? _____
28. Are the total cash investment required and the terms for financing the balance satisfactory? _____
29. Does the cash investment include payment for fixtures and equipment? _____
30. If you will be required to participate in company-sponsored promotion and publicity by contributing to an "advertising fund," will you have the right to veto any increase in contributions to the "fund?" _____
31. If the parent company's product or service is protected by patent or liability insurance, is the same protection extended to you? _____
32. Are you free to buy the amount of merchandise you believe you need rather than required to purchase a certain amount? _____
33. Can you, as the franchisee, return merchandise for credit? _____
34. Can you engage in other business activities? _____
35. If there is an annual sales quota, can you retain your franchise if it is not met? __ __
36. Does the contract give you an exclusive territory for the length of the franchise? _____
37. Is your territory protected? _____
38. Is the franchise agreement renewable? _____
39. Can you terminate your agreement if you are not happy for some reason? _____
40. Is the franchisor prohibited from selling the franchise out from under you? _____
41. May you sell the business to whomever you please? _____
42. If you sell your franchise, will you be compensated for the goodwill you have built into the business? _____
43. Does the contract obligate the franchisor to give you continuing assistance after you are operating the business? _____
44. Are you permitted a choice in determining whether you will sell any new product or service introduced by the franchisor after you have opened your business? _____
45. Is there anything with respect to the franchise or its operation which would make you ineligible for special financial assistance or other benefits accorded to small business concerns by federal, state, or local governments? _____
46. Did your lawyer approve the franchise contract after he studied it paragraph by paragraph? _____
47. Is the contract free and clear of requirements which would call upon you to take any steps which are, according to your lawyer, unwise or illegal in your state, county, or city? _____

*Check if answer is "yes"*

*The Franchisor*

48. Does the contract cover all aspects of your agreement with the franchisor? _____

49. Does it really benefit both you and the franchisor?

*Your Market*

50. Are the territorial boundaries of your market completely, accurately, and understandably defined? _____

51. Have you made any study to determine whether the product or service you propose to sell has a market in your territory at the prices you will have to charge? _____

52. Does the territory provide an adequate sales potential? _____

53. Will the population in the territory given you increase over the next 5 years? _____

54. Will the average per capita income in the territory remain the same or increase over the next 5 years? _____

55. Is existing competition in your territory for the product or service not too well entrenched? _____

*YOU—The Franchisee*

56. Do you know where you are going to get the equity capital you will need? _____

57. Have you compared what it would take to start your own similar business with the price you must pay for the franchise? _____

58. Have you made a business plan—for example:
    a. Have you worked out what income from sales or services you can reasonably expect in the first 6 months? The first year? The second year? _____
    b. Have you made a forecast of expenses, including a regular salary for yourself? _____

59. Are you prepared to give up some independence of action to secure the advantages offered by the franchise? _____

60. Are you capable of accepting supervision, even though you will presumably be your own boss? _____

61. Are you prepared to accept rules and regulations with which you may not agree? _____

62. Can you afford the period of training involved? _____

63. Are you ready to spend much or all of the remainder of your business life with this franchisor, offering his product or service to the public? _____

SOURCE: U.S. Small Business Administration.

Franchising has created opportunities for thousands of American entrepreneurs. Many of these individuals could not have pursued self-employment without the introduction and growth of the franchise concept. But the franchise route does not guarantee success by any means. Even with the backing of a strong and reputable franchisor, success can only be achieved by hard work and the intelligent use of time and money.

## Look Before You Leap

Before venturing into self-employment, an individual must conduct adequate investigation to insure that a business being started or purchased stands a chance of success. Information concerning various aspects of internal and external conditions facing a prospective owner must be sought and candidly scrutinized. Lack of data or the unwillingness to pursue questions can lead to disaster.

Below are described the more common considerations that should be addressed when contemplating entrepreneurship. Approach each one with an open mind and try to avoid personal bias that may cloud the facts.

### MARKET

Determine the ability of the market to carry all existing businesses serving it and prospective firms considering an introduction. There are occasions where a new or existing business can be so efficient and well managed, relative to its competitors, that it can survive in an overly competitive or declining market and, in some cases, even prosper. When analyzing the market as the only seller with a new product or service, make sure a real need is present before committing resources. Only through the use of statistical analysis can these conclusions be reached. Examining data in reference to community growth patterns, levels of economic activity, traffic counts, etc., may reveal some interesting facts. Opinion surveys may also prove useful. Part of Chapter VII deals with estimating market conditions relative to sales forecasting.

### COMPETITIVE CONDITIONS

Evaluate the degree of competition within the marketplace in question. How many competitors exist? Who are they? Where are they located? What are their strengths and weaknesses? Who is growing, stagnating, declining, and why?

### REGULATORY ENVIRONMENT

In some cases, fortunes are made or lost depending upon the actions of local government officials. Changing zoning regulations and patterns, alterations of traffic flows, changes in building codes, decisions concerning public transportation and parking, etc., can have a significant effect on any business. Many motels and restaurants have met with demise due to the redirection of traffic flows. Most local communities have short- and long-range growth plans. It is wise to study these plans carefully and ask local officials questions regarding the existing or potential location.

Also, keep in mind the impact of existing and potential state and federal government regulations. Examination of these is of paramount importance. Seeking the advice of officials representing agencies charged with any regulatory responsibilities may be wise.

## HUMAN RELATIONS

Before purchasing an existing operation, look into the current state of employee relations. Negative attitudes on the part of needed and hard to replace workers may be compromising the firm's existence. If starting a business, it would be wise to examine the general nature of employee relationships which may be common within local areas. Many business owners interact and establish informal standards. It is amazing how consistent these standards can be from business to business in the same community.

## PRIOR CLAIMS

In reference to buying a business, always have an attorney investigate any legal claims that may exist against the operation before purchasing. Unpaid taxes, wages, bills, and/or mortgage liabilities can exist and are usually passed on to the new owner upon acquisition.

## PHYSICAL FACILITIES

Physical condition of all buildings and equipment should be given careful consideration before purchasing a business. Professional appraisers can determine the fair value of tangible assets. Obsolete and inefficient facilities are normally expensive to replace, especially if an exorbitant price was paid initially for these assets.

## PRODUCTS/SERVICES

Evaluate existing or future product/service lines. Determine the positive and negative features in relation to price, promotion, distribution, and competition.

ENVIRONMENTAL RISKS

Is the proposition in question susceptible to external uncontrollable events? If so, which ones and to what extent? For example, governmental actions, international events, or reactions by competitors may cause difficulties. Evaluate all facets of the environment and determine how the business in question will be effected. External threats are listed in Table 23 on page 154.

**Buyer Beware**

A seller always has a motivation for disposing of property. It may or may not be candidly revealed to prospective purchasers. This is why it's important that proper investigation be conducted into the reasons for selling. Hiring a competent consultant, accountant, or attorney can help in identifying and analyzing various aspects of the proposition. Surprising situations may be discovered that are not apparent to the untrained observer.

Below are listed some of the more common explanations for someone's selling out. Make sure the truth is known before committing time and money.

Wants to retire
Too old to pursue
Not interested anymore
Going back to the corporate world
Not making enough money
Loss of profits, sales, and/or markets
Sickness
Desires to relocate outside the immediate area
Wants to pursue other business endeavors
Competitive pressures
Tired of the problems and headaches associated with business
     ownership

**Watch Out for the Lemon**

A failing business can be easily detected if the right elements are examined and understood. Generally, an operation ceases to be viable for more than one specific reason, although it centers around a single broad deficiency—managerial incompetence on the part of owners and managers. Dun and Bradstreet, the well-known financial reporting firm, states that 92.1 percent of small firms that fail do so because of managerial ineptness. They further break down statistics to account for exact causes of demise, all relating to management deficiencies, which can be found by referring to Table 4 illustrated earlier in this chapter.

Below are mentioned some of the more specific reasons attributed to small business failure. If one or more of these conditions exists, it should be quite obvious to the professionally trained eye and may even be apparent to anyone taking a close look.

### LACK OF MARKET POTENTIALS

Many businesses fail due to the lack of an adequate market for their products or services. Also, the total existing market may be contracting at a rate faster than the ability or willingness of the firm to react and shift emphasis. Only through sufficient market examination and evaluation can these threats be revealed. Chapter VII goes into detail about determining market potentials.

### CAPITAL STARVATION

Many new businesses and existing enterprises tend to underestimate their capital requirements, thereby creating a capital squeeze somewhere down the pike, generally at an inopportune time. In many cases, adequate capital is present, but mismanagement of funds causes difficulties. These factors will affect the firm's ability to generate sales, thus adversely affecting profits. Many lenders and investors will simply be reluctant to advance and risk their money if these conditions prevail, probably forcing the closing or scaling back of operations.

### HEAVY COMPETITION

Many entrepreneurs, before purchasing or starting a business, fail to account for competitive factors in the market to be served by their new operation. Severe competition can have a detrimental effect on any organization, forcing it to close, in many cases, before it gets off the ground. Consequently, a comprehensive examination is necessary to determine if existing and potential demand can support all firms currently serving the market and projected newcomers.

### UNCONTROLLED GROWTH

Many businesses expand too quickly, thereby causing strains on their financial and/or managerial structures. Both large and small organizations fall victim to this deadly sin. Several large corporations have recently gone bankrupt because of expansion beyond their resource capabilities. Once profits begin to decline or evaporate, lenders and investors run for the hills. Growth should be planned well in advance, making sure that adequate resources are available to support endeavors before committing to expansion goals.

### INAPPROPRIATE LOCATION

A bad location can be difficult to spot initially. Therefore, adequate investigation is necessary to determine the history of the location and whether it is suitable. How many businesses have been at the location in the past twenty years? What types of businesses were there? Why did they leave? Always conduct research concerning the location of an existing business being contemplated for purchase or the suitability of placing a business in a particular locale. Collecting information such as opinion surveys and analyzing data in reference to traffic counts and parking facilities will reveal considerable information about the viability of any location whether new or old.

### DISASTROUS EVENTS

Is the business subject to catastrophic events that can drain its vitality and resources to the point where it cannot recover? Has it occurred before?

### UNUSUAL AGREEMENTS

Examine the existence of any agreements the business has with present owners, employees, and third parties. Do these contracts compromise the present or future profitability of the enterprise? Can they be broken if the firm is purchased? Always have an attorney evaluate and comment on any agreements that may exist to insure flexibility in business operations. On some occasions, owners who are selling out may attempt to lock-in favored employees with contractual agreements, whereby the new owners cannot replace those workers for a given period of time.

## What to Expect

If one or more of the conditions mentioned in the preceding section exists, expect any number of the following situations to prevail within a business.

— Uncontrolled Expenses—Costs may be increasing faster on a proportionate basis than sales revenues, thus eating into or eliminating profits and creating losses. Many business operations fail to maintain adequate accounting procedures that would alert management to excessive cost increases.

— Falling Profits—Consistently falling profits is probably an indication of deteriorating sales revenues or due to expenses increasing faster than sales on a relative basis.

— Accelerated Debt Service—If indebtedness becomes too great, the ability of the business to serve its debts becomes questionable. It may spell trouble in the near future. If this condition exists, the business will probably attempt to pay debts by borrowing additional funds (borrow from Peter to pay Paul), which is only a quick fix in most cases. Eventually, both Peter and Paul come collecting at the same time.

— Falling Sales—A steady trend of falling sales can produce negative consequences for any business. Normally, "expenses do not decline relative to sales," thereby squeezing or eliminating profit margins. In addition to the conditions reviewed in the previous section that could cause a decline in sales revenues, poor internal management in reference to product/service planning, market research, promotion efforts, and distribution can also result in declining sales.

If one or more of the just-mentioned conditions prevail within a business enterprise, the firm may have some degree of difficulty meeting its current obligations. Its liquid position, also known as working capital, may be deteriorated to the point where current bills can't be paid on time.

## What Is the Fair Price?

There are two basic approaches used to determine the fair price for a business. The methods are described below.

### BOOK VALUE/GOODWILL METHOD

This approach is simple to compute. Subtract the liabilities of the business (debts) from its assets. What's left over is called book value. It is assumed that if the assets of a business were sold and the debts paid in full, what would remain in the form of cash is the true money worth of an operation. In addition to computing this figure when selling a business, an intangible asset called goodwill is taken into account and given a dollar value. Goodwill is simply described as the reputation or positive condition achieved by a business because of sound management or, in some cases, just good fortune. Once goodwill is financially evaluated, the value established will be added to the book value in order to determine the selling price.

### ANTICIPATED PROFIT METHOD

Many experts feel that using the book value and goodwill approach is inadequate and not a reliable indicator of true business worth. In fact, they support the contention that expected profits should dictate the selling price for a business. For example, in the real estate business, a house's value is not based upon the cost of materials (tangibles) and labor (intangibles) but is determined by what the market will pay for the structure.

When using this method, an estimation of future profits will need to be made. This can be done by examining past and current performance, present and anticipated market conditions, and environmental threats facing the business. After profits are projected, they can be compared against the selling price (potential investment) in order to determine an adequate value. To illustrate, suppose a buyer is interested in purchasing a business priced at $150,000. The potential buyer also wants to return his investment in 10 years, not counting salary draw. It has been determined that an average annual net profit of $14,000 can be generated by the business over the next decade. By using the simple formula shown below, the following conclusion can be determined.

$$\frac{\text{Purchasing Price}}{\text{Average Annual Net Profits}} = \frac{\$150,000}{14,000} = \begin{array}{l} 10.7 \text{ years to} \\ \text{return investment} \end{array}$$

Obviously, the buyer must either accept a longer pay-back period or negotiate a lower price. Another factor that may enter into the discussion about price is the degree of risk inherent in the business proposition. A greater risk generally demands a faster pay-back and if average net income is set at $14,000 per year, the price of the business should come down to reflect those uncertainties. For example, a purchase price of $125,000 will be returned in 8.9 years as illustrated below:

$$\frac{\text{Purchase Price}}{\text{Average Annual Net Profits}} = \frac{\$125,000}{14,000} = 8.9 \text{ years}$$

Conversely, a lesser risk may demand a longer pay-back period because of the higher price demanded.

When using the net tangible asset/goodwill or anticipated profit methods, also seek the assistance of competent accountants and attorneys to help in assigning values and making projections. Profit estimation is reviewed in Chapter VII.

## Using Financial Information

When analyzing business opportunities, serious consideration must be given to the "nuts and bolts" aspects. Financial information, when used and presented in proper format, can weed out the losers from the winners in short order. In addition, it may help to reveal the "right price" to pay for a business if acquisition is contemplated. When starting a business from the ground floor, financial data can be obtained to assist in determining the necessary capital base needed to begin and support operation until profits are generated. Once in operation, the information provided by financial statements can help insure sound fiscal management.

FINANCIAL STATEMENTS

Financial statements can say a whole lot about a firm's viability. Consequently, it is imperative to know the major financial statements generally available for evaluation purposes. First, the balance sheet is used to list a firm's assets and liabilities. These two major elements are further divided into sub-classifications (Current Assets, Non-Current Assets, Current Liabilities, Non-Current Liabilities, and Owners Equity). Second, the profit and loss statement, also known as the income statement, is used in listing and analyzing revenue and expense accounts to determine the firm's profitability. Third, a cash-flow statement is sometimes used as a supplement to the two major elements just mentioned. Its purpose is to get a closer look at how a firm manages liquid (cash) resources. Segments of Chapter VII, including Tables 18, 19, and 20, describe and illustrate these financial statements and discuss their functional purpose.

Financial information is useless without a means of comparison. A firm's financial statement should be compared to similar businesses and against the industry as a whole before attempts are made to analyze its performance. To accomplish this task, various accounts within the balance sheet and income statement can be divided into each other, thereby creating what are called financial ratios. Since ratios are compiled and published on many firms and industries by several research organizations, standards of comparison are easy to make for existing businesses. Some research outlets maintain ratios and cost information dealing with starting a new business.

An intense discussion of ratio analysis is way beyond the scope of this publication. It would be wise to write the Superintendent of Documents, U.S. Government Printing Office, Washington, D.C. 20402, and request copies of the following booklets. They cost $4.50 each.

*Ratio Analysis for Small Business*
*Handbook of Small Business Finance*

## COMMON RATIOS USED TODAY

| Ratio | Used to Determine |
|-------|-------------------|
| Current Assets / Current Liabilities | Cash position (ability to pay short-term debts) |
| Quick Assets / Current Liabilities | Cash position (ability to pay short-term debts) |
| Current Liabilities / Net Worth | Relationship between capital invested and short-term (year to year) debt obligations |
| Net Sales / Net Worth | How often capital is being recycled |
| Net Sales / Inventory | How many times inventory is turned over to generate sales |
| Fixed Assets / Net Worth | Relationship between invested capital and hard assets such as plant and equipment |
| Total Debt / Net Worth | Relationship between invested capital and all debt obligations |
| Net Profit / Net Sales | Rate of return on sales generated |

| *Ratio* | *Used to Determine* |
|---|---|
| Net Profit / Net Worth | Efficient use of invested capital |
| Net Sales / Working Capital | How much working capital should be maintained in relation to a given level of sales |
| Accounts Receivables / Daily Credit Sales | If customer accounts are being paid according to terms |

Table 7 contains an example of a ratio table compiled and published by Dun and Bradstreet. The ratios shown deal with general automotive repair shops ranging in asset size from $50,000 to $2,000,000 and above. The figure shown in parenthesis above each asset category is the number of firms giving financial information. Also, use the center number of the three given under each asset classification as a means of comparison. That is the median figure between the high and low numbers.

Appendix A contains a list of research organizations (names and addresses) offering financial ratios and other useful data to prospective entrepreneurs and current business owners. Information about specific types of businesses is available from these outlets and listed under each address.

## Additional Insight

You might want to make some final considerations before pressing ahead with your plans. Answering the following questions might provide additional insights into your readiness for business ownership. If you have already decided to purchase a franchise, many of the following questions will be answered automatically by the franchise organization and/or previous series of questions. But it wouldn't hurt to go ahead and answer the questions for your own protection, just in case something was overlooked.

Consider these questions carefully before answering. Be honest and fair with yourself because it's your time and money at stake. Answer all that apply to your situation. Obviously, some will not. If you respond to most in a favorable way (yes) and feel comfortable with the rest, then the next step in the actualization of your own business involves obtaining capital.

TABLE 7

ECONOMIC SECTOR: SERVICES

SIC: 7538 GENERAL AUTOMOTIVE REPAIR SHOPS

| | TO 50M | 50-2MM | 2MM+ | TOTAL |
|---|---|---|---|---|
| CURRENT ASSETS TO CURRENT DEBT (TIMES) | (1045) | (764) | (130) | (1939) |
| | 4.55 | 6.11 | 4.50 | 5.12 |
| | 1.95 | 3.01 | 2.25 | 2.34 |
| | 1.10 | 1.65 | 1.47 | 1.33 |
| NET PROFITS ON NET SALES (PERCENT) | 16.20 | 13.70 | 10.75 | 14.79 |
| | 7.18 | 7.85 | 6.22 | 7.44 |
| | 2.44 | 3.56 | 3.26 | 3.11 |
| PROFITS ON NET WORTH (PERCENT) | 87.99 | 40.29 | 25.84 | 62.25 |
| | 42.74 | 21.44 | 10.91 | 27.98 |
| | 16.71 | 10.96 | 5.33 | 11.45 |
| PROFITS ON WORKING CAPITAL (PERCENT) | 182.14 | 106.07 | 57.10 | 144.58 |
| | 71.38 | 44.38 | 32.46 | 54.84 |
| | 10.14 | 17.17 | 13.77 | 14.77 |
| SALES TO NET WORTH (TIMES) | 11.21 | 5.41 | 5.01 | 7.94 |
| | 6.13 | 2.90 | 1.98 | 4.22 |
| | 2.91 | 1.34 | .55 | 1.82 |
| SALES TO WORKING CAPITAL (TIMES) | 20.00 | 11.49 | 11.08 | 16.38 |
| | 9.95 | 6.26 | 4.94 | 7.68 |
| | 3.35 | 3.02 | 2.19 | 3.06 |
| COLLECTION PERIOD (DAYS) | 26 | 36 | 36 | 31 |
| | 12 | 20 | 20 | 16 |
| | 5 | 9 | 9 | 7 |
| SALES TO INVENTORY (TIMES) | 40.0 | 25.0 | 21.3 | 33.3 |
| | 20.0 | 11.3 | 8.5 | 15.4 |
| | 10.0 | 5.6 | 4.5 | 7.5 |
| FIXED ASSETS TO NET WORTH (PERCENT) | 112.3 | 79.0 | 70.2 | 94.6 |
| | 67.4 | 43.3 | 29.0 | 55.5 |
| | 34.5 | 19.6 | 16.7 | 24.3 |
| CURRENT DEBT TO NET WORTH (PERCENT) | 106.7 | 52.8 | 82.8 | 84.2 |
| | 36.8 | 24.2 | 27.1 | 30.0 |
| | 9.7 | 7.5 | 6.1 | 8.3 |
| TOTAL DEBT TO NET WORTH (PERCENT) | 204.4 | 101.8 | 102.3 | 144.8 |
| | 67.4 | 47.1 | 43.5 | 53.7 |
| | 14.5 | 16.2 | 17.8 | 15.9 |
| INVENTORY TO WORKING CAPITAL (PERCENT) | 97.8 | 96.7 | 118.5 | 98.4 |
| | 60.6 | 62.2 | 75.7 | 62.4 |
| | 16.0 | 25.6 | 32.8 | 20.0 |
| CURRENT DEBT TO INVENTORY (PERCENT) | 293.0 | 165.3 | 178.5 | 236.7 |
| | 131.3 | 81.9 | 95.6 | 100.0 |
| | 47.7 | 38.0 | 45.1 | 42.8 |
| FUNDED DEBTS TO WORKING CAPITAL (PERCENT) | 304.3 | 222.2 | 221.6 | 251.0 |
| | 101.4 | 81.0 | 62.2 | 87.3 |
| | 12.5 | 22.2 | 9.4 | 18.2 |

SOURCE: By permission of Dun & Bradstreet Credit Services, a company of The Dun & Bradstreet Corporation.

## ARE YOU THE TYPE?

Have you rated your personal qualifications using a scale similar to that presented earlier in this section?          _____

Have you had some objective evaluators rate you on such scales?          _____

Have you carefully considered your weak points and taken steps to improve them or to find an associate whose strong points will compensate for them?          _____

## WHAT BUSINESS SHOULD YOU CHOOSE?

Have you written a summary of your background and experience to help you in making this decision?          _____

Have you considered your hobbies and what you would like to do?          _____

Does anyone want the service you can perform?          _____

Have you studied surveys and/or sought advice and counsel to find out what fields of business may be expected to expand?          _____

Have you considered working for someone else to gain more experience?          _____

## WHAT ARE YOUR CHANCES FOR SUCCESS?

Are general business conditions good?          _____

Are business conditions good in the city and neighborhood where you plan to locate?          _____

Are current conditions good in the line of business you plan to start?          _____

## WHAT WILL BE YOUR RETURN ON INVESTMENT?

Do you know the typical return on investment in the line of business you plan to start?          _____

Have you determined how much you will have to invest in your business?          _____

Are you satisfied that the rate of return on the money you invest in the business will be greater than the rate you would probably receive if you invested the money elsewhere?          _____

## HOW MUCH MONEY WILL YOU NEED?

Have you filled out worksheets similar to those shown in Chapter V of this book?          _____

In filling out the worksheets, have you taken care not to overestimate income?          _____

Have you obtained quoted prices for equipment and supplies you will need?          _____

Do you know the costs of goods which must be in your inventory?          _____

Have you estimated expenses only after checking rents, wage scales, utility and other pertinent costs in the area where you plan to locate?          _____

*Check if*
*answer*
*is "yes"*

Have you found what percentage of your estimated sales your projected inventory and each expense item is and compared each percentage with the typical percentage for your line of business? _____

Have you added an additional amount of money to your estimates to allow for unexpected contingencies? _____

## WHERE CAN YOU GET THE MONEY?

Have you counted up how much money of your own you can put into the business? _____

Do you know how much credit you can get from your suppliers—the people you will buy from? _____

Do you know where you can borrow the rest of the money you need to start your business? _____

Have you selected a progressive bank with the credit services you may need? _____

Have you talked to a banker about your plans? _____

Does the banker have an interested, helpful attitude toward your problems? _____

## SHOULD YOU SHARE OWNERSHIP WITH OTHERS?

If you need a partner with money or know-how that you don't have, do you know someone who will fit—someone you can get along with? _____

Do you know the good and bad points about going it alone, having a partner, and incorporating your business? _____

Have you talked to a lawyer about it? _____

## WHERE SHOULD YOU LOCATE?

Have you studied the make-up of the population in the city or town where you plan to locate? _____

Do you know what kind of people will want to buy what you plan to sell? _____

Do people like that live in the area where you want to locate? _____

Have you checked the number, type and size of competitors in the area? _____

Does the area need another business like the one you plan to open? _____

Are employees available? _____

Have you checked and found adequate: utilities, parking facilities, police and fire protection, available housing, schools and other cultural and community activities? _____

Do you consider costs of the location reasonable in terms of taxes and average rents? _____

Is there sufficient opportunity for growth and expansion? _____

Have you checked the relative merits of the various shopping areas within the city, including shopping centers? _____

In selecting the actual site, have you compared it with others? _____
Have you had a lawyer check the lease and zoning? _____

## SHOULD YOU BUY A GOING BUSINESS?

Have you considered the advantages and disadvantages of buying a going business? _____

Have you compared what it would cost to equip and stock a new business with the price asked for the business you are considering buying? _____

## HOW MUCH SHOULD YOU PAY FOR IT?

Have you estimated future sales and profits of the going business for the next few years? _____

Are your estimated future profits satisfactory? _____

Have you looked at past financial statements of the business to find the return on investment, sales and profit trends? _____

Have you verified the owner's claims about the business with reports from an independent accountant's analysis of the figures? _____

Is the inventory you will purchase a good buy? _____

Are equipment and fixtures fairly valued? _____

If you plan to buy the accounts receivable, are they worth the asking price? _____

Have you been careful in your appraisal of the company's good will? _____

Are you prepared to assume the company's liabilities and are the creditors agreeable? _____

Have you learned why the present owner wants to sell? _____

Have you found out about the present owner's reputation with his employees and suppliers? _____

Have you consulted a lawyer to be sure that the title is good? _____

Has your lawyer checked to find out if there is any lien against the assets you are buying? _____

Has your lawyer drawn up an agreement covering all essential points, including a seller's warranty for your protection against false statements? _____

## SHOULD YOU INVEST IN A FRANCHISE?

Have you considered how the advantages and disadvantages of franchising apply to you? _____

Have you made a thorough search to find the right franchise opportunity? _____

Have you evaluated the franchise by answering the questions asked earlier in this section? _____

## HAVE YOU WORKED OUT PLANS FOR BUYING?

Have you estimated what share of the market you think you can get? _____

Do you know how much or how many of each item of merchandise you will buy to open your business?

Have you found suppliers who will sell you what you need at a good price?

Do you have a plan for finding out what your customers want?

Have you set up a model stock assortment to follow in your buying?

Have you worked out stock control plans to avoid over-stocks, under-stocks, and out-of-stocks?

Do you plan to buy most of your stock from a few suppliers rather than a little from many, so that those you buy from will want to help you succeed?

HOW WILL YOU PRICE YOUR PRODUCTS AND SERVICES?

Have you decided upon your price ranges?

Do you know how to figure what you should charge to cover your costs?

Do you know what your competitors charge?

WHAT SELLING METHODS WILL YOU USE?

Have you studied the selling and sales promotion methods of competitors?

Have you studied why customers buy your type of product or service?

Have you thought about why you like to buy from some salesmen while others turn you off?

Have you decided what your methods of selling will be?

Have you outlined your sales promotion policy?

HOW WILL YOU SELECT AND TRAIN PERSONNEL?

If you need to hire someone to help you, do you know where to look?

Do you know what kind of person you need?

Have you written a job description for each person you will need?

Do you know the prevailing wage scales?

Do you have a plan for training new employees?

Will you continue training through good supervision?

WHAT OTHER MANAGEMENT PROBLEMS WILL YOU FACE?

Do you plan to sell for credit?

If you do, do you have the extra capital necessary to carry accounts receivable?

Have you made a policy for returned goods?

Have you planned how you will make deliveries?

Have you considered other policies which must be made in your particular business?  _____

Have you made a plan to guide yourself in making the best use of your time and effort?  _____

## WHAT RECORDS WILL YOU KEEP?

Have you planned a system of records that will keep track of your income and expenses, what you owe other people, and what other people owe you?  _____

Have you worked out a way to keep track of your inventory so that you will always have enough on hand for your customers but not more than you can sell?  _____

Have you planned on how to keep your payroll records and take care of tax reports and payments?  _____

Do you know what financial statements you should prepare?  _____

Do you know how to use these financial statements?  _____

Have you obtained standard operating ratios for your type of business which you plan to use as guides?  _____

Do you know an accountant who will help you with your records and financial statements?  _____

## WHAT LAWS WILL AFFECT YOU?

Have you checked with the proper authorities to find out what, if any, licenses to do business are necessary?  _____

Do you know what police and health regulations apply to your business?  _____

Will your operations be subject to interstate commerce regulations? If so, do you know to which ones?  _____

Have you received advice from your lawyer regarding your responsibilities under federal and state laws and local ordinances?  _____

## HOW WILL YOU HANDLE TAXES AND INSURANCE?

Have you worked out a system for handling the withholding tax for your employees?  _____

Have you worked out a system for handling sales taxes? Excise taxes?  _____

Have you planned an adequate record system for the efficient preparation of income tax forms?  _____

Have you prepared a worksheet for meeting tax obligations?  _____

Have you talked with an insurance agent about what kinds of insurance you will need and how much it will cost?  _____

## WILL YOU SET MEASURABLE GOALS FOR YOURSELF?

Have you set goals and sub-goals for yourself?  _____

Have you specified dates when each goal is to be achieved?  _____

*Check if*
*answer*
*is "yes"*

Are these realistic goals; that is, will they challenge you but at the same time not call for unreasonable accomplishments?          _____

Are the goals specific so that you can measure performance?          _____

Have you developed a business plan, using one of the SBA Aids to record your ideas, facts, and figures?          _____

Have you allowed for obstacles?          _____

WILL YOU KEEP UP TO DATE?

Have you made plans to keep up with improvements in your trade or industry?          _____

Have you prepared a business plan which will be amended as circumstances demand?          _____

SOURCE OF QUESTIONS: U.S. Small Business Administration.

Chapter III

# SOURCES OF HELP
## Ripe for the Picking

### Help Galore

Few individuals are aware of the reservoir of assistance available from public and private organizations directed to the small business community. Taking advantage of these services may mean the difference between success and failure for many struggling businesses and entrepreneurs. Many of these informational outlets will help when evaluating business opportunities and specific propositions.

### Where to Look

U.S. SMALL BUSINESS ADMINISTRATION (SBA)

One of the primary objectives of the U.S. Small Business Administration is to promote the economic well being of small firms and entrepreneurs. This is partly accomplished by providing an array of business and managerial assistance programs that are available upon request. The next several pages will be devoted to describing these non-financial services. Information concerning SBA financial assistance programs can be found later in the book.

SCORE (Service Corps of Retired Executives)—Retired business executives within this program offer advice to the small business community on a free basis. The combined experience of SCORE counselors spans the entire spectrum of American business. Volunteers meet with small business owners and prospective entrepreneurs to determine and discuss their difficulties. After careful consideration and evaluation, the counselor will formulate a plan of action designed to help minimize or eliminate the problem areas. In addition, the individual(s) requesting assistance will be guided through this sometimes difficult process. If the problem is extremely difficult or complex, several SCORE representatives may be asked to assist. Sometimes, other SBA and outside resources may be brought to bear. Currently, there are over 6,000 SCORE advisors located throughout the country.

ACE (Active Corps of Executives)—ACE is designed to supplement SCORE activities by providing business and managerial counseling on an on-going basis. Members of this organization are practicing executives, professionals, and academicians. Normally, ACE volunteers, numbering about 2,500, can provide the latest expertise that may not be available from SCORE chapters.

University Business Development Centers (UBDCs)—These organizations are established in tandem with the U.S. Small Business Administration to provide additional counseling services to the small business community. UBDC's are simply college- or university-based counseling centers utilizing institutional resources, including faculty and students. In addition, these centers muster community involvement and volunteers to accomplish their task of providing help to small firms and people wanting to start businesses. Appendix B provides a listing of current university business development centers.

Small Business Institutes (SBIs)—The U.S. Small Business Administration has contracted with over 400 colleges and universities to establish small business institutes. This program, although similar to the UBDC approach, does have distinct differences. Counseling services provided by SBI's are limited in one respect but more extensive in others. SBI student and faculty counselors are assigned to certain projects with the objective of providing detailed verbal and written recommendations to specific problem areas that a prospective entrepreneur or business owner may face. This approach enables students to experience real life business situations. The cost for this service is free to individuals or businesses seeking assistance.

Call Contracting Program—This SBA-financed program is designed to give free professional advice and expertise to small firms and individuals who qualify. The agency contracts with reputable and reliable accounting and/or consulting firms to carry out the objectives of this program. Generally, problems of a very difficult or technical nature are handled under call contracting.

Management Training—The SBA co-sponsors several types of training functions. Working in unison with private experts, the SBA provides courses, conferences, problem clinics, and workshops designed to deliver counseling services to local communities throughout the country. Checking with the regional SBA office can yield a schedule of events in particular areas served.

SBA Publications—The Small Business Administration has many inexpensive publications available to any individual upon request. These booklets and pamphlets provide valuable business and managerial tips on how to run a small business successfully. In addition, publications concerning the start-up of specific types of businesses are also available.

Business Development pamphlets are broken into three classifications which are as follows:

| | |
|---|---|
| Financial Management and Analysis | Marketing |
| | Personnel Management |
| General Management and Planning | New Products/Ideas/ Inventions |
| Crime Prevention | Miscellaneous |

The titles of these publications are reviewed in Appendix C located at the end of this book.

Business Development booklets are broken into four categories. They are:

— Small Business Management Series—These detailed books deal with specific management problems faced by many start-up firms and existing operations.
— Starting and Managing Series—These publications yield specific and detailed information about starting and managing different types of small firms.
— Business Basics—This series of books attempts to teach various aspects of small business management.
— Nonseries Publications—These helpful publications deal with management topics but do not fall under any category listed thus far.

A listing of these publications can be found in Appendix D. Publications may be ordered by writing to the Superintendent of

Documents, U.S. Government Printing Office, Washington, D.C. 20402.

In addition, when seeking SBA managerial assistance services, call or write the field offices maintained by the agency. They are listed in Appendix E. They will send an assistance form that is to be completed and returned to the field office. This form is illustrated in Appendix F.

## DEPARTMENT OF COMMERCE

The U.S. Department of Commerce maintains an array of informational resources that are available to anyone. This department is constantly collecting economic, financial, and business data relating to the economy, different industries, states, and, in some cases, individual firms. Over the last decade, the Commerce Department has been heavily involved in the promotion of American products abroad. It has enormous amounts of data that can be used by domestic exporters when studying overseas markets. In addition, the department gets actively involved in setting up channels of distribution for any business (new or existing) wanting to exploit foreign market potentials. Department of Commerce field offices can be contacted for details concerning their publications and assistance programs. Refer to Appendix G for a listing of these offices.

The Minority Business Development Agency (MBDA), which is part of the Commerce Department, provides basic services to minority-owned firms. Their regional and district offices are listed in Appendix H. They will refer the entrepreneur to MBDA funded local offices providing services within certain geographic areas.

## U.S. FEDERAL TRADE COMMISSION (FTC)

The FTC was set up to protect consumers and businesses against firms that would promote restraint of trade and use unfair competitive methods. It publishes material on what constitutes illegal practices when conducting business. Write to the address below and request the publications concerning these matters. Knowing what to avoid initially may save many headaches later. Also, the publications might provide some insights into whether competitors are acting appropriately or not.

Federal Trade Commission
Washington, D.C. 20580

GOVERNMENTAL PROCUREMENT ASSISTANCE

The U.S. Small Business Administration provides help to small firms wishing to do business with the federal government through the SBA's procurement automated source system (PASS); a small firm's capabilities are matched to those government agencies requiring what the firm has to offer. Also, PASS will identify large companies that have obtained government procurement contracts and are in need of small sub-contractors to fulfill requirements in the agreements. Appendix I illustrates the PASS application form used by the SBA.

In addition, the U.S. Superintendent of Documents publishes the *Commerce Business Daily*, which reports most procurement opportunities available from Uncle Sam. Most of the PASS information received by the SBA is also contained in this publication. Therefore, subscribing to this daily report may be unnecessary. However, it does provide information on other opportunities that can be examined for potential exploitation. A subscription can be obtained by writing to:

Superintendent of Documents
Government Printing Office
Washington, D.C. 20402

The cost for the publication is broken down as follows:

$175 per year by 1st Class mail
$150 per year by 2nd Class mail
$ 90 for six months by 1st Class mail
$ 50 for six months by 2nd Class mail

Allow six weeks for delivery of the first issue.

Many state and local governments actively encourage small businesses to bid on their purchasing requirements. Contact their procurement offices for additional details. Also, foreign governments are always seeking American products and services. SBA and Department of Commerce field offices, listed in Appendices E and G, can provide assistance in reaching foreign government procurement offices located in the U.S. Contacting their embassies in Washington or consulate offices in major cities may also help.

Reading these publications will be of great help to you in understanding governmental procurement procedures and may open up opportunities not apparent before.

## U.S. INTERNAL REVENUE SERVICE

The IRS can provide information related to business taxation. It publishes many useful and free reports concerning the tax obligation of business enterprises. Some of the publications will assist in establishing the necessary accounting procedures for the proper handling and payment of taxes. Write or call the nearest IRS office and request the booklets needed. They are listed in Appendix K. IRS personnel will also answer questions personally.

## STATE GOVERNMENTS

Most state governments are realizing the importance of small business activity to their economy. Many have developed assistance programs aimed at helping prospective entrepreneurs and existing small firms. Services may include managerial, procurement and/or funding help. The degree of assistance varies from state to state. To find out what may be available, write or call the offices listed in Appendix J for more information. Also, referring to Appendix L will give broad information about the services provided by different states.

## LOCAL GOVERNMENTS

Most municipalities maintain records in reference to local economic activity. Statistics dealing with retail sales, personal income, construction permits, traffic counts, and growth patterns can be obtained and are useful when analyzing general business prospects or specific propositions. For example, when evaluating several possible store locations, traffic counts and area growth patterns should be carefully reviewed.

## ACCOUNTANTS

In addition to their traditional role as bookkeeper and auditor, many accountants provide invaluable information and assistance relative to decisions concerning business propositions. Included below are some of the more common services that can be expected from most accountants.

— Of course, record keeping and auditing
— Corporate and individual tax planning

— Sales and income projection
— Budget construction
— Identification and exploitation of capital sources
— Construction of past, present, and pro forma (future) financial statements
— Cost containment analysis and procedures
— Determination and projection of working capital requirements
— Overall financial analysis

Although most are listed in the phone book, it is wise to consult a banker, attorney, or business consultant when seeking a suitable accountant. Bankers and lawyers are in constant contact with the accounting profession and they generally know the accountants that can provide adequate help at reasonable cost. A good approach is to seek out owners in similar lines of business and ask for advice. This can be the best source of reference available because of the direct contact between accountant and owner. In addition, there are two national, professional accounting associations that may provide referrals upon request. They are listed below. Also, try state associations. Many are more familiar with their membership than the national groups.

American Institute of Certified Public Accountants
1211 Avenue of the Americas
New York, New York 10036
(212) 575-6200

National Society of Public Accountants
1010 North Fairfax Street
Alexandria, Virginia 22314
(703) 549-6400

Accountants can save a tremendous amount of pain and expense if they are used wisely. Always have an accountant explore a prospective business proposition before purchasing, for obvious reasons cited earlier in the book. If already in business, you need accountants to evaluate any large investment decision contemplated. Even if a business has an internal accountant, outside opinion should be sought. It can be helpful in spotting difficulties that may not be apparent from the inside. The small price paid for the information is an investment if it helps avoid a bad deal which potentially could cause severe losses. Remember, it's better to pay a little now than a whole lot later.

## ADVERTISING FIRMS

Advertising agencies can be a source of marketing assistance overlooked by many existing firms and prospective entrepreneurs. Many agencies provide services over and above their traditional function of selling media. These include:

— Evaluation of marketing objectives
— Planning of advertising strategy and tactics
— Selection of correct media outlets
— Production of ad layouts and commercials
— Coordination and execution of strategy and tactics
— Evaluation of advertising results

Generally, small advertising accounts will have to pay for the additional services rendered over and above the cost of media purchased from the agency. However, larger accounts can expect some, if not all, of the aforementioned services, to be included as a part of the media fee paid. In other words, these services may be performed free of charge if large amounts of media are purchased.

Advertising agencies are located in the yellow pages of most phone books. In addition, talking to various media and other businesses may provide information concerning the services and reputation of various agencies. Also, several professional advertising associations might provide referrals upon request. The names and addresses are listed below.

American Advertising Federation
1225 Connecticut Avenue, N.W.
Washington, D.C. 20036
(202) 659-1800

American Association of Advertising Agencies
666 Third Avenue
New York, New York 10017
(212) 682-2500

Mutual Advertising Agency Network
8335 Jefferson Avenue
Detroit, Michigan 48214
(313) 821-0120

National Advertising Agency Network
245 5th Avenue
New York, New York 10016
(212) 481-3022

Referring to the publication entitled *Standard Directory of Advertising Agencies* will provide comprehensive information on most agencies, including their areas of specialty. This work can normally be found in a library. If not, write to the publisher and request the three-volume set. The cost is $157, at last word. It may seem expensive but consider the time and money associated with an extensive search.

National Register Publishing Company, Inc.
5201 Old Orchard Road
Skokie, Illinois 60077
(312) 470-3100

## ASSOCIATIONS (TRADE AND PROFESSIONAL)

Trade and professional associations represent a specific group of businesses or individuals that find themselves in the same or similar line of business. Many trade associations maintain assistance programs designed to help and serve the firms they represent. Newsletters, seminars, toll free hotline, etc., are but a few services offered by many of these trade organizations. In addition, quite a few associations collect and analyze financial data in reference to the whole industry it serves as well as individual firms. This information is organized, and in many cases made available to members and prospective entrepreneurs wishing to enter the industry through a start-up operation or by purchasing an existing firm.

A list of trade and professional associations can be found by referring to the two publications given below. One or both should be found in most libraries. If not found, write or call the publishers for details and the cost to acquire the books.

*Encyclopedia of Associations*
Publisher—Gale Research Company
645 Griswold
Detroit, Michigan 48226
(313) 961-2242

*National Trade and Professional Associations of the United States*
Publisher—Columbia Books, Inc.
   1350 New York Avenue, N.W.
   Washington, D.C. 20005
   (202) 737-3777

There are many associations that represent the interest of the small business community in general. Some will provide useful information that could be utilized by an entrepreneur or existing firm when evaluating overall business conditions and trends and, in some cases, specific opportunities. These organizations are listed in Appendix L.

## BANK OF AMERICA

The prestigious Bank of America constantly collects and analyzes data on the problems of starting a small business. These studies are made public through the bank's own publication called the *Small Business Reporter*. Individual reports on the businesses mentioned in Appendix M can be obtained by writing to the following address:

Bank of America
Department 3120
P.O. Box 37000
San Francisco, California 94137

## CHAMBERS OF COMMERCE

Local chambers of commerce can provide valuable assistance to prospective entrepreneurs and existing small businesses. Besides facilitating interaction between local business people, civic groups, and professionals, CC's can be an important source of community contacts that could help any business. In addition, many chambers of commerce maintain small business committees that are used to promote and/or assist small firms within the area they serve. Also, some chambers have strong ties to the U.S. Small Business Administration and other governmental bodies, including state and local agencies that represent the interests of small enterprises.

Some chambers collect statistical data on the communities they serve and make this information publicly available. Facts concerning sales, income structure, growth patterns, etc., may be acquired so as to assist in the planning function. A listing of all chambers of commerce in the world can be obtained by referring to a publication entitled,

*World Wide Chamber of Commerce Directory.* If it cannot be found in a library, write the publisher mentioned below. The book costs less than $10, at last word.

> Johnson Publishing Company, Inc.
> P.O. Box 455, 8th and Van Buren
> Loveland, Colorado 80537

## COMPETITION

Competitors are almost always looked upon as "the enemy." However, with a little creative thinking, competitors can be viewed as a source of vital information. Some will candidly provide useful data upon being asked and others will not. Even if some competitors are strict about conveying ideas and information, their actions in the market place can reveal interesting particulars worth noting. For example, an unanticipated price hike may indicate that a competitor is experiencing unusually strong demand, falling profit margins, or increasing cost pressures. It may also signal a shift in marketing strategy or tactics. So, always ask questions, listen, and observe.

## CUSTOMERS

Customers can yield valuable tips about the firm's image to the public at large. Many small business entrepreneurs have been shocked to hear the comments about their business from their clientele. Before starting a small business, it is wise to speak with potential customers. They might reveal some pros and cons that may not have been apparent upon initial or later evaluation. In reference to buying a going concern, seeking out current and potential customers could be an excellent way to gauge the viability of the enterprise being considered for acquisition.

## FINANCIAL INSTITUTIONS

Local financial institutions have an intimate knowledge of the community they serve. Therefore, they can be an important source of information concerning business prospects. Many will help in analyzing financial data concerning the local economy and specific business opportunities. Most know what businesses can work in the community and which ones have a high chance of failure. Some even know which locations are good or bad for particular types of businesses.

## FRIENDS, FAMILY, AND ASSOCIATES

Personal and professional relationships can yield valuable information even though extensive research is being conducted. Drawing on the combined experiences of friends, relatives, and associates can augment existing research efforts and in some cases fill knowledge vacuums that may exist. Soliciting advice can also bring to bear some interesting insights often under-emphasized or overlooked in the research endeavor. In some cases, it may provide profit opportunities, and in other situations, help avoid financial disaster.

U.S. presidents have been known to call on family members and friends when delineating major policy directions. John Kennedy constantly consulted his father on civil rights issues and Jimmy Carter drew on his mother and Southern friends for advice. Even his daughter, Amy, was consulted on nuclear arms questions.

Soliciting advice can be like picking peaches. Generally, a yield of good, average, and rotten fruit is collected. Therefore, when absorbing advice from friends, family, and/or associates, consider the source very carefully. Was previous advice and information solid and sound? If so, to what degree? If not, watch out.

## INSURANCE COMPANIES

Insurance companies and their local agents can provide useful information relating to the reduction of liability under a number of conditions. Besides providing the traditional business insurance services such as casualty, health, and life protection, many are involved in the reduction of risks relating to defective products or services, non-payment of client accounts, international transactions, etc.

To find out which companies are involved in comprehensive risk reduction programs may require some time and energy. It may take time in finding the right kind of insurance combination required at a good price. Generally, calling local agents will reveal vital and necessary information. Again, talking to bankers, attorneys, accountants, and consultants will usually provide insight into the types of insurance required and where to find it.

Some insurance companies provide additional services to small firms and prospective entrepreneurs. These services can range anywhere from setting up pension and profit sharing plans to providing in-house consulting services on such things as cash-flow and resource management.

## LEGAL COMMUNITY

Attorneys are important in the business process and should be utilized when there are any doubts and/or unanswered questions about any proposition. An existing enterprise should use an attorney when examining situations that can have legal ramification either now or in the future. Start-up firms need to seek out legal assistance on matters such as legal structure, personal and business liabilities, permits, licenses, etc. Besides the items just mentioned, attorneys can help in the following areas:

— Analysis and evaluation of contracts
— Negotiation with investors, lenders, and suppliers
— Compliance with legal statutes and codes
— Defense in legal matters
— Identification of capital sources

Attorneys are listed in the yellow pages of the phone book. In addition, calling or writing the state bar association, which is usually located in the capital city of a particular state, will yield a list of lawyers located in a given area of that state, if requested. However, the best source of contact information concerning competent legal help will come from bankers, accountants, and business consultants. Most work with legal expertise on a regular basis and are in a position to know the best lawyer for a given situation. Also, try other businesses in a related field. Some good legal contacts may surface.

Consulting the publication entitled *The Lawyer's Register By Specialties and Fields of Law* may provide some helpful sources. If not located in a library, the book may be obtained by contacting the publisher at the address below.

Lawyer's Register Publishing Company
5325 Naiman Parkway
Cleveland, Ohio 44139

The cost is $49.50

## LIBRARIES (PUBLIC, PRIVATE AND COLLEGE)

Most large and medium-sized libraries maintain an array of business books and periodicals that can be helpful to any existing or prospective entrepreneur. In addition, some have learning resource centers with the latest in business-related audio and visual aids. Normally, cities with a population of around 5,000 have at least one library, although they generally lack adequate materials and facilities. There is an exception to this rule. Small towns harboring universities or colleges may have the advantage of the institution's library resources. Libraries within population centers exceeding 100,000 are more sophisticated and detailed in their information delivery capabilities. All things being equal, college and university libraries tend to be the best for business research purposes.

Many of the large state universities collect, assimilate, and publish an array of economic information on local areas within the state it serves. The quality of this data tends to be very high and can provide a small firm or prospective entrepreneur with valuable information when planning or analyzing opportunities.

## PLANNING DISTRICTS
### (ECONOMIC DEVELOPMENT CENTERS)

Many localities belong to planning districts. These districts maintain offices and are funded by one or more communities for the purpose of coordinating growth objectives. They gather, dissiminate, organize, and publish an array of data about the areas they serve. The information tends to be somewhat technical, but it can prove helpful to any firm or individual examining potentials within a locality. Market trends, population shifts, income patterns, activity in certain lines of business, are but a few of the types of information available from the office of a good planning district. Call the municipal manager of the local government to find out if such an organization exists and how to make contact if it does.

Some local governments call planning districts economic development companies or centers.

## MANAGEMENT CONSULTANTS

Every business occasionally finds itself in a management situation that it cannot directly control or correct. When this condition prevails, a management consultant can be hired to help with the difficulties. In addition, a prospective entrepreneur may want to use a consultant to assist in the start-up phase of a new enterprise. Keep in mind that most of these consultants specialized in particular segments of management, although some generalists remain.

The management consulting profession is an unregulated industry requiring no certification. Consequently, many calling themselves consultants actually lack in the necessary education and expertise needed to be a good advisor. Given these circumstances, carefully examine the educational background and experience of any consultant before signing a service contract. Ask for client references and check them out thoroughly to insure the credibility and capability of the consultant.

Bankers, lawyers, and accountants can be excellent sources in providing contact with management consultants. Also, talking with potential or existing competitors may reveal some consultants willing to provide services in the area of business contemplated or currently being exploited. Another source of referrals are the professional associations that represent management consultants. Some maintain codes of ethics to enhance the credibility of their membership. These organizations are listed below.

Associations of Management Consultants
500 North Michigan Avenue, Suite 1400
Chicago, Illinois 60611
(312) 661-1700

Association of Consulting Management Engineers
230 Park Avenue
New York, New York 10169
(212) 697-9693

Institute of Management Consultants
19 West 44th Street
New York, New York 10036
(212) 921-2885

Society of Professional Management Consultants
16 West 56th Street
New York, New York 10019
(212) 586-2041

## MARKETING CONSULTANTS

Like management problems, marketing difficulties can also surface demanding the attention of outside expertise. Market consultants should possess the same combination of education and experience as management advisors, except in different fields, of course. The types of assistance to expect from a marketing consultant include, but is not limited to, the following:

— Market research
— Market planning
— Mail order
— Direct mail
— Distribution
— Market testing
— Merchandising

Keep in mind that marketing consultants also tend to specialize in a particular field and a generalist may be difficult to locate. Checking the yellow pages of the phone books in larger cities will reveal some prospects. In addition, bankers, accountants, and attorneys may provide good contacts. The best leads are generally given by firms that are currently using or have employed a marketing consultant. When initially talking to consultants, always ask for background information and client references. Check the information out carefully to insure credibility. A bad consultant can be costly in terms of loss of time, markets, and money.

## PERIODICALS

There are several excellent periodicals that serve the small business community. Reading and studying the contents contained within their covers can prove to be helpful to the individual wishing to start or buy a business. Also, existing enterprises can find useful material relating to the operational matters. Some of the information to be found in these publications include, but is not limited to, the following:

— Successful management techniques
— Dealing with lenders and investors
— Sources of capital
— Government assistance programs
— Marketing techniques and tips
— Bartering of goods and services
— Exporting

Appendix N contains the names and addresses of these small-business oriented periodicals.

## PUBLIC RELATIONS FIRMS AND CONSULTANTS

These organizations and consultants provide publicity services to firms or individuals wishing to exploit the news value of particular business happenings. Publicity is usually an inexpensive means of creating an image and/or generating sales. However, the public relations (PR) function does have limits and it should never be viewed as a substitute for advertising. In fact, PR is normally seen as an extension of the marketing effort.

Public relations firms and consultants are listed in the yellow pages of phone books in large and medium-sized cities. However, the best sources of contacts include business consultants, bankers, accountants, lawyers, and other businesses who have used PR services. In addition, contacting the professional association listed below might provide some referrals. When talking to potential firms or consultants, always ask for background information and investigate thoroughly.

Public Relations Society of America
33 Irving Place
New York, New York 10003
(212) 228-7228

Also, it is important to remember that many advertising agencies perform public relations services. When searching for advertising expertise, ask about PR functions as well.

## SUPPLIERS

Some vendors provide a wealth of information and help to new or existing businesses in the field they serve. A few suppliers will even go so far as to set up an entrepreneur in business by providing location, inventory, and financial assistance. Most do not go to those extremes, but many will help in one or more vital areas.

Constantly search for new suppliers. Evaluate their services and credit terms carefully. It is not unethical to play them against each other. In fact, it makes good business sense. Tell one or more suppliers that a better deal can be obtained elsewhere. Watch for their reactions. Some will bend and others will not.

Suppliers can be located in a set of publications known as *The Thomas Registers*. Most libraries have the volumes. If not available otherwise, they can be obtained by writing to the publisher whose address and phone number appears below. Inquire concerning information and the cost involved.

> Thomas Publishing Company
> One Penn Plaza
> New York, New York 10001
> (212) 290-7200

## UNIVERSITIES AND COLLEGES

Many institutions of higher education have resources available for use by the small business community. Most college and universities maintain large numbers of books, magazines, and newsletters in the fields of business and economics that can be used for research or other related purposes. In addition, these institutions offer numerous classes which, if taken, may provide helpful information. Currently, over 300 business schools offer courses in "small business management" and/or "entrepreneurism." The U.S. Small Business Administration is compiling a list of these colleges and it should be available soon. A call to the regional SBA office may reveal how to get the list. Also, many business professors moonlight as free-lance, part-time consultants offering their expertise at rates normally below those charged by established consulting firms. They can be a source of valuable information.

Some business schools want their students to work on outside projects so as to allow them real-life experiences. Many schools make it a requirement. These colleges are always looking for challenging situations that can be used as a proving ground for their students. Generally, no fee is charged to the entrepreneur or small firm and these students can provide valuable talent in most problem situations.

Seminars and workshops are additional services provided by some institutes of higher education to existing businesses of all sizes and to prospective entrepreneurs. Topics can cover the entire business spectrum and the fees are normally low. Many of these interaction meetings are held in unison with the U.S. Small Business Administration, U.S. Department of Commerce, state or local chambers of commerce, or other bodies representing business interests.

Call the local college or university for details.

Chapter IV

# CORRECT LEGAL STRUCTURE
## Evaluation Is Necessary

---

## Legal Forms of Organization

It is vitally important that entrepreneurs select the correct form of legal structure. Whether it is a new business just starting out or an existing operation, the legal form will determine to a great extent the way in which business is conducted, not to mention tax affairs. It will also affect the degree of freedom to operate within the total business environment.

Selecting the most appropriate form of legal organization is easier said than done. Many aspects must be examined, taking into account both personal and business considerations.

Five kinds of legal structure are in general use today. They are as follows: sole proprietorship, general partnership, limited partnership, corporation, and subchapter S corporation. Each has unique characteristics with certain advantages and disadvantages that need to be evaluated. Only the form which maximizes the interests of the entrepreneur and business should be selected.

### SOLE PROPRIETORSHIP

Over 95 percent of all businesses in the country are classified as proprietorships. It is the simplest form of legal structure generally requiring only a local business license to operate. Normally, the owner also serves as manager. The primary advantages of this structure are as follows:

— Easy to form—Establishing a sole proprietorship is simple and inexpensive, requiring little or no government approval. Check with the local court clerk to determine if there are any licensing requirements.
— Owner keeps all of the profit—The owner is entitled to all profits generated by the business.
— Freedom from government regulation—Most government agencies direct their regulatory efforts toward large corporate entities, although the government paperwork requirement for small businesses has increased somewhat over the last decade. Whatever the case, small firms are expected to comply with all local, state, and federal regulations even though governmental policing is held to a minimum.
— Low Taxes—The owner of a sole proprietorship is taxed as an individual, at a rate normally lower than the corporate tax rate.
— Complete control—The owner makes all of the decisions and determines management policy.
— Quick decisions—Generally, one person can make quicker decisions than a number of individuals.
— Little working capital needed—In many cases, sole proprietorship can be operated with limited capital requirements.
— Easy to terminate—A sole proprietorship can quickly and easily cease operations without red tape.

Disadvantages of the sole proprietorship form of legal organization are listed below.

— Lack of continuity—If the owner becomes ill and/or dies, the business may terminate.
— Unlimited liability—The owner is legally responsible for all debts of the business without question. If the business fails and there are debts outstanding, creditors may sue the owner to satisfy their claims. The owner's personal assets could be at risk. Certain types of loss (physical, personal injury, theft, etc.) can be prevented by maintaining adequate insurance programs.
— Capital starvation—Some proprietorships have difficulty raising money because of the limited funding alternatives available to the legal form (only one owner, can't sell stock, etc.).
— Owner spread too thin—The owner has to wear many hats performing a number of diverse business functions (marketing, purchasing, bookkeeping, etc.).

— Lack of Expertise—Generally, a proprietorship is a "one person" show with limited experience in many facets of business operations and unable to attract needed expertise because of its small size and/or little growth potential.

— Difficult to transfer ownership—Selling all or part of a sole proprietorship can be equated to the difficulty in transacting real estate. In fact, many times real estate is involved.

## GENERAL PARTNERSHIP

A partnership is defined by the Uniform Partnership Act "as an association of two or more persons to carry on as co-owners of a business for profit." Most general partnerships are evidenced by a written agreement called "Articles of Partnership." Though these articles are not required by law, most individuals involved in partnerships agree it is in the best interest of all to have a written agreement. In addition, the articles should be recorded with the clerk of the local court as a matter of public record for the protection of all individuals associated with the partnership. Articles of Partnership are designed mainly to spell out the contributions made by each partner to the business, whether by money or property, and the responsibilities of the partners in the firm. Table 8 lists the different types of partners that may be involved in partnership activities.

### TABLE 8

#### TYPES OF PARTNERS

*Ostensible (General) Partner*—Active in the business and publicly known as being a partner.

*Active Partner*—Active in the business and may or may not be publicly known as being associated with the firm.

*Secret Partner*—Active in the firm but not presented publicly as a partner.

*Dormant Partner*—Inactive in the firm and not presented publicly as a partner.

*Silent Partner*—Inactive in the firm but can be presented as being associated with the partnership.

*Nominal Partner*—Not a partner in the firm but held out publicly to be a partner, usually for prestigious reasons. In some cases, these partners can be held liable for partnership activity if their names are used to represent the firm.

*Subpartner*—Not a partner but contracts with an active partner so as to participate in the partner's business and profits.

*Limited Partner*—Is not involved in managing the partnership, therefore his/her liability is limited to the amount invested and no more.

Below are some of the more common components of a general partnership agreement:

Name of the partnership
Its purpose
Date of formation
Its address
Name and address of partners
Duration of the partnership
Contributions made by each partner
How business expenses are handled
Division of profits and losses among partners
Duties and responsibilities of each partner
Salary and/or draw of each partner
Procedure for selling partnership interest
Method of accounting and recordkeeping
Handling the death of a partner
How to change the partnership agreement
How to handle disagreements
Dealing with absence and disability
Required and prohibited actions
Protection of remaining partners if a partner dies
Provisions for the retirement of partners

Advantages to the general partnership form of legal structure are mentioned below:

— Easy to form—Procedures and expenses are minimized.
— Enhanced capital availability—Two or more people will be providing and searching for capital. In addition, funding sources are more likely to entertain financing requests because of the broader capital base.
— Low tax rate—General partners are taxed as individuals. The individual tax rate is normally lower than that of a corporation.
— Broader management base—Two or more heads are better than one.
— Better quality employees—Partnerships tend to attract good employees because of the possibility of becoming a principal in the firm.
— Managerial flexibility—Generally, important decisions can be made quickly, although not as fast as in a sole proprietorship.
— Limited government interference—Like sole proprietorships, partnerships are normally free of extensive governmental scrutiny, although compliance with regulations is a must.

Disadvantages inherent in the general partnership include the following:

— Unlimited liability—The general partners are personally liable for the debts of the partnership. General partners can legally bind each other. This is why it is extremely important to know intimately the partners involved in the firm. Make sure all general partners are credible.
— Lack of continuity—Normally, a general partnership has a limited life and is terminated on the date specified in the Articles of Partnership or upon the death of a general partner. Termination can be avoided by stating in the articles that the partnership is perpetual.
— Divided authority—General partners may disagree, causing organization disharmony.
— Profits divided—Profits are shared by all general partners.
— Scarcity of suitable partners—Appropriate partners can be difficult to locate.

## LIMITED PARTNERSHIP

Basically, limited and general partnerships share the same characteristics, with a few distinct differences worth noting. A limited partnership is defined as an association of at least one general partner and one limited partner. The limited partner is an individual who only invests capital and does not participate in managing the firm. In fact, the limited partnership form of business organization is viewed by many as a capital generating mechanism used quite frequently in real estate, oil and gas development, and mining deals. Very attractive tax benefits can be passed to investors involved in a limited partnership agreement.

The main thing to remember is that the general partner(s) in a limited partnership has unlimited liability for the debts of the business without question. On the other hand, limited partners are not liable for partnership debts if they do not participate in managing the business. Their personal assets are not at stake if the limited partnership incurs debts. They can only lose the amount invested and nothing more. Keep in mind that recent court rulings have determined that limited partners who actively get involved in management functions and affairs are not, in fact, limited partners and should be considered general partners, thereby assuming unlimited risk for the debts of the partnership.

If the limited partnership generates profits, the general partners are normally rewarded by receiving between one and 20 percent of all income produced after expenses are paid. The remaining 80 to 99 percent is divided among the limited partners. Percentages vary among different propositions.

## CORPORATION

The corporation is the most complex legal structure discussed thus far. In 1819, Chief Justice Marshall defined a corporation as an "artificial being, invisible, intangible, and existing only in contemplation of the law." Consequently, the corporation is a legal entity separate from the people who own or operate it.

Corporations are normally formed subject to approval of the state government in the state in which the corporation will reside. If doing business in a number of states, the corporation needs to get the approval of each state and will be classified as a "foreign corporation" within those borders.

In order to form a corporation, an organizational meeting must take place. The organizer(s) must draft a corporate charter, also known as "Articles of Incorporation" which outline the powers and limitations of the proposed corporation. Table 9 shows an example of actual articles of incorporation that can be used by a Virginia corporation. The charter is then submitted to the secretary of state in the domicile state for approval. If the charter is disapproved, the secretary's office will probably recommend changes in the articles of incorporation so as to facilitate a positive decision. Table 9 illustrates an approved charter issued after articles of incorporation were submitted and accepted by the State of Virginia.

Typical articles of incorporation would include the following elements:

— Name of the corporation—Most states will not allow a corporation to pick a name similar to a corporate name already in existence, in order to avoid confusion. In addition, the name chosen may not be offensive or deceptive to the public. It is wise to call the State Corporation Commission or secretary of state to determine if the name selected can be used before submitting the articles of incorporation. Time and energy may be saved by avoiding disapproval and return of the articles. Some states will allow corporate organizers to reserve a name until the articles of incorporation are sent to the appropriate agency. Normally, there is a small fee for this service.

TABLE 9

*ARTICLES OF INCORPORATION*
of
*Telemedia, Inc.*

FIRST.—The name of this corporation is Telemedia, Inc.

SECOND.—Its registered office in the State of Virginia is located at *100 Anywhere Drive* in the City of *Winchester.* The registered agent in charge thereof is James L. Silvester who is a resident of the State of Virginia and who is a director of the corporation and whose business office is the same as the registered office of the corporation.

THIRD.—The purposes for which the corporation is organized are as follows:

A. To contract for and fund the development and production of television programs for distribution to cable television networks, on a syndicated basis to independent and major network owned and affiliated commercial television stations, to pay television systems, to public television stations and systems, and to such additional outlets as become available for programming. The Company intends to develop the ancillary marketing potential of these projects, and other projects independent of the television market, for distribution to the video disk and video cassette markets, audiocassette markets, records, radio, books, newspapers, and other print media, so as to enhance merchandising opportunities.

B. To do all other things lawful, necessary, or incident to the accomplishment of the purposes set forth above; to exercise all lawful powers now possessed by Virginia corporations of similar character; and to engage in any business in which a corporation organized under the laws of Virginia may engage except any business that is required to be specifically set forth in the articles of incorporation.

FOURTH.—The amount of the total authorized capital stock of this corporation is 10,000 common shares—par value 5 dollars per share, which equals fifty thousand dollars ($50,000).

FIFTH.—The number of directors constituting the initial board of directors is *three,* and the names and addresses of the persons who are to serve as the initial directors are:

(Names and addresses are listed here)

SIXTH.—The directors shall have power to make and to alter or amend the By-Laws; subject to stockholders' rights under Section 13.1-24 of the codes of the State of Virginia; to fix the amount to be reserved as working capital, and to authorize and cause to be executed, mortgages and liens without limit as to the amount, upon the property and franchise of the corporation.

The By-Laws shall determine whether and to what extent the accounts and books of this corporation, or any of them shall be open to the inspection of the stockholders; and no stockholder shall have any right of inspecting any account, or book or document of this corporation, except as conferred by the law or the By-Laws, or by resolution of the stockholders.

The stockholders and directors shall have power to hold their meetings and keep the books, documents and papers of the corporation outside the State of Virginia, at such places as may be from time to time designated by the By-Laws or by resolutions of the stockholders or directors, except as otherwise required by the laws of the State of Virginia.

The object, powers, and purposes specified in any clause or paragraph herein above contained shall be construed as general powers conferred by the laws of the State of Virginia; and it is hereby expressly provided that the foregoing enumeration of specific powers shall in no wise limit or restrict any other power, object, or purpose of the corporation, or in any matter affect any general powers or authority of the corporation.

I, the UNDERSIGNED, for the purpose of forming a corporation under the laws of the State of Virginia, do make, file, and record these articles, and do certify that the facts herein are true; and I have accordingly hereunto set my hand.

DATED: _____                    SIGNED: _____
                                                INCORPORATOR

— Purpose—The purpose for which the corporation was formed must be stated in precise terminology. Some states allow the use of broad language when stating corporate purpose, such as, "The purpose of the corporation is to engage in any lawful act or activity for which a corporation may be organized." However, most states want exact purposes clearly stated. Many corporate organizers use both approaches, for good reason. Making a specific statement of purpose will satisfy most states without question. In addition, others (such as funding sources) may look more favorably on the corporation if specific purposes are stated. Also, other states will be more willing to let the corporation do business within its borders without changing the corporate charter (articles of incorporation). A broad statement of purpose will give the corporation maneuvering room to expand into other profitable areas when opportunities arise.

— Life of the business—A statement of how long the corporation is to remain in business. It may be for months, years, or perpetuity. Some states will not require that this be answered, but will assume that the life is perpetual unless otherwise stated.

— Location—The address of the corporation's registered office must be stated. If the corporation wishes to incorporate in a state other than the one in which it resides, an office may be required in the other state. However, the establishment of the office can be avoided if the corporation appoints a "registered agent" in the state to act in behalf of its interests. The agent will be required to maintain certain corporate records and to accept communications between the state of incorporation and the corporation. Some states will require the agent representing the corporation to maintain an office. Some agents offer their services to many corporations wanting to incorporate in other states. Their fees for agent services are very reasonable. Call the State Corporation Commission or secretary of state in the state where incorporation is desired and ask for a list of registered agents.

— Incorporator(s)—The names and addresses of the incorporator(s) (organizers) need to be stated. Most states require that at least one incorporator be a resident of the state in which incorporation will take place.

— Capital Structure—The type of capital stock and the maximum amount authorized to be issued must be stated. The corporation must promulgate the number and class of shares to be offered. In addition, the privileges and limitations of each class of shares must be detailed in some states.

— Capital Requirement—Many states require a minimum capital infusion before the corporate charter (articles of incorporation) is approved.

— Preemptive Rights—A statement detailing the rights or restrictions of existing stockholders to purchase additional shares if issued by the corporation in proportion to their existing ownership interest before offering the new stock to prospective shareholders. Allowing preemptive rights gives existing shareholders the right to maintain their percentage control of the business.

— Initial Directors—The names and addresses of the individuals who will serve as initial directors must be given. These people serve until the first stockholder's meeting, after which they will either continue to serve or be replaced.

— Internal Affairs—A statement of how the corporation will be regulated. In most cases, by-laws are acknowledged as being the internal law of the corporation, and will be discussed below.

— Charter Changes—Procedures for changing the articles of incorporation should be stated even though it is defined in state law.

After the charter is approved by the state, stockholders need to have a meeting to adopt corporate by-laws and elect the board of directors. The board will in turn appoint the corporate officers. The by-laws are designed to serve as internal regulations that govern the operation of the corporation by establishing rights and limitations. Some by-laws will duplicate provisions of the articles of incorporation (charter) and state law. The most common by-laws used in corporation include, but are not limited to, the following:

— Address of the principal office. If preferred, all offices can be listed.
— Time, place, and required notification of annual stockholder meeting.
— Procedure for calling special stockholders' meetings.
— Required quorum and voting rights and limitations of stockholders.
— Number of corporate directors involved along with their compensation, if any. Lengths of terms of office, methods for electing and reelecting, and procedures for creating or dealing with vacancies on the board.
— Time, place, and required notification of regular board meetings.
— Procedures for calling special board meetings.
— Required quorum and voting rights and limitations of directors.
— Method of selecting corporate officers.
— Statement of major corporate officers (titles such as Chairman of the Board, Vice Chairman of the Board, President, Vice President, Treasurer, Secretary, etc.), including responsibilities and term of office.
— Procedures for creating new corporate positions and dealing with vacancies.
— Procedures for the issuance of stock.
— Form of stock certificate to use, including the terminology on the certificate.
— Procedures for handling stock transfers and record keeping.
— Procedure for the approval and issuance of dividends on a regular or irregular basis.
— Statement of the fiscal year.
— Sample of the corporate seal.
— Authorization to open financial accounts and sign checks.
— Procedures for issuing the annual statement and other periodic reports to the stockholders. Who's responsible.
— Steps and procedures for changing the by-laws.

The corporate form of legal structure has definite pros and cons. Advantages are listed below:

— Limited Liability—Stockholders are liable only for the amount of their investment, in most cases. In rare situations, stockholders may be at risk for more than the amount invested if the stock they purchase is assessable. Check the stock certificate. If it says "fully paid and assessable," liability may be greater than investment. However, most certificates read "fully paid and non-assessable" which means the risk is limited. Also, if the corporation is sued, stockholders are normally free of liability. However, managers may be subject to suit.

— Ease of Transferability—Ownership can be easily transferred by signing the stock certificate(s).
— Legal Entity—A corporation is a separate entity standing by itself, divorced from its owners and managers in the eyes of the law.
— Diversified Management—Some corporations have the ability to attract and draw on the skills of several individuals.
— Continuous Life—Corporations are generally perpetual in nature and can only be terminated by a vote of the stockholders. The state may revoke a corporate charter if laws are being broken by the corporation. Rarely, a corporation will elect to limit its life. This limitation must be stated in the articles of incorporation. If the corporation decides at a later date to be perpetual, the articles may be changed to reflect that wish.
— Ease in Raising Capital—Money can be generated by issuing shares of stocks and/or issuing bonds, in addition to the same funding methods available to other legal structures.

The corporate structure can present a number of difficulties to its owners and managers. Below are listed the most common:

— Government Interference—Corporations are more regulated than the other forms of legal organizations.
— Double Taxation—Corporations are taxed twice, in that they pay taxes on business income and then the stockholders must pay tax on their dividends. In addition, many states require corporations to pay a tax on their total capital.
— Corporate Formation—Starting a corporation is more difficult and usually more expensive than other legal forms.
— Charter Restrictions—The activities of a corporation may be limited by its articles of incorporation and laws not affecting other legal forms.
— Records—Normally, corporations require more bookkeeping responsibilities than do sole proprietorships or partnerships.

— Possible Liability—Many lenders will require the managers and major stockholders of a small corporation to endorse and guarantee loan agreements. This procedure may extend to other contractual agreements as well. This situation puts the personal assets of the managers and stockholders at risk.

It is not really difficult to form a corporation in most states. In fact, many entrepreneurs form their own without legal assistance, thereby saving hundreds or even thousands of dollars. Generally, states will assist in incorporation by providing booklets, forms, and samples to use in the process. Table 10 shows the sample "articles of incorporation" provided by the State of Virginia to prospective incorporators. Some states actually promote individuals to incorporate within their boundaries by using incentives. For example, Delaware, Nevada, and Wyoming are very popular incorporation states because of low capital taxes and a friendly attitude toward corporations. Also, these states have no corporate income taxes. Table 11 gives the names and addresses of the offices to contact in the above-mentioned states.

Normally, individuals can incorporate their businesses and expect no legal problems. There are instances in which the complexities of the business might necessitate an attorney being involved in the incorporation process. For example, a firm with many investors and/or engaged in interstate commerce might consider using legal assistance in putting the corporation together. The entrepreneur will have to decide for himself/herself if an attorney is needed. Whatever the case, most small business people should never pay over $300 in legal fees for incorporation services unless the business affairs of the business are complex. If self-incorporation is the desired approach, get a copy of the book, *How to Form Your Own Corporation Without a Lawyer for Under $50*, by Ted Nicholas. The publisher is Enterprise Publishing, Inc., located at 725 Market Street in Wilmington, Delaware 19801. It costs $14.95. This publication is considered the bible of self-incorporators, with over 750,000 in print. It includes ready-made forms to use along with the names, addresses, and fees for all state agencies involved in the incorporation process.

## SUBCHAPTER S CORPORATION

A number of years ago, Congress recognized the need to increase the flexibility of small firms that use the corporate form of legal structure. Therefore, the subchapter S corporation was created and

## TABLE 10

### MODEL FORM FOR ARTICLES OF INCORPORATION

**For a Virginia stock corporation for general business purposes**

**NOTE:** This is designed as a model of the shortest permissible form of articles of incorporation; it contains all the required provisions. Other provisions may be added as desired in accordance with specific Sections of the Act to which reference should be made.

### ARTICLES OF INCORPORATION
### OF

_____

We hereby associate to form a stock corporation under the provisions of Chapter 1 of Title 13.1 of the Code of Virginia and to that end set forth the following:

(a)   The name of the corporation is

(b)   The purpose or purposes for which the corporation is organized are:

(c)   The aggregate number of shares which the corporation shall have authorized to issue and the par value per share are as follows:

| CLASS AND SERIES | NUMBER OF SHARES | PAR VALUE PER SHARE OR NO PAR VALUE |
|---|---|---|

**NOTE:** If there is to be more than one class of stock, the preferences, limitations and relative rights of the different classes should be set forth in this article.

(d)   The post-office address of the initial registered office is

_____, Virginia.

(Number)        (Street)                                    (Post Office)        (Zone)

The name of the city or the name of the county in which the initial registered office is located is_____

of_____ . The name of its registered agent is _____,

who is a resident of Virginia and who is a director of the corporation or who is a member of Virginia State Bar, and whose business office is the same as the registered office of the corporation.

(e)   The number of directors constituting the initial board of directors is _____ and the names and addresses of the persons who are to serve as the initial directors are:

| _Name_ | _Address_ |
|---|---|

Dated_____ . 19_____ .

_____

_____

_____

FEES ARE ON THE BACK OF THIS FORM                    _Incorporators_

USE AS GUIDE ONLY

## TABLE 11

Secretary of State
State of Delaware
Dover, Delaware 19901

Secretary of State
State of Nevada
Carson City, Nevada 89710

Secretary of State
State of Wyoming
Capitol Building
Cheyenne, Wyoming 82002

designed to permit closely held "small business corporations" to be treated as partnerships from a tax perspective, thereby eliminating double taxation. A standard corporation is taxed on two occasions. It must pay tax on its business income and then shareholders (owners) are taxed on the portion of net profits distributed and paid as dividends. Subchapter S provisions allow shareholders to absorb all corporate income or losses as partners and report it as individual taxpayers. In essence, the subchapter S corporation is not affected by corporate income taxes, thereby eliminating the double taxation feature of standard corporations. Aside from being treated as a partnership from a tax standpoint, the subchapter S and standard corporation share most of the same pros and cons, with a few exceptions.

A corporation must meet certain requirements before the subchapter S alternative becomes feasible. They are:

— The corporation must be a domestic entity (incorporated within the United States).
— The corporation can only have one class of stock.
— Only individuals or estates can be shareholders.
— The corporation cannot be part of another organization.
— The number of shareholders may not exceed 40.
— The corporation cannot have any nonresident alien shareholders.
— 20 percent or more of its revenue must be domestically generated.
— Dividends, interests, royalties, rents, annuities, and securities transactions cannot account for more than 20 percent of total revenues.

If the corporation meets all of the above requirements and wants to adopt the subchapter S option, it must do so within 75 days of starting business activity. In the case of an existing firm, adoption must be executed sometime within the initial 75 days of the firm's fiscal year. All shareholders in the business must give consent to electing the subchapter S structure. Their willingness will be evidenced by signing IRS Form 2553 which can be obtained by writing the local or regional IRS office. Table 12 illustrates this document. The adoption will remain effective until the corporation decides to cancel the status or the IRS revokes it because the firm has failed to maintain the required conditions. Cancellation will prevent the firm from adopting the subchapter S structure a second time in the near future. There is a waiting period of several years before the status can be renewed.

Subchapter S corporations do provide a few very attractive benefits to family corporations. Recent tax legislation has made it extremely advantageous to establish retirement programs under subchapter S provisions. In addition, family members who are shareholders can shift income from one member to another in order to minimize the tax bite. For example, a father in a high tax bracket can shift income to his son whose tax rate is lower, thereby reducing the tax burden on the whole family.

The major negative aspect of the subchapter S legal structure is its limitation on the number of shareholders it can assume (40 maximum). If the corporation is in an expansion mode and needs to raise additional funds over and above the financial capabilities of its present shareholders, the subchapter S status may have to be forfeited. The firm's management will need to evaluate the benefits of receiving the additional capital versus the cost of dropping the subchapter S form of legal organization. In addition, many states refuse to officially acknowledge the subchapter S form; therefore, corporate income or loss is not given preferential treatment under the income tax codes of the hostile state, although federal income tax advantages still exist.

## Section 1244 Stock

Before forming a corporation it is wise to remember that certain tax incentives are available to make a business an attractive investment to prospective investors who may want to purchase stock (ownership) in the enterprise. When the directors have the first board meeting, they

88 CORRECT LEGAL STRUCTURE

## TABLE 12

| Form **2553** (Rev. October 1981) Department of the Treasury Internal Revenue Service | **Election by a Small Business Corporation** (Under section 1372 of the Internal Revenue Code) ▶ For Paperwork Reduction Act Notice, see instructions on back. | OMB No. 1545-0146 Expires 8-31-84 |
|---|---|---|

**Note:** This election under section 1372(a) to be treated as an "electing small business corporation" for income tax purposes can be approved only if all the tests in Instruction B are met.

| Name of corporation (see instructions) | Employer identification number (see instructions) | Principal business activity and specific product or service (see instructions) |
|---|---|---|
| Number and street | | Election is to be effective for tax year beginning (month, day, year) |
| City or town, State and ZIP code | | Number of shares issued and outstanding (see instructions) |

Is the corporation the outgrowth or continuation of any form of predecessor? . . . . . ☐ Yes ☐ No

If "Yes," state name of predecessor, type of organization, and period of its existence ▶ ......................

Date and place of incorporation

If this election takes effect for the first tax year the corporation exists, complete A through H below, otherwise complete E through H.

| A Date corporation first had shareholders | B Date corporation first had assets | C Date corporation began doing business | D Annual return will be filed for tax year ending (month) |
|---|---|---|---|
| | | | |

| E Name of each shareholder, person having a community property interest in the corporation's stock, and each tenant in common, joint tenant, and tenant by the entirety. (A husband and wife (and their estates) are treated as one shareholder. However, both must be listed below if both own interest in stock of the corporation.) | F Shareholders' Consent Statement. We, the undersigned shareholders, consent to the corporation's election to be treated as an "electing small business corporation" under section 1372(a). *(Shareholders sign and date below.) | G Stock owned | | H. Social security number (employer identification number of estate or trust) |
|---|---|---|---|---|
| | | Number of shares | Dates acquired | |
| 1 | | | | |
| 2 | | | | |
| 3 | | | | |
| 4 | | | | |
| 5 | | | | |
| 6 | | | | |
| 7 | | | | |
| 8 | | | | |
| 9 | | | | |
| 10 | | | | |
| 11 | | | | |
| 12 | | | | |
| 13 | | | | |
| 14 | | | | |
| 15 | | | | |

*For this election to be valid, the consent of each shareholder, person having a community property interest in the corporation's stock, and each tenant in common, joint tenant, and tenant by the entirety must either appear above or be attached to this form. (See instructions for column F.)

Under penalties of perjury, I declare that I have examined this election, including accompanying schedules and statements, and to the best of my knowledge and belief it is true, correct, and complete.

Signature and Title of Officer ▶                                                                    Date ▶

should consider the election of a section under the Internal Revenue Code (Number 1244) that allows an investor to treat a loss in "small business stock" as an ordinary instead of a capital loss, thereby enhancing its positive tax impact. In order for a corporation to qualify its shares as "section 1244 stock," it must approve the concept at the first director's meeting and before the issuances of any equity. Also, the shares issued can only be common stock and must be sold by the firm in exchange for money or property subject to a promulgated plan, with a few restrictions. Another legal limitation states that the amount of capital received for the shares may not exceed certain dollar limits that have been established.

## Question Thyself

Before deciding what legal form to select, consider the following questions very carefully.

— What is the nature of liability from a personal standpoint?
— Would the business continue if the entrepreneur or other key principals of the firm became ill and/or died? Is it important that it does continue?
— Which legal structure would allow the greatest flexibility in management?
— Can additional capital be easily sought if needed?
— Can additional expertise be attracted if needed?
— Does the degree of regulation hamper business activity?
— What legal form can best fulfill the goals of the entrepreneur and business?

## If in Doubt Look About

Many people lack the legal and accounting expertise needed to make a sound judgment about legal structure. Therefore, it is advisable to seek out the help of a competent tax attorney or certified public accountant (CPA) to insure the correct selection.

### For Further Help

*How to Form Your Own Corporation Without a Lawyer for Under $50*, by Ted Nicholas. Enterprise Publishing, Inc., 725 Market Street, Wilmington, DE 19801. Price—$14.95

*Tax and Business Organization Aspects of Small Business,* by Jonathan Sobeloff. Joint Committee on Continuing Legal Education of The American Law Institute and The American Bar Association, 4025 Chestnut Street, Philadelphia, PA 19104

*Selecting the Legal Structure for Your Firm.* Free publication available from the U.S. Small Business Administration, P.O. Box 15434, Ft. Worth, Texas 76119. Ask for management aid number 231.

*Incorporating a Small Business.* Free publication available from the U.S. Small Business Administration, P.O. Box 15434, Ft. Worth, Texas 76119. Ask for management aid number 223.

*Partnership Desk Book,* by Burton J. Defren. Institute for Business Planning, IBP Plaza, Englewood Cliffs, NJ 07632.

# Chapter V

# NATURE OF SMALL BUSINESS FINANCING
## Be Prepared

---

## Capital and Small Business

That old maxim that suggests it takes money to make money is as true today as it was a century ago. Both new and existing businesses must have access to financial resources in order to take advantage of profitable situations that may arise. Funds are needed to market new products, pay vendors, meet payrolls, buy equipment, and extend credit to customers, just to mention a few business activities.

Money alone will not insure you a successful operation. Capital, like any resource, must be managed efficiently in order to maximize profits. Many cash rich firms have failed to turn profits because of poor or inadequate financial management. For example, a company that has large cash deposits on hand in a checking account, earning nominal interest income, may feel secure in the short term. But these are idle funds, not being used to generate revenues, which are vital in creating adequate profits.

Many new and operating small businesses suffer from undercapitalization and/or funds mismanagement. These afflictions are major causes of business failures. Generally, the end result is a capital squeeze forcing the owners to close down. The trick is to recognize the problem, early in the ball game, before it becomes reality and unmanageable, thereby avoiding the squeeze altogether.

## Capital and the New Business

The capital requirements to start a new business will vary depending upon many factors. These need to be analyzed and investigated with great care so as to avoid underestimating financial resources needed to start and carry the business until profits are generated internally to support operations. For example, the type of operation you are starting will determine, to a great extent, your initial capital needs. A manufacturing operation will require more capital than a retail establishment. Wholesaling outlets tend to require more funds than service firms. Other items that need to be considered include location of the enterprise, current and projected economic climate, product/service to be offered, credit policies, etc.

A lot of thought and consideration should be given when studying your initial capital requirements. Many entrepreneurs, with good products and services, fail in their business attempts because of underestimating capital requirements in the beginning.

Tables 13 and 14 are provided courtesy of the Small Business Administration. If used correctly, they will provide you with estimates of capital needs to start any small business. It is advisable to have your lawyer and/or accountant assist you in completing the sheets. This will help in making accurate estimates. Once capital needs have been determined, the next step is to obtain the necessary funds to commence operation. These procedures will be discussed in Chapters VI-VIII.

## Capital and the Existing Business

Many entrepreneurs fail to anticipate capital needs for present and future operations. Eventually, cash flow problems develop because of the undercapitalization and existing funds will prove inadequate in paying current obligations. This situation is not reserved exclusively for the small business person. Some large firms have met their demise because of failing to project funding needs. W.T. Grant, the giant discount chain, collapsed because it grew too quickly before uncovering sources of funds to finance the expansion. Cash flow problems developed that could not be reversed and the rest is history.

As a business expands, so do its capital needs. If growth increases faster than capital availability, a cash squeeze will occur causing financial hardship. Likewise, if the business is stagnant due to economic conditions and the availability of capital contracts, cash flow difficulties will ensue.

## TABLE 13

| ESTIMATED MONTHLY EXPENSES | | | |
|---|---|---|---|
| Item | Your estimate of monthly expenses based on sales of $ _____ per year | Your estimate of how much cash you need to start your business (See column 3.) | What to put in column 2 (These figures are typical for one kind of business. you will have to decide how many months to allow for in your business.) |
| | Column 1 | Column 2 | Column 3 |
| Salary of owner-manager | $ | $ | 2 times column 1 |
| All other salaries and wages | | | 3 times column 1 |
| Rent | | | 3 times column 1 |
| Advertising | | | 3 times column 1 |
| Delivery expense | | | 3 times column 1 |
| Supplies | | | 3 times column 1 |
| Telephone and telegraph | | | 3 times column 1 |
| Other utilities | | | 3 times column 1 |
| Insurance | | | Payment required by insurance company |
| Taxes, including Social Security | | | 4 times column 1 |
| Interest | | | 3 times column 1 |
| Maintenance | | | 3 times column 1 |
| Legal and other professional fees | | | 3 times column 1 |
| Miscellaneous | | | 3 times column 1 |
| **STARTING COSTS YOU ONLY HAVE TO PAY ONCE** | | | Leave column 2 blank |
| Fixtures and equipment | | | Fill in table 14 and put the total here |
| Decorating and remodeling | | | Talk it over with a contractor |
| Installation of fixtures and equipment | | | Talk to suppliers from who you buy these |
| Starting inventory | | | Suppliers will probably help you estimate this |
| Deposits with public utilities | | | Find out from utilities companies |
| Legal and other professional fees | | | Lawyer, accountant, and so on |
| Licenses and permits | | | Find out from city offices what you have to have |
| Advertising and promotion for opening | | | Estimate what you'll use |
| Accounts receivable | | | What you need to buy more stock until credit customers pay |
| Cash | | | For unexpected expenses or losses, special purchases, etc. |
| Other | | | Make a separate list and enter total |
| **TOTAL ESTIMATED CASH YOU NEED TO START WITH** | | $ | Add up all the numbers in column 2 |

Source: U.S. Small Business Administration.

TABLE 14

## LIST OF FURNITURE, FIXTURES, AND EQUIPMENT

| Leave out or add items to suit your business. Use separate sheets to list exactly what you need for each of the items below. | If you plan to pay cash in full, enter the full amount below and in the last column. | If you are going to pay by installments, fill out the columns below. Enter in the last column your downpayment plus at least one installment. | | | Estimate of the cash you need for furniture, fixtures, and equipment |
|---|---|---|---|---|---|
| | | Price | Downpayment | Amount of each installment | |
| Counters | $ | $ | $ | $ | $ |
| Storage shelves, cabinets | | | | | |
| Display stands, shelves, tables | | | | | |
| Cash register | | | | | |
| Safe | | | | | |
| Window display fixtures | | | | | |
| Special lighting | | | | | |
| Outside sign | | | | | |
| Delivery equipment if needed | | | | | |
| **TOTAL FURNITURE, FIXTURES, AND EQUIPMENT** (Enter this figure also in table 13 under "Starting Costs You Only Have To Pay Once.") | | | | | $ |

Source: U.S. Small Business Administration.

TABLE 15

**Cash Budget**

(For three months, ending March 31, 19 _____)

| | January | | February | | March | |
|---|---|---|---|---|---|---|
| | Budget | Actual | Budget | Actual | Budget | Actual |
| **Expected Cash Receipts:** | | | | | | |
| 1. Cash sales | ___ | ___ | ___ | ___ | ___ | ___ |
| 2. Collections on accounts receivable | ___ | ___ | ___ | ___ | ___ | ___ |
| 3. Other income | ___ | ___ | ___ | ___ | ___ | ___ |
| 4. Total cash receipts | ___ | ___ | ___ | ___ | ___ | ___ |
| **Expected Cash Payments** | | | | | | |
| 5. Raw materials | ___ | ___ | ___ | ___ | ___ | ___ |
| 6. Payroll | ___ | ___ | ___ | ___ | ___ | ___ |
| 7. Other factory expenses (including maintenance) | ___ | ___ | ___ | ___ | ___ | ___ |
| 8. Advertising | ___ | ___ | ___ | ___ | ___ | ___ |
| 9. Selling expense | ___ | ___ | ___ | ___ | ___ | ___ |
| 10. Administrative expense (including salary of owner-manager) | ___ | ___ | ___ | ___ | ___ | ___ |
| 11. New plant and equipment | ___ | ___ | ___ | ___ | ___ | ___ |
| 12. Other payments(taxes, including estimated income tax; repayment of loans; interest; etc.) | ___ | ___ | ___ | ___ | ___ | ___ |
| 13. Total cash payments | ___ | ___ | ___ | ___ | ___ | ___ |
| 14. **Expected Cash Balance** at beginning of the month | ___ | ___ | ___ | ___ | ___ | ___ |
| 15. Cash increase of decrease (item 4 minus item 13) | ___ | ___ | ___ | ___ | ___ | ___ |
| 16. Expected cash balance at end of month (item 14 plus item 15) | ___ | ___ | ___ | ___ | ___ | ___ |
| 17. Desired working cash balance | ___ | ___ | ___ | ___ | ___ | ___ |
| 18. Short-term loans needed (item 17 minus item 16, if item 17 is larger) | ___ | ___ | ___ | ___ | ___ | ___ |
| 19. Cash available for dividends, capital cash expenditures, and/or short investments (item 16 minus item 17, if item 16 is larger than item 17) | ___ | ___ | ___ | ___ | ___ | ___ |
| **Capital Cash:** | | | | | | |
| 20. Cash available (item 19 after deducting dividends, etc.) | ___ | ___ | ___ | ___ | ___ | ___ |
| 21. Desired capital cash (item 11, new plant equipment) | ___ | ___ | ___ | ___ | ___ | ___ |
| 22. Long-term loans needed (item 21 less item 20, if item 20 is larger than item 20) | ___ | ___ | ___ | ___ | ___ | ___ |

Source: U.S. Small Business Administration.

Capital needs arise because of many factors. Economic conditions on the local, state, or national level can cause revenues to temporarily decline, thereby making it difficult to meet obligations. Abnormal increases in accounts receivable (customer accounts) due to asset mismanagement and/or unexpected growth can cause a need for financial resources. Increasing inventory levels to support revenue growth and the purchase of new equipment to increase productivity will call for additional capital input. Purchasing merchandise before suppliers increase their prices and seasonal factors will increase the need to finance these inventories until sales are made and receivables collected. In addition, the exploitation of unexpected profit opportunities as they arise will call for capital over and above that which is normally available. Also, excessive withdrawal of earnings from the business and a reduction in credit or payment terms by suppliers will also increase capital needs.

Causes of capital shortages cannot be traced to any single event. There is a combination of factors that create the problems. Identification and positive reaction to these anticipated funding problems will insure proper cash flow and help avoid a potentially injurious capital squeeze. The cash budget in Table 15 will help project the capital needs for a business already in operation. The table, listing only three months, should be expanded to include an entire year, taking into consideration yearly objectives.

An accountant should assist when recording the projections. If expense records are maintained and posted to the table on a monthly basis, a comparison between budget estimates and actual expenditures can be made. Any variances that exist (differences between what was budgeted and actually spent) can be analyzed to determine the effects upon the financial structure of the business.

# Chapter VI

# UNDERSTANDING MONEY SOURCES
## The Bank Isn't the Final Stop

### Never Enough Money

Once you start or buy a small business, your need for capital is constant. Money is needed to finance current operations, expansion, seasonal inventories, and, in some cases, just to stay afloat. Unfortunately, traditional sources of funding for entrepreneurs have been less accommodating lately. Commercial banks, which supply over 65 percent of small business capital requirements, have downgraded their commitment to small firms. Many banks are raising service fees to small businesses above that which is charged their larger business customers. What's more, small firms usually are charged higher interest rates on loans than are larger businesses. Aspiring entrepreneurs, wishing to start their own businesses, have been left out in the cold almost completely. Banks claim that financing new, unproven enterprises is just too risky. To make matters worse, the U.S. Small Business Administration, which has come to be known as the lender of last resort, and other government funding outlets, have fallen victim to the Reagan budget ax.

Individuals wishing to start new businesses or expand existing operations do have alternatives when seeking capital beyond the traditional avenues of friend, family, self, and banks. Many of these are overlooked by entrepreneurs in the search process.

**Capital Evolution**

The capital needs of a business will be determined, to a great extent, by its stage of evolution. Each stage will demand different funding requirements. An understanding of these are needed in order to adequately project the need for financial resources.

- Seed Stage—This is capital to formulate an idea. The product or service is still on the drawing board being developed. At this stage market feasibility studies are conducted and examined. Most of this funding is provided by the entrepreneur and/or close associates, although it should be pointed out that some financial organizations have begun to fund businesses in the seed stage.

- Start-up Stage—This type of financing is used to get the new company off the ground. Product/service development is being completed and it has been determined that a market exists. Major emphasis is placed on developing managerial expertise, completing final market studies, projecting financial resources, etc. Generally, the product or service is not being marketed at this point.

- First Stage—This funding is provided to launch production of the product or service and to initiate marketing efforts.

- Second Stage—Capital is made available to finance initial cash flow and facilitate expansion of the new company. At this point, the company is not usually showing a profit. Money is needed to support inventories and accounts receivable (customer accounts) until sufficient profits are generated to support operations.

- Third Stage—Normally this money is provided to expand the business on a large scale. Sales are growing very rapidly and profits are being generated. Very little of the market for the firm's product or service has been exploited and funds are needed to support additional marketing endeavors, production, and working capital.

- Fourth Stage (also referred to as bridge financing)—This capital is used as interim financing until financial resources are obtained through a public offering of stock. At times, the bridge money is repaid out of the proceeds of the stock offering once executed. In this stage the company is attempting to make the transition from small firm to medium-size business. Subsequent public offerings can be made in order to continue expansion and growth.

- Acquisition Funding—Resources made available to allow a company to expand by purchasing other firms is an example of acquisition financing. Mergers and consolidations are common results of using this method of funding.

- Leverage Buyout—This financing technique can be used when the existing net assets of a company exceed its selling price. Since most companies are sold based upon a multiple of earnings, and that multiple has been decreasing over the last decade due to economic conditions, companies can be purchased by third parties utilizing assets as collateral for loans provided to these parties by financial outlets and/or previous owners. Management and employees can use this method to purchase their company. There have been cases reported where management teams have bought entire firms, using leverage techniques, without investing a penny of their own funds.

## Capital Generation—Two Forms

Profits generated within a business can be used to finance various aspects of a firm's operation. This is referred to as *internal funding* and is an inexpensive source of money. Internal capital generation can be achieved in several ways. Cutting costs, selling surplus inventories and equipment, speeding up collection of accounts receivable, and retaining more profits in the business are a number of ways to augment internal capital.

In contrast, capital generated outside the business is called *external* financing. Outlets such as banks, suppliers, commercial finance companies, and investment bankers would be examples of sources external to the firm. Generally there are costs associated with this form of financing and they will be discussed later in this chapter.

Before utilizing external sources, a company should determine if its capital requirements can be met internally. Even though this may not generate all capital requirements needed, it will reduce dependency on external funding, thereby reducing interest costs and/or loss of control. Furthermore, the demonstrated capability to maximize internal capital will enhance the confidence of lenders and investors in the company and its management. This will increase their incentive to commit financial resources on a reasonable basis.

Utilizing internal funding can be costly at times. For example, selling assets to generate cash may have to be done at a loss; unloading certain fixed assets now may force the business to pursue costly sources of materials later on down the road; rigorous inventory reductions may cause stock shortages needed to generate production and/or sales; and the tightening of credit policies may result in loss of customers.

Generally speaking, a business that uses internal financing to the maximum will benefit from the approach. Although, this policy may have to be altered if at some point in the future external funding is needed, especially equity capital. Many equity investors are interested in dividend income. These investors may be discouraged if the firm's policies mandate reinvesting all net income in the business without rewarding investors in the form of dividends. Some speculative investors may be interested only in the capital gain potential of an investment (increase in the value of their investment) without expecting dividend income. Normally, investors expect both dividend yield and capital gains.

## What Kind of Capital

When seeking funding alternatives for your small business, it is important to analyze carefully the purpose for which the capital will be used. This will determine the kinds of funds needed to carry out your objectives. Deciding what type of capital to employ can be a difficult task since many of the kinds of capital available, although different in name, can be used at the same time and for similar or identical purposes.

In general terms, there are two ways to fund a new or existing business. Many firms use a combination of these to finance operations. *Debt financing* is simply money borrowed from a lender, where you promise to repay the principal amount of the loan plus interest on agreed-upon terms, usually evidenced by a contract (loan agreement). *Equity financing* is somewhat different. This technique allows a business owner to exchange ownership in the firm for capital re-sources. These funds do not have to be repaid like a loan, but the equity investor will expect a return on investment in the form of stock dividends and/or capital gains upon selling the stock back to you or a third party. The major disadvantage to this form of financing is your loss of some control over the business because of the new owners.

Debt comes in several forms. A loan can be *unsecured,* in which no collateral is used to back the note. Your credit reputation is the only security available to the lender in this agreement. On the other hand, the *secured* loan is backed by some form of asset to insure the lender against loss due to nonrepayment. Even borrowers with good credit histories may be required to pledge assets occasionally due to economic conditions, bank policy changes, and industry shifts. Generally, it depends on the lender's perception of your financial condition. For example, if a prospective borrower's financial statements are in question as to ability to support a loan, the lender will be inclined to ask for collateral. The more common types of loan security are:

- Guarantor—This individual or firm guarantees payment of an obligation as evidenced by signing a contract (guarantor agreement).

- Endorsers—An endorser signs the obligation agreement and in some cases may have to post collateral. If the principal borrower defaults, the endorser is expected to pay.

- Comaker—A comaker is a principal in an obligation agreement. The borrower and comaker share joint responsibility.

- Accounts Receivable (Customer accounts)—These are commonly used as collateral on short-term loans. Repayment is made when customers pay on their accounts.

- Equipment—A lender will consider making loans against equipment that has been paid in full. The lender will determine the fair market value of the equipment and will lend up to a certain percentage (usually 60 percent) of that value.

- Marketable Securities (stocks and bonds)—Lenders will accept securities as collateral if they are readily marketable. Generally, financial sources will advance no more than 70 percent of the market value so as to protect against price declines. If the security prices drop below what the lender considers acceptable, then the borrower might have to post additional assets. These terms are spelled out in the loan contract.

- Real Estate—Most financial outlets consider real estate excellent collateral and will normally lend up to 90 percent of market value of the property.

- Savings Accounts—Certificates of deposit and savings accounts can be used to secure loans. The lender will hold the certificate or passbook as collateral with the right to the funds if default occurs. In most cases, lower rates of interest are offered on these loans because of the liquid nature of the pledged assets. These are commonly referred to as passbook or certificate loans.

- Chattel Mortgage—This instrument is somewhat like a real estate mortgage in that they both secure loans with property. In this case equipment is being used for collateral purposes. The lender will evaluate the present and future market value of the equipment and then advance funds amounting to something less than the present value. The business will be expected to make up the difference through a down payment and/or trade-in. If default occurs, the lender can foreclose on the equipment. The business must maintain the equipment and insure it against accidental loss.

- Insurance Policies—Lenders will accept life insurance policies as collateral for loans. They will advance up to the cash value of the policy and it must be assigned to them. When the terms of the loan contract are fulfilled, the policy can be reassigned back to its original status.

- Warehouse Merchandise—Financial institutions will lend up to a certain percentage of the market value of merchandise being stored in a bonded warehouse. The goods must be marketable and evidenced by a warehouse receipt, which is the collateral document used to secure the loan.

- Display Merchandise—Cars, appliances, furniture, etc., can be financed through a technique known as floor planning by using trust receipts as collateral. Lenders will advance funds against display merchandise, held in trust by the borrower, to be repaid when the items are sold.

- Leases—A lender holding a mortgage on property involved in a lease transaction may demand assignment of the lease such that rent payments are made directly to the lender. This will help insure loan repayments.

Collateral requirements and lender demands can place limitations upon your business activities. If the company is considered a good credit risk, limitations will be minimized. Conversely, a bad risk will be met with stiff conditions. Knowing the kinds of restrictions which a lender may demand will help you understand their possible effect on your business. Below are some of the more common loan restrictions used in lending transactions.

— Restriction of your ability to take on additional debt
— Limitation of the selling of accounts receivable and/or excess inventories to raise cash
— Prevention of dividend (earnings) pay-out beyond a certain level to ensure that enough funds are left in the business to retire debt
— Maintenance of certain levels of working capital
— Necessity of supplying the lender with appropriate financial statements on a periodic basis

All lending restrictions are known as covenants and appear in the loan contract. Negative covenants limit the borrower's ability to act in certain areas without the permission of the lender. In contrast, positive covenants outline specifically the things which the borrower must do. The first three aforementioned loan restrictions are examples of negative covenants and the last two are positive.

When negotiating with lenders, keep in mind that they have three primary objectives. First and foremost on their minds is repayment of the loan. Lenders will evaluate a prospective borrower's ability to repay by analyzing the loan application and supporting documentation required to be completed. This will be explained in more detail in Chapter VIII. These forms will determine the ability to generate adequate cash to make loan payments without adversely affecting other organizational needs, such as working capital. Second, lenders are concerned with protecting their lending position. It is the nature of financial outlets to insure the money they lend with collateral agreements and loan restrictions (some were mentioned earlier). Third, lenders will attempt to charge the highest interest rate possible so as to maximize profits. Keep in mind that they are subject to market forces and must compete with other financial institutions. Letting them know that you have other alternatives might help in achieving a lower rate.

Before signing a loan agreement, make sure you and your attorney and/or accountant read the documentation carefully. No matter how desperate you are for the funds, make sure your interests are represented and protected. Attempt to negotiate terms that limit your restrictions. You will find· that lenders will bargain on certain loan conditions. Also, keep in mind that after the loan is made, many financial outlets will amend loan restrictions, on a periodic basis, depending upon the financial health of your business at the time. For example, if after a year into the loan your business is expanding and profits growing, some loan restrictions may be removed by the lender. You might be able to assume additional debt or sell your accounts receivable to generate cash. On the other hand, if your business deteriorates, additional security and limitations could be called for under the terms of the loan agreement. The point to remember is that lenders are flexible and will negotiate loan conditions.

Time factors are also important in understanding debt financing. In many cases these factors will determine the interest rate to be charged on a loan and whether collateral should be used.

*Short-term* borrowings are used to finance inventories and accounts receivable. When inventories are sold and outstanding accounts paid by customers, the loans are expected to be repaid. Many lenders will do this on either a secured or unsecured basis depending upon the business. Firms that have seasonal needs will generally have to operate on a secured basis. Some financial outlets offer borrowers *lines of credit*. These allow access to funds for short-term demands without having to apply for a loan every time the need arises. There is an upper limit that can be borrowed, established by the lender, based on the firm's ability to repay. Lines of credit, like all short-term credit, are expected to be paid in full within a period of one year.

*Intermediate loans* run longer than one year but less than five. These loans can be secured with collateral or can be unsecured, and are used to finance equipment purchases. *Long-term borrowings* extend beyond five years. They are collateralized and used to finance acquisitions, leveraged buyouts, and major plant expansions.

The specific kind of money used can also be distinguished by the source of repayment. As we mentioned earlier, short-term notes are paid from funds generated by retiring customer accounts and inventory turnover. Intermediate and long-term loans are repaid out of business earnings.

**Evaluation of Capital Alternatives**

In considering your funding situation, you must evaluate the implications of choosing a course of action. This can be accomplished by studying the factors listed below. Your reactions to these will determine, to some extent, the kinds of capital sources pursued.

- Risk—Lenders are always exposed to some degree of risk when they invest their funds. Likewise, the recipient of the capital is also at risk. Debt funds must be repaid in the form of principal and interest. This can place strains upon the cash flow of the company. If debt burden becomes too great, default is a possibility and with it a host of other problems such as credit denial, foreclosure, and maybe even bankruptcy. Even if you recover, your ability to raise funds in the future could be impaired. Lenders will either refuse to do business with you or will charge exceptionally high interest rates because they perceive you to be a questionable credit risk.

- Maneuverability—Many lenders will require that you place restrictions on the firm's assets. They may ask that you refrain from selling or borrowing against accounts receivable, equipment, and/or inventories. These limitations will be written into the loan contract. If you break the agreement, the lender may have the right to call in the loan or charge a higher rate of interest. Loan restrictions were discussed in detail on pages 103-104.

  Another example of reduced flexibility is the reliance on just a few sources of capital. Avail yourself of as many financial outlets as possible. This will enhance your access to funding when needed.

  In addition, relying too much on internal financing as opposed to external, and vice versa, could also prove to be restricting. Capital that is available and is not being utilized to generate sales, will result in loss of growth and profits.

- Cost—Capital costs are determined by their effects on business profits and the current owners. There are situations in which business profits could be higher if equity financing were used instead of debt. But since the current owners' profit participation would be diluted by taking on new stockholders, the equity alternative is rejected. For example, consider a firm that is comparing the cost of debt with that of equity financing. The company has the option of borrowing $50,000 at 16 percent interest or selling 20 percent of the stock to equity investors. Net income is expected to reach $100,000 this year and the company's effective income tax rate is 30 percent. The cost of debt in this case can be determined by using the following formula:

Cost of Debt to the Present Owners
$$= \text{Interest Rate} \times (1 - \text{Effective income tax rate})$$
$$= 16 \times (1 - .30)$$
$$= 16 \times (.70)$$
$$= 11.2\%$$

Assuming a one-year loan to be repaid in one installment, the interest expense would equal $5,600, reducing net income to $94,400. Since debt is used, the present owners are entitled to all profits. If the equity alternative is used by the firm, net income would be $100,000 because no interest expense would be incurred. However, only $80,000 could be claimed by the present investors, since $20,000 would be directed to the new owners for their investment. This is generally viewed by the current owner as a cost of doing business and can be determined in the formula below:

Cost of Equity to the Present Owners
$$= \frac{\text{Earnings Directed to New Investors}}{\text{Investment}}$$
$$= \frac{\$20,000}{\$50,000}$$
$$= .40 \text{ or } 40\%$$

Even though the equity alternative produces higher net income, it will probably be rejected due to the loss of control and earnings on the part of the current owners. The losses are a cost to them as evidenced in the computation above.

- Availability—A business may find that its preferred sources of capital have dried up for any number of reasons (economic conditions, industry status, international events, company factors, etc.). At this point, the firm must pursue other funding alternatives. For example, a company may be using retained earnings (internal financing) and short-term debt to finance operations. If a recession sets in and profits contract, internal funds will become strained. In addition, high interest rates, which usually accompany economic downturns, will discourage borrowing. The business might be forced to seek equity funding despite loss of control and earnings in order to survive.

- Control—Using debt and internal financing will not compromise control of the present ownership in most cases. If lenders do get nervous, they might demand a representation in the firm's management structure which could affect control somewhat. The use of equity financing will reduce the control of present owners. The degree of loss will depend on the amount of equity exchanged for capital. New firms will need to give more equity (ownership) for the same amount of funds than the more established companies with track records. Normally, equity investors are entitled to managerial voting rights in proportion to the stock they own in the business.

## Where to Turn—Private and Government Outlets

The capital sources outlined in this section represent only a broad overview of what is available to small businesses and prospective entrepreneurs. Specific and detailed information regarding these financial outlets can be found in Chapter XI.

### SELF

In the early stages of your business endeavors, capital may be hard to find. If this is the case, you might have to rely on personal resources to finance operations until you gain the trust of creditors.

There are a number of ways to tap your hidden wealth. You might consider using the money in your savings accounts and/or certificates of deposit. This prospect may be disquieting to you, but there is a way to borrow against these accounts without disturbing the funds. It's called "passbook borrowing" and bankers don't like to talk about it. You can borrow up to the amount that is on deposit using savings accounts and certificates of deposit as collateral. The unique feature to this alternative is the interest rates. According to current regulations, financial institutions can charge between 1 and 5 percent above the rate being paid on the accounts. Most charge 2 or 3 percent. For example, let's say you want to borrow $25,000 to finance a start-up business. You have $12,000 in your savings account paying 5½ percent and $20,000 in a certificate of deposit drawing a 13 percent rate. You can borrow the $12,000 from your savings account for approximately 8 percent with the additional $13,000 coming from your certificate account costing in the neighborhood of 16 percent. Your total cost of capital, about 13 percent, is well below that which is currently charged by financial outlets for small business lending purposes. Your savings and certificate accounts will remain intact, earning interest income. In fact, some or all of that interest income can be used to offset the interest charges against the passbook loan. If you use this approach the cost of the loan can be reduced to below 13 percent, depending upon the amount of interest income used. Of course, the money in your savings and certificate accounts will fail to grow in proportion to the amount of interest income utilized to reduce loan cost.

Another possibility you might want to consider is the cash value of your life insurance policies. This money can be borrowed and repaid over a long period of time. Loan rates vary among insurance companies, but generally run between 6 and 8 percent. You might wonder if this affects your life insurance coverage. It does to a degree. For example, if $10,000 is borrowed from your $50,000 life insurance policy and soon after something happens to you, those policies will only pay $40,000, minus interest charges incurred, to your estate. This assumes that you do not make any principal or interest payments. If you did, the amount paid would increase accordingly. So in essence, your insurance is reduced by the amount owed against the policy. It would be wise to purchase inexpensive term life insurance to cover the amount you borrow so as not to adversely affect your beneficiaries.

The house in which you live is another source of financing worth exploring. Equity you have built in your home can be borrowed by getting a second mortgage. Many lenders will advance up to 80 or 90 percent of the value of your home minus the first mortgage. Some will go as high as 95 and a few will lend up to 100 percent, although this is very rare. Lenders want to protect themselves against a dip in housing prices that could negatively affect their collateral position. These loans can run as long as 15 years, but most lenders prefer a seven- to ten-year payback period.

To illustrate how a second mortgage can be used, let's say that you purchased a house in 1972 for $30,000. Currently, its fair market value, as determined by a certified appraiser, is $70,000. The first mortgage amounts to $22,000. Your borrowing ability based upon the above information is calculated as follows:

$$85\% \text{ of } \$70,000 = \$59,500$$
$$-\ \underline{22,000} \text{ first mortgage}$$
$$= \$37,500 \text{ equity available for borrowing}$$

## FAMILY AND FRIENDS

Relatives and acquaintances might be willing to help in financing your business venture. They can raise funds in the same manner as yourself, which was described in the previous section. Keep in mind that these individuals expect to be repaid with interest and/or profits which can reduce your future earnings. Some may want the business to post collateral in the form of plant and equipment, inventories, accounts receivable, etc. Many will demand a "piece of the action," thereby diluting your control, although if investors do buy in, specific collateral does not have to be offered. Their investment is secured by the stock they own.

If you face any of the above situations, be ready with some answers. Offer your friends and relatives a reasonable interest rate on loans. A few may seek a chunk of the profits generated. Make sure that your future interest is protected. Agree that profits should reward their investment with an adequate return to a point. After that has been achieved, attempt to get their hands out of your pockets. If some want ownership, don't panic. Try to negotiate an agreement whereby you have the right to buy them out, at a profit of course, sometime in the future when you and the business can afford to do so. Management can also become a problem. Some of your friends and relatives, upon advancing funds, might feel compelled to help you run the business whether you like it or not. In some cases this cannot be avoided. If they own stock in the business, certain voting rights are guaranteed, in proportion to their investment, under state laws. Of course, if more than 50 percent of the stock is owned by you, control is in your hands. To avoid hard feelings, make sure it is made clear up front that you are the boss and interference in running the business will not be tolerated. A legal agreement outlining that requirement may be appropriate. Check with your attorney.

If at all possible, it is advisable to steer clear of family and friends for funding purposes. These sources can be less than amiable at times, creating more ill will than happy endings. In fact, these individuals can become adversaries very quickly, especially when it comes to money. They tend to do so more frequently than lenders/investors who are not acquainted with you on a personal basis. If no other financing alternative exists, the answer becomes academic. Take their money.

### BANKS

Many large banks, located in metropolitan areas, are severing relationships with their small business clients. They cite risk factors and increasing costs of servicing small accounts as the primary reasons for the shift in emphasis. Most are at least raising service fees to small firms above those which are charged larger businesses. In addition, small businesses are charged higher interest rates on loans than are larger businesses. These changes will adversely affect entrepreneurs located in these areas, not to mention the whole American economy, although some banks, especially the ones found in smaller cities and rural areas, continue to provide financial services to small businesses and many are actively seeking new accounts.

Banks active in small business funding will either lend on a conventional basis or in tandem with a government agency. With conventional financing the bank utilizies its own funds without government involvement. Lending programs, including local, state, or federal entities, are normally in the form of loan participations involving direct government funds or loan guarantees. When an agency participates in a lending situation, part of the funds are advanced by the government and the remainder is supplied by the bank. Under guaranteed programs, banks that provide funds to businesses are protected against non-repayment to a certain percent of the loan amount (usually 90 percent). Banks like government-backed loans because the guaranteed portion can be sold to investors, in the secondary markets, for handsome profits. In addition, this frees capital to be used to make additional guaranteed loans to be sold at a profit. The lending process can be repeated continuously.

Banks offering conventional or government-sponsored loans to existing firms or start-ups will demand stiff collateral requirements in most cases. Business assets such as customer accounts, inventories, equipment, and land will have to be pledged in order to secure capital. Security in the form of personal assets might also be requested. Savings accounts, cars, residential property, jewelry, etc., can be used as collateral for business loans. Of course, tying up too many assets can adversely affect business operations. This was described earlier in the chapter. Remember, bankers have to compete for loans among themselves. Letting them know that other alternatives exist will probably bring collateral terms that can be tolerated.

Even though banks are one of the most conservative sources of capital available, they still supply 67 percent of small business funding needs. In the future, some of this burden will be shifted to other financial outlets more amiable to small firms. But for now, those seeking funds should locate banks actively involved with helping small enterprises and prospective entrepreneurs.

## VENTURE CAPITAL COMPANIES

Venture capital firms are private concerns that pool the financial resources of wealthy individuals and organizations interested in making investments in small businesses. Some are subsidiaries of major corporations. Exxon and General Electric own venture capital companies. Recent federal legislation has provided tax benefits for venture capital outlets involved in funding projects. Consequently, this form of financing has increased dramatically, augmenting the money available to small enterprises and prospective entrepreneurs.

These firms will invest their capital in a number of ways. They might make loans, buy bonds (debt), or invest in companies by purchasing equity through stock ownership. A combination of the above may be used. Generally, their preferred approach is an equity purchase. Also, they might acquire bonds with equity kickers. In other words, the bond can be converted to stock ownership at the option of the investor.

Venture capital firms expect to receive an average of five times their original investment within five to seven years. This is why loans are not favored by venture capitalists. Small business loan rates seldom exceed 20 percent a year, in which case the return on investment would be somewhat less than is considered normal for the venture capital industry. At this point one might question the advantages of seeking out venture firms if they require such a large return. It must be remembered that a business receiving equity funds does not have to worry about principal and interest payments, which can make life easier in the early years of operation. The investor is expecting the business to grow rapidly and someday return a handsome profit. In most cases, before selling out, the venture firm will give the entrepreneur the option to purchase its interest in the business before offering it to a third party. The right of first refusal can be stipulated in the venture capital agreement.

Conversely, the disadvantage of equity participation is the loss of control. When ownership is exchanged for capital resources, the entrepreneur's ability to influence business affairs will be diluted. Investor input must be taken into consideration. The degree of loss will depend on several factors. Firms that have been in operation showing track records can normally convince venture capital firms to take less equity than if it was a start-up situation. Also, entrepreneurs providing a large portion of the money required for a start-up company can strike a better deal with venture capital organizations than entrepreneurs supplying little of their own personal funds. In any case, most of these financial outlets will not acquire more than 50 percent of the company receiving assistance. Therefore, ultimate control is left to the entrepreneur and managing team. Many venture firms will require that they be represented in management, but will make waves only if they feel it's in their best interest. Besides, these firms can provide valuable insight into running an operation successfully.

Venture capital companies will invest only in prospects that have bright futures and the potential for rapid growth. Small businesses such as gas stations, corner grocery stores, dry cleaners, etc., will not be able to pursue this alternative unless they plan to expand through chain operations.

The professional association representing the venture capital industry is listed in Appendix O. It may provide valuable information concerning finding appropriate funding sources.

### SMALL BUSINESS INVESTMENT COMPANIES (SBICs)

SBICs are private profit making concerns created under the Small Business Investment Act of 1958. Their primary goal is to provide financial resources to existing small businesses and prospective entrepreneurs. All SBICs that fall under the above act are licensed, regulated, and partially funded by the U.S. Small Business Administration. Some financial organizations call themselves small business investment companies but prefer not to fall under the jurisdiction of the SBA. They generally operate on the same basis as licensed SBICs with one exception. Low-interest government money, provided by the SBA, will not be available to them for relending purposes, thereby reducing their funding flexibility. Approximately 400 SBICs are in existence today across the nation.

Like venture capital companies, these financial outlets will invest in equity (stock), make loans, or buy bonds. They prefer to acquire debt as opposed to making equity investments because of their capital structure. Many SBICs borrow from the government and then relend to small businesses. If they make stock purchases, returns on their investment may be a long time coming. On the other hand, making loans and buying bonds will generate immediate income to pay the government for the funds borrowed.

SBICs prefer to finance small businesses with track records of at least six months or more. They will consider start-up situations in some cases. Only those prospects or firms that have promising futures are given consideration by small business investment companies.

Minority Enterprise Small Business Investment Companies (MES-BICs) provide funding specifically to minority-owned businesses. In addition, capital is made available to minorities interested in starting a new business or purchasing an existing operation. MESBICs are basically the same as SBICs. They are regulated and licensed by the U.S. Small Business Administration and receive part of their capital from the agency. Today over 125 are in existence.

Appendix P contains a list of professional associations representing small business investment companies. Contacting them may result in funding contracts.

### COMMERCIAL FINANCE COMPANIES

Many small businesses snubbed by banks can turn to commercial finance companies for help in certain areas. Even businesses experiencing financial difficulties can turn to these sources for assistance. Since these financial outlets tend to charge higher interest rates than banks, it is wise to try the banks first. If unsuccessful in that regard, a firm has the option of pursuing over 2,500 commercial finance companies now operating in this country.

Commercial finance companies will lend on a short- and/or intermediate-term basis with collateral always being required. For example, these companies will grant short-term (less than a year) loans using accounts receivable and inventories as collateral. Generally you can borrow up to 90 percent of the value of good receivables and 60 percent of inventory value. In addition, intermediate loans (one to five years) can be granted for equipment purchase. The finance company will collateralize the equipment for security purposes.

Leasing is another service offered by many commercial finance organizations. If a business is in need of some new equipment but lacks the necessary financial resources to purchase, lending is an alternative. The finance company will buy the equipment and lease it to the business. Monthly rental payments must be made that usually last three to seven years. The advantages to leasing are many. Little or no down payment is required; the equipment can be bought at the end of the lease agreement for a fraction of original cost; the business is protected against obsolescence; leases do not appear as liabilities on the financial statements of the business, thus not reducing its ability to borrow for other reasons; and lease payments are fully deductible as expenses. Other advantages are pointed out in Table 16.

TABLE 16

LEASING ADVANTAGES

- 100 percent financing—leasing generally requires little or no down payment
- preserves working capital that can be used for other revenue generating projects
- does not compromise control of the business
- does not disrupt existing financing arrangements
- lease payments are paid out of pre-tax revenues, thereby creating a tax write-off as opposed to purchasing capital equipment out of retained earnings (net income-dividends pay to investors, if any) and thereby losing important tax advantages
- lease liabilities are not generally reported on the firm's financial statements, thereby preserving its financial position
- provides the ability to obtain the latest and most efficient equipment that might not otherwise be available due to financial constraints
- facilitates the expansion or replacement of aging equipment
- provides a protection against inflation, since lease payments are made in current money
- provides protection against rapid obsolescence—if property becomes obsolete before the end of the lease period, it is generally possible to trade-up without much difficulty or cost
- after the lease term is completed, it is the responsibility of the leasing firm to dispose of the equipment
- the cost of leasing is higher than most other financing methods, but earnings on the capital that would otherwise be used outweigh the cost
- leasing can be used as an alternative or supplement to bank credit when borrowing conditions become too restrictive or uneconomical
- lease payments are entirely deductible as business expenses

Commercial finance companies can also factor (buy) accounts receivable. They will purchase your receivables at a discount ranging between one and 15 percent. Their fees are determined by a number of considerations, including volume of sales, general quality of the firm's customers, credit policies within the firm, and average size of an account. The factoring procedure can be conducted on a non-notification basis, which means customers are not aware that their accounts have been sold. Factoring is believed to be a costly financial tool to be utilized only if bank credit is unattractive or not available. There are some reasons to believe this may not be true. When evaluating expenses associated with factoring, you should carefully analyze the services being rendered. If receivables bookkeeping, collection, and credit risks are being assumed, either partially or wholly by the factor, internal costs associated with these functions will decrease in proportion to the increased participation of the factor. In addition, factoring service provides freed cash, otherwise tied up in receivables, that can be used to generate revenues. So, the elimination or reduction of the credit function within the business plus the profits created from unencumbered cash may make the factoring decision an attractive alternative or supplement to existing bank relationships. Table 17 outlines the advantage in dealing with a factor.

TABLE 17

ADVANTAGES TO FACTORING

• factors will collect accounts receivable

• factors will do all the bookkeeping relative to the credit function

• factoring can be used as a supplement or substitute to bank credit when borrowing conditions become too restrictive or uneconomical

• factors will conduct credit investigations on the firm's existing and prospective accounts. In fact, factors are experts in credit analysis. This will establish confidence in the ability to collect the accounts receivable.

• factors assume all the credit risks associated with accounts receivable

• factors allow firms to utilize all available cash for revenue generation. Banks may require that a business maintain compensating balances on hand (ranging between 5 and 15 percent of the loan amount). In addition, certain factoring arrangements can free cash that would otherwise be set aside to meet projected current obligations.

• factoring can actually enhance a firm's relationship with banks and other funding outlets. If lenders and investors are confident that a factoring organization will purchase the accounts receivable of a firm if the cash is needed, they will be more willing to provide assistance.

In addition, these commercial finance companies will advance funds for leveraged buyouts and acquisitions if sufficient collateral is made available. For example, a business might be interested in purchasing another firm but lacks the immediate financial resources to do so. A commercial finance company will fund all or part of the acquisition if enough collateral in the form of nonpledged (clean) assets is available in the firm to be acquired.

The two major associations representing the commercial finance industry are listed in Appendix Q. They may provide information about funding outlets.

## LIFE INSURANCE COMPANIES

Traditionally, life insurance companies have been very insensitive to small business funding needs. In fact, most of these firms prefer to invest in amounts of one million dollars or more per business deal. Obviously, this is beyond the financial requirements of most small enterprises. This is not to suggest that insurance companies should be forgotten as a viable source. Many of these insurers are starting to realize the profit potential in financing small businesses and some are currently active in providing funding programs. Most insurance companies will not entertain start-up situations. They prefer going concerns with profitable track records that have potential for future growth. Long-term lending is their favorite form of financing. The loans are expected to finance internal expansion. Funds can also be used for external growth through acquisition and leveraged buyouts.

## PENSION FUNDS

Like insurance companies, pension funds prefer to finance only existing operations with attractive growth prospects. In fact, many insurers are partially pension funds. Start-up funding is avoided, with most consideration being given to long-term loans. Historically, these financial outlets have favored large businesses, but some are looking in the direction of small firms.

## INVESTMENT BANKERS (UNDERWRITERS)

There are some investment banking houses that specialize in raising capital for small businesses with growth potential. They will make a *public offering* of securities in the business to the investment community. What happens, in fact, is that the underwriter (investment banker) sells stock and/or bonds for the small firm to individual investors willing to buy. Start-ups and existing firms can use this funding alternative to raise needed capital.

Underwriters will demand to be paid a minimum commission of 10 percent on the gross dollar amount they sell. In addition, fees called accountable and non-accountable expenses are charged, and they can be substantial. After everything is considered, the cost of raising capital through a public offering can exceed 35 percent of amount sought. In other words, raising $300,000 can cost in excess of $100,000. If the offering is unsuccessful (not enough money raised), any stock purchased must be returned to the investor for a refund. The underwriter will not charge you for those sales, but some expenses incurred will be passed on to the small firm or entrepreneur. All conditions of a public offering are normally covered in an underwriting agreement between the investment banker and the business to be financed. Attorneys for both parties should review this contract to determine if it suits the requirements of all involved.

In addition, an interstate public offering must be approved by the Securities Exchange Commission in Washington, D.C., and every state in which securities are sold. If the offering is intrastate (located within the confines of a particular state), only approval from that state is needed. The underwriter will take care of the details involved in notifying and registering with the appropriate government agencies.

## SMALL BUSINESS ADMINISTRATION (SBA)

The U.S. Small Business Administration has been called the lender of last resort by small business advocates. One of its primary objectives is to help entrepreneurs secure financial resources to start businesses or expand existing operations. It is authorized to make participation loans and provide loan guarantees, and in some cases make direct loans to those firms classified as small by the agency. Consequently, many small businesses and prospective owners, frustrated by strained relations with their local bankers and economic conditions, have turned to the SBA for lending support.

To be considered for a loan, an individual or business firm must meet certain conditions. They are:

— must have adequate credentials
— must not be dominant in its field
— must comply with all federal employment laws
— must pursue traditional lending sources (only upon rejection by private lenders does the SBA alternative become a possibility)
— must be classified as small business by SBA size standards (these classifications are based on number of employees or the value of sales stated in dollars)

The criteria for determining if a business is small will vary depending upon the type of business. The specific criteria are as follows:

|                             | *Annual Sales*                                    |
|-----------------------------|---------------------------------------------------|
| *Type of Business*          | *Not Exceeding*                                   |
| Retail                      | 3.5-13.5 Million)  Limits will depend             |
| Wholesale                   | 100 employees or less)  on industry               |
| Service                     | 3.5-13.5 Million)                                 |
| General Construction        | 17 Million                                        |
| Special Trade Construction  | 7 Million                                         |

Manufacturing firms are constrained by number of employees. The maximum employment cannot exceed 500 workers.

These fundamental criteria are only the beginning. Many exceptions are allowed specific businesses and industries. The local SBA field office will prove helpful in determining which criteria apply to any business.

Assuming all SBA conditions are met, an entrepreneur can submit a business proposal to the agency for consideration. It will be carefully evaluated to determine positive and negative aspects. In the final analysis, if the project has merit (adequate market, good management, sufficient collateral, possibility of loan repayment, etc.), the SBA will offer a loan guarantee. It must be kept in mind that this is not a loan. The agency simply guarantees that a lender will be protected against default if funds are advanced to a small business concern. Up to 85 percent of the principal loan amount is covered for non-repayment to a maximum of $500,000; in other words, risk exposure is minimized. In addition, interest charges on these loans generally run a couple of points above the prime rate. It is hoped that the guarantees will induce lenders to advance the necessary financial resources to initiate and carry out the business project. Using the maximum guarantee limit, a loan for $588,235 can be granted with a 85 percent guarantee to the lender. A larger loan will reduce the guarantee below 85 percent and may increase lender resistance.

The SBA does provide direct loans to Vietnam era and disabled veterans as well as to handicapped individuals.

## FARMERS HOME ADMINISTRATION (FMHA)

This agency falls under the jurisdiction of the U.S. Department of Agriculture. Its primary goal is to enhance the quality of rural life through upgrading the economic environment. This is accomplished by an array of funding programs to promote industrial, business, and agricultural development. It is the intention of the agency to provide supplemental financial support, augmenting the efforts of private lending sources, rather than competing with them. Under most FmHA programs, borrowers are required to pursue private funding when financially able to do so. The programs directed to agriculture are designed to build the family farm system, which is the economic base of many rural areas. Borrowers must be family-size operators, living on and operating the farm, at least on a part-time basis. Funding is available also for any type of agricultural activity. Business and industrial loans are made available to large and small businesses to promote economic development in communities with a population base below 50,000. Preference is given to applications for projects in open country, rural communities, and in towns of 25,000 people or less. These funds can be used to develop and finance business or industry, increase employment, and control or abate pollution. Within this broad framework, uses include, but are not limited to, the following:

— Business and industrial acquisition, construction, conversion, enlargement, repair, and modernization
— Purchasing and development of land, easements, right-of-ways, buildings, facilities, leases, materials, and custom feed lots
— Purchasing of equipment, lease-hold improvements, machinery, and supplies
— Start-up costs and working capital

FmHA will provide loan guarantees to private lenders who advance funds under its programs. The agency guarantees to limit any loss due to loan default to a certain percentage of the total amount involved (usually 90 percent). Interest rates are negotiated between the borrower and private lender unless the rate is mandated by statute. Insured loans are also offered. These funds are originated and made by the Farmers Home Administration directly. The agency sells the loans to private investors and insures repayment. Interest rates on insured funds are about the same as the current cost of federal borrowing. Some rates may be established by law.

Certain programs provide grants (which do not have to be repaid) and low interest loans to individual and organizations involved in certain agricultural pursuits. In addition, the FmHA provides emergency and disaster loan assistance to the farming community at very attractive interest rates.

## FARM CREDIT ADMINISTRATION (FCA)

The Farm Credit Administration is an independent federal organization which oversees the nationwide farmer-owned and managed farm credit system. This network provides funding to the U.S. agricultural community through a number of programs. Federal Land Banks, located in most communities, supply long-term mortgage credit to purchase, enlarge, and improve farms. These banks will also finance mortgages on farm property and lend for other farming endeavors. Production Credit Associations, which are also supervised by FCA, make short- and intermediate-term loans for farm production, farm home, and/or farm family purposes. In addition, Cooperative Banks provide loan services to cooperatives supplying agricultural needs.

## ECONOMIC DEVELOPMENT ADMINISTRATION (EDA)

The Economic Development Administration, which is part of the U.S. Department of Commerce, provides funding programs to businesses of all sizes. Start-up and existing firms are eligible to apply. EDA will consider only those requests that will have a positive impact upon areas designated as needing economic assistance. Its purpose is to enhance the earning levels of people within these areas by increasing job opportunities. EDA also provides assistance to firms, regardless of size, that have been adversely affected by foreign imports. The agency does not have funding limits, as is the case with the Small Business Administration. In fact, many firms that have exhausted SBA funds may turn to EDA for additional capital, although private funding outlets must be pursued first. Only after rejection by these firms does EDA funding become a possibility.

Sounds easy. Well, it's not. The EDA is a very tough cookie to deal with. Few funding requests are approved. The loan application procedure is long and cumbersome and conditions are numerous. Funding terms and restrictions prove to be too stringent for most firms. For example, the agency requires that at least 15 percent of the proposed project be funded by equity (ownership) or other secondary loans. One-third of the 15 percent must come from the state or organizations located within the community benefiting from the project. Also, loans used to finance capital purchases (buildings, land, equipment, machinery) cannot exceed 65 percent of the cost. In addition, an applicant for EDA funding must supply a large amount of the required working capital before a loan will be approved.

The agency will provide loan guarantees to lenders willing to fund borrowers. These arrangements also require collateral.

## DEPARTMENT OF ENERGY (DOE)

The U.S. Department of Energy maintains funding programs directed to all businesses, regardless of size, operating in certain energy areas. In the past, the agency tended to favor large corporations. Recent evidence has shown that small firms are much more innovative than large ones, forcing the DOE to redirect some of its financial resources.

Most DOE programs provide grants to firms exploring ways to enhance domestic energy efficiency through conservation, new methods of energy utilization, and the development of alternative energy sources. This money does not have to be repaid. In addition, the department is providing loan guarantees to financial outlets lending to companies that develop new and old sources of coal. Guarantees run as high as 30 million dollars. DOE also has a similar program available to firms operating in the geothermal energy field. Up to 200 million dollars can be guaranteed.

## MARITIME ADMINISTRATION

The Maritime Administration falls under control of the U.S. Department of Commerce. It provides an array of programs designed to aid large and small firms in the construction, reconstruction, or reconditioning of vessels in the American Merchant Marine. Most programs give direct payments to private ship owners. In one case, 45 million dollars was given just for a single ship. In addition, loan guarantees up to 126 million dollars per ship are offered to commercial lenders willing to provide funding.

## NATIONAL OCEANIC AND ATMOSPHERIC ADMINISTRATION

Under the U.S. Department of Interior, this agency provides funding to assist in strengthening the domestic fishing industry. Loans are made to finance and refinance the cost of purchasing, constructing, equipping, maintaining, repairing, or operating new or used commercial fishing vessels or gear. Only American citizens with experience in the fishing trade are advised to apply.

## BUREAU OF INDIAN AFFAIRS

The Bureau, which falls under the jurisdiction of the U.S. Department of Interior, offers programs to encourage the economic development of federal Indian reservations. Grants, direct government loans, and loan guarantees (up to one million dollars) are made available to Native Americans for this purpose.

## EXPORT-IMPORT BANK (EXIMBANK)

The Export-Import Bank is an independent government agency established to promote American exports overseas. This is accomplished through a number of programs directed to firms involved in exporting and to commercial banks.

Eximbank can authorize the Foreign Credit Insurance Association (FCIA) to issue policies insuring exporters against political and/or commercial risks on short- and medium-term credit extended to foreign buyers. Insurance can be bought from banks participating in FCIA programs or directly from the Association. In addition, Eximbank itself will offer guarantees to U.S. businesses covering political and commercial risks involved in the performance of services overseas and in the leasing, consignment, or exhibition of U.S. goods abroad. The agency will also guarantee payment of medium-term export loans held by commercial banks. The aforementioned programs are designed to help U.S. exporters compete in the international marketplace. Without Eximbank-sponsored guarantees, many exporters would not offer foreign customers credit terms, thereby placing them at a competitive disadvantage with suppliers in other nations offering attractive terms. In short, Eximbank insurance programs provide reimbursement coverage to American exporters and bankers should foreign customers fail to pay.

Some lenders will advance only a certain amount of funds to finance exports. After this limit is reached, export money will be cut off or higher interest rates will be charged to international firms. Now, Eximbank will purchase export loans from commercial banks to provide additional capital, at reasonable interest rates, to firms wishing to sell overseas. Another program designed to facilitate U.S. exports provides direct loans to overseas buyers of American goods and services.

### OVERSEAS PRIVATE INVESTMENT CORPORATION (OPIC)

The Overseas Private Investment Corporation is an independent federal agency that promotes U.S. investment abroad. It offers an array of programs that can benefit American firms wishing to start new operations or expand existing facilities in less developed nations. The agency provides loan guarantees (up to 100 percent) to lenders that assist organizations in exploiting international opportunities. Direct loans are also made available. All funding programs are long term (exceeding five years) in nature and commercial interest rates are charged. Capital advanced under OPIC cannot finance more than 50 percent of the foreign venture. Therefore, additional money must be provided from other sources.

Insurance programs are also offered to protect companies against certain investment losses arising from operations in other countries. The coverage reduces the risk associated with nationalization, war, revolution, insurrection, civil strife, and currency inconvertibility.

### FEDERAL RESERVE BOARD (FRB)

The Federal Reserve Board will offer loan guarantees to lenders who financially assist firms engaged in producing goods or services for national defense purposes. Specifically, its intention is to facilitate and expedite the funding of contractors, subcontractors, and others engaged in operations deemed necessary for defense of the U.S. The interest rates on these loans are low and 100 percent loan guarantees are provided.

### NATIONAL SCIENCE FOUNDATION (NSF)

The National Science Foundation provides grant money to assist small firms conducting scientific research in the areas of new product/process development. Some grants have exceeded one million dollars. The money, which does not have to be repaid, is designed for basic research and is not to be used to commercially market anything created. After research and testing is conducted utilizing NSF resources, the firm is expected to have private funding available in order to execute any marketing endeavors.

Given the scientific emphasis of NSF funding, only those small companies that are technical in nature should seek this funding alternative.

### STATE DEVELOPMENT COMPANIES (SDC)

A SDC is sanctioned by state law to provide financial and managerial assistance to all businesses located within the state it serves. These development companies receive their capital from traditional funding outlets such as banks, pension funds, insurance companies, etc. In addition, SDCs can borrow from the U.S. Small Business Administration to provide loans to qualified small firms located in the state.

### STATE GOVERNMENTS

Most state governments maintain programs to promote the economic well being of small businesses located within their jurisdiction. In many cases, assistance is also provided to individuals wishing to start a new business or purchase an existing operation. Appendix J contains a listing of state agencies

### LOCAL GOVERNMENTS

Some local governments are actively involved in providing managerial and/or financial assistance to prospective entrepreneurs and existing small firms located within the municipality. Contact the city or county administrator's office to determine which agencies are responsible for this function.

Many local governments are providing help to firms of all sizes through the use of a relatively new financing mechanism referred to as industrial revenue bonds. A business may get approval from a local government to raise funds through the sale of tax-exempt bonds if the project provides direct benefits to the locality in the form of increased revenues, taxes, and employment. The project must also fit into the overall growth plan of the municipality. The principal advantage to this form of financing is its low cost. Generally, interest rates on the bonds sold run one to two percentage points below other conventional funding sources. Investors like these bonds because the interest income paid to them is free from federal, state, and local income taxes. There are two major drawbacks with industrial revenue bonds. Start-up firms are normally discouraged from pursuing this funding alternative due to the lack of operating history. It may be difficult to convince local officials and investors that a new business just starting out deserves consideration. In addition, using industrial revenue bonds may disqualify a business from utilizing other attractive government funding programs.

Some states allow their local municipalities to use this funding technique more than others. Check with the municipal manager to determine what projects may be funded. It is also wise to talk with officials of any state or federal government agency from which assistance may be forthcoming. See if the bonds will disturb anticipated help from this direction.

## CERTIFIED DEVELOPMENT COMPANIES (CDC)
## LOCAL DEVELOPMENT COMPANIES (LDC)

Local development companies (LDC) and certified development companies (CDC) are profit or non-profit corporations started by local business people with the intention of stimulating economic development within their immediate community. They are a little-known source of small business funding and assistance and are often overlooked by many existing businesses and prospective entrepreneurs. LDCs/CDCs.do not see profit as their motivating objective. Primary consideration is given to positive economic impact on the community they serve. Like state development companies, LDCs/CDCs receive a large portion of their funding capability from the U.S. Small Business Administration for relending purposes to qualified small firms and entrepreneurs. SBA money passing through LDCs/CDCs may be loaned for up to 25 years at prevailing interest rates.

These organizations can provide valuable help because of their local nature. Many have established contacts within the immediate area allowing opportunity seekers access to conventional funding and managerial assistance. These firms are listed in Chapter XI.

## Application Procedures

All private and government financial outlets require initial application forms to be completed. Appendix S contains the forms required by the U.S. Small Business Administration. The forms are elementary and easy to answer. But don't be fooled. The real work is just beginning. Additional documentation will be required. Most lenders and investors will request a detailed report outlining all particulars of a prospective business proposal. It's used in the funding decision to evaluate the soundness of the project and is called a business plan. Its construction can be a long, difficult, and tedious process. Some exceed

Form Approved
OMB No. 3245-0016

U.S. Small Business Administration

## APPLICATION FOR BUSINESS LOAN

**I. Applicant**

| Trade Name of Borrower | | Street Address | | | |
|---|---|---|---|---|---|
| City | County | State | Zip | | Tel. No. (Inc. A/C) |
| Employer's ID Number | Date of Application | Date Application Received by SBA | | Number of Employees (including subsidiaries and affiliates) | |
| Type of Business | Date Business Established | ☐ Existing Business | | At Time of Application _____ | |
| Bank of Business Account | | ☐ New Business ☐ Purchase Existing Business | | If Loan is Approved _____ | |

**II. Management** (Proprietor, partners, officers, directors and stockholders owning 20% or more of outstanding stock)

| Name | Address | % Owned | Annual Comp. | *Military Service From | To | *Race | *Sex |
|---|---|---|---|---|---|---|---|
| | | | $ | | | | |
| | | | $ | | | | |
| | | | $ | | | | |
| | | | $ | | | | |

*This data is collected for statistical purposes only. It has no bearing on the credit decision to approve or decline this application.

**III. Use of Proceeds** (Enter Gross Dollar Amounts Rounded to Nearest Hundreds)

| | Loan Requested | SBA USE ONLY Approved |
|---|---|---|
| (5) Land Acquisition | $ | |
| (6) New Plant or Building Construction | | |
| (7) Building Expansion or Repair | | |
| (8) Acquisition and/or Repair of Machinery and Equipment | | |
| (9) Inventory Purchase | | |

2 ( ) SBA Office Code     1 ( 1 ) SBA Loan Number

**IV. Summary of Collateral:**

If your collateral consists of (A) Land and Building, (D) Accounts Receivable and/or (E) Inventory, fill in the appropriate blanks. If you are pledging (B) Machinery and Equipment, (C) Furniture and Fixtures, and/or (F) Other, please provide an itemized list (labeled Exhibit A) that contains serial and identification numbers for all articles that had an original value greater than $500. Include a legal description of Real Estate offered as collateral.

| | | | | Present Market Value | Present Mortgage Balance | Cost Less Depreciation |
|---|---|---|---|---|---|---|
| (10) Working Capital (Including Accounts Payable) | | | | | | |
| (11) Acquisition of all or part of Existing Business | | A. Land and Building | | $ | $ | $ |
| (12a) Payoff SBA Loan | | B. Machinery & Equipment | | | | |
| (12b) Payoff Bank Loan (Non SBA Associated) | | C. Furniture & Fixtures | | | | |
| (12c) Other Debt Payment (Non SBA Associated) | | D. Accounts Receivable | | | | |
| (13) All Other | | E. Inventory | | | | |
| (14) Total Loan Requested | $ | F. Other | | | | |
| Term of Loan | | Total Collateral | | $ | $ | $ |

**V. Previous Government Financing.** If you or any principals or affiliates have ever requested Government Financing (including SBA), complete the following:

| Name of Agency | Amount | Date of Request | Approved or Declined | Balance | Status |
|---|---|---|---|---|---|
| | $ | | | $ | |
| | $ | | | $ | |
| | $ | | | $ | |

(3) Previous SBA Financing (Check One)
☐ (1) No   ☐ (2) Repaid/Other   ☐ (3) Present Borrower

(4) Loan Number of 1st SBA Loan

**VI. Indebtedness.** Furnish the following information on all installment debts, contracts, notes, and mortgages payable. Indicate by an asterisk (*) items to be paid by loan proceeds and reason for paying same (present balance should agree with latest balance sheet submitted).

| To Whom Payable | Original Amount | Original Date | Present Balance | Rate of Interest | Maturity Date | Monthly Payment | Security | Current or Delinquent |
|---|---|---|---|---|---|---|---|---|
| | $ | | $ | | | $ | | |
| | $ | | $ | | | $ | | |
| | $ | | $ | | | $ | | |
| | $ | | $ | | | $ | | |

SBA Form 4 (11-82) REF SOP 50 10          PREVIOUS EDITIONS ARE OBSOLETE                    (OVER)

First page of Application for Business Loan (see Appendix S).

100 pages in duration. Length and detail depend on the amount of money requested, use of funds, type of business or industry, and whether the funding is used for a start-up or existing operation. Generally the more capital requested, the greater amount of information needed. Likewise, start-ups will require more data than firms already conducting business because of the increased uncertainty involved.

There are some exceptions to the above rules. For example, a business that has an established relationship with lenders may not have to go through the pains of constructing a business plan every time capital needs arise. Many lenders, acquainted with their clients, will request only a completed application form, business and personal financial statements, tax returns, and owner guarantees.

The business plan is discussed in the next chapter. The information provided is appropriate for most private and government funding requests.

# Chapter VII

# THE BUSINESS PLAN
## Roadmap to Success

### Design

Most individuals seeking capital to finance a business proposition fail to realize the importance of a properly structured business plan. One entrepreneur recently asked, "Why do I need to spend the time developing a business plan when it's the greatest idea in the world— everybody will invest." Because of this kind of thinking, over 90 percent of all plans requesting funds are rejected by financial outlets.

A business plan is essentially a sales tool used to stimulate investor interest. It must be packaged correctly in order to attract the necessary money sources. The design and construction can be a major undertaking challenging the most astute. An adequate business plan should run between 40 and 60 pages (typed and double spaced) with an adequate number of appendices for purposes of illustrations and detail. Hundreds of hours and many months will be consumed putting it together and perfecting the final document. In some cases, it may be costly. Entrepreneurs who lack business experience and expertise in one or more areas may have to pay professionals to research and/or write part or all of the plan. Its importance in the funding decision cannot be overstated. Prospective capital sources use it as an instrument to evaluate the merits of a proposal before risking their money. In addition, the plan lets potential investors know that the entrepreneur/ managing team has given deep and serious consideration to the business proposition and that they are capable of managing profitably. A well documented and convincing business plan portraying the potential for future profits is what capital sources are seeking. It should touch on all pertinent areas without being detailed to the point where investors get bored reading it.

The business plan should never be viewed as solely for the use of financial outlets. Indeed, it can be utilized by businesses as a guide pointing to the most profitable and least hazardous way to carry out an idea. It allows for a careful consideration of different objectives, alternatives, strategies and tactics, and analyzes available resources before committing funds. These initial evaluations will prevent many costly mistakes from becoming reality. In fact, the plan gives a five year path to follow by forcing entrepreneurs to set realistic goals, predict resource allocation, and project future earnings. Also, problems concerning competitive conditions, promotional opportunities, industry trends, etc., are addressed. Such a practice over a period of time will enhance the decision making ability of the entrepreneur and others involved in the enterprise.

In the final analysis, the business plan is the roadmap directing energies in a coherent fashion. It outlines what must be accomplished and how to carry it out. Developing a plan that can stand up to critical evaluation and the extreme scrutiny of investors is the initial hurdle which must be cleared.

The next major section of this chapter deals with the proper construction of an appropriate business plan. It should be reviewed and studied very carefully. The following is reprinted by permission of the copyright holder, Institute for New Enterprise Development, Cambridge, Massachusetts. This material, which begins with the sub heading "Table of Contents" and ends with "Proposed Company Offering," is a most useful guide when preparing a business plan.

## TABLE OF CONTENTS

3. MARKETING PLAN
   A. Overall Marketing Strategy
   B. Pricing
   C. Sales Tactics
   D. Service and Warranty Policies
   E. Advertising and Promotion

4. DESIGN AND DEVELOPMENT PLANS
   A. Development Status and Tasks
   B. Difficulties and Risks
   C. Product Improvement and New Products
   D. Costs

5. MANUFACTURING AND OPERATIONS PLAN
   A. Geographic Location
   B. Facilities and Improvements
   C. Strategy and Plans
   D. Labor Force

6. MANAGEMENT TEAM
   A. Organization
   B. Key Management Personnel
   C. Management Compensation and Ownership
   D. Board of Directors
   E. Management Assistance and Training Needs
   F. Supporting Professional Services

7. OVERALL SCHEDULE

8. CRITICAL RISKS AND PROBLEMS

9. COMMUNITY BENEFITS
   A. Economic Development
   B. Human Development
   C. Community Development

10. THE FINANCIAL PLAN
   A. Profit and Loss Forecast
   B. Pro Forma Cash Flows Analysis
   C. Pro Forma Balance Sheets
   D. Breakeven Chart
   E. Cost Control

   PRO FORMA INCOME STATEMENTS
   PRO FORMA CASH FLOWS STATEMENTS
   PRO FORMA BALANCE SHEETS
   BREAKEVEN CHART

11. PROPOSED COMPANY OFFERING
   A. Desired Financing
   B. Securities Offering
   C. Capitalization
   D. Use of Funds

## THE SUMMARY

Many investors like to read through a one or two page summary of a business plan that highlights its important features and opportunities, and allows them to determine quickly whether or not the venture described is of interest.

Do not write your summary until you have written your plan. As you draft each section, circle one or two sentences that you think are important enough to be included in a summary.

Allow plenty of time to write an appealing and convincing summary, remembering that the summary is the first thing about you and your venture that the would-be investor is going to read. Unless it is appealing and convincing, it will also be the last. You may have spent many weeks on the rest of your plan and it may be very good. However, if that quality does not come through in your summary, you may not get a chance to make a presentation at which you can convincingly rebut criticism and clear up misunderstandings.

It is recommended that, as a minimum, your summary should contain brief statements about the following features of your venture.

*The Company and Its Founders:* You should indicate when the company was formed, what it will do, and what is special or unique about its product or technology. Also indicate what in the backgrounds of the entrepreneurs makes them particularly qualified to pursue the business opportunity.

If your company has been in business for a few years, indicate what its sales and profits were in its most recent fiscal year and the trend of sales and profits.

*Market Opportunity:* Identify and briefly explain the market opportunity. This explanation should include information on the size and growth rate of the market for your company's product or service, and a statement indicating the percentage of that market that will be captured. A brief statement about industry-wide trends is useful. You might also indicate any plans for expanding the initial product line.

*Products and Technology:* Identify any proprietary technology, trade secrets or unique skills that give you a competitive edge in the market place.

*Financial Projections:* State your sales and profit projections for the first and second year of operation after obtaining the necessary financing.

*Proposed Financing:* Briefly indicate how much equity financing you want, how much of your company you are prepared to offer for that financing, and what use will be made of the capital raised.

## 1. *THE INDUSTRY, THE COMPANY AND ITS PRODUCTS*

The purpose of this section is to give the investor some context in which to fit all that you are about to say concerning your product and its market. This section should clearly present the business that you are in, the product you will offer, the nature of your industry and the opportunities available to market your product.

## The Industry

Present the current status and prospects for the industry in which the proposed business will operate. Discuss any new products or developments, new markets and customers, new requirements, new companies, and any other national or economic trends and factors that could affect the venture's business positively or negatively. Identify the source of all information used to describe industry trends.

## The Company

Describe briefly what business area your company is in, or intends to enter; what products or services it will offer; and who are or will be its principal customers.

As background give the date your venture was incorporated and describe the identification and development of its products and the involvement of the company's principals in that development.

If your company has been in business for several years and is seeking expansion financing, review its history and cite its prior sales and profit performance. If your company has had set-backs or losses in prior years, discuss these and emphasize what has and will be done to prevent a recurrence of these difficulties and to improve your company's performance.

## The Products or Services

The potential investor will be vitally interested in exactly what you are going to sell, what kind of product protection you have, and the opportunities and possible drawbacks to your product or service.

A. *Description:* Describe in detail the products or services to be sold. Discuss the application of your product or service. Describe the primary end-use as well as any significant secondary applications. Emphasize any unique features of your product or service, and highlight any differences between what is currently on the market and what you will offer that will account for your market penetration.

Define the present state of development of the product or service. For products, provide a summary of the functional specifications. Include photographs when available.

B. *Proprietary Position:* Describe any patents, trade secrets or other proprietary features. Discuss any head start that you might have that would enable you to achieve a favored or entrenched position in your industry.

C. *Potential:* Describe any features of your product or service that give it an advantage over the competition. Discuss any opportunities for the expansion of the product line or the development of related products or services. Emphasize your opportunities and explain how you will take advantage of them.

Discuss any product disadvantage or the possibilities of rapid obsolescence because of technological or styling changes, or marketing fads.

## 2. MARKET RESEARCH AND ANALYSIS

The purpose of this section of the plan is to present enough facts to convince the investor that your venture's product or service has a substantial market in a growing industry and can achieve sales despite the competition. The discussion and the guidelines given below should help you do this.

This section of the plan is one of the most difficult to prepare and also one of the most important. Almost all subsequent sections of the business plan depend on the sales estimates that are developed in this section. The sales levels you project based on the market research and analysis directly influence the size of the manufacturing operation, the marketing plan, and the amount of debt and equity capital you will require. Yet most entrepreneurs seem to have great difficulty preparing and presenting market research and analyses that will convince potential investors that the venture's sales estimates are sound and attainable.

Because of the importance of market analysis and the dependence of other parts of the plan on the sales projections, we generally advise entrepreneurs to prepare this section of the business plan before they do any other. We also advise entrepreneurs to take enough time to do this section very well and to check alternate sources of market data for key numbers such as "market size" and "market growth rates".

A. *Customers:* Discuss who the customers are for the anticipated application of the product or service. Classify potential customers into relatively homogeneous groups (major market segment) having common, identifiable characteristics. For example, an automotive part might be sold to automotive manufacturers or to parts distributors supplying the replacement market.

Who and where are the major purchasers for the product or service in each market segment? What is the basis for their purchase decisions: price, quality, service, personal contacts, political pressures or some combination of these factors?

List any potential customers who have expressed an interest in the product or service and indicate why. List any potential customers who have shown no interest in the proposed product or service and explain why this is so. Explain what you will do to overcome negative customer reaction. If you have an existing business, list your current principal customers and discuss the trend in your sales to them.

B. *Market Size and Trends:* What is the total size of the current market for the product or service offered? This market size should be determined from available market data sources and from a knowledge of the purchases of competing products by potential customers in each major market segment. Discussions with potential distributors, dealers, sales representatives and customers can be particularly useful in establishing the market size and trends. Describe the size of the total market in both units and dollars. If you intend to sell regionally, show the regional market size. Indicate the sources of data and methods used to establish current market size. Also state the credentials of people doing market research.

Describe the potential annual growth of the total market for your product or service for each major customer group. Total market projections should be made for at least three future years. Discuss the major factors affecting market growth (industry trends, socio-economic trends, government policy, population shifts). Also review previous trends in the market. Any differences between past and projected annual growth rates should be explained. Indicate the sources of all data and methods used to make projections.

C. *Competition:* Make a realistic assessment of the strengths and weaknesses of competitive products and services and name the companies that supply them. State the data sources used to determine which products are competitive and the strengths of the competition.

Compare competing products or services on the basis of price, performance, service, warranties and other pertinent features. A table can be an effective way of presenting these data. Present a short discussion of the current advantages and disadvantages of competing products and services and say why they are not meeting customer needs. Indicate any knowledge of competitors' actions that could lead you to new or improved products and an advantageous position.

Review the strengths and weaknesses of the competing companies. Determine and discuss each competitor's share of the market, sales, distribution and production capabilities. Also review the profitability of the competition and their profit trend. Who is the pricing leader; quality leader? Discuss why any companies have entered or dropped out of the market in recent years.

Discuss your three or four key competitors and why the customer buys from them. From what you know about their operations, explain why you think you can capture a share of their business. Discuss what makes you think it will be easy or difficult to compete with them.

D. *Estimated Market Share and Sales:* Summarize what it is about your product or service that will make it saleable in the face of current and potential competition.

Identify any major customers who are willing to make purchase commitments. Indicate the extent of those commitments and why they were made. Discuss which customers could be major purchasers in future years and why.

Based upon your assessment of the advantages of your product or service; the market size and trends; customers; the competition and their products, and the sales trends in prior years; estimate your share of the market, and your sales in units and dollars for each of the next three years. The growth of the company's sales and its estimated market share should be related to the growth of its industry, the customers and the strengths and weaknesses of competitors. This data can be presented in a table, as shown below.

The assumptions used to estimate market share and sales should be clearly stated. If yours is an existing business indicate the total market, and your market share and sales for two prior years.

Sales and Market Share Data

|  |  | 1st Year | | | | Year | |
| --- | --- | --- | --- | --- | --- | --- | --- |
|  |  | 1Q | 2Q | 3Q | 4Q | 2 | 3 |
| Estimated Total Market | Units |  |  |  |  |  |  |
|  | Dollars |  |  |  |  |  |  |
| Estimated Sales | Units |  |  |  |  |  |  |
|  | Dollars |  |  |  |  |  |  |
| Estimated Market Share, % | Units |  |  |  |  |  |  |
|  | Dollars |  |  |  |  |  |  |

E. *Ongoing Market Evaluation:* Explain how you will evaluate your target markets on a continuing basis to assess customer needs; to guide product improvement and new product programs; to plan for expansions of your production facility; and to guide product/service pricing.

### 3. MARKETING PLAN

The marketing plan describes how the sales projections will be attained. It should detail the overall marketing strategy, sales and service policies, pricing, distribution and advertising strategies that will be used to achieve the estimated market share and sales projections. It should describe specifically *what* is to be done, *how* it will be done, and *who* will do it.

A. *Overall Marketing Strategy:* Describe the general marketing philosophy and strategy of the company. This should be derived partly from the market research and evaluation. It should include a discussion of: What kinds of customer groups will be targeted for initial intensive selling effort? What customer groups for later selling efforts? How will specific potential customers in these groups be identified and how will they be contacted? What features of the product or service—e.g., quality, price, delivery, warranty—will be emphasized to generate sales? Are there any innovative or unusual marketing concepts that will enhance customer acceptance—e.g., leasing where only sales were previously attempted?

Indicate whether the product or service will be introduced initially, nationally or on a regional level. If on a regional level, explain why and indicate if and when you plan to extend sales to other sections of the country.

Discuss any seasonal trends and what can be done to promote sales out of season.

Describe any plans to obtain government contracts to support product development costs and overhead.

B. *Pricing:* Many entrepreneurs have told us that they have a superior product that they plan to sell for a lower price than their competitors' product. This makes a bad impression for two reasons. First, if their product is as good as they say it is, they must think they are very poor sales people to have to offer it at a lower price than the competition. Second, costs tend to be underestimated. If you start out with low costs and prices, there is little room to maneuver; and price hikes will be tougher to implement than price cuts.

The pricing policy is one of the more important decisions you will have to make. The "price must be right" to penetrate the market, maintain a market position and produce profits. Devote ample time to considering a number of pricing strategies and convincingly present the one you select.

Discuss the prices to be charged for your products or services and compare your pricing policy with those of your major competitors. Discuss the gross profit margin between manufacturing and ultimate sales costs. Indicate whether this margin is large enough to allow you a profit and also allow for distribution and sales; warranty; service; amortization of development and equipment costs; and price competition.

Explain how the price you set will enable you to:

• Get the product or service accepted

• Maintain and profitably increase your market share in the face of competition

• Produce profits.

Justify any price increases over competitive items on the basis of newness, quality, warranty, and service.

If your product is to be priced lower than your competition's, explain how you will do this and maintain profitability—e.g., greater effectiveness in manufacturing and distributing the product, lower labor costs, lower overhead, or lower material costs.

Discuss the relationship of price, market share and profits. For example, a higher price may reduce volume but result in a higher gross profit. Describe any discount allowance for prompt payment of volume purchases.

C. *Sales Tactics:* Describe the methods that will be used to make sales and distribute the product or service. Will the company use its own sales force; sales representatives; distributors? Can you use manufacturers' sales organizations already selling related products? Describe both the initial plans and longer range plans for a sales force. Discuss the margins to be given to retailers, wholesalers, and salesmen and compare them to those given by your competition.

If distributors or sales representatives are to be used, describe how they have been selected, when they will start to represent you and the areas they will cover. Show a table that indicates the build-up of dealers and representatives by month and the expected sales to be made by each dealer. Describe any special policies regarding discounts, exclusive distribution rights, etc.

If a direct sales force is to be used, indicate how it will be structured and at what rate it will be built up. If it is to replace a dealer or representative organization, indicate when and how. Show the sales expected per salesperson per year, what commission incentive and/or salary they are slated to receive, and compare these figures to the average for your industry.

Present as an exhibit a selling schedule and a sales budget that includes all marketing, promotion and service costs. This sales expense exhibit should also indicate when sales will commence and the lapse between a sale and a delivery.

D. *Service and Warranty Policies:* If your company will offer a product that will require service and warranties, indicate the importance of these to the customers' purchasing decision and discuss your method of handling service problems. Describe the kind and term of any warranties to be offered, whether service will be handled by a company service organization, agencies, dealers and distributors, or factory return. Indicate the proposed charge for service calls and whether service will be a profitable or breakeven operation. Compare your service and warranty policies and practices to those of your principal competitors.

E. *Advertising and Promotion:* Describe the approaches the company will use to bring its product to the attention of prospective purchasers. For OEM and industrial products indicate the plans for trade show participation, trade magazine advertisements, direct mailings, the preparation of product sheets and promotional literature, and the use of advertising agencies. For consumer products indicate what kind of advertising and promotional campaign is contemplated to introduce the product and what kind of sales aids will be provided to dealers. The schedule and cost of promotion and advertising should be presented. If advertising will be a significant part of company expenses, an exhibit showing how and when these costs will be incurred should be included.

## 4. DESIGN AND DEVELOPMENT PLANS

If the product, process or service of the proposed venture requires any design and development before it is ready to be placed on the market, the nature and extent of this work should be fully discussed. The investor will want to know the extent and nature of any design and development and the costs and time required to achieve a marketable product. Such design and development might be the engineering work necessary to convert a laboratory prototype to a finished product; or the design of special tooling; or the work of an industrial designer to make a product more attractive and saleable; or the identification and organization of manpower, equipment and special techniques to implement a service business—e.g., the equipment, new computer software and skills required for computerized credit checking.

A. *Development Status and Tasks:* Describe the current status of the product or service and explain what remains to be done to make it marketable. Describe briefly the competence or expertise that your company has or will acquire to complete this development. Indicate the type and extent of technical assistance that will be required, state who will supervise this activity within your organization and his experience in related development work.

B. *Difficulties and Risks:* Identify any major anticipated design and development problems and approaches to their solution. Discuss their possible effect on the schedule, cost of design and development, and time of market introduction.

C. *Product Improvement and New Products:* In addition to describing the development of the initial products, discuss any on-going design and development work that is planned to keep your product or service competitive and to develop new related products that can be sold to the same group of customers.

D. *Costs:* Present and discuss a design and development budget. The costs should include labor, materials, consulting fees, etc. Design and development costs are often underestimated. This can seriously impact cash flow projections. Accordingly, consider and perhaps show a 10%-20% cost contingency. These cost data will become an integral part of the financial plan.

## 5. MANUFACTURING AND OPERATIONS PLAN

The manufacturing and operations plan should describe the kind of facilities, plant location, space requirements, capital equipment and labor force (part- and full-time) that are required to provide the company's product or service. For a manufacturing business, discuss your policies regarding inventory control, purchasing, production control, and "make or buy decisions" (i.e., which parts of the product will be purchased and which operations will be performed by your work force). A service business may require particular attention and focus on an appropriate location, an ability to minimize overhead, lease the required equipment, and obtain competitive productivity from a highly skilled or a trained labor force.

The discussion guidelines given below are general enough to cover both product and service businesses. Only those that are relevant to your venture—be it product or service—should be addressed in the business plan.

A. *Geographic Location:* Describe the planned location of the business and discuss any advantages or disadvantages of the site in terms of wage rates, labor unions, labor availability, closeness to customers or suppliers, access to transportation, state and local taxes and laws, utilities and zoning. For a service business, proximity to customers is generally a "must."

B. *Facilities and Improvements:* If yours is an existing business, describe the facilities currently used to conduct the company's business. This should include plant and office space; storage and land areas; machinery, special tooling and other capital equipment.

If your venture is a start-up, describe how and when the necessary facilities to *start* production will be acquired. Discuss whether equipment and space will be leased or acquired (new or used) and indicate the costs and timing of such actions. Indicate how much of the proposed financing will be devoted to plant and equipment. (These cost data will become part of the financial plan.)

Discuss how and when plant space and equipment will be expanded to the capacities required for future sales projections. Discuss any plans to improve or add to existing plant space or move the facility. Explain future equipment needs and indicate the timing and cost of such acquisitions. A three year planning period should be used for these projections.

C. *Strategy and Plans:* Describe the manufacturing processes involved in your product's production and any decisions with respect to subcontracting component parts rather than manufacturing in-house. The "make or buy" strategy adopted should consider inventory financing, available labor skills and other non-technical questions as well as purely production, cost, and capability issues. Justify your proposed "make or buy" policy. Discuss any surveys you have completed of potential subcontractors and suppliers, and who these are likely to be.

Present a production plan that shows cost-volume information at various sales levels of operation with breakdowns of applicable material, labor, purchased components and factory overhead. Discuss the inventory required at various sales levels. These data will be incorporated into cash flow projections. Explain how any seasonal production loads will be handled without severe dislocation—e.g., by building inventory or using part-time help in peak periods.

Briefly, describe your approach to quality control, production control, inventory control. Explain what quality control and inspection procedures the company will use to minimize service problems and associated customer dissatisfaction.

Discuss how you will organize and operate your purchasing function to ensure that adequate materials are on hand for production, the best price has been obtained, and that raw materials and in-process inventory, and hence, working capital, have been minimized.

D. *Labor Force:* Exclusive of management functions (discussed later), does the local labor force have the necessary skills in sufficient quantity and quality (lack of absenteeism, productivity), to manufacture the products or supply the services of your company. If the skills of the labor force are inadequate to the needs of the company, describe the kinds of training that you will use to upgrade their skills. Discuss whether the business can provide training and still offer a competitive product both in the short-term (first year) and longer-term (2-5 years).

## 6. MANAGEMENT TEAM

The management team is the key to turning a good idea into a successful business. Investors look for a committed management team with a balance of technical, managerial and business skills, and experience in doing what is proposed.

Accordingly, this section of the business plan will be of primary interest to potential investors and will significantly influence their investment decisions. It should include a description of the key management personnel and their primary duties; the organizational structure; and the board of directors.

A. *Organization:* In a table, present the key management roles in the company and the individual who will fill each position

Discuss any current or past situations where the key management people have worked together that indicate how their skills complement each other and result in an effective management team. If any key individuals will not be on hand at the start of the venture, indicate when they will join the company.

In a new business, it may not be possible to fill each executive role with a full-time person without excessively burdening the overhead of the venture. One solution is to use part-time specialists or consultants to perform some functions. If this is your plan, discuss it and indicate who will be used and when they will be replaced by a full-time staff member.

If the company is established and of sufficient size, an organization chart can be appended as an exhibit.

B. *Key Management Personnel:* Describe the exact duties and responsibilities of each of the key members of the management team. Include a brief (three or four sentence) statement of the career highlights of each individual that focuses on accomplishments that demonstrate his or her ability to perform the assigned role.

Complete resumes for each key management member should be included here or as an exhibit to the business plan. These resumes should stress training, experience and accomplishments of each person in performing functions similar to that person's role in the venture. Accomplishments should be discussed in such concrete terms as profit and sales improvement; labor management; manufacturing or technical achievements; and ability to meet budgets and schedules. Where possible it should be noted who can attest to accomplishments and what recognition or rewards were received—e.g., pay increases, promotions, etc.

C. *Management Compensation and Ownership:* The likelihood of obtaining financing for a start-up is small when the founding management team is not prepared to accept initial modest salaries. If the founders demand substantial salaries in excess of what they received at their prior employment, the potential investor will conclude that their psychological commitment to the venture is a good deal less than it should be.

State the salary that is to be paid to each key person and compare it to the salary received at his/her last independent job. Set forth the stock ownership planned for the key personnel, the amount of their equity investment (if any), and any performance-dependent stock option or bonus plans that are contemplated.

D. *Board of Directors:* Discuss the company's philosophy as to the size and composition of the board. Identify any proposed board members and include a one or two sentence statement of the member's background that shows how he or she can benefit the company.

E. *Management Assistance and Training Needs:* Describe, candidly, the strengths and weaknesses of your management team and Board of Directors. Discuss the kind, extent and timing of any management training that will be required to overcome the weaknesses and obtain effective venture operation. Also discuss the need for technical and management assistance during the first three years of your venture. Be as specific as you can as to the kind, extent and cost of such assistance and how it will be obtained.

F. *Supporting Professional Services:* State the legal (including patent), accounting, advertising and banking organizations that you have selected for your venture. Capable, reputable and well known supporting service organizations can not only provide significant direct, professional assistance, but can also add to the credibility of your venture. In addition, properly selected professional organizations can help you establish good contacts in the business community, identify potential investors and help you secure financing.

## 7. OVERALL SCHEDULE

A schedule that shows the timing and interrelationship of the major events necessary to launch the venture and realize its objectives is an essential part of a business plan. In addition to being a planning aid and showing deadlines critical to a venture's success, a well-prepared schedule can be an extremely effective sales tool in raising money from potential investors. A well-prepared and realistic schedule demonstrates the ability of the management team to plan for venture growth in a way that recognizes obstacles and minimizes risk.

Prepare, as a part of this section, a month-by-month schedule that shows the timing of activities such as product development, market planning, sales programs, and production and operations. Sufficient detail should be included to show the timing of the primary tasks required to accomplish an activity.

Show on the schedule the deadlines or milestones critical to the venture's success. This should include events such as:

- Incorporation of the venture (for a new business)

- Completion of design and development

- Completion of prototypes (a key date; its achievement is a tangible measure of the company's ability to perform)

- When sales representatives are obtained

- Displays at trade shows

- When distributors and dealers are signed up

- Order of materials in production quantities

- Start of production or operation (another key date because it is related to the production of income)

- Receipt of first orders

- First sales and deliveries (a date of maximum interest because it relates directly to the company's credibility and need for capital)

- Payment of first accounts receivable (cash in)

The schedule should also show the following and their relation to the development of the business:

- Number of management personnel

- Number of production and operations personnel

- Additions to plant or equipment

Discuss in a general way the activities most likely to cause a schedule slippage, and what steps you would take to correct such slippages. Discuss the impact of schedule slippages on the venture's operation, especially its potential viability and capital needs. Keep in mind that the time to do things tends to be underestimated—even more than financing requirements. So be realistic about your schedule.

## 8. CRITICAL RISKS AND PROBLEMS

The development of a business has risks and problems, and the business plan invariably contains some implicit assumptions about them. The discovery of any unstated negative factors by potential investors can undermine the credibility of the venture and endanger its financing.

On the other hand, identifying and discussing the risks in your venture demonstrates your skills as a manager and increases your credibility with a venture capital investor. Taking the initiative to identify and discuss risks helps you demonstrate to the investor that you have thought about them and can handle them. Risks then tend not to loom as large black clouds in the investor's thinking about your venture.

Accordingly, identify and discuss the major problems and risks that you think you will have to deal with to develop the venture. This should include a description of the risks relating to your industry, your company and its personnel, your product's market appeal and the timing and financing of your start-up. Among the risks that might require discussion are:

- Price cutting by competitors

- Any potentially unfavorable industry-wide trends

- Design or manufacturing costs in excess of estimates

- Sales projections not achieved

- Product development schedule not met

- Difficulties or long lead times encountered in the procurement of parts or raw materials

- Difficulties encountered in obtaining bank credit lines because of tight money

- Larger than expected innovation and development costs to stay competitive

- Availability of trained labor

This list is not meant to be complete but only indicative of the kinds of risks and assumptions that might be discussed.

Indicate which of your assumptions or potential problems are most critical to the success of the venture. Describe your plans for minimizing the impact of unfavorable developments in each risk area on the success of your venture.

## 9. COMMUNITY BENEFITS

The proposed venture should be an instrument of community and human development as well as economic development, and it should be responsive to the expressed desires of the community.

Describe and discuss the potential economic and non-economic benefits to members of the community that could result from your venture.

Among the potential benefits that may merit discussion are:

*Economic Development*

- number of jobs generated in each of the first three years of the venture

- number and kind of new employment opportunities for previously unemployed or underemployed individuals

- number of skilled and higher paying jobs

- ownership and control of venture assets by community residents

- purchase of goods and services from local suppliers

*Human Development*

- new technical skills development and associated career opportunities for community residents

- management development and training

- employment of unique skills within the community that are not unused

*Community Development*

- development of community's physical assets

- improved perception of CDC responsiveness and their role in the community

- provision of needed, but unsupplied, services or products to the community

- improvements in the living environment

- community support, participation and pride in the venture

- development of community-owned economic structure and decreased absentee business ownership

Describe any compromises or time lags in venture profitability that may result from trying to achieve some or all of the kinds of benefits cited above. Any such compromises or lags in profitability should be justified in the context of all the benefits achieved and the role of the venture in a total, planned program of economic, human and community development.

## 10. THE FINANCIAL PLAN

The financial plan is basic to the evaluation of an investment opportunity and should represent the entrepreneur's best estimates of future operations. Its purpose is to indicate the venture's potential and the timetable for financial viability. It can also serve as an operating plan for financial management of the venture.

In developing the financial plan, three basic forecasts must be prepared:

a. Profit and Loss Forecasts for three years

b. Cash Flows Projections for three years

c. Pro Forma Balance Sheets at start-up, semi-annually in the first year and at the end of each of the first three years of operation

In the case of an existing venture seeking expansion capital, balance sheets and income statements for the current and two prior years should be presented in addition to these financial projections.

Sample forms for preparing financial projections have been provided as Tables 18-20.[1] It is recommended that the venture's financial and marketing personnel prepare them, with assistance from an accountant if required. In addition to these three basic financial exhibits, a breakeven chart (Table 21) should be presented that shows the level of sales required to cover all operating costs.

After you have completed the preparation of the financial exhibits, briefly highlight in writing the important conclusions that can be drawn. This might include the maximum cash requirement, the amount to be supplied by equity and debt; the level of profits as a percent of sales; how fast any debts are repaid; etc.

## A. *Profit and Loss Forecast (Table 18)*

The preparation of pro forma income statements is the profit planning part of financial management. Crucial to the earnings forecasts—as well as other projections—is the sales forecast. You have already developed sales forecasts while completing your Market Research and Analysis section. The sales data projected should be used here.

Once the sales forecasts are in hand, production costs (or operations costs for a service business) should be budgeted. The level of production or operation that is required to meet the sales forecasts and also to fulfill inventory requirements must be determined. The material, labor, service and manufacturing overhead requirements must be developed and translated into cost data. A separation of the fixed and variable elements of these costs is desirable, and the effect of sales volume on inventory, equipment acquisitions and manufacturing costs should be taken into account.

Sales expense should include the costs of selling the distribution, storage, discounts, advertising and promotion. General and administrative expense should include management salaries, secretarial costs, and legal and accounting expenses. Manufacturing or operations overhead includes rent, utilities, fringe benefits, telephone, etc.

[1]Robert Morris Associates (The National Association of Bank Loan Officers and Credit Men) also publishes forms for preparing financial projections as well as instructions for preparing supporting worksheets for Accounts Payable Disbursements, Accounts Receivables Collections, Material Flow and Purchases, etc. These instructions and forms are: Charles G. Zimmerman, "Projection of Financial Statements—And the Preparatory Use of Work Sheet Schedules for Budgets" and RMA Form C-117, "Projection of Financial Statements," (Philadelphia, Pennsylvania: Robert Morris Associates, 1961).

## TABLE 18

### PRO FORMA INCOME STATEMENTS

| | 1st Year – Months | | | | | | | | | | | | 2nd Year Quarters | | | | 3rd Year Quarters | | | |
|---|---|---|---|---|---|---|---|---|---|---|---|---|---|---|---|---|---|---|---|---|
| | 1 | 2 | 3 | 4 | 5 | 6 | 7 | 8 | 9 | 10 | 11 | 12 | 1Q | 2Q | 3Q | 4Q | 1Q | 2Q | 3Q | 4Q |
| Sales | | | | | | | | | | | | | | | | | | | | |
| Less: Discounts | | | | | | | | | | | | | | | | | | | | |
| Less: Bad Debt Provision | | | | | | | | | | | | | | | | | | | | |
| Less: Materials Used | | | | | | | | | | | | | | | | | | | | |
| Direct Labor | | | | | | | | | | | | | | | | | | | | |
| Manufacturing Overhead[1] | | | | | | | | | | | | | | | | | | | | |
| Other Manufacturing Expense (Leased Equipment) | | | | | | | | | | | | | | | | | | | | |
| Total Cost of Goods Sold | | | | | | | | | | | | | | | | | | | | |
| Gross Profit (or Loss) | | | | | | | | | | | | | | | | | | | | |
| Less: Sales Expense | | | | | | | | | | | | | | | | | | | | |
| Engineering Expense | | | | | | | | | | | | | | | | | | | | |
| General and Administrative Expense[2] | | | | | | | | | | | | | | | | | | | | |
| Operating Profit (or Loss) | | | | | | | | | | | | | | | | | | | | |
| Less: Other Expense (e.g., interest, depreciation) | | | | | | | | | | | | | | | | | | | | |
| Profit (Loss) Before Taxes | | | | | | | | | | | | | | | | | | | | |
| Income Tax Provision | | | | | | | | | | | | | | | | | | | | |
| Profit (Loss) After Taxes | | | | | | | | | | | | | | | | | | | | |

(1) Includes rent, utilities, fringe benefits, telephone.
(2) Includes office supplies, accounting and legal services, management, etc.

Earnings projections should be prepared monthly in the first year of operation and quarterly for the second and third years.

If these earnings projections are to be useful they must represent management's realistic, best estimates of probable operating results. Sales or operating cost projections that are either too conservative or too optimistic have little value as aids to policy formulation and decision-making.

*Discussion of Assumptions:* Because of the importance of profit and loss projections as an indication of the potential financial feasibility of a new venture to potential investors, it is extremely important that any assumptions made in its preparation be fully explained and documented. Such assumptions could include the amount allowed for bad debts and discounts, and any assumptions made with respect to sales expenses or general and administrative costs which are fixed percentages of costs or sales.

*Risks and Sensitivity:* Once the income statements have been prepared, draw on Section 8 of these guidelines to highlight any major risks that could prevent the venture's sales and profit goals from being attained, and the sensitivity of profits to these risks.

This discussion should reflect the entrepreneur's thinking about the risks that might be encountered in the firm itself, the industry, and the environment. This could include such things as the effect of a 20% reduction in sales projections, or the impact over time of a learning curve on the level of productivity.

## B. *Pro Forma Cash Flows Analysis (Table 19)*

For a new venture the cash flows forecast can be more important than the forecasts of profits because it details the amount and timing of expected cash inflows and outflows. Usually the level of profits, particularly during the start-up years of a venture, will not be sufficient to finance operating asset needs. Moreover, cash inflows do not match the outflows on a short-term basis. The cash flows forecast will indicate these conditions and allow management to plan cash needs.

Given a level of projected sales and capital expenditures over a specific period, the cash forecast will highlight the need for and timing of additional financing and indicate peak requirements for working capital. Management must decide how this additional financing is to be obtained, on what terms, and how it is to be repaid. Part of the needed financing will be supplied by the equity financing (that is sought by this business plan), part by bank loans for one to five years, and the balance by short-term lines of credit from banks. This information becomes part of the final cash flows forecast.

If the venture is in a seasonal or cyclical industry, or is in an industry in which suppliers require a new firm to pay cash, or if an inventory build-up occurs before the product can be sold and produce revenues, the cash flows forecast is crucial to the continuing solvency of the business. A detailed cash flows forecast which is understood and used by management can help them

TABLE 19

PRO FORMA CASH FLOWS

| | 1st Year - Months | | | | | | | | | | | | 2nd Year Quarters | | | | 3rd Year Quarters | | | |
|---|---|---|---|---|---|---|---|---|---|---|---|---|---|---|---|---|---|---|---|---|
| | 1 | 2 | 3 | 4 | 5 | 6 | 7 | 8 | 9 | 10 | 11 | 12 | 1Q | 2Q | 3Q | 4Q | 1Q | 2Q | 3Q | 4Q |
| Cash Balance: Opening | | | | | | | | | | | | | | | | | | | | |
| Add: Cash Receipts | | | | | | | | | | | | | | | | | | | | |
| Collection of Accounts Receivable | | | | | | | | | | | | | | | | | | | | |
| Miscellaneous Receipts | | | | | | | | | | | | | | | | | | | | |
| Bank Loan Proceeds | | | | | | | | | | | | | | | | | | | | |
| Sale of Stock | | | | | | | | | | | | | | | | | | | | |
| Total Receipts | | | | | | | | | | | | | | | | | | | | |
| Less: Disbursements | | | | | | | | | | | | | | | | | | | | |
| Trade Payables | | | | | | | | | | | | | | | | | | | | |
| Direct Labor | | | | | | | | | | | | | | | | | | | | |
| Manufacturing Overhead | | | | | | | | | | | | | | | | | | | | |
| Leased Equipment | | | | | | | | | | | | | | | | | | | | |
| Sales Expense | | | | | | | | | | | | | | | | | | | | |
| Warranty Expense | | | | | | | | | | | | | | | | | | | | |
| General and Administrative Expense | | | | | | | | | | | | | | | | | | | | |
| Fixed Asset Additions | | | | | | | | | | | | | | | | | | | | |
| Income Tax | | | | | | | | | | | | | | | | | | | | |
| Loan Interest @ ____ % | | | | | | | | | | | | | | | | | | | | |
| Loan Repayments | | | | | | | | | | | | | | | | | | | | |
| Other Payments | | | | | | | | | | | | | | | | | | | | |
| Total Disbursements | | | | | | | | | | | | | | | | | | | | |
| Cash Increase (Decrease) | | | | | | | | | | | | | | | | | | | | |
| Cash Balance: Closing | | | | | | | | | | | | | | | | | | | | |

direct their attention to operating problems without distractions caused by periodic cash crises that should have been anticipated. Cash flows projections should be made for each month of the first year of operation and quarterly for the second and third years.

*Discussion of Assumptions:* This should include assumptions made about the timing of collections receivables, trade discounts given, terms of payments to vendors, planned salary and wage increases, anticipated increases in any operating expenses, seasonality of the business as it affects inventory requirements, inventory turnovers per year, and capital equipment purchases. Thinking about such assumptions when planning your venture is useful for identifying issues which may later require attention if they are not to become significant problems.

*Cash Flow Sensitivity:* Once the cash flow has been completed, discuss the impact on cash needs that possible changes in some of the crucial assumptions would have; e.g., slower receivables collection or scales below forecasts. This will enable you to test the sensitivity of the cash budget based on differing assumptions about business factors, and to view several possible outcomes. Investors are vitally interested in this because it helps them estimate the possibility that you will need more cash sooner than planned.

## C. *Pro Forma Balance Sheets (Table 20)*

The balance sheets detail the assets required to support the projected level of operations and show how these assets are to be financed (liabilities and equity). Investors and bankers look at the projected balance sheets to determine if debt to equity ratios, working capital, current ratios, inventory turnover, etc., are within the acceptable limits required to justify future financings projected for the venture.

Pro forma balance sheets should be prepared at start-up, semi-annually for the first year, and at the end of each of the first three years of operation.

## D. *Breakeven Chart (Table 21)*

A breakeven chart shows the level of sales (and hence, production) needed to cover all your costs. This includes those costs that vary with the production level (manufacturing labor, material, sales costs) and those that do not change with production (rent, interest charges, executive salaries, etc.). The sales level that exactly equals all costs is the breakeven level for your venture.

It is very useful for the investor and the management to know what the breakeven point is and whether it will be easy or difficult to attain. It is very desirable for your projected sales to be sufficiently larger than the breakeven sales so that small changes in your performance do not produce losses. You should prepare a breakeven chart and discuss how your breakeven point might be lowered in case you start to fall short of your sales projections. You should also discuss the effect on your breakeven point of lower production capacity requirements.

## TABLE 20
### PRO FORMA BALANCE SHEETS

| | Start-up | End of 6 Months | End of First Year | End of Second Year | End of Third Year |
|---|---|---|---|---|---|
| **ASSETS** | | | | | |
| Current | | | | | |
|   Cash | | | | | |
|   Marketable Securities | | | | | |
|   Accounts Receivable | | | | | |
|   Inventories | | | | | |
|     Raw Materials and Supplies | | | | | |
|     Work in Process | | | | | |
|     Finished Goods | | | | | |
|   Total Inventory | | | | | |
|   Prepaid Items | | | | | |
| Total Current Assets | | | | | |
| Plant and Equipment | | | | | |
|   Less: Accumulated Depreciation | | | | | |
| Net Plant and Equipment | | | | | |
| Deferred Charges | | | | | |
| Other Assets (Identify) | | | | | |
| **TOTAL ASSETS** | | | | | |
| **LIABILITIES AND STOCKHOLDERS' EQUITY** | | | | | |
|   Notes Payable to Banks | | | | | |
|   Accounts Payable | | | | | |
|   Accruals | | | | | |
|   Federal and State Taxes | | | | | |
|   Other | | | | | |
| TOTAL CURRENT LIABILITIES | | | | | |
|   Long Term Notes | | | | | |
|   Other Liabilities | | | | | |
|   Common Stock | | | | | |
|   Capital Surplus | | | | | |
|   Retained Earnings | | | | | |
| **TOTAL LIABILITIES AND STOCKHOLDERS' EQUITY** | | | | | |

## TABLE 21

## SAMPLE BREAKEVEN CHART

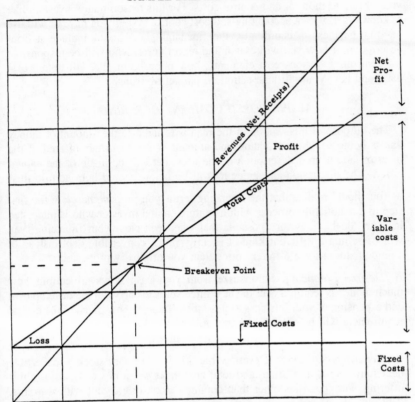

Units Produced

### E. *Cost Control*

Your ability to meet your income and cash flows projections will depend on your ability to monitor and control costs. For this reason many investors like to know what type of accounting and cost control system you have or will use in your business. Accordingly, the financial plan should include a brief description of how you will obtain and report costs, who will be responsible for controlling various cost elements, how often he or she will obtain cost data, and how you will take action on budget overruns.

## 11. *PROPOSED COMPANY OFFERING*

The purpose of this section of the plan is to indicate the amount of money that is being sought, the nature and amount of the securities offered to the investor, and a brief description of the uses that will be made of the capital raised. The discussion and guidelines given below should help you do this.

You should realize that the financing terms you propose here are the first step in a negotiation process with a venture capital investor who is interested in your "deal." It is very possible that when you close your financing, you will be selling a different kind of security (e.g., convertible debt instead of common stock) for a different price than you originally proposed.

A. *Desired Financing:* Summarize from your cash flows projections how much money is required over the next three years to carry out the development and expansion of your business as described. Indicate how much of the capital requirement will be obtained by this offering and how much will be obtained from term loans, lines of credit or other sources.

B. *Securities Offering:* Describe the kind (common stock, convertible debenture, etc.), unit price, and total amount of securities to be sold in this offering. For securities other than common stock (e.g., debt with warrants, debt plus stock) indicate interest, maturity, and conversion conditions. Also show the percentage of the company that the investors of this offering will hold after it is completed, or after exercise of any stock conversion or purchase rights in the case of convertible debentures or warrants.

If the securities are being sold as a "private placement" (that is, exempt from SEC registration), you should include the following statement in this part of the plan:

"The shares being sold pursuant to this offering are restricted securities and may not be resold readily. The prospective investor should recognize that such securities might be restricted as to resale for an indefinite period of time. Each purchaser will be required to execute a Non-Distribution Agreement satisfactory in form to corporate counsel."

C. *Capitalization:* Present in tabular form the current and proposed (post-offering) number of outstanding shares of common stock. Indicate any shares offered by key management people and show the number of shares that they will hold after completion of the proposed financing.

Indicate how many shares of your company's common stock will remain authorized but unissued after the offering and how many of these will be reserved for stock options for future key employees.

D. *Use of Funds:* Investors like to know how their money is going to be spent. Provide a description of how the capital raised will be used. Summarize, as specifically as possible, what amount will be used for such things as product design and development; capital equipment; marketing; and general working capital needs.

The main body of the business plan ends here. Appendices begin at this point.

## Final Note

All projections within a business plan must be based on realism. Accurate planning and performance measurement is dependent on realistic projections of future outcomes. In addition, projections will be the basis for critical decisions relating to all aspects of the firm's operation. Unreasonable expectations can cause resources to be spent unwisely and create suspicion among potential lenders and investors.

Every projection stated must be firmly documented, giving reasonable evidence that it can be achieved. A plan of action must be detailed, discussing strategy and tactics. For example, in a market forecast a firm must undertake an analysis of market opportunities and the capability of the firm to exploit those potentials. Once the sales projection is made, it should be backed by reasonable assurances of an expanding market. After this is accomplished, specific marketing steps to achieve the stated objective must be discussed. These endeavors might include the opening of new offices; introduction of new or modified products/services; addition of new sales personnel; new customer identification; expanding needs of existing customers; and/or enhanced promotion effort.

Whether it is sales projections, profit and loss estimates, cash-flow forecasts, or other financial predictions, realistic appraisals and approaches are mandatory in order to prevent unwise application of resources and disappointment among managers, creditors, and investors.

An entrepreneur should also consider and evaluate internal and external forces that affect the business in question and report their impact in the business plan under the section entitled "Critical Risks and Problems." These forces are listed in Tables 22 and 23.

TABLE 22

INTERNAL FACTORS

Expansion Plans
Pricing Structure
Operational Limitations
Financial Limitations
Research and Development
Introduction of New Product/Services
Marketing Dynamics
Revenue and Earnings Projections
Market Expansion

TABLE 23

ENVIRONMENTAL (EXTERNAL) FACTORS

Economic Cycles
Business Trends
Government Regulations
State of Technology
Competitive Conditions
Changing Demand Patterns
Industry Trends
Unions
Inflation
Changes in Population Profile
International Events

It is the opinion of many small business experts that entrepreneurs/ managing teams should not attempt to construct statements or attempt forecasting. Most simply lack the marketing, financial, and accounting expertise to accomplish these feats adequately and to the satisfaction of funding outlets. Therefore, competent business consultants and/or accountants should be sought out to complete this laborious and tedious task. Chapter III and Table 24 provide information on individuals and/or organizations that may provide assistance.

## TABLE 24

OUTSIDE SOURCES OF INFORMATION

ECONOMIC

*General*
Chamber of Commerce
Business friends
Social friends
Advisory board
Local service clubs
Customers
Advertising, sales
Board of Directors
Newspapers
Competition—unknown

↑

| TECHNOLOGICAL | COMPANY | POLITICAL |
|---|---|---|
| *Professional* | | *Educational and* |
| *Services* | | *Governmental* |
| Accountants | | Universities |
| Lawyers | | Private and public libraries |
| Technical consultants | *Internal* | Small Business Administration |
| Management consultants ← | | → U.S. Department of |
| Advertising agency | Owner-manager | Commerce |
| Insurance | Key subordinates | Department of Agriculture |
| Bankers | Employees | Other Federal, State, |
| Investment bankers | | and local agencies |

↓

SOCIAL

*Trade*

Trade associations
Suppliers
Professional journals
Competition—known

Chapter VIII

# APPROACHING THE INVESTOR
## What Is Expected

### Beefing Up the Business Plan

The success of any business endeavor will hinge on the decisions made by the entrepreneur and managers involved. A comprehensive business plan will assist in the decision-making function by allocating the firm's limited resources and evaluating managerial decisions. In addition, it forces the business to establish reasonable objectives and make logical choices. The plan should be viewed and conveyed as a path to follow. It allows the business to guide itself through anticipated and unexpected economic environments by forcing the entrepreneur to identify and deal with real and potential problems before they threaten the business.

In reference to what was mentioned earlier, the business plan should run between 40 and 60 pages (typed and double spaced), with an adequate number of appendices for purposes of illustration and detail. There are exceptions to this rule. Some plans can get by with fewer pages and others take more. It depends on many factors, some of which include product/service being marketed, age of the firm, type of industry, nature of funding, etc. Whatever the case, the business plan must be detailed enough to tell the whole story without being so long and drawn out as to bore the reader. Copies of the finished plan will need to be made for prospective investors. All reproductions should have nice-looking protective covers so as to project a professional image. Do an adequate job, but don't go overboard. Too much attention to cosmetics will give investors the immediate impression that substance is being compromised for image purposes, even though this may not be the case. If it is apparent that lots of time and money was spent to produce an "attention getter" cover, investors will feel that extravagance is the name of the game. Recently, an entrepreneur and managing team of a small wholesale business submitted a business plan with an expensive gold-embossed cover to a New York venture capital firm. To make matters worse, the first page of the business plan contained a smiling photograph of the entrepreneur. Well, it was good for a couple of laughs before being returned with a rejection letter.

Keep in mind that certain aspects of the business plan are more important than others. Quality and capability of management is generally given the highest consideration and must be emphasized accordingly. "Good managers can sell anything. Look at the pet rock, it was really nothing, but they made it sell," quoted an investor. He went on to say that "management is given approximately 60 percent weight in a funding decision, with the rest divided among the various components of the business plan." In addition, the marketing research segment of the plan is of great importance because it attempts to convey the marketability of the firm's product or service. Therefore, this section should be given added emphasis.

## Initial Contacts with Money Sources

Most financial outlets have specific investment preferences. Many will invest only in selected geographic areas and in certain types of businesses. Also, they limit themselves as to the amount invested. Many will entertain proposals only for existing firms while others welcome start-up situations. Some do both. Studying these particulars will save countless hours pursuing the wrong funding sources. Most of the investors mentioned in Chapter XI have been listed with their preferences. After matching proposition with correct source, the next step involves contact.

Financial outlets generally don't like phone calls. They prefer that entrepreneurs mail them a cover letter and a two- or three-page summary of the business plan for initial consideration. The summary section of the completed plan can be used for this purpose. Make sure a competent business consultant, attorney, or accountant has reviewed the summary before sending it to the investors. In fact, several people should evaluate the summation to determine its merits. Their recommendation should be carefully considered. Any changes that strengthen the document should be made without reservation. Just remember that the summary must never exceed three pages. It is strictly an attention getter designed to spark investors' interest in reading the entire business plan. If they are pleased with what they see, the whole plan will be requested for additional consideration. Don't get discouraged if this process takes some time. An excellent way to determine an investor's interest in the proposition is the amount of time he spends looking over the plan. Extensive evaluation is a positive signal, without question.

While the business plan is being examined, the entrepreneur should be making a background investigation of the investor. This must be done to protect the business from hooking up with an unethical or otherwise difficult capital source. Ask for references. Contacting firms that have received funds from the prospective funding outlet is an ideal way to get valuable insight into the nature of the investor. In addition, checking with the U.S. Small Business Administration in Washington might prove to be helpful. Also, speaking with the local chamber of commerce in the city where the investor resides should yield some information. Some investors belong to professional trade organizations (listed in appendices O and P). Give them a call to check the credentials of the funding source. Potential investors should be carefully reviewed in reference to their relationships with affiliated entrepreneurs and to the degree in which they provide initial and ongoing managerial assistance. Taking these inexpensive and cautious measures in the beginning may eliminate costly headaches down the road.

After the investors have critically evaluated and scrutinized the business plan, the entrepreneur will be informed of the decision by letter or phone. If the response is negative, ask why and what can be done to improve chances of successful funding. Maybe they know another source that may be interested. A positive answer will invoke an invitation to meet the money source personally.

The aforementioned procedure just outlined applies to most financial outlets. The exceptions are banks and governmental sources of funding. These outlets will normally meet with entrepreneurs beforehand to discuss the proposal. They may even request that a simple application form be completed. Ultimately, these sources will also demand a comprehensive business plan.

## Presentation of the Business Plan

When a financial outlet requests a verbal presentation of the business plan, respond at once to set an appointment. Go to the meeting dressed appropriately. Appear mildly confident and poised. Avoid excessive zeal. In addition, conducting oneself in a polite, professional and dignified manner is a must. Many entrepreneurs with good business plans have failed to obtain capital because they didn't project a solid character image to investors.

The presentation is used to evaluate the entrepreneur and/or management team more than the business plan. After all, the investors have already read the plan at this point. The entrepreneur and others involved must be prepared to discuss all facets of the proposal in an intelligent and convincing manner, with a command of the facts. Below are some observations that will probably be made during the presentation stage:

— Does the entrepreneur and/or managing team appear structured and systematic?
— Is there enough business and technical expertise involved in the proposition? Can it be obtained if lacking?
— Is the entrepreneur and others involved realistic in their estimates of projections, risks, time, resources, etc.?
— How is criticism handled? Can helpful comments be accepted?
— Is forthrightness displayed? Are inconsistencies admitted frankly or evaded?
— Does the entrepreneur and/or managing team communicate effectively?

Specific questions will be asked. Even though most have been covered extensively in the business plan, a verbal response will be expected. Remember, the investors are searching for weaknesses. They will attempt to detect contradictions between the verbal presentation and what is stated in the plan. The most common questions put to entrepreneurs during the presentation are as follows:

— How much capital is requested?
— For what purposes will it be used?
— How will it be repaid?

— What security is being offered?
— Describe the product or service to be marketed.
— Who are the customers?
— Why will they buy?
— Who are the competitors?
— Why is this product/service better than the competition?
— By how much is the total market for the product/service growing?
— How long will it take to gear up for marketing?
— When will marketing endeavors begin?
— What are the background and track record of the company's management relative to the product/service and industry?
— What are their relevant management and business skills?
— What are the risks involved in this venture?
— What are the strengths of the proposal?
— What are the weaknesses of the proposal?
— What is the credit history of the principals involved in the project?
— How much capital do the principals intend on investing in the project?
— Has all the appropriate personal and business insurance been considered?
— Does the business have a competent attorney? Accountant? Who are they?

The responses received from the aforementioned questions will determine to a great extent whether funding is approved. A good presentation will substantially enhance the chances of getting funds.

## Give and Take in Final Funding Negotiations

If the entrepreneur and business plan live up to investor expectations, the next barrier to overcome regards funding terms. This is a major bone of contention between investor and management which demands careful consideration. Many good deals have fallen apart during this stage of discussion. In a lending situation, the point of confrontation centers around the interest rate to be charged. Most businesses feel that financial outlets are demanding too much while the lenders contend it's not enough. When equity (ownership) is involved in the discussions, the argument rages over how much ownership the entrepreneur and others involved must forfeit to investors in exchange for their capital. The question of who controls what takes center stage.

It all boils down to perceived risks by the investors. Greater risks will force the entrepreneur to give up a larger portion of ownership in an equity deal or pay higher interest rates if lending is the financing vehicle. There is no steadfast rule used by investors to determine the pitfalls in prospective business propositions. Each financial outlet sees things differently and will act accordingly, although there are some general guidelines used in analyzing risks. Knowing these before going into negotiations will reduce frustration from the outset. They are:

— The less capital invested by the entrepreneur and others involved in the business, the more ownership demanded by investors in an equity arrangement. If loans are contemplated, higher rates of interest will be required. Most investors prefer that management invest in the business proposition to the maximum degree possible. One venture capitalist recently commented that he sleeps better knowing individuals running the business have invested money. "If their money is on the line, you can bet they will try harder to make things work."

— A start-up company will need to give up more ownership and/or pay higher interest rates than a going operation. This reasoning is quite obvious. An existing concern has a greater chance of survival.

— A business that operates in a high growth industry (computers, medical technology, alternative energy, information transfer, etc.) will be able to negotiate better equity terms or lower interest rates on loans than a firm that finds itself in a less promising sector of the economy.

— The general economic climate will affect investor attitude. Periods of recession and stagnation will find financial outlets wary and extremely cautious, probably demanding more equity or higher interest rates than would be the case in an expanding economy.

— Anticipated earnings growth will also affect investor reactions. If the prospects for continued profits are good, a better equity or lending deal can be arranged with the funding outlets.

Before entering into negotiations with investors, do some homework. Study similar funding arrangements. Know what to expect. Consult attorneys, accountants, and consultants in reference to the business proposition. Being well informed will impress the investors and help insure a fair funding agreement. When negotiating, keep in mind that both parties must give and take. Try to establish a relationship with the investor by establishing a candid and friendly rapport. Disagreements will happen, but it is critically important to maintain a positive and professional posture at all times. Communication is an absolute necessity during the negotiation process. Each party must clearly state their goals and let the other know if changes in position occur. Without this interreaction, negotiation will eventually come to a halt.

The entrepreneur/managing team should be keen negotiators. Investors will respect shrewdness. If a loan is being discussed, tell the lender that a high interest rate will retard earnings and adversely affect the firm's rate of growth. Attempt to prove this with hard figures. In an equity situation, mention that giving up too much ownership will have a negative impact on managerial incentive. Throw the investors a "high ball." Tell them that a high percentage of ownership must be retained by management. Use this as a starting point in the discussions.

Always appear willing to negotiate. Investors expect to give and take. Above all, don't get greedy. It's a turn-off to serious funding sources. Recently, an inventor created a number of ingenious energy efficient products and several investors expressed interest in providing capital to finance marketing endeavors. The inventor refused to give up more than 75 percent ownership in the business for what he called "control purposes." Because the products were new and unproven the investors refused to provide funding under his conditions. They made a counter-offer to hold 60 percent of ownership and would further reduce it to 40 percent once earnings were generated, thereby giving the inventor control later down the road. He still declined the offer and the deal broke apart. Realizing his mistake, the inventor decided to accept the offer, but it was too late. The investors wouldn't have anything to do with the proposition.

Too much emphasis on the idea of control can kill a good deal as it did in the case mentioned above. Remember, it's better to have 20 percent of a watermelon than 80 percent of a raisin. A properly structured deal can insure the entrepreneur and others involved eventual control of the business. Many investors will negotiate incentive/equity deals. This is where the entrepreneurs are given a smaller percentage of ownership in the beginning, which will increase as the business grows.

Whatever the case, don't get desperate and accept anything that comes along, even though the money is desperately needed. Most businesses would be wise not to accept poor or inadequate funding offers. The ideal scenario would be teaming up with reputable investors who are willing to assist in making the proposition operate and function successfully. Investors willing to help rather than hinder should be sought out. Appendix R provides an outline of a typical investment agreement.

## Twenty-four Reasons Why Funds Requests Are Rejected

Listed below are some of the more common reasons why financial outlets refuse funding requests. The problems stem from deficiencies within the business and/or because of difficulties with the entrepreneur/ managing team.

— Lack of Continuity—The business plan must demonstrate that the firm will continue uninterrupted if key employees of the firm leave or die.
— Unwillingness to Part with Equity—Too many entrepreneurs are unduly concerned over giving up ownership and/or control of the business. Overemphasis on this issue can kill a good deal in short order.
— Inability to Take Criticism—Many investors will make helpful suggestions concerning the proposal. Defensive reactions on the part of the entrepreneur/managing team will leave a bad impression. It denotes immaturity.
— Underestimating Capital Needs—Many entrepreneurs tend to underestimate capital requirements for the business. In some cases, it is a deliberate attempt to impress investors that something can be accomplished with less. Well, it doesn't. In fact, it displays a lack of good business sense. One of the major reasons for business failure is lack of adequate capitalization.
— Lack of a Total Plan—Most business plans that are submitted to funding outlets are strictly financial in nature. They fail to consider non-financial aspects such as production considerations.
— Unrealistic, Low Expense Forecasts—Reasonable expense projections must be made in order to accurately predict earnings

flow. Overstated profit expectations based on erroneous expense data will only give investors the impression that numbers are being "churned" in order to create an attractive picture.

— Overstated Revenue Projections—If revenues fail in living up to expectation, the chances are that profits will do the same. Since the technical aspects of funding deals rely heavily on projected revenues and profits, realistic projections need to be made. In fact, investors will not allow overstated forecasts. They will use their financial expertise to adjust the figures appearing in the business plan. It's nice to have it done right the first time around. It shows that the entrepreneur/managing team know what they are doing.

— Little or No Experience in the Area of Operation—Investors will feel uncomfortable knowing that the firm's management is weak in the product/service area. The firm can compensate for this by hiring a consultant and/or managers with experience and knowledge in the product/service and industry.

— Self-centered—Many entrepreneurs don't like delegating authority to others when it needs to be done. they tend to be egocentric and think everything must evolve around them. Most fear losing control. "Ego in itself is not bad," stated one investor. "It's the unrestrained ego that causes problems, and we steer clear of that type of individual."

— Too Much Show—Trying to impress investors with fancy offices and cars will have only a negative impact. They will feel that too much is being spent on cosmetics and not enough on substance. Normally it gives the impression of extravagance.

— Seeking More Than Is Needed—This is called "Fudging" and is considered a no-no. It is easy to detect, and invokes the question, why is the extra money needed? The entrepreneur will find that it's an embarrassing situation and could weaken the relationship with the investor.

— Using Investors Against Each Other—Don't try to pit money sources against each other to enhance the bargaining position. It's a turn-off to investors and will not work. Many will refuse to talk after being exposed to this tactic. Now don't get the wrong idea. It is okay to have other funding alternatives. Just don't use them as bait to squeeze out what might be considered a better deal. It shows lack of tact.

— Lack of Appreciation for the Learning Process—The ability to learn rapidly is essential in today's business environment. Entrepreneurs must convince investors that they are capable of catching on quickly. Formal and informal discussion between investor and entrepreneur will reveal this quality. Learn from what the investor has to say. If learning ability is not shown to investors, funding may not be forthcoming.

— Sweet Talk—Don't butter up the investors. It's obvious and they do not like it one bit. Being too sweet and nice could kill a deal in short order. The investors know something is up and it creates suspicion from the very beginning, and that is "strike one" against the entrepreneur.

— Lack of Managerial Wholeness—Management is the most important consideration in the funding decision. Without the proper breadth of management and business experience to run the operation with a good chance of success, the probability of securing funds is nil.

— Wrong Timing—The product or service may not be ready for the market at this time, or the right time has already passed and there are too many existing competitors.

— Lack of Pragmatism—Entrepreneurs must remember that funding negotiations are a give and take situation requiring compromise on both sides. Unreasonable demands denote lack of practicality and will result in an invitation out the door. "One entrepreneur demanded to keep 65 percent of the business and invest only $10,000," says a New York venture capitalist. "Hell, he wanted us to foot $500,000 and retain only 35 percent of the business, and it was a start-up situation with no track record." The entrepreneur refused to compromise and the deal fell apart quickly.

— Inability to Communicate—Entrepreneurs who can't convey their ideas clearly and concisely in written or verbal form stand little chance of being funded. A banker for Chase Manhattan Bank recently stated that "if the entrepreneur and managing team can't explain and answer questions about the proposal in a clear and logical fashion, how are they going to market their service or product?"

— Lack of Trust—Many entrepreneurs feel that funding outlets can't be trusted and are cheats. It becomes obvious very quickly.

Information is withheld, former relationships are criticized, and complaints are made about rotten terms they got from other funding sources. One investor recently remarked that "When a paranoid entrepreneur comes down the pike, we run for the hills. It's trouble from the start."

— Lack of Appreciation for the Team Approach— "The entrepreneur who thinks he/she can do it all is a danger signal," stated an investor recently. He went on to say that "entrepreneurs who fail to recognize the need for a unified effort are being naïve. Today's business environment demands it."

— Intolerance—Information about personality and background will be sought by the prospective investors. Entrepreneurs who get insulted and upset when probing questions are asked leave a bad impression.

— Lack of Appreciation for a Buck—If the entrepreneur/managing team fail to show investors that their money is going to be treated with a lot of consideration and prudence, the deal will come apart. One of the biggest fears on the part of investors is that once their money is given to the entrepreneurs, it will be spent indiscriminately and recklessly. Entrepreneurs need to dispel this fear by showing the investor exactly how funds will be employed.

— Lack of Testing—A product or service should be tested on a small scale to evaluate results before attempting large distribution efforts. Testing reveals potentially costly faults that can be corrected before large efforts are executed. Telling investors that the product/service is ready to be marketed on a large scale without appropriate testing because "it's the greatest thing ever developed" is giving the wrong impression and will scare off serious investors. The business plan should make reference to testing procedures. If testing has already taken place, the results should be revealed.

— Lack of Caution—Studies have shown that most successful entrepreneurs are moderate risk takers and not the "high stakes rollers" they are publicized to be.

Chapter IX

# MAKE IT SUCCESSFUL
## Sweat and Money Are at Stake

### Aim Toward the Future

Setting long-term goals and objectives can prove to be a roadmap guiding the business along a path to future profits and success. One of the foremost reasons for America's lack of competitive success in the international marketplace is the unwillingness of domestic business leaders to plan for the future. U.S. managers have been criticized throughout the industrial world for being "short termers," exploiting only immediate opportunities and, therefore, compromising long-term considerations that could prove to be more profitable. In reality, it is not the fault of the managers, but of society at large. American business leaders are rewarded by shareholders for their yearly performance. Consequently, they will do their best to look good on a short-term basis in order to enhance their immediate compensation and position. This problem is cultural and needs to be addressed by the country's political, business, and academic leadership.

Whatever the case, when looking to the future, an entrepreneur must also consider the past and present. By analyzing past and current business performance, insight can be gained into the forecasting function. Evaluating the firm's strengths and weaknesses, relative to financial performance, will set the stage for accurate projections. In addition, knowing the environmental conditions besetting the marketplace should play a significant role in the process of establishing forecasts.

Always plan at least five years into the future. Be flexible enough to allow for emergency situations that may or may not be anticipated (this is called "crisis planning"). For example, prior to the predicted gasoline crunch of 1979, Mayor Kelley of Ocean City, Maryland, which is a large eastern summer resort, stockpiled gas supplies and promised every visitor that he would have enough gas to get them home. He saved the resort from financial disaster that year.

Failure to plan for the long haul will result in short-term adventurism, thereby mis-allocating the firm's limited resources and compromising greater profit potentials.

## Intimate Knowledge Is Critical for Success

It is important to know every aspect of the business inside and out. Knowledge of what makes the firm tick and move can be valuable in successfully overcoming present and future problems. Good information resources and personal experiences can be used to gain this valuable insight.

## Managing for Success

Management is a broad topic covering many different disciplines. It is impossible to discuss all facets of the subject in the confines of this book. However, the important managerial elements of running a small business must be highlighted, and they are broadly reviewed here.

### MANAGING CASH AND CREDIT

Always remember that money is a commodity that is bought and sold for a price (interest rates). It is one of the most precious resources available to a business and requires effective management if the firm is to survive and prosper.

Send out invoices consistently and promptly at about the same time each month. The bills should contain all relevant information about the sale (date purchased, cost, account balance, terms, etc.). When income is received from receivables or cash sales, deposit it promptly in interest bearing checking accounts or other insured accounts that can be drawn on readily. After paying obligations due, put the remaining cash back into the operation immediately so as to generate additional sales and profits. Idle cash or money sitting in low yielding accounts is not an example of effective money management.

Make sure that accounts receivable are current and take steps to keep them that way. Past dues can be costly if money must be borrowed or existing funds used to finance operations until accounts are collected. Therefore, credit and collection control procedures are critical to successful operation. Grant credit based upon certain conditions that may vary depending on the customer. This can be accomplished by evaluating potential accounts relative to their ability to pay. After that, payment terms and credit limits can be established. Also, existing accounts should be reviewed periodically in order to determine if changes in credit arrangements are necessary.

All prospective and existing accounts must be required to fill out a credit application form. The form should include a promise to pay according to the terms of the credit agreement and it can be used to investigate customers' credit history. Make sure the application has a release statement allowing permission to conduct a credit investigation.

If accounts are offered to customers, expect some problems to surface, especially during periods of economic recession. Normally, it is advisable and advantageous to work with slow payers instead of being overly rigid and maybe losing business as a result. Set up procedures for dealing with slow or delinquent accounts. Degrees of slowness should be established with the objective of applying increasing measures of pressure the longer the overdue remains unpaid. Extreme cases may have to be pursued legally. Many of these delinquent situations can be avoided if standards are developed and instituted to disallow existing or prospective customers from billing beyond their ability to repay.

When the business decides to use credit, always exercise conservatism and precedence. Pay bills on or before due dates so as to maintain a healthy credit history. A bad payment record can be expensive in terms of loss of credit privilege and higher interest charged by worried lenders. Take advantage of early payment discounts if they are economically favorable from a cash float standpoint (savings generated from the payment discount must be greater than the income that could be created by using the money in another way before the invoice is due).

In addition, maintaining good relations with all creditors, including bankers, can prove to be beneficial in the long run. Keep them informed as to what is happening with the business. Below are some tips that may help to accomplish this information function.

— Be candid about positive and negative situations. Many creditors will work with a business in a difficult environment if they are aware of the problems besetting the enterprise and its industry.
— Help the creditors to understand the business and industry. Sometimes ignorance is the biggest stumbling block to effective relationships.
— Provide some insight into management and control functions. This will gain the creditor's confidence and faith in that it shows a willingness to make things operate smoothly and efficiently.
— Be specific about short-term, intermediate-term, long-term, and crisis planning. Creditors dislike unanticipated disruptions. Tell them when things are going to take place.

It is not necessary to incorporate the aforementioned tips into creditor relationships, but they will help relieve some of the natural and obvious tensions that exist between borrowers and creditors. An atmosphere of mutual trust and respect will also be fostered leading to a lasting and growing relationship.

## MANAGING OTHER FINANCES

Existing and prospective small business owners should attempt to understand the financial complexities involved in business operations. A thorough understanding of financial statements (balance sheet, profit and loss statement, cash flow statement) will provide a solid foundation for making good business decisions. These statements, showing all revenue, expense, asset, and liability accounts, should be prepared and examined once a month by a competent accountant and reviewed by the firm's owner(s). Each account within the statements should be shown for the current period and the same period for last year. In addition, current year-to-date totals can be given for financial control purposes.

Good financial statements will also serve to contain costs. Studying past and present information concerning cost accounts may provide valuable insight into the conditions affecting expense figures. Also, an examination of revenue accounts may indicate the degree of product/ service mark-up or mark-down required to maintain adequate levels of sales and profits. It may show a need to alter existing lines through modification, new introductions, and/or phase-out.

Financial statements are discussed extensively in Chapter VII.

## Managing Growth

Growing too fast can be as hazardous as a no-growth situation, if not more so. Growth must be implemented and managed carefully to insure that the business does not expand beyond its ability to control and/or finance operation. Many firms have met with demise because of uncontrollable expansion. The giant, W. T. Grant, failed because it grew beyond its capability to finance expansion internally and externally. The result was bankruptcy.

Growth should be mapped out well in advance. Within these plans a reasonable estimation of resources necessary in carrying out objectives must be evaluated and scrutinized to determine the feasibility of expansion. If resources will be lacking because of internal constraints and/or environmental factors, expansion objectives should be altered to meet with the realities of the situation.

## Managing Inventory

Proper inventory management can mean the difference between profit or loss, and in some cases survival. Excessive inventories will lock up needed cash that would otherwise be used to generate sales and profits.

If an inventory system is to be effective, its main objectives should be cost containment and efficient delivery. A study of purchase activity relative to finished goods and raw materials will need to be performed in order to accomplish these goals. Once the study and evaluation is completed, a minimum amount of inventory within each item and raw material classification can be stored to satisfy short-term customer orders. In addition, production can be maintained.

Below are some additional tips for addressing the inventory problem.

— Compare prices among suppliers.
— Purchasing should be controlled by one individual or department. Duplication of effort is a waste of time and money.
— All finished goods or raw material orders should be confirmed in writing, outlining every cost and condition, to avoid misunderstandings which do occur at times.
— When goods are delivered, check to make sure that everything is received in proper condition.
— Cross-reference the supplier's invoice with the written quotation. This will avoid overcharges which occasionally happen.

Whatever inventory procedure is implemented, the cost of the endeavor must be less than its potential savings. Excessive inventory control can inflict the same harm as too little. A balance must be struck. The optimum solution is hard to find, but it is imperative if the business is to manage resources correctly.

There are complex statistical methods used to determine optimum inventory levels. Discussion of these are beyond the scope of this book. Therefore, seek out a competent business consultant when faced with inventory problems. Talking with other business owners who have faced similar difficulties may provide a wealth of helpful information. Also, seeking out college professors with specialties in the field of information sciences may prove to be useful in solving problems related to inventory control.

## MANAGING MARKETS

All businesses survive based upon their ability to react to changes in market conditions and consumer tastes. If a business expects to prosper, it should be constantly on guard for future trends that may provide opportunities if exploited or even help avoid costly disasters. Expanding markets must be carefully evaluated against available resources to determine the possibility of further penetration or introduction. Stagnating markets require serious review if the business is involved. Can existing sales be maintained profitably? Is there any room for new sales? If so, why and how can they be achieved? Does the firm possess unique advantages allowing it to beat competition in stagnant markets? Declining markets are equally important to understand, especially when existing sales are at stake. Are sales holding firm or declining slower than the total market? Can further profits be squeezed out? When should market exit take place?

Addressing the reality of changing markets will help insure continual existence and profitable operation. Constantly be aware of trends and try to determine how the business may be affected.

## MANAGING PEOPLE

Many business experts contend that people are a firm's most important resource. This reasoning revolves around the fact that labor is generally the largest expenditure faced by most businesses. Therefore, it would make economic sense to manage labor resources efficiently.

Periodically analyze and evaluate personnel requirements. Make sure there are enough people to get the job done. Failure to operate at demand capacity will result in lost opportunities and increased costs. If too many workers are employed, expenses will increase faster than sales or profits on a percentage basis, thereby suggesting a reduction in force. In addition, all positions within the business should be reviewed regularly to determine their relative importance and worth to the business. Time will constantly change perceptions. This job analysis may reveal such things as redundant effort, reduced work load, down time, etc., that would justify employment cuts. It may be discovered that full-time positions should be reduced to part-time status. Generally, it is less costly to maintain two part-timers than one full-timer doing the same job, although there are hazards to this approach. Small businesses have enough problems attracting good help because of financial constraints. Emphasizing part-time positions too heavily may turn good employees or prospective candidates away.

Employment cutback decisions are difficult to make because of the human element involved. But remember, "It is better to rule from the head than to be dominated by the heart in a business situation." Employees singled out for cuts should be given ample warning. Try to assist them in finding new jobs. In addition, explaining the reasons for cuts to terminated and remaining employees will lessen the negative impact on morale.

It is also wise to develop a plan for absenteeism, which can be costly in terms of lost efficiency and the paying of overtime to someone else to perform the necessary work. For example, most absenteeism occurs on Monday which, of course, follows the weekend. One large company adopted a policy of distributing paychecks on Monday, and no-shows were reduced by 50 percent within two weeks of the decision. Another illustration explaining the effectiveness of a policy directed toward controlling absenteeism can be found in the Small Business Administration's management aid number 206, written by Jack H. Feller. It states that an "owner/manager of one small company eliminated vacations and sick leave. Instead, this owner/manager gave each employee thirty days' annual leave to use as the employee saw fit. At the end of the year, the employees were paid at regular rates for the leave they didn't use. To qualify for the year-end pay, the employee had to prove that sick leave was taken only for that purpose. Nonsick leave had to be applied for in advance. As a result, unscheduled absences and overtime pay were reduced significantly. In addition, employees were happier and more productive than they were under the old system."

When approaching worker incentives, always recognize and compensate exceptional work and effort. Both monetary (money and fringes) and psychological (non-monetary benefits) rewards should be used to stimulate interest, productivity, and satisfaction. In addition, always try to involve employees in the management of the business. Seek out their advice and counsel. Many employees have ideas that may not be apparent to the owners and/or managers. Giving them a feeling of worth and allowing their input into the decision-making function will usually provide positive reinforcement for all concerned.

Keeping good records is also an important part of people management. It can also protect the business from unwarranted legal actions taken by disgruntled employees or governmental bodies. The firm should make all employees fill out application forms that conform to federal government standards. Asking the wrong questions on the form can bring legal suit, but the procedure is necessary to insure accurate information on employees. In addition, records concerning work history (absenteeism, sick leave, vacation time, promotion, demotion, salary/wage increases or decreases) should be verified by appropriate documentation. For example, use written appraisal forms when evaluating employees. Review the contents of the forms with workers and then ask them to sign the final appraisal documents. This will protect the firm in the event that certain employees pursue legal action because of the firm's reactions due to the results appearing on the appraisal form. Also, interviewing and asking exiting employees to sign an exit document outlining their reason for leaving can save the firm expenses incurred because of unjust unemployment insurance claims.

Businesses employing workers must have an in-depth knowledge of every job within the firm. First, a job analysis needs to be completed which attempts to identify the specific tasks within each position and how the particular jobs relate to their immediate environment. Table 25 contains a checklist for conducting a job analysis. Second, after the job analysis is performed, a description of each position must be written detailing the responsibilities and conditions of each position in the business. This job description, as it is called, is utilized for purposes of promoting, demoting, selecting, transferring, and training existing or prospective employees. An outline of a job description appears in Table 26. Third, job specifications must be developed and used to identify and describe the physical and mental qualifications needed to perform the tasks in question. Generally, this document will also outline the

## TABLE 25

### SUMMARY/REVIEW CHECKLIST FOR CONDUCTING A JOB ANALYSIS

\_\_\_\_ 1. Gather data concerning the duties and qualifications of the job:

    \_\_\_\_a. think about the various duties, responsibilities and qualifications of the job and write them down.

    \_\_\_\_b. utilize the job analysis outline form to help you organize your thoughts.

    \_\_\_\_c. ask an employee who now holds the job to list the duties and responsibilities of the job as well as the qualifications which he or she believes are needed.

    \_\_\_\_d. review the duties, responsibilities and qualifications for the job with the person who supervises the job, if you are not doing that yourself directly.

    \_\_\_\_e. combine all job analysis notes to create a clear picture of the job.

\_\_\_\_ 2. Keep in mind the ultimate goals of the analysis: to simplify and improve employee recruitment, training and development; to evaluate jobs so that appropriate salary and wage rates can be set.

SOURCE: U.S. Small Business Administration.

## TABLE 26

### OUTLINE FOR WRITING A JOB DESCRIPTION

INSTRUCTIONS: Determine the positions for which you would like to write job descriptions. Remember that job descriptions are particularly useful in areas where job turnover is high, since they aid in recruitment, selection, and training of new employees. Now, complete the information below.

### JOB DESCRIPTION

Date: _____

*JOB TITLE:*

*STATEMENT OF THE JOB*
(A brief summary of the job, stating its general nature)

*MAJOR DUTIES*
(including responsibilities for quantity and quality of work, safety of others, equipment, decisions to be made, and schedules to be met. Most jobs can be described in outline form with three to eight duties)

1.

*MINOR DUTIES*
(include those duties only performed occasionally)

*RELATIONSHIPS*
(whom does a person in this position supervise? report to? work with?)

SOURCE: U.S. Small Business Administration.

hazards inherent in these positions. Test requirements may also be included in order to evaluate the capabilities of existing or potential employees. The job specification procedure will protect the firm against legitimate discrimination decision. For example, the specification document might state that individuals over six feet tall are unsuitable for a particular task. Therefore, people exceeding six feet in height will probably be hard-pressed to bring suit unless they can prove that the job specification itself is flawed. An outline for writing a job specification is shown in Table 27. Fourth, a job classification is needed to evaluate the value of particular positions to a business. This is determined by examining job complexities, duties, and contribution to the firm. Once this procedure is completed, pay scales are developed.

TABLE 27

OUTLINE FOR WRITING A JOB SPECIFICATION

*INSTRUCTIONS:* Determine the positions for which you would like to write job specifications. (Remember that job specifications are particularly useful in areas where job turnover is high, since they aid recruitment, selection, and training of new employees.) Now, complete the information below.

JOB SPECIFICATION

*JOB TITLE:*                                                               *Date:* _____

*Education* (List only that which is really necessary for the job, e.g., high school, college, trade schools, or other special training.)

*Experience* (The amount of previous and related experience which a new employee should have.)

*Knowledge/Skills* (List the specific knowledge and skills which the job may require.)

*Physical and Mental Requirements* (Mention any special physical or mental abilities required for the job, e.g., 20/20 eyesight, ability to lift 80 lb. bags, availability for irregular work hours, ability to work under time pressure, etc.)

SOURCE: U.S. Small Business Administration.

Many employers are learning the benefits of conducting orientation programs for new employees. Their purpose should be to familiarize new workers with the firm and their work environment. The objective is to reduce early turnovers, which can be a costly business expense. Generally, most firms do not begin to recover their cost of maintaining new inexperienced employees until after the first six months of employment. Unfortunately, this is when the greatest amount of turnover takes place. Most is due to misunderstandings or lack of communication between the firm and new workers. It may result in employees feeling out of place and/or overwhelmed. Involuntary termination or voluntary departure normally follows suit. Table 28 contains a checklist for establishing a job orientation program.

TABLE 28

JOB ORIENTATION CHECKLIST

____Explain:

    ____company purpose
    ____company image
    ____kind of clients catered to

____Introduce to other employees and positions

____Explain relationship between new employee's position and other positions

____Tour the building:

    ____working areas
    ____management office
    ____rest facilities
    ____records
    ____employee locker room or closet
    ____other relevant areas

____Explain facilities and equipment

____Review the duties and responsibilities of the job from the job description

____Introduce to emergency equipment and safety procedures

____Questions and answers

SOURCE: U.S. Small Business Administration.

## MANAGING PRODUCTS/SERVICES

Those products or services offering the greatest potential for sales and/or profits should be given highest priority in the marketing effort. Individual items or services being sold should have enough mark-up to cover all costs associated with it, including handling, warranties, and servicing arrangements, plus an adequate profit margin.

Products and services travel through "life cycles" and most will become less appealing to the marketplace as time passes on. Therefore, it is essential that business owners be constantly aware of changing conditions and customer tastes. Modify existing lines when necessary and move into new product or service areas when market forces demand to shift. Look at insurance companies today. A decade ago "whole-life" policies were in style and now they won't sell. Inflation made them obsolete because of their low dividend yields on the cash values built into the policies. Consequently, the insurance industry has replaced the "whole-life" concept with what is called "universal-life" which pays higher yields on the cash values. Incidentally, "whole-life" policies can still be purchased, but the primary marketing thrust, on the part of many insurance companies, has been directed to "universal-life."

## MANAGING RISK

Understanding risk is an important aspect of running any business. Some experts contend that an adequate insurance program designed to reduce risk is just as vital to the success of a firm as are other business functions. Without question, assets left unprotected could compromise the future existence of the business if loss occurred. Therefore, a sound risk reduction plan should be implemented and carefully managed to insure economic viability in the event of loss due to unanticipated events.

The items listed below should be considered by all existing business owners and prospective entrepreneurs thinking about purchasing a small enterprise.

— Determine how loss may occur—Recognizing the probability of loss is the initial step in understanding risk. Realistic appraisal is a must in order to protect the firm's assets and livelihood.
— Seek professional advice—Talk to agents employed by insurance companies and independent agents representing different companies. Ask for their assistance in determining insurance needs. To insure the credibility of the agents, request references and check them out. In addition, talking to other business owners may provide reliable agent contacts.
— Shop around for the best buy—Insurance products are subject to competitive forces; therefore, prices will differ among companies. Following a few simple rules will help to reduce the cost of carrying insurance coverage.

• Identify risks and the potential for loss.

- Insure the largest risk factor initially.

- Try to use deductibles. High deductibles will reduce insurance costs.

- Eliminate all overlapping insurance coverage. It is a waste of money, since most companies share the burden of loss as opposed to the owner getting extra coverage.

- Purchase insurance in large units, if possible. Avoid many small policies, since they tend to be more expensive for the same coverage.

- Some insurance companies sell consolidated policies incorporating all coverage into one central agreement. In addition, many professional and trade associations have insurance products at discount group rates. For example, the National Small Business Association located at 1604 K. Street, N.W., in Washington, DC 20006, provides some attractive insurance programs at reasonable prices.

- Always evaluate the firm's risk exposure on a timely and regular basis for purposes of upgrading or downgrading. This will insure adequate coverage at reasonable cost, and, in some cases, the phase out of protection that has become unnecessary.

— Structure an insurance program—A formalized plan outlining all aspects of the insurance program should be set forth for management purposes. The plan may include, but is not limited to, the following procedures:

- State the objective of the insurance plan.

- Try to deal with only one agent, if possible. Dealing with several may create confusion and disinformation.

- Assign responsibility for the program to one individual.

- Prevent or minimize losses through safety and inspection procedures.

- State the potential for loss candidly. Failure to acquire needed coverage because of disinformation can be a threat to the viability of the firm.

- No matter how small the chance for loss, all risks should be covered. Avoid underestimation of asset value to save money. If loss does occur, the firm may not recover its investment.

- Periodically, evaluate the insurance program to determine the need for modification. Some risk programs have automatic cost-of-living increases built in to protect against loss caused by increasing asset value due to inflation. All assets should be appraised occasionally to determine insurance requirement.

- Always maintain adequate records concerning the risk reduction program. This information may be helpful later when attempting to change or modify coverage.

The following insurance checklist is provided courtesy of the U.S. Small Business Administration; it was written by Professor Mark R. Greene. It is designed to provide insight into the insurance needs of small businesses.

Points reviewed in the checklist are classified into three groups. They are as follows: essential coverage, desirable but non-essential coverage, and employee coverage. After reading each statement, place a check under the column entitled "No action needed" if the statement and how it affects the insurance plan is understood. If it isn't, check the column entitled "Look into this." After completing the study, evaluate existing and/or prospective insurance coverage, keeping in mind the points covered in the checklist. Discuss any problems or concerns with an agent.

### Essential Coverage

Four kinds of insurance are essential: fire insurance, liability insurance, automobile insurance, and workers' compensation insurance. In some areas and in some kinds of businesses, crime insurance, which is discussed under "Desirable Coverages," is also essential.

Are you certain that all the following points have been given full consideration in your insurance program?

*Fire Insurance*

1. You can add other perils—such as windstorm, hail, smoke, explosion, vandalism, and malicious mischief—to your basic fire insurance at a relatively small additional cost.                    ____  ____

2. If you need comprehensive coverage, your best buy may be one of the all-risk contracts that offer the broadest available protection for the money.                    ____  ____

3. The insurance company may indemnify you—that is, compensate you for your losses—in any one of several ways: (1) It may pay actual cash value of the property at the time of loss. (2) It may repair or replace the property with material of like kind and quality. (3) It may take all the property at the agreed or appraised value and reimburse you for your loss.                    ____  ____

4. You can insure property you don't own. You must have an insurable interest—a financial interest—in the property when a loss occurs but not necessarily at the time the insurance contract is made. For instance, a repair shop or drycleaning plant may carry insurance on customers' property in the shop, or a person holding a mortgage on a building may insure the building although he doesn't own it.                    ____  ____

5. When you sell property, you cannot assign the insurance policy along with the property unless you have permission from the insurance company.                    ____  ____

6. Even if you have several policies on your property, you can still collect only the amount of your actual cash loss. All the insurers share the payment proportionately. Suppose, for example, that you are carrying two policies—one for $20,000 and one for $30,000—on a $40,000 building, and fire causes damage to the building amounting to $12,000. The $20,000 policy will pay $4,800; that is,                    ____  ____

$\frac{20,000}{50,000}$ , or $\frac{2}{5}$ , of $12,000. The $30,000 policy will pay

$7,200; which is $\frac{30,000}{50,000}$, or $\frac{3}{5}$, of $12,000.

7. Special protection other than the standard fire policy is needed to cover the loss by fire of accounts, bills, currency, deeds, evidences of debt, and money and securities.                    ____  ____

8. If an insured building is vacant or unoccupied for more than 60 consecutive days, coverage is suspended unless you have a special endorsement to your policy cancelling this provision.                    ____  ____

*Fire Insurance*

9. If, either before or after a loss, you conceal or misrepresent to the insurer any material fact or circumstance concerning your insurance or the interest of the insured, the policy may be voided.                                          ____   ____

10. If you increase the hazard of fire, the insurance company may suspend your coverage even for losses not originating from the increased hazard. (An example of such a hazard might be renting part of your building to a drycleaning plant.)   ____   ____

11. After a loss, you must use all reasonable means to protect the property from further loss or run the risk of having your coverage cancelled.                               ____   ____

12. To recover your loss, you must furnish within 60 days (unless an extension is granted by the insurance company) a complete inventory of the damaged, destroyed, and un-damaged property, showing in detail quantities, costs, actual cash value, and amount of loss claimed.         ____   ____

13. If you and the insurer disagree on the amount of loss, the question may be resolved through special appraisal procedures provided for in the fire-insurance policy.        ____   ____

14. You may cancel your policy without notice at any time and get part of the premium returned. The insurance company also may cancel at any time with a 5-day written notice to you.   ____   ____

15. By accepting a co-insurance clause in your policy, you get a substantial reduction in premiums. A co-insurance clause states that you must carry insurance equal to 80 or 90 percent of the value of the insured property. If you carry less than this, you cannot collect the full amount of your loss, even if the loss is small. What percent of your loss you can collect will depend on what percent of the full value of the property you have insured it for.                                    ____   ____

16. If your loss is caused by someone else's negligence, the insurer has the right to sue this negligent third party for the amount it has paid you under the policy. This is known as the insurer's right of subrogation. However, the insurer will usually waive this right upon request. For example, if you have leased your insured building to someone and have waived your right to recover from the tenant for any insured damages to your property, you should have your agent request the insurer to waive the subrogation clause in the fire policy on your leased building.                                        ____   ____

| | No Action Needed | Look Into This |
|---|---|---|

*Fire Insurance*

17. A building under construction can be insured for fire, lightning, extended coverage, vandalism and malicious mischief.                                                 ____  ____

*Liability Insurance*
1. Legal liability limits of $1 million are no longer considered high or unreasonable even for a small business.        ____  ____

2. Most liability policies require you to notify the insurer immediately after an incident on your property that might cause a future claim. This holds true no matter how unimportant the incident may seem at the time it happens.       ____  ____

3. Most liability policies, in addition to covering bodily injuries, may now cover personal injuries (libel, slander, and so on), if these are specifically insured.               ____  ____

4. Under certain conditions, your business may be subject to damage claims even from trespassers.                    ____  ____

5. You may be legally liable for damages even in cases where you used "reasonable care."                              ____  ____

6. Even if the suit against you is false or fraudulent, the liability insurer pays court costs, legal fees, and interest on judgments in addition to the liability judgments themselves.     ____  ____

7. You can be liable for the acts of others under contracts you have signed with them. This liability is insurable.       ____  ____

8. In some cases you may be held liable for fire loss to property of others in your care. Yet, this property would normally not be covered by your fire or general liability insurance. This risk can be covered by fire legal liability insurance or through requesting subrogation waivers from insurers of owners of the property.                                                ____  ____

*Automobile Insurance*
1. When an employee or a subcontractor uses his own car on your behalf, you can be legally liable even if you don't own a car or truck yourself.                                     ____  ____

2. Five or more automobiles or motorcycles under one ownership and operated as a fleet for business purposes can generally be insured under a low-cost fleet policy against both material damage to your vehicle and liability to others for property damage or personal injury.                        ____  ____

*Automobile Insurance*

3. You can often get deductibles of almost any amount—say $250 or $500—and thereby reduce your premiums.                        ____   ____

4. Automobile medical-payments insurance pays for medical claims, including your own, arising from automobile accidents regardless of the question of negligence.                        ____   ____

5. In most states, you must carry liability insurance or be prepared to provide other proof (surety bond) of financial responsibility when you are involved in an accident.                        ____   ____

6. You can purchase uninsured-motorist protection to cover your own bodily-injury claims from someone who has no insurance.                        ____   ____

7. Personal property stored in an automobile and not attached to it (for example, merchandise being delivered) is not covered under an automobile policy.                        ____   ____

*Workers' Compensation*
1. Common law requires that an employer (1) provide his employees a safe place to work, (2) hire competent fellow employees, (3) provide safe tools, and (4) warn his employees of an existing danger.                        ____   ____

2. If an employer fails to provide the above, under both common law and workers' compensation laws he is liable for damage suits brought by an employee.                        ____   ____

3. State law determines the level or type of benefits payable under workers' compensation policies.                        ____   ____

4. Not all employees are covered by workers' compensation laws. The exceptions are determined by state law and therefore vary from state to state.                        ____   ____

5. In nearly all states, you are not legally required to cover your workers under workers' compensation.                        ____   ____

6. You can save money on workers' compensation insurance by seeing that your employees are properly classified.                        ____   ____

7. Rates for workers' compensation insurance vary from 0.1 percent of the payroll for "safe" occupations to about 25 percent or more of the payroll for very hazardous occupations.                        ____   ____

8. Most employers in most states can reduce their workers' compensation premium cost by reducing their accident rates

below the average. They do this by using safety and loss-
prevention measures.                                      ___   ___

## DESIRABLE COVERAGES

Some types of insurance coverage, while not absolutely essential,
will add greatly to the security of your business. These coverages
include business interruption insurance, crime insurance, glass insurance, and rent insurance.

### Business Interruption Insurance

1. You can purchase insurance to cover fixed expenses that
would continue if a fire shut down your business—such as
salaries to key employees, taxes, interest, depreciation, and
utilities—as well as the profits you would lose.              ___   ___

2. Under properly written contingent business interruption
insurance, you can also collect if fire or other peril closes down
the business of a supplier or customer and this interrupts your
business.                                                      ___   ___

3. The business interruption policy provides payments for
amounts you spend to hasten the reopening of your business
after a fire or other insured peril.                          ___   ___

4. You can get coverage for the extra expenses you suffer if an
insured peril, while not actually closing your business down,
seriously disrupts it.                                        ___   ___

5. When the policy is properly endorsed, you can get business
interruption insurance to indemnify you if your operations are
suspended because of failure or interruption of the supply of
power, light, heat, gas, or water furnished by a public utility
company.                                                      ___   ___

### Crime Insurance

1. Burglary insurance excludes such property as accounts,
articles in a showcase window, and manuscripts.               ___   ___

2. Coverage is granted under burglary insurance only if there
are visible marks of the burglar's forced entry.             ___   ___

3. Burglary insurance can be written to cover, in addition to
money in a safe, inventoried merchandise and damage incurred
in the course of a burglary.                                  ___   ___

|                        | *No Action Needed* | *Look Into This* |
| ---------------------- | --- | --- |

*Crime Insurance*

4. Robbery insurance protects you from loss of property, money, and securities by force, trickery, or threat of violence on or off your premises. ___ ___

5. A comprehensive crime policy written just for small businessmen is available. In addition to burglary and robbery, it covers other types of loss by theft, destruction, and disappearance of money and securities. It also covers thefts by your employees. ___ ___

6. If you are in a high-risk area and cannot get insurance through normal channels without paying excessive rates, you may be able to get help through the federal crime insurance plan. Your agent or State Insurance Commissioner can tell you where to get information about these plans. ___ ___

*Glass Insurance*
1. You can purchase a special glass insurance policy that covers all risk to plate-glass windows, glass signs, motion-picture screens, glass brick, glass doors, showcases, countertops, and insulated glass panels. ___ ___

2. The glass insurance policy covers not only the glass itself, but also its lettering and ornamentation, if these are specifically insured, and the costs of temporary plates or boarding up when necessary. ___ ___

3. After the glass has been replaced, full coverage is continued without any additional premium for the period covered. ___ ___

*Rent Insurance*
1. You can buy rent insurance that will pay your rent if the property you lease becomes unusable because of fire or other insured perils and your lease calls for continued payments in such a situation. ___ ___

2. If you own property and lease it to others, you can insure against loss if the lease is cancelled because of fire and you have to rent the property again at a reduced rental.

## EMPLOYEE BENEFIT COVERAGES

Insurance coverages that can be used to provide employee benefits include group life insurance, group health insurance, disability insurance, and retirement income. Key-man insurance protects the company

*Group Life Insurance*

against financial loss caused by the death of a valuable employee or partner.

*Group Life Insurance*
1. If you pay group-insurance premiums and cover all employees up to $50,000, the cost to you is deductible for Federal income-tax purposes, and yet the value of the benefit is not taxable income to your employees.    ⎯    ⎯

2. Most insurers will provide group coverages at low rates even if there are 10 or fewer employees in your group.    ⎯    ⎯

3. If the employees pay part of the cost of the group insurance, state laws require that 75 percent of them must elect coverage for the plan to qualify as group insurance.    ⎯    ⎯

4. Group plans permit an employee leaving the company to convert his group-insurance coverage to a private plan, at the rate for his age, without a medical exam if he does so within 30 days after leaving his job.    ⎯    ⎯

*Group Health Insurance*
1. Group health insurance costs much less and provides more generous benefits for the worker than individual contracts would.    ⎯    ⎯

2. If you pay the entire cost, individual employees cannot be dropped from a group plan unless the entire group policy is cancelled.    ⎯    ⎯

3. Generous programs of employee benefits, such as group health insurance, tend to reduce labor turnover.    ⎯    ⎯

*Disability Insurance*
1. Workers' compensation insurance pays an employee only for time lost because of work injuries and work-related sickness, not for time lost because of disabilities incurred off the job. But you can purchase, at a low premium, insurance to replace the lost income of workers who suffer short-term or long-term disability not related to their work.    ⎯    ⎯

2. You can get coverage that provides employees with an income for life in case of permanent disability resulting from work-related sickness or accident.    ⎯    ⎯

|                    | No Action Needed | Look Into This |
|--------------------|:----------------:|:--------------:|

*Retirement Income*

1. If you are self-employed, you can get an income tax deduction for funds used for retirement for you and your employees through plans of insurance or annuities approved for use under the Employees Retirement Income Security Act of 1974 (ERISA).                                                         ____  ____

2. Annuity contracts may provide for variable payments in the hope of giving the annuitants some protection against the effects of inflation. Whether fixed or variable, an annuity can provide retirement income that is guaranteed for life.        ____  ____

*Key-Man Insurance*
1. One of the most serious setbacks that can come to a small company is the loss of a key man. But your key man can be insured with life insurance and disability insurance owned by and payable to your company.                                         ____  ____

2. Proceeds of a key-man policy are not subject to income tax, but premiums are not a deductible business expense.              ____  ____

3. The cash value of key-man insurance, which accumulates as an asset of the business, can be borrowed against, and the interest and dividends are not subject to income tax as long as the policy remains in force.                                         ____  ____

## MANAGING TAXES

Prospective entrepreneurs and existing business owners must realize the importance of paying and managing their tax liabilities. Improper use of taxes due can be costly in terms of penalties imposed by state, local and federal revenue agencies, not to mention the time involved in audits that will surely ensue. Effective management of tax obligations entails the following major points.

— Know the degree of tax liability in reference to the taxes imposed, their dollar amounts, and when they are due.
— Make sure that funds are available to pay the tax obligations.
— Always pay on or before the due date to avoid costly late payment charges which can exceed 25 percent of the amount due in some cases.
— Seek competent tax advice from an expert in the field (CPA and/ or Tax Attorney).

Below is a list of taxes that a business owner may expect to face when running an operation. Types and amounts of taxes will vary depending upon many factors such as line of business, state residency, and profitability, to mention but a few. For example, five state governments do not have income taxes imposed on business profits.

— Federal Income Tax
— State Income Tax
— Local Income Tax
— Social Security Tax
— Federal Unemployment Tax
— State Unemployment Tax
— Excise Taxes
— State Sales Tax
— Local Sales Tax

Taxes are normally paid on a periodic basis to the various government agencies. Payments are accompanied with a form supplied by the governing body. Check with the appropriate agency responsible for the collection of taxes to determine payment procedures. Table 29 contains a worksheet that can be used by a business when analyzing and computing tax obligations.

## Managing Problems

A good manager has been defined as an individual with the ability to solve potential problems before they become real problems and threaten the business. Most management experts agree that solving difficulties should be a sequential process involving a number of specific procedures. They are listed below.

— Problem Definition: The problem must be clearly stated and understood. An evaluation concerning the direct and indirect effects of the difficulty must be made. Problem identification is the single largest stumbling block to effective decision making. Also, the unwillingness or inability to deal with difficulties once apparent will greatly impede progress toward goal attainment.

— Initial Investigation: This stage attempts to obtain a concise definition of the problem and its potential ramifications.

## TABLE 29

| Kind of Tax | Due Date | Amount Due | Pay to | Date For Writing The Check |
|---|---|---|---|---|
| **FEDERAL TAXES** | | | | |
| Employee Income Tax and Social Security Tax | | | | |
| Excise Tax | | | | |
| Owner-Manager's and/or corporation's income tax | | | | |
| Unemployment Tax | | | | |
| **STATE TAXES** | | | | |
| Unemployment Taxes | | | | |
| Income Taxes | | | | |
| Sales Taxes | | | | |
| Franchise Tax | | | | |
| Other | | | | |
| **LOCAL TAXES** | | | | |
| Sales Tax | | | | |
| Real Estate Tax | | | | |
| Personal Property Tax | | | | |
| Licenses (retail, vending machine, etc.) | | | | |
| Other | | | | |

— Identify and Select Alternative Courses of Action: Several plans should be developed with the objective of defusing the problem or minimizing its impact.

— Collection of Relevant Data: Information in relation to each course of action must be collected, organized, and evaluated to determine which one is the suitable solution. Statistical analysis is often used in this stage.

— Selection of the Alternative: Once the optimum alternative is identified it should be officially adopted as the solution to the problem.

— Implement the Course of Action: Put the solution into effect.

— Evaluate the Course of Action Taken: Periodic examination of the action implemented is needed in order to determine its effectiveness. Evaluation may reveal a need for modification of the existing alternative or the employment of a new course of action.

The experiences gained and recorded by using problem solving procedures and solutions will help to develop and refine the decision-making abilities of owners/managers.

**Decision Making Is Necessary**

When the time comes for decision making, business owners and managers should not procrastinate. Hesitation is one of the foremost reasons for missed opportunities and the assumption of unreasonable costs. This is not to say that an owner should react without due consideration. On the contrary, when lacking appropriate information, it may be a good idea to delay a decision, but dangers and opportunities may still present themselves. The delayed decision must be weighed against the potential losses due to inaction.

The optimum solution is to have reliable and accurate information available at all times. This will help to avoid the unpleasant situation of making decisions using inadequate data or taking no action at all.

**Knowing When to Seek Advice**

When the need for outside assistance becomes apparent, get it immediately without hesitation. Delay can be costly, especially if problems grow to the point of unmanageability. Also, avoid being egotistical and trying to solve insurmountable problems without assistance or by utilizing limited in-house staff. Businesses that are both large and small occasionally need the help of outside expertise when facing environmental or internal problems. Sources of professional assistance were discussed earlier in Chapter III.

Chapter X

# IMPORTANT CONSIDERATIONS
## Before Venturing

## Cover the Bases

Every prospective or practicing entrepreneur must consider and evaluate certain critical elements before starting or, in some cases, relocating operations. Failure to do so could lead to disastrous consequences. It is impossible to discuss all the different small businesses relative to these important features within the confines of this book. Therefore, the four major categories of business classification (retail, wholesale, service, and manufacturing) will be used as a means of broad comparison.

Table 30 shows which elements should be considered by the various business categories. An asterisk (*) means evaluation is definitely necessary while an (X) means some critical analysis is needed. Blanks indicate little or no relationship.

## Consider These Carefully

### CAPITAL

All businesses must be concerned that an adequate amount of capital is available to begin and support operations. Service firms, by their very nature, are generally less capital intensive than other types of businesses. Therefore, they can operate on the proverbial shoestring.

Capital needs are discussed extensively in Chapter V.

## CHANNELS OF DISTRIBUTION

Most manufacturers must worry about getting their products in the hands of the ultimate consumer. In many cases, this is accomplished through the use of intermediaries which are commonly referred to as "middlemen." These intermediaries are links in a channel of distribution and help move the product to its destination. Wholesalers must also be concerned with this matter because many employ middlemen known as agents and brokers to facilitate the flow of their products to retailers. Service businesses should not be overly concerned with channels of distribution since most services are performed by the originator. Some businesses franchise their operations to achieve growth. In these cases, the franchisee would serve as the distributor for the franchisor.

TABLE 30
ELEMENTS TO CONSIDER BEFORE VENTURING

|  | Retail | Wholesale | Service | Manufacturing |
|---|---|---|---|---|
| 1. Capital | * | * | X | * |
| 2. Channels of Distribution |  | X |  | * |
| 3. Climate | X |  |  | * |
| 4. Competition | * | * | * | * |
| 5. Credit Policies | * | * | * | * |
| 6. Delivery | X | * |  | * |
| 7. Demographics | * | * | * | * |
| 8. Economic Climate | * | * | * | * |
| 9. Financial Control | * | * | * | * |
| 10. Government Regulation | X | * | X | * |
| 11. Industry Trends | * | * | * | * |
| 12. Inflation | * | * | * | * |
| 13. International Events | X | X |  | * |
| 14. Labor | * | * | * | * |
| 15. Licenses | X | * | X | * |
| 16. Location | * | * |  | * |
| 17. Market Research | * | * | * | * |
| 18. Operations Policy | * | * | * | * |
| 19. Pricing | * | * | * | * |
| 20. Product/Service | * | * | * | * |
| 21. Raw Materials |  |  |  | * |
| 22. Research & Development |  |  |  | * |
| 23. Service | * | * | X | * |
| 24. State of Technology | X | X | X | * |
| 25. Storage | X | * |  | * |
| 26. Topography | X | * | X | * |
| 27. Trade Credit | * | * |  | * |
| 28. Vendors (Suppliers) | * | * | X | * |
| 29. Warranties | * | * | * | * |

Below are listed the more common channels of distribution:

Manufacturer-Wholesaler-Retailer-Customer
Manufacturer-Broker-Wholesaler-Retailer-Customer
Manufacturer-Broker-Agent-Wholesaler-Retailer-Customer
Manufacturer-Broker-Jobber-Wholesaler-Retailer-Customer
Manufacturer-Broker-Retailer-Customer
Manufacturer-Jobber-Retailer-Customer
Service Originator-Customer
Service Originator-Agent-Customer

Many products and industries have standardized channels of distribution that have been used for years. Some companies mistakenly think they can reduce costs and increase profits by eliminating middlemen. Most firms that attempt to do this fail in their efforts. Always remember that intermediaries are specialists in their fields and they know the ropes. Consequently, they are cost effective to use even though they charge commissions and represent an added link in the channel. The only way a company can make money by eliminating these organizations is to gain the necessary expertise and apply it better than the middlemen being replaced. A few large discount chains have accomplished this feat.

## CLIMATE

Some manufacturing and retailing establishments must consider the effects of climatic conditions on their business. Failure to do so could be detrimental to profitable operations. For example, some years ago the Del Monte Corporation built a large pineapple cannery in Mexico on a river. The fruit groves were located up-river. During picking season the fruit was to be barged down-river to the cannery for processing and shipment. Management failed to consider one very important point and it was a costly mistake. The river's flood stage and picking season just so happened at the same time. Consequently, the river could not support barge movement and the factory was never used. Millions were lost due to failure in considering the climate's effect on operations.

Retail firms can also be affected by climate. Stores and shops located along coastal resorts can be adversely affected if unseasonably cold weather grips their areas for a season or two. Likewise, retail businesses in winter resorts can experience the same fate if a warmer than normal winter occurs.

Wholesaling and servicing enterprises are not affected by weather as compared to the aforementioned. Wholesalers sell to retailers and, therefore, it is the retailer's responsibility to get the product to the ultimate customer. Service firms normally take the product directly to the customer, thereby minimizing the impact of weather on a potential customer. For example, an electrician or plumber will work rain or shine. Of course, extreme weather conditions can stymie any operation.

## COMPETITION

The impact of competition is important to any business operation. The degree and strength of competitive forces within a particular market should be considered and evaluated very carefully to determine the effects on existing or prospective endeavors. Is there room for another seller? If the market is crowded with competitors, can an enterprise with exceptional management skills survive or prosper, forcing other less efficient firms to concede market share.

More details concerning competitive factors can be found in Chapter VII.

## CREDIT POLICIES

Most businesses are forced to give customers credit privileges because of competitive forces within most markets. A standardized credit policy is a must in order to establish uniformity and minimize the possibility of credit discrimination. In addition, it will establish procedures for granting credit and collecting past dues. A good policy will facilitate the entire credit function. More insight about credit can be gained by referring to Chapter IX.

## DELIVERY

Product delivery is a primary concern for wholesale and manufacturing operations. These organizations must deliver their products to the appropriate link in the channel of distribution in order to ultimately sell the goods. Some retail firms, such as mail order companies, are also involved in the process of delivery, although to a much lesser extent than the previously mentioned types of business. Service companies normally do not worry about delivery, since services are delivered when performed. There are exceptions. For example, consulting firms, research firms, photo-copy centers, etc., may be involved in the delivery of various papers and reports.

## DEMOGRAPHICS

All businesses must be concerned with the characteristics of the marketplace they are trying to exploit. An understanding of demographics will help accomplish this by classifying the total market into various segments. This is called market segmentation. The most common classifications are listed below:

> Age
> Income
> Geographic Area
> Marital Status
> Religion
> Sex
> Occupation

## ECONOMIC CLIMATE

The systematic risk inherent in the overall economy will affect all businesses. Having an idea when recessions will occur can help insure proper preparation and thus defense against the impact of economic downturns. It is interesting to note the number of companies who fail to take heed of a recession's warning signals and fall victim. Businesses that are on guard normally weather the storm and some even prosper.

Below are listed the more common recession signals:

— Steady increase in the general level of interest rates. (When short-term rates exceed long-term rates it is called an "inversion" and a recession will generally follow suit.)
— Falling economic output
— Falling corporate profits
— Leading economic indicators constantly down
— Consumer and business confidence constantly negative
— Consistently rising levels of business inventories

Most of these statistics are reported monthly in a government publication known as *The Survey of Current Business,* available at many libraries or directly from The Superintendent of Documents, U.S. Government Printing Office, Washington, D.C. 20402. The cost is $30 per year.

## FINANCIAL CONTROL

Maintaining financial control of a business is contingent upon managing resources so as to generate adequate profit levels. The management of physical, financial, and intangible assets would fall in this category. Chapter IX deals heavily with this subject.

## GOVERNMENT REGULATION

Local, state, and federal government regulations affect all businesses, both large and small, costing the American business community approximately 175 billion dollars per year. Even though the larger firms tend to be watched more closely, small firms are expected to abide by all codes and statutes. Writing to government agencies and requesting information on laws affecting a particular line of business would be wise.

## INDUSTRY TRENDS

All businesses must be concerned with events taking place within their industries. Even though the overall economy is recovering from the recession, many industries are failing to respond. Some will never regain their former strength and a few will slowly die. The service industries have, for the most part, been unaffected by economic downturns. In fact, services which now account for 60 percent of the nation's output will climb to 80 percent of economic activity by the end of this decade.

Checking activities within a particular industry in question will help gain insight into the dynamic forces working to strengthen, stagnate, or weaken performance in that area.

## INFLATION

Inflation affects all businesses. Initially, the results of rising inflation are quite positive, with sales and profits increasing, although much of the increase is artificial. For example, if a business achieves a ten percent return on investment (ROI) one year and inflation for that same period runs at eight percent, the firm has only realized a two percent gain on its investment, although most companies would report a ten percent increase. Many establishments actually base expansion plans on inflated figures and later down the pike experience a capital squeeze because (inflation adjusted) accounting records were not used to make the decision.

All financial and accounting records should reflect the damage caused by inflation. Failure to do so could lead to disaster. In addition, high levels of inflation (exceeding ten percent per year) generally cause recessions. So inflation can be viewed as an indicator of future economic vitality. Conversely, lower levels of inflation (two to four percent) are considered good for the economy. An economic system experiencing either no inflation or deflation (declining price levels) is thought to be in serious trouble.

## INTERNATIONAL EVENTS

Whether or not it is a popular nation, the United States has joined the world economic community out of necessity because of resource dependency. Consequently, the American economy is subject to forces beyond the immediate control of domestic leaders. Some lines of businesses are more affected than others. A knowledge of international forces that may do harm to particular industries and firms will help to insure survivability if negative events occur. For example, what should petroleum retailers and wholesalers do if OPEC imposes another embargo? How can American automobile manufacturers and dealers respond to the ever-increasing tide of foreign competition?

Much has been said about the inability of American manufacturers to compete with the more efficient and productive foreign counterparts. This is largely true, and domestic producers will have to respond in order to survive. On the other hand, retailers and wholesalers may be affected only temporarily due to overseas competition, because they can always change to more marketable foreign products. Service firms are generally insulated from foreign competition since most nations haven't concentrated upon exporting services as of this date. In fact, the service sector is considered an area where American firms could compete successfully in the international marketplace.

## LABOR

All firms must insure that adequate human resources are available to support operations. A manufacturing firm should be concerned that a particular location has enough skilled, semi-skilled, and managerial talent. Businesses offering technical services may be interested in the number of qualified technical personnel who could be hired in a given location.

Firms failing to consider the implications of inadequate labor supply before starting or relocating operations will suffer the additional cost of attracting needed individuals located outside the immediate area of operation.

## LICENSES

Most local and state agencies require business establishments to apply for any number of licenses. In addition, many want payment of a flat and/or percentage of estimated sales fee before granting permits. Requirements vary from one area to another. Larger concerns may need federal permits. For example, a license must be acquired from the U.S. Department of Commerce before a firm may engage in export activities.

Small firms should check with the local Clerk of the Court. He/she will have information concerning any local, state, or federal licensing requirements for particular types of businesses.

## LOCATION

It is important for manufacturing businesses to be located near their markets. Transportation costs can be minimized. Some manufacturers may also decide to locate in the proximity of its needed raw materials. For example, steel mills in Pennsylvania are located near large coal deposits which are critical to the steel-making process. Transportation charges for coal are astronomical, thereby necessitating a location near the source of the raw material. Wholesaling firms normally attempt to optimize their distribution facilities between the many retail customers they serve. Retail establishments want to locate where traffic flow is adequate enough to support operations. Specialty retail stores need not worry to the same degree because customers will make special efforts to obtain items of specific characteristics and quality. Finally, only those service firms that provide in-house services need not worry about location. When the customer must come to the place of business, location can be of prime importance.

## MARKET RESEARCH

Market research is necessary to determine whether a product or service can be successfully sold. This research, if conducted properly, will reveal the threats inherent in the marketplace as well as any opportunities that may exist. Many small businesses fail because of not considering the impact of competitive forces and overestimating customer base. Market research will address these weaknesses.

Chapter VII addresses the topic of market research extensively.

## OPERATIONS POLICY

An operations policy explains the procedures to follow in maintaining effective operations. Generally, the need for operations policy increases as a firm grows. It is not surprising to find many small retail or service businesses operating efficiently without an operations policy, although they probably maintain at least an employee policy to insure compliance with employment laws.

The standard operations policy should include a description of key functions within the business and who is in charge of each. An organizational chart would normally be part of the policy manual, along with a description of responsibilities and spans of control to reduce administrative overlap. Standard operating procedures (SOPs) would be established for each function. A statement relating to events not covered by SOPs is generally incorporated with policy to reduce confusion if an exceptional situation were to occur.

## PRICING

All businesses must worry about pricing their products and services. After all, the prices chosen will affect a firm's ability to successfully compete. Price setting can be a complicated task. Many things need to be considered carefully. For example, if the product/service is new, a higher price can normally be set. Conversely, strong competitive forces within the market would force a lower price. Pricing strategy should also be integrated with long-term goals. A "skimming" price policy means that a firm is setting a high price in order to achieve large profit margins. However, a lower market share is achieved. Consequently, when competitors enter the field, the ability to survive will be in question due to a thin customer base. On the other hand, a "penetration" policy sets a lower price to achieve a wider market acceptance, which helps to fight off competitive threats.

An interesting illustration of these two pricing policies can be found in analyzing the battle between Texas Instruments and Bomar Corporation. Bomar introduced one of the first hand-held calculators and chose a skimming price policy. Therefore, only a small market share was gained. Texas Instruments came out with their calculator (basically the same product), but adopted a penetration policy to achieve a wider market share. The rest is history. Bomar went out of business because its market share was too small to support operations after competition set in.

Pricing is discussed in Chapter VII.


## PRODUCT/SERVICE

The product or service offered will determine business success. Obviously, many products and services are widely available today from many different sources. Some will continue to be in demand while others will stagnate or die. New ones will come and go. The trick is to find a line that has achieved some degree of success in the marketplace with a lot of growth potential left and yet only a few competitors. Chapter VII contains information about product development.

Franchising is staged to make a comeback, but a franchise is only as good as the product or service it represents. Details concerning franchise ownership are discussed in Chapter II.

Below are listed some good and bad business prospects that exist today. Keep in mind that changing economic conditions could alter what constitutes a positive or negative proposition.


*Good Prospects:*
— Information Services
— Computer Software and Hardware
— Medical Instruments, Services, and Supplies
— Aerospace and Defense-Related Products and Services
— Entertainment Products and Services
— Sports Products and Services
— Educational Products and Services
— Specialty Retailing
— Financial and Tax Services
— Convenience Stores
— Fast-Food Outlets
— Precision Instruments
— Do-It-Yourself Stores
— Consulting Services

*Bad Prospects:*
— Domestic Car Dealers
— Gasoline Service Stations
— Conventional Grocery Stores
— General Department Stores
— Residential Construction
— Steel Related Businesses
— Textile Related Businesses

## RAW MATERIALS

The location of raw materials is of primary concern to manufacturing outfits. Some will locate their operations near sources of raw materials in order to minimize the cost of transportation that is usually passed on to the manufacturer. This is usually the case where raw materials are extremely heavy and bulky. For example, many steel mills will locate near coal mines. In addition, availability is a major consideration. Manufacturers must insure that adequate raw materials and/or components are available to keep production flowing. Failure to deliver finished goods to customers on time may result in a loss of goodwill.

Some manufacturers may attempt to optimize their location between major customers and sources of materials needed for production. In some cases, it may be more advantageous to locate near markets as opposed to suppliers. It could be that both market and raw material locations are minimized in favor of a location that is more favorable because of wages, taxes, and/or climate.

## RESEARCH AND DEVELOPMENT (R&D)

Research and Development is a primary concern for manufacturing firms for survival reasons. Without the new products or processes initially created through R&D efforts, a company's ability to compete effectively would be compromised. In fact, many economists feel that the United States manufacturers are becoming less competitive than foreign firms because industry as a whole is spending much less on R&D in real terms (inflation adjusted) than it did a decade ago. At the same time foreign manufacturers have been increasing their R&D emphasis. This situation underscores the necessity in maintaining an adequate R&D program if the future is to be met with success.

Retail, wholesale, and service businesses should concern themselves with research and development to the extent that trends affect their marketing endeavors. Obviously, existing products and services will give way to new ones. The trick is to know when these events will happen and how they can be exploited. Research will tell how.

## SERVICE

Some products need periodic servicing. The work can be done either by the retailer, wholesaler, or manufacturer. Generally, there exist cooperative agreements between the aforementioned to decide who will handle what and when. In any case, the need to service products sold must be taken into account. Making sure the proper service capability is available can be of primary importance to potential customers. Even a service business should be concerned. For example, let's say a management consultant performs a market study for a firm. Six or seven weeks after the study is finished the consultant should call or visit the firm to determine if the study has indeed been of assistance. This is called "servicing the service." If everybody is happy with the previous work, it would be an ideal time to push additional services.

## STATE OF TECHNOLOGY

Technology is changing the way all firms conduct themselves in the marketplace. Failure to acknowledge and use the latest in technical innovations will insure demise. To illustrate, many American manufacturers have failed to innovate to the same degree as their foreign counterparts. Consequently, international markets have been losing to the more productive foreign producers. Even on a smaller scale, those retailers and service firms failing to consider the impact of technology on their existing lines will fall victim to changing demand patterns.

Determine which emerging technologies will affect existing and/or prospective lines and to what degree. Outline how these changes may be exploited profitably.

## STORAGE

A retail business must store inventory in order to fulfill customer wants when immediate demand occurs. Some retail outlets succeed or fail based on their ability to provide a quick and adequate supply of their product, especially in a competitive market. Wholesalers and manufacturers generally need larger storage facilities to accommodate the enormous volume of finished and unfinished material that must be stored until production or shipment is made. Storage is not a big problem for service firms, since services are intangibles and cannot be warehoused.

The right amount of storage space is important. Too little might cause production and delivery delays, thereby resulting in a loss of customer goodwill. On the other hand, under-utilized space is wasteful and is an overhead expense not covered by revenues.

## TOPOGRAPHY

Many areas are not conducive to manufacturing facilities because of land contour. There is one county in the state of Virginia where 85 percent of the land has an incline exceeding 15 degrees, which is considered restrictive for manufacturing and large wholesaling purposes. Normally, this situation would not affect retail or service establishments which tend to be smaller by nature, although any area that is largely inaccessible would be bad for businesses dependent on traffic flow. Another thing to be considered is the impact of no industrial growth. Opportunities for any type of business may be restricted if growth is stymied. To illustrate, the seat of the aforementioned county is a town of 8,000 people. It has one of the highest failure rates for small businesses in the state. Main Street is littered with empty storefronts and many existing operations are barely afloat.

## TRADE CREDIT

It is wise to check with prospective suppliers about their credit arrangements. If the business is new it can expect to pay cash on delivery for merchandise and supplies during the first few months of operation. This obstacle can be overcome if the owner has a good credit rating and is willing to personally guarantee payment. Then immediate credit terms are normally available.

Many businesses fail to follow through in getting better terms with a supplier after a relationship has been established. One small motorcycle and repair shop in Virginia was dealing with four different suppliers for 18 months and all were demanding cash on delivery. A consultant advised the owners to write and demand favorable credit terms or other vendors would be found. Three graciously gave credit while one refused. Luckily, the one that resisted was the smallest and least important of the four. In addition, ask suppliers for a discount upon making early payments. Many will grant a one or two percent reduction for paying bills within ten days. Evaluate the cost of paying cash, taking into consideration the discount against the advantage of using the float (suppliers' credit). The answer will be determined by analyzing the rate of return on utilized dollars. For example, if the average annual rate of return on invested capital exceeds the annual adjusted rate of the suppliers' discount, it would not be wise to make early payments because the business can make more return by using the suppliers' float. If the rate is less, early payments may be appropriate.

Also, playing one supplier against the other for purposes of securing better credit terms might be a good idea at times. Many businesses have found that some vendors will extend payment terms from the traditional net 30 days to 45 or 60 days. In some industries, terms of 90 to 180 days have been achieved.

## Vendors (Suppliers)

Most small retailers purchase from wholesalers who in turn buy from manufacturers and/or jobbers. Manufacturing firms must buy their raw materials and components from other sources. The point to remember is that all businesses should have several sources of supplies readily available. Relying on a single vendor can be risky. What happens if the vendor goes out of business or changes marketing approaches so as not to include particular types of businesses?

In addition, it may be wise to let suppliers know that several vendors are being used. It will keep them on their toes. Again, it may be useful to play them against each other to negotiate better prices.

## Warranties

For competitive reasons, most businesses must give warranties that guarantee the successful performance of their products or services. Warranties, whether implied or expressed, are contracts that must be taken seriously. Broken warranties can lead to costly legal battles with disenfranchised customers, not to mention governmental agencies. In addition, the possibility of bad press must be taken into account, and the loss of goodwill it will cause. When considering warranties, try to estimate the cost of making such guarantees and what means will be used to deliver what is promised.

When projecting warranties, try to do it in a novel and unique way. A new slant can do wonders to stimulate sales. For example, a couple of years ago a mail order firm decided to incorporate a unique approach to making a guarantee. The company in question told potential buyers that their checks or money orders would not be cashed for 30 days and if they were not satisfied with the product it could be returned within a month. Upon the return of the merchandise, the uncashed monies would be sent back. The favorable result of this new twist was tremendous.

## Basic Business Start-up*

Starting a new business is at best a dubious adventure in itself. It is of utmost importance to be organized from the beginning, to have a plan, to know what information is already in hand and what remains to be discovered. The value of being organized cannot be over-emphasized. Certain tasks must be completed, some in a definite sequence; without organization, something is likely to be overlooked.

In the next four sections, we will examine the most basic steps to starting up four different businesses: one retail, one wholesale, one manufacturing and one service business. Some basic steps are common to all businesses from the point where market research is completed, the type of business has been established and the financing for the venture is in hand. Following these basic steps will make the new business expedition somewhat less dubious and increase the potential for success.

### THE RETAIL BUSINESS: "PENNY'S HOT SHOP"

Penny Reynolds, a private caterer, decided to open a sandwich shop for business people in the downtown district of her community. Several restaurants were already established, but they were either geared for full meal and high atmosphere, or they were small specialty shops serving limited ethnic cuisine. Penny determined there was a market for a restaurant which would serve only sandwiches of a traditional sort, with a minimum of side dishes, and emphasis on fast service.

With business plan and financing in hand, the steps Penny took to open her shop were:

1. She looked at available rental property in the area she wanted to service. She talked with several realtors to find the best location for the best price and made a tentative agreement to rent a space which had been an ice-cream parlor under previous renters.

*This section is provided by Alicelee Riley, who is a small business consultant located in Winchester, Virginia. She is owner of Riley Management Services.

2. She met with the building and fire inspectors from the city to determine what must be done to bring the building in line with regulations for her type of business. In addition, she needed to find out restrictions, limits on seating capacity, and other regulations that might apply.

3. Penny then met with the sanitation inspector to determine what regulations for food preparation and storage would apply.

4. Once she was sure she could afford to make the necessary improvements to the space (after consulting her business counsellor and checking with local contractors), she signed a lease and arranged for utilities and telephone.

5. Penny went to city hall and applied for her business license and obtained other information she needed regarding local taxes and regulations.

6. The state government had a sales tax, so she applied for the necessary reporting forms, tax tables, and book of regulations.

7. Knowing she would have employees, Penny applied to the Internal Revenue Service for a federal employer identification number. (The federal government supplies a book of instructions and forms when the number is assigned).

8. While work was being completed on the space, Penny began negotiating with restaurant equipment dealers to provide the necessary equipment and fixtures for her shop. She ordered what was needed.

9. Next, she located food distributors and gathered information from them.

10. The actual menu was selected and she worked closely with her business counsellor to plan mark-ups on the menu items and initial stock levels.

11. Her record-keeping system (as a sole proprietorship) and other important files were established.

12. After meeting with several agents, Penny purchased a comprehensive business insurance plan which suited her needs.

13. Penny decided initially to hire one full-time and one part-time employee. She placed a request with the local state employment office and interviewed prospects. By the time her space was completed and equipment began arriving, she had her employees and they were helping with the final stages.

14. The menu and advertising handbills were designed and printed.

15. Penny and her employees did the interior decorating to create a pleasing atmosphere in the shop.

16. All food items were ordered, along with serving, storage and cleaning supplies.

17. Penny paid for advertising on radio and in the local newspaper to announce the opening of her shop. Handbills were distributed.

18. The staff was trained and a couple of warm-up exercises were given so that opening day could go smoothly.

19. Finally, the sanitation inspector was called in one final time, after all was ready, to make sure the shop was in compliance with local codes.

Always remember, however, that extensive decision-making was necessary at every step. Items such as employee compensation, advertising, budgeting, etc., required close attention. But by following this basic sequence, Penny was able to open on schedule with a minimum of difficulty.

### THE WHOLESALE BUSINESS: "POTTERY CENTRAL"

Fred Jenkins was a plant nursery specialist. On a vacation trip to Mexico, he encountered a number of pottery makers who were producing decorative pots which were much less costly than undecorated domestic ones. He determined there would be a market for such pottery in the U.S. and decided to start a wholesale pottery business. After Fred obtained the necessary financing and developed a plan of action, he went to work.

1. Since Fred's concept involved importing, he contacted the U.S. Commerce Department and Customs Service for information regarding importing, licensing, etc.

2. He met with his accountant and attorney to wade through the information because of the tax implications and the complexities of both importing and engaging in interstate trade.

3. He met with representatives of various trucking firms to learn about shipping rates and regulations.

4. Fred went shopping for warehouse-office space. As a wholesaler, Fred did not need a fancy building, but adequate space with easy access for shipping was necessary. He made a tentative agreement for renting a small warehouse with an attached office just outside of town.

5. He checked with the zoning, building and fire authorities about regulations and needed improvements.

6. Once he had consulted with local contractors, he signed a lease for the building and arranged for the improvements, utilities, and telephone.

7. He then applied for a business license, a federal employer identification number, and requested information on state and local taxes applicable to wholesaling.

8. He contacted Chambers of Commerce, advertising agencies, friends, and business associates for names of nurseries and florists in the region.

9. He worked closely with his business advisors to determine initial stock levels, mark-ups, and equipment requirements. Also, he contacted the Mexican potters and placed his first orders, including packing supplies. Fred also negotiated orders with domestic potters for some of their pottery pieces to complement his imported products.

10. Next, Fred decided to hire a secretary-bookkeeper, shipping clerk, and warehouseman because he planned to spend a good deal of his time on the road visiting potential customers. He placed want ads in the newspaper and with the local employment office. It wasn't long before he interviewed prospects and chose his employees.

11. Working with his accountant, Fred set up his sole proprietor record-keeping system and inventory system, and developed invoicing forms, billing policies, and other necessary items and procedures.

12. He met with various agents and purchased a sound business insurance plan.

13. With the help of a small advertising agency, business cards, sales literature, and company stationery were developed and printed. Other advertising approaches were explored and decisions made.

14. Once the space was ready, Fred and his employees organized the storage areas. Office equipment and furniture were then purchased.

15. The staff received training about business operation and Fred spent some of his time pre-selling several customers.

16. When the first shipments arrived, Fred sent a mass mailing to all the potential customers on his list and opened the doors for business.

Obviously, there are major differences between this wholesale business and the retail approach. Space requirements and marketing emphases differ widely. Once again, many details have been excluded, particularly regarding importing and shipping. Nevertheless, this scenario contains the basic start-up logic.

### THE SERVICE BUSINESS: "CLEAN SWEEPERS"

Jim Black and John Simmons were servicemen for a woodstove firm. They observed a need for chimney sweep services in their community and decided to form a partnership to open a chimney sweep business. Together they met with an accountant and attorney to develop a business plan and a viable partnership agreement. Shortly thereafter, they met with their banker to arrange financing. Once these major preliminaries were concluded, they got down to the start-up details:

1. Jim owned several acres of property on the outskirts of town. On the property was a small barn in fairly good condition. The two men decided to use this building for their business. However, the area was zoned as residential. It was necessary for them to obtain a zoning variance through the city zoning board in order to locate their business in the barn.

2. Along with obtaining the variance, they met with the building and fire inspectors to determine what work was needed to bring the building in compliance with local codes. Arrangements were made with local contractors for the work to be completed.

3. The two men then applied for local business licenses and obtained other necessary information on state and local taxes applicable to their business.

4. They arranged for utilities and telephone service for their building.

5. Anticipating they would need to hire at least one employee, they filed for a federal employer identification number and accompanying forms and information.

6. They obtained information prices from various distributors regarding equipment and supplies. Orders were soon placed.

7. Since they would be traveling to their customers, a large van was purchased to accommodate all their equipment.

8. With the help of their business advisors, they set up a partnership record-keeping system, developed billing forms and procedures, and established a pricing structure for their services.

9. They consulted with several insurance agents and purchased a comprehensive business insurance plan.

10. They contacted the local employment agency, interviewed prospects, and hired a secretary-bookkeeper, their only other employee.

11. Working with a local ad agency, they developed business cards, stationery, and an advertising plan, which was executed right away.

12. After their equipment arrived and the final building inspections were made, they opened for business.

A service business is often one of the easiest to start, but frequently takes more intense marketing to convince the consumer that he needs the service, since it is an intangible. Depending on the cost of equipment and supplies, a service business, especially if it can be run from home, may have less overhead expense than other types of businesses. Pricing for services, however, is critical, since many people tend to undervalue their time, and therefore do not have enough income to keep the business operating. Sound advice is very important.

### THE MANUFACTURING BUSINESS: "NATURALURES, INC."

George McDonald, Ed Frye and Paul Smith were fishing buddies. For years they had fished the waters of the region and the problem of inexpensive and realistic lures was a frequent topic of discussion. Ed was a chemist for a gasket company. Paul was a machinist and George was a salesman. They tinkered with making their own plastic lures in Ed's workshop. Finally, they developed some fine products and decided to manufacture these lures to sell to tackle wholesalers.

After pooling their financial resources and developing a plan with the aid of their accountant, they began to build their business:

1. Before going further, they met with their attorney and accountant to prepare and file their articles of incorporation with the state. A board of directors was appointed and stock apportioned among the three stockholders.

2. Ed's workshop was too small to produce lures in quantity, so they sought a basic warehouse building which could be set up for manufacturing. They found a small location in the county industrial park and made a tentative agreement to rent.

3. They then contacted the building and fire inspectors and determined what improvements were needed to the site to bring it up to code for their type of business. The OSHA representative was contacted to determine what federal regulations affected their operation.

4. Contractors were hired to do the work. Also, a lease was signed for the building and utilities were arranged.

5. Meanwhile, since the men felt they had developed a new concept in manufacturing plastic lures, it was necessary to find out if their method could be patented and if the name, "Naturalures," could qualify for trademark. Their local attorney referred them to a lawyer who specialized in patents and trademarks. He handled those transactions for them.

6. They applied for local business licenses and obtained other information on taxes and regulations affecting a manufacturing business.

7. They filed for a federal employer identification number for the corporation in anticipation of hiring several employees.

8. Working closely with their board of directors and accountant, pricing and start-up production levels were developed.

9. Suppliers for needed machinery and raw materials were found, and queried for their best prices and terms. Orders were then placed.

10. Meetings with various shippers were held and packaging decisions were made as part of nailing down the details on shipping.

11. They contacted the local employment agency and hired a secretary-bookkeeper, shipping-inventory clerk, and two other individuals to assist with production.

12. They purchased a business insurance plan through a reputable agent after thorough study of various alternatives.

13. Their accountant helped them set up a corporate record-keeping system, inventory system, production system, and billing systems. All special forms were designed and printed.

14. Office equipment and furniture were ordered and installed.

15. With the help of an advertising agency, business cards, stationery, and a marketing plan were designed and developed to target the wholesale market.

16. Through local sporting goods stores, they gathered the names of major wholesalers of fishing gear, contacted them and sent samples of their lures.

17. Employees were trained and special safety instruction was provided to all production workers, based on OSHA regulations.

18. Following a final building inspection, the production of "Naturalures" began.

Manufacturing requires certain technical knowledge very different from retailing and wholesaling. Generally, establishing a manufacturing business is more costly because of the equipment involved.

Likewise, a manufacturing business can be more risky, especially if it involves developing new markets. Marketing effectiveness and quality control are critical factors in this field.

There are many factors to consider in any business venture. All these considerations may seem overwhelming to the person starting a business for the first time. Keeping overhead down, purchasing wisely, pricing competitively, and marketing effectively are important to early success. Investigating licensing regulations, building codes, and taxing regulations are critical. But as much as any of these, it is absolutely necessary for the novice entrepreneur to have a clear objective, to be motivated, to know as much about the pitfalls as he or she does about the potentials, and to stay organized. Following a logical plan and understanding the basic steps will help make the business adventure a more pleasant, fulfilling and profitable experience.

# Chapter XI

# DIRECTORY OF CAPITAL SOURCES
## Something for Everyone

---

## Private Sources

### PRIVATE CAPITAL COMPANIES

This section contains a list of venture capital firms, small business investment companies (SBICs), minority enterprise small business investment companies (MESBICs), consulting firms, and other organizations specializing in small business funding. These organizations have provided detailed information concerning their investment preferences. Chapter VI describes the differences between these funding outlets and how they operate.

*ALABAMA*

Hickory Venture Capital Corp.
699 Gallatin St., Ste. A-2
Huntsville, AL 35801
205 539 1931

CONTACT: Monro Lanier
TYPE OF FIRM: SBIC
FUNDING PREFERENCE:
  First-Round Funding
  Second-Round Funding
  Leveraged Buyouts

INDUSTRY PREFERENCE:
  Diversified
  Medical Technology
  Wholesale Distribution
GEOGRAPHIC PREFERENCE:
  Southeast
  Mid-West
  Southwest
TYPES OF FUNDS:
  Equity (stock purchases)
  Minimum: $500,000
  Maximum: $2,500,000


The Remington Fund, Inc.
PO Box 10686; 1927 First Avenue North
Birmingham, AL 35202
205 324 7709

CONTACT: Lana Sellers, Ruffner Page
TYPE OF FIRM: Venture Capital Firm
FUNDING PREFERENCE:
  Later-Stage Funding
  Leveraged Buyouts
  Acquisitions
INDUSTRY PREFERENCE:
  Manufacturing
GEOGRAPHIC PREFERENCE:
  Southeast
TYPES OF FUNDS:
  Equity (stock purchases)
  Loans With Equity Kickers
  Minimum: $150,000
  Maximum: $1,200,000


Tuskegee Capital Corporation
4453 Richardson Road
Montgomery, AL 36108
205 281 8059

CONTACT: A. G. Bartholomew
TYPE OF FIRM: MESBIC
FUNDING PREFERENCE:
  Start-Up Funding
  First-Round Funding

INDUSTRY PREFERENCE:
  Diversified
GEOGRAPHIC PREFERENCE:
  Southeast
TYPES OF FUNDS:
  Loans
  Minimum: $25,000
  Maximum: $120,000


*ARIZONA*


Norwest Growth Fund, Inc.
8777 East Via De Ventura, Suite 335
Scottsdale, AR 85258-3346
602 483 8940
602 483 7449 (FAX)

CONTACT: Steve Schewe
TYPE OF FIRM: Venture Capital Firm
FUNDING PREFERENCE:
  Start-Up Funding
  First-Round Funding
  Second-Round Funding
  Third-Round Funding
  Fourth-Round Funding
  Later-Stage Funding
  Leveraged Buyouts
  Acquisitions
INDUSTRY PREFERENCE:
  Diversified
  Communications Technology
  Computer Hardware
  Computer Software
  Manufacturing
  Medical Technology
  Other High Technologies Not Mentioned
  Retail
  Franchise
GEOGRAPHIC PREFERENCE:
  Mid-West
  Rocky Mountain States
  Northwest
  Far West
  Southwest

TYPES OF FUNDS:
  Equity (stock purchases)
  Loans With Equity Kickers
  Bonds With Equity Kickers
  Minimum: $1,000,000
  VC: $6,000,000   LBO: $15,000,000


*CALIFORNIA*


Accel Partners
One Embarcadero Center, Suite 2102
San Francisco, CA 94111
415 989 565

CONTACT: James W. Breyer
TYPE OF FIRM: Venture Capital Firm
FUNDING PREFERENCE:
  Seed Funding
  Start-Up Funding
  First-Round Funding
  Third-Round Funding
  Fourth-Round Funding
  Later-Stage Funding
  Leveraged Buyouts
INDUSTRY PREFERENCE:
  Communications Technology
  Computer Hardware
  Computer Software
  Media
  Medical Technology
  Services
GEOGRAPHIC PREFERENCE:
  No Preference (U.S.A.)
TYPES OF FUNDS:
  Equity (stock purchases)
  Minimum: $250,000
  Maximum: $2,000,000


Advanced Technology Ventures
1000 El Camino Real, Suite 210
Menlo Park, CA 94025
415 321 8601

CONTACT: Joseph C. Henkens
TYPE OF FIRM: Venture Capital Firm
FUNDING PREFERENCE:
Seed Funding
Start-Up Funding
First-Round Funding
INDUSTRY PREFERENCE:
Communications Technology
Computer Hardware
Computer Software
Medical Technology
Other High Technologies Not Mentioned
GEOGRAPHIC PREFERENCE:
No Preference (U.S.A.)
TYPES OF FUNDS:
Equity (stock purchases)
Minimum: $230,000
Maximum: $1,000,000


Alpha Partners
2200 Sand Hill Rd., Suite 250
Menlo Park, CA 94025
415 854 7024

CONTACT: Brian J. Grossl, Wallace F. Davis
TYPE OF FIRM: Venture Capital Firm
FUNDING PREFERENCE:
Seed Funding
Start-Up Funding
INDUSTRY PREFERENCE:
Communications Technology
Computer Hardware
Computer Software
Manufacturing
Media
Medical Technology
Other High Technologies Not Mentioned
GEOGRAPHIC PREFERENCE:
Immediate Area: San Francisco Bay Area
TYPES OF FUNDS:
Equity (stock purchases)
Minimum: $250,000
Maximum: $2,500,000

Arscott, Worton & Associates
375 Forest Ave.
Palo Alto, CA 94301
415 853 0766

CONTACT: David Arscott, Leal Norton, Dean Campbell
TYPE OF FIRM: Venture Capital Firm
FUNDING PREFERENCE:
  Start-Up Funding
  First-Round Funding
  Second-Round Funding
INDUSTRY PREFERENCE:
  Diversified
GEOGRAPHIC PREFERENCE:
  No Preference (U.S.A.)
TYPES OF FUNDS:
  Equity (stock purchases)
  Minimum: Open
  Maximum: Open


Associated Venture Investors
3000 Sand Hill Road, Building 3, Suite 280
Menlo Park, CA 94025
415 854 4470

CONTACT: Chuck K. Chan
TYPE OF FIRM: Venture Capital Firm
FUNDING PREFERENCE:
  Seed Funding
  Start-Up Funding
  First-Round Funding
INDUSTRY PREFERENCE:
  Communications Technology
  Computer Hardware
  Computer Software
  Other High Technologies Not Mentioned
GEOGRAPHIC PREFERENCE:
  West Coast
  Home State: California
TYPES OF FUNDS:
  Equity (stock purchases)
  Minimum: $500,000
  Maximum: 2,000,000

California Capital Investors, Ltd.
11812 San Vicente Blvd.
Los Angeles, CA 90049
213 820 7222

CONTACT: Lynda S. Gibson, Investment Officer
TYPE OF FIRM: SBIC
FUNDING PREFERENCE:
  Second-Round Funding
  Third-Round Funding
  Leveraged Buyouts
INDUSTRY PREFERENCE:
  Diversified
GEOGRAPHIC PREFERENCE:
  Northwest
  Far West
  Home State: California
TYPES OF FUNDS:
  Loans With Equity Kickers
  Minimum: $250,000
  Maximum: $500,000

Charter Venture Capital
525 University Avenue, Suite 1500
Palo Alto, CA 94301
415 324 6953

CONTACT: A. Barr Dolan
TYPE OF FIRM: Venture Capital Firm
FUNDING PREFERENCE:
  Seed Funding
  Start-Up Funding
  First-Round Funding
  Second-Round Funding
  Third-Round Funding
INDUSTRY PREFERENCE:
  Communications Technology
  Computer Hardware
  Computer Software
  Medical Technology
  Other High Technologies Not Mentioned
GEOGRAPHIC PREFERENCE:
  No Preference (U.S.A.)
TYPES OF FUNDS:
  Equity (stock purchases)

Minimum: $100,000
Maximum: $1,000,000


Concord Partners
435 Tasso St.
Palo Alto, CA
415 327 2600

CONTACT: Philip M. Young
TYPE OF FIRM: Venture Capital Firm
FUNDING PREFERENCE:
  Seed Funding
  Start-Up Funding
  First-Round Funding
  Second-Round Funding
  Leveraged Buyouts
  Acquisitions
INDUSTRY PREFERENCE:
  Alternative Energy
  Conventional Energy (oil, natural gas, and coal)
  Communications Technology
  Computer Hardware
  Computer Software
  Medical Technology
  Services
GEOGRAPHIC PREFERENCE:
  No Preference (U.S.A.)
TYPES OF FUNDS:
  Equity (stock purchases)
  Minimum: $500,000
  Maximum: $5,000,000


Cornerstone Ventures
3000 Sand Hill Road, 3-260
Menlo Park, CA 94025
415 854 2876

CONTACT: Barbara Anderson
TYPE OF FIRM: Venture Capital Firm
FUNDING PREFERENCE:
  Start-Up Funding
INDUSTRY PREFERENCE:
  Communications Technology

Computer Hardware
Computer Software
Manufacturing
Other High Technologies Not Mentioned
GEOGRAPHIC PREFERENCE:
  Far West
TYPES OF FUNDS:
  Equity (stock purchases)
  Minimum: $250,000
  Maximum: $750,000


Cypress Funds
2740 Sand Hill Rd.
Menlo Park, CA 94025
415 854 4193


CONTACT: Val E. Vaden
TYPE OF FIRM: Venture Capital Firm
  LBO Firm
FUNDING PREFERENCE:
  Seed Funding
  Start-Up Funding
  Leveraged Buyouts
  Acquisitions
INDUSTRY PREFERENCE:
  Communications Technology
  Computer Hardware
  Computer Software
  Manufacturing
  Medical Technology
  Retail
  Services
  Wholesale Distribution
GEOGRAPHIC PREFERENCE:
  No Preference (U.S.A.)
  Mid-West
  Rocky Mountain States
  Northwest
  Far West
  Southwest
TYPES OF FUNDS:
  Equity (stock purchases)
  Minimum: VC: $1,000,000   LBO: $3,000,000
  Maximum: VC: $5,000,000   LBO: $20,000,000

DFC Ventures Limited
100 Spear Street, Suite 1430
San Francisco, CA 94105
415 777 2847

CONTACT: Chris C. Ellison
TYPE OF FIRM: Venture Capital Firm
FUNDING PREFERENCE:
  Seed Funding
  Start-Up Funding
  First-Round Funding
  Second-Round Funding
  Third-Round Funding
  Fourth-Round Funding
  Later-Stage Funding
INDUSTRY PREFERENCE:
  Communications Technology
  Computer Hardware
  Computer Software
  Medical Technology
  Other High Technologies Not Mentioned
GEOGRAPHIC PREFERENCE:
  Northwest
  Far West
TYPES OF FUNDS:
  Equity (stock purchases)
  Loans With Equity Kickers
  Minimum: $250,000
  Maximum: $1,000,000


Dougery, Jones & Wilder
2003 Landings Dr.
Mountain View, CA 94043
415 968 4820

CONTACT: Jeanne M. Mitchell
TYPE OF FIRM: Venture Capital Firm
FUNDING PREFERENCE:
  Seed Funding
  Start-Up Funding
  First-Round Funding
  Second-Round Funding
  Third-Round Funding
  Fourth-Round Funding
  Later-Stage Funding
  Leveraged Buyouts

INDUSTRY PREFERENCE:
  Diversified
  Communications Technology
  Computer Hardware
  Computer Software
  Medical Technology
  Other High Technologies Not Mentioned
GEOGRAPHIC PREFERENCE:
  Mid-West
  Rocky Mountain States
  Northwest
  Far West
  Southwest
TYPES OF FUNDS:
  Equity (stock purchases)
  Minimum: $250,000
  Maximum: $2,500,000


Draper Associates
3000 Sand Hill Rd #4-235
Menlo Park, CA 94025
415 854 1712

CONTACT: Timothy C. Draper
TYPE OF FIRM: Venture Capital Firm
FUNDING PREFERENCE:
  Seed Funding
INDUSTRY PREFERENCE:
  Communications Technology
  Computer Hardware
  Computer Software
  Medical Technology
  Other High Technologies Not Mentioned
GEOGRAPHIC PREFERENCE:
  No Preference (U.S.A.)
TYPES OF FUNDS:
  Equity (stock purchases)
  Minimum: $100,000
  Maximum: $500,000


Glenwood Venture Management
3000 Sand Hill Rd, Suite 230, Bldg. Four
Menlo Park, CA 94025
415 854 8070

CONTACT: Dag Tellefsen
TYPE OF FIRM: Venture Capital Firm
FUNDING PREFERENCE:
  Seed Funding
  Start-Up Funding
INDUSTRY PREFERENCE:
  Communications Technology
  Computer Hardware
  Computer Software
  Medical Technology
  Other High Technologies Not Mentioned
GEOGRAPHIC PREFERENCE:
  Rocky Mountain States
  Northwest
  Immediate Area: Western U.S.
TYPES OF FUNDS:
  Equity (stock purchases)
  Minimum: $250,000
  Maximum: $2,000,000


Glynn Ventures
Suite 235, Bldg. 4, 3000 Sand Hill Rd.
Menlo Park, CA 94025
415 854 2215

TYPE OF FIRM: Start-Up Funding
  First-Round Funding
  Second-Round Funding
INDUSTRY PREFERENCE:
  Communications Technology
  Computer Hardware
  Computer Software
  Medical Technology
GEOGRAPHIC PREFERENCE:
  Far West
TYPES OF FUNDS:
  Equity (stock purchases)
  Minimum: $250,000
  Maximum: $500,000


Grace Ventures Corp.
20300 Stevens Creek Blvd., Suite 330
Cupertino, CA 95014
408 725 0774

CONTACT: Dr. Christian Horn
TYPE OF FIRM: Venture Capital Firm
FUNDING PREFERENCE:
  Seed Funding
  Start-Up Funding
  First-Round Funding
INDUSTRY PREFERENCE:
  Diversified
GEOGRAPHIC PREFERENCE:
  No Preference (U.S.A.)
TYPES OF FUNDS:
  Equity (stock purchases)
  Minimum: $250,000
  Maximum: $1,000,000


Henry & Co.
9191 Towne Centre Dr., Suite 230
San Diego, CA 92122
619 453 1655

TYPE OF FIRM: Venture Capital Firm
FUNDING PREFERENCE:
  First-Round Funding
  Second-Round Funding
INDUSTRY PREFERENCE:
  Communications Technology
  Computer Hardware
  Computer Software
  Manufacturing
  Medical Technology
  Other High Technologies Not Mentioned
GEOGRAPHIC PREFERENCE:
  Far West
TYPES OF FUNDS:
  Equity (stock purchases)
  Minimum: $500,000
  Maximum:


INDOSUEZ Technology Group
3000 Sand Hill Rd., Bldg. Two, Suite 160
Menlo Park, CA 94025
415 854 0587

CONTACT: David E. Gold
TYPE OF FIRM: Venture Capital Firm
FUNDING PREFERENCE:
  Seed Funding
  Start-Up Funding
  First-Round Funding
  Second-Round Funding
  Third-Round Funding
  Fourth-Round Funding
  Later-Stage Funding
INDUSTRY PREFERENCE:
  Communications Technology
  Computer Hardware
  Computer Software
  Medical Technology
  Other High Technologies Not Mentioned
  Retail
GEOGRAPHIC PREFERENCE:
  No Preference (U.S.A.)
TYPES OF FUNDS:
  Equity (stock purchases)
  Minimum: Open
  Maximum: $1,500,000


InterVen Partners
333 South Grand Ave., Suite 4050
Los Angeles, CA 90071
213 622 1922

CONTACT: David B. Jones
TYPE OF FIRM: Venture Capital Firm
FUNDING PREFERENCE:
  Seed Funding
  Start-Up Funding
  First-Round Funding
  Second-Round Funding
  Leveraged Buyouts
  Acquisitions
INDUSTRY PREFERENCE:
  Diversified
GEOGRAPHIC PREFERENCE:
  Northwest
  Far West
  Immediate Area: Southern California

TYPES OF FUNDS:
  Equity (stock purchases)
  Minimum: $500,000
  Maximum: $3,000,000

Institutional Venture Partners
3000 Sand Hill Rd., #2-290
Menlo Park, CA 94025
415 854 0132

CONTACT: Geoffrey Y. Yang
TYPE OF FIRM: Venture Capital Firm
FUNDING PREFERENCE:
  Seed Funding
  Start-Up Funding
  First-Round Funding
INDUSTRY PREFERENCE:
  Communications Technology
  Computer Hardware
  Computer Software
  Medical Technology
  Other High Technologies Not Mentioned
  Retail
GEOGRAPHIC PREFERENCE:
  Far West
TYPES OF FUNDS:
  Equity (stock purchases)
  Minimum: $1,000,000
  Maximum: $2,500,000

Ivanhoe Venture Capital, Ltd.
737 Pearl St., Ste. 201
La Jolla, CA 92037

TYPE OF FIRM: Venture Capital Firm
  SBIC
FUNDING PREFERENCE:
  Second-Round Funding
  Third-Round Funding
  Leveraged Buyouts
INDUSTRY PREFERENCE:
  Diversified
GEOGRAPHIC PREFERENCE:
  Far West

TYPES OF FUNDS:
  Loans With Equity Kickers
  Minimum: $50,000
  Maximum: $200,000


JAFCO America Ventures
2180 Sand Hill Rd., Suite 320
Menlo Park, CA 94025

CONTACT: William V. Shelander
TYPE OF FIRM: Venture Capital Firm
FUNDING PREFERENCE:
  Start-Up Funding
  First-Round Funding
  Second-Round Funding
  Third-Round Funding
  Fourth-Round Funding
INDUSTRY PREFERENCE:
  Communications Technology
  Computer Hardware
  Computer Software
  Manufacturing
  Medical Technology
  Other High Technologies Not Mentioned
GEOGRAPHIC PREFERENCE:
  No Preference (U.S.A.)
TYPES OF FUNDS:
  Equity (stock purchases)
  Minimum: $300,000
  Maximum: $2,000,000


J. H. Whitney & Co.
3000 Sand Hill Rd., #1-270
Menlo Park, CA 94025
415 854 0500

CONTACT: Edward Ryan
TYPE OF FIRM: Venture Capital Firm
FUNDING PREFERENCE:
  Start-Up Funding
  First-Round Funding
  Leveraged Buyouts
INDUSTRY PREFERENCE:
  Diversified

GEOGRAPHIC PREFERENCE:
  No Preference (U.S.A.)
TYPES OF FUNDS:
  Equity (stock purchases)
  Minimum: $2,000,000
  Maximum: $5,000,000


Julian, Cole & Stein
11777 San Vicente Blvd., Suite 522
Los Angeles, CA 90049
213 826 8002

CONTACT: James M. Julian
TYPE OF FIRM: Venture Capital Firm
FUNDING PREFERENCE:
  Seed Funding
INDUSTRY PREFERENCE:
  Communications Technology
  Other High Technologies Not Mentioned
GEOGRAPHIC PREFERENCE:
  Southwest
TYPES OF FUNDS:
  Equity (stock purchases)
  Minimum: $500,000
  Maximum: $15,000,000


Kleiner Perkins Caufield & Byers
Four Embarcadero Center, Suite 3520
San Francisco, CA 94111
415 421 3110

CONTACT: Dina Downey
TYPE OF FIRM: Venture Capital Firm
FUNDING PREFERENCE:
  Seed Funding
  Start-Up Funding
  First-Round Funding
INDUSTRY PREFERENCE:
  Communications Technology
  Computer Hardware
  Computer Software
  Medical Technology
  Other High Technologies Not Mentioned

GEOGRAPHIC PREFERENCE:
  Far West
TYPES OF FUNDS:
  Equity (stock purchases)
  Minimum: Open
  Maximum: $5,000,000


Magna Pacific Investments
977 North Broadway, Suite 301
Los Angeles, CA 90012
213 680 2505

CONTACT: David Wong
TYPE OF FIRM: MESBIC
FUNDING PREFERENCE:
  Seed Funding
INDUSTRY PREFERENCE:
  Diversified
GEOGRAPHIC PREFERENCE:
  No Preference (U.S.A.)
TYPES OF FUNDS:
  Loans With Equity Kickers
  Minimum: $50,000
  Maximum: $300,000


MBW Management Inc.
350 Second Street, Suite 7
Los Altos, CA 94022
415 941 2392

CONTACT: James R. Weersing
TYPE OF FIRM: Venture Capital Firm
FUNDING PREFERENCE:
  Start-Up Funding
  First-Round Funding
  Second-Round Funding
  Third-Round Funding
  Fourth-Round Funding
  Later-Stage Funding
  Leveraged Buyouts
INDUSTRY PREFERENCE:
  Diversified
  Communications Technology
  Computer Hardware
  Computer Software

  Manufacturing
  Media
  Medical Technology
  Other High Technologies Not Mentioned
GEOGRAPHIC PREFERENCE:
  No Preference (U.S.A.)
TYPES OF FUNDS:
  Equity (stock purchases)
  Loans With Equity Kickers
  Minimum: $500,000
  Maximum: $2,000,000


MedVenture Associates
Pier 33 South, 2nd Floor
San Francisco, CA 94111
415 956 6818

CONTACT: Annette Campbell-White
TYPE OF FIRM: Venture Capital Firm
FUNDING PREFERENCE:
  Seed Funding
  Start-Up Funding
  First-Round Funding
INDUSTRY PREFERENCE:
  Medical Technology
  Other High Technologies Not Mentioned
GEOGRAPHIC PREFERENCE:
  Rocky Mountain States
  Far West
  Southwest
TYPES OF FUNDS:
  Equity (stock purchases)
  Minimum: $300,000
  Maximum: $600,000


Menlo Ventures
3000 Sand Hill Rd., Bldg. Four, Suite 100
Menlo Park, CA 94025
415 854 8540

CONTACT: H. DuBose Montgomery
TYPE OF FIRM: Venture Capital Firm
FUNDING PREFERENCE:
  Seed Funding

Start-Up Funding
First-Round Funding
Second-Round Funding
Third-Round Funding
Fourth-Round Funding
Later-Stage Funding
Leveraged Buyouts
INDUSTRY PREFERENCE:
  Diversified
  Communications Technology
  Computer Hardware
  Computer Software
  Manufacturing
  Media
  Medical Technology
  Other High Technologies Not Mentioned
  Services
GEOGRAPHIC PREFERENCE:
  No Preference (U.S.A.)
TYPES OF FUNDS:
  Equity (stock purchases)
  Minimum: $500,000
  Maximum: $5,000,000


MIP Equity Fund
3000 Sand Hill Rd., Bldg. 4-280
Menlo Park, CA 94025
415 854 2653


CONTACT: J. C. Severiens, Sylvia Bardes
TYPE OF FIRM: Venture Capital Firm
FUNDING PREFERENCE:
  Later-Stage Funding
INDUSTRY PREFERENCE:
  Communications Technology
  Computer Hardware
  Computer Software
  Medical Technology
  Other High Technologies Not Mentioned
GEOGRAPHIC PREFERENCE:
  Northeast
  Far West
TYPES OF FUNDS:
  Equity (stock purchases)
  Minimum: $2,000,000
  Maximum: $4,000,000

Newtek Ventures
500 Washington St., #720
San Francisco, CA 94111
415 986 5711

TYPE OF FIRM: Venture Capital Firm
FUNDING PREFERENCE:
  Seed Funding
  Start-Up Funding
  First-Round Funding
  Second-Round Funding
  Third-Round Funding
  Leveraged Buyouts
INDUSTRY PREFERENCE:
  Alternative Energy
  Communications Technology
  Computer Hardware
  Computer Software
  Medical Technology
  Other High Technologies Not Mentioned
GEOGRAPHIC PREFERENCE:
  No Preference (U.S.A.)
TYPES OF FUNDS:
  Equity (stock purchases)
  Minimum: $250,000
  Maximum: $1,000,000


Oak Investment Partners
3000 Sand Hill Rd., Bldg. 3-240
Menlo Park, CA 94025
415 854 8825

CONTACT: Catherine Pierson Goodrich
TYPE OF FIRM: Venture Capital Firm
FUNDING PREFERENCE:
  Seed Funding
  Start-Up Funding
  First-Round Funding
INDUSTRY PREFERENCE:
  Communications Technology
  Computer Hardware
  Computer Software
  Medical Technology
  Other High Technologies Not Mentioned
  Retail

GEOGRAPHIC PREFERENCE:
  No Preference (U.S.A.)
TYPES OF FUNDS:
  Equity (stock purchases)
  Minimum: $500,000
  Maximum: $5,000,000


Olympic Venture Partners
101 California St., Suite 4035
San Francisco, CA 94111
415 362 4433

CONTACT: Charles P. Waite, Jr.
TYPE OF FIRM: Venture Capital Firm.
FUNDING PREFERENCE:
  Start-Up Funding
INDUSTRY PREFERENCE:
  Communications Technology
  Computer Hardware
  Computer Software
  Medical Technology
GEOGRAPHIC PREFERENCE:
  Northwest
TYPES OF FUNDS:
  Equity (stock purchases)
  Minimum: $1,000,000
  Maximum: $2,000,000


OSCCO Ventures
3000 Sand Hill Rd., 4-140
Menlo Park, CA 94025
415 854 2222

CONTACT: J. G. Rudolph
TYPE OF FIRM: Venture Capital Firm
FUNDING PREFERENCE:
  Seed Funding
.  Start-Up Funding
  First-Round Funding
INDUSTRY PREFERENCE:
  Diversified
  Communications Technology
  Computer Hardware
  Computer Software

Medical Technology
Other High Technologies Not Mentioned
GEOGRAPHIC PREFERENCE:
  Northwest
  Far West
  Southwest
  Home State: California
  Immediate Area: N. Calif.
TYPES OF FUNDS:
  Equity (stock purchases)
  Minimum: $500,000
  Maximum: $2,500,000


Pacific Capital Fund, Inc.
675 Mariners Island Blvd., Ste. 103
San Mateo, CA 94404
415 574 4747

CONTACT: Gina Marie C. Guerrero
TYPE OF FIRM: MESBIC
FUNDING PREFERENCE:
  First-Round Funding
INDUSTRY PREFERENCE:
  Diversified
GEOGRAPHIC PREFERENCE:
  Home State: California
TYPES OF FUNDS:
  Equity (stock purchases)
  Loans
  Loans With Equity Kickers
  Minimum: $100,000
  Maximum: $300,000


Peregrine Ventures
1299 Ocean Ave., Ste. 306
Santa Monica, CA 90401
213 458 1441

CONTACT: Gene Miller, General Partner
TYPE OF FIRM: Venture Capital Firm
FUNDING PREFERENCE:
  Start-Up Funding
  First-Round Funding

INDUSTRY PREFERENCE:
  Communications Technology
  Computer Hardware
  Computer Software
  Medical Technology
GEOGRAPHIC PREFERENCE:
  Northeast
  Far West
TYPES OF FUNDS:
  Equity (stock purchases)
  Minimum: $750,000
  Maximum: $1,500,000


R & D Funding Corp.
3945 Freedom Circle, Suite 800
Santa Clara, CA 95054
408 980 0990

CONTACT: Michael Hasley, Jonathan Baer
TYPE OF FIRM: R & D Finance/Venture Capital
FUNDING PREFERENCE:
  Second-Round Funding
INDUSTRY PREFERENCE:
  Diversified
GEOGRAPHIC PREFERENCE:
  No Preference (U.S.A.)
TYPES OF FUNDS:
  R & D Contacts with warrants
  Minimum: Open
  Maximum: Open


Sand Hill Venture Group, Inc.
3000 Sand Hill Rd., Bldg. 2, Suite 256
Menlo Park, CA 94025
415 854 9600

CONTACT: D McCrea Graham II
TYPE OF FIRM: Venture Capital Firm
FUNDING PREFERENCE:
  Start-Up Funding
INDUSTRY PREFERENCE:
  Diversified
GEOGRAPHIC PREFERENCE:
  Far West

TYPES OF FUNDS:
  Equity (stock purchases)
  Minimum: $300,000
  Maximum: $1,000,000


Sigma Partners
2099 Gateway Pl., Suite 310
San Jose, CA 95110
408 279 6300

CONTACT: Cliff Haas
TYPE OF FIRM: Venture Capital Firm
FUNDING PREFERENCE:
  Seed Funding
  Start-Up Funding
  First-Round Funding
  Second-Round Funding
INDUSTRY PREFERENCE:
  Communications Technology
  Computer Hardware
  Computer Software
  Medical Technology
  Other High Technologies Not Mentioned
GEOGRAPHIC PREFERENCE:
  Northeast
  Far West
TYPES OF FUNDS:
  Equity (stock purchases)
  Minimum: $500,000
  Maximum: $2,000,000


Southern California Ventures
9920 Lacienega Blvd., Suite 510
Ingelwood, CA 90301
213 216 0544

CONTACT: Lois Fisher
TYPE OF FIRM: Venture Capital Firm
FUNDING PREFERENCE:
  Seed Funding
  Start-Up Funding
INDUSTRY PREFERENCE:
  Diversified

GEOGRAPHIC PREFERENCE:
  Far West
TYPES OF FUNDS:
  Equity (stock purchases)
  Minimum: $200,000
  Maximum: $1,250,000


Spout Group
3000 Sand Hill Rd., Bldg. 1, Suite 285
Menlo Park, CA 95124
415 854 1550

CONTACT:
  High Tech: Keith Geeslin
  Retail: Jon Stone
  Service, Graphics: Russell Pyne
TYPE OF FIRM: Venture Capital Firm
FUNDING PREFERENCE:
  Seed Funding
  Start-Up Funding
  First-Round Funding
  Second-Round Funding
  Third-Round Funding
  Fourth-Round Funding
  Later-Stage Funding
  Leveraged Buyouts
  Acquisitions
INDUSTRY PREFERENCE:
  Diversified
  Communications Technology
  Computer Hardware
  Computer Software
  Manufacturing
  Media
  Medical Technology
  Other High Technologies Not Mentioned
  Retail
  Services
  Wholesale Distribution
GEOGRAPHIC PREFERENCE:
  No Preference (U.S.A.)
TYPES OF FUNDS:
  Equity (stock purchases)
  Minimum: $1,000,000
  Maximum: $5,000,000

Thompson Clive, Inc.
3000 Sand Hill Rd., Bldg. 4, Suite 240
Menlo Park, CA 94025
415 854 0314

CONTACT: Michael Elias
TYPE OF FIRM: Venture Capital Firm
FUNDING PREFERENCE:
  Start-Up Funding
  First-Round Funding
  Second-Round Funding
  Third-Round Funding
INDUSTRY PREFERENCE:
  Diversified
GEOGRAPHIC PREFERENCE:
  Far West
TYPES OF FUNDS:
  Equity (stock purchases)
  Loans
  Minimum: $100,000
  Maximum: $1,500,000


Trinity Ventures, Ltd.
20813 Stevens Creek Blvd. Suite 101
Cupertino, CA 95014
408 446 9690

CONTACT: Noel Fenton
TYPE OF FIRM: Venture Capital Firm
FUNDING PREFERENCE:
  Seed Funding
  Start-Up Funding
  First-Round Funding
  Second-Round Funding
  Third-Round Funding
INDUSTRY PREFERENCE:
  Diversified
  Alternative Energy
  Communications Technology
  Computer Hardware
  Computer Software
  Medical Technology
GEOGRAPHIC PREFERENCE:
  Far West

TYPES OF FUNDS:
  Equity (stock purchases)
  Loans
  Minimum: $250,000
  Maximum: $3,000,000


Union Venture Corporation
445 S. Figueroa Street
Los Angeles, CA 90071
213 236 4092

CONTACT: Jeff Watts, President
TYPE OF FIRM: Venture Capital Firm SBIC
FUNDING PREFERENCE:
  Third-Round Funding
  Fourth-Round Funding
  Later-Stage Funding
  Leveraged Buyouts
  Acquisitions
INDUSTRY PREFERENCE:
  Diversified
  Communications Technology
  Computer Hardware
  Computer Software
  Manufacturing
  Medical Technology
  Other High Technologies Not Mentioned
GEOGRAPHIC PREFERENCE:
  No Preference (U.S.A.)
  Far West
TYPES OF FUNDS:
  Equity (stock purchases)
  Loans With Equity Kickers
  Minimum: $1,000,000
  Maximum: Open


Vanguard Associates
300 Hamilton Ave. 5-500
Palo Alto, CA 94301
415 324 8400

CONTACT: Dr. Jack M. Gill
TYPE OF FIRM: Venture Capital Firm

FUNDING PREFERENCE:
  Seed Funding
INDUSTRY PREFERENCE:
  Communications Technology
  Computer Hardware
  Computer Software
  Medical Technology
GEOGRAPHIC PREFERENCE:
  Far West
  Southwest
  Home State: Calif. & Texas
TYPES OF FUNDS:
  Equity (stock purchases)
  Minimum: $250,000
  Maximum: $1,000,000


Woodside Fund
850 Woodside Drive
Woodside, CA 94062
415 368 5545

CONTACT: Craig L. Davidson
TYPE OF FIRM: Venture Capital Firm
FUNDING PREFERENCE:
  Seed Funding
  Start-Up Funding
  First-Round Funding
INDUSTRY PREFERENCE:
  Diversified
GEOGRAPHIC PREFERENCE:
  Far West
  Home State: California
  Immediate Area: Northern Calif.
TYPES OF FUNDS:
  Equity (stock purchases)
  Loans With Equity Kickers
  Minimum: $100,000
  Maximum: $1,000,000

*CONNECTICUT*

Abacus Ventures
411 West Putnam Ave.
Greenwich, CT 06830
203 629 1100

CONTACT: Yung Wong
TYPE OF FIRM: Venture Capital Firm
FUNDING PREFERENCE:
  Seed Funding
  Start-Up Funding
  First-Round Funding
INDUSTRY PREFERENCE:
  Communications Technology
GEOGRAPHIC PREFERENCE:
  No Preference (U.S.A.)
TYPES OF FUNDS:
  Equity (stock purchases)
  Minimum: $500,000
  Maximum: $3,000,000


Advanced Materials Partners, Inc.
49 Locust Avenue, PO Box 1022
New Canaan, CT 06840
203 966 6415

CONTACT: Warner K. Babcock
TYPE OF FIRM: Venture Capital Firm
FUNDING PREFERENCE:
  Seed Funding
  Start-Up Funding
  First-Round Funding
  Second-Round Funding
  Third-Round Funding
  Fourth-Round Funding
  Later-Stage Funding
  Leveraged Buyouts
  Acquisitions
  Public Offerings
INDUSTRY PREFERENCE:
  Advanced Materials
GEOGRAPHIC PREFERENCE:
  No Preference (U.S.A.)
TYPES OF FUNDS:
  Equity (stock purchases)
  Minimum: $250,000
  Maximum: $3,000,000

Anchorage Properties Limited
53 Binney Lane
Old Greenwich, CT 06870
203 637 0451

CONTACT: Fred Hirschhorn, Jr.
TYPE OF FIRM: Venture Capital Firm
FUNDING PREFERENCE:
  Seed Funding
  Start-Up Funding
  First-Round Funding
INDUSTRY PREFERENCE:
  Diversified but No High Tech
GEOGRAPHIC PREFERENCE:
  Northeast
  Far West
TYPES OF FUNDS:
  Equity (stock purchases)
  Minimum: $20,000
  Maximum: $750,000


APT Leasing, Inc.
53 Unquowa Place
Fairfield, CT 06430
203 255 6421

CONTACT: Anne P. Toth
TYPE OF FIRM: Individual Investor
FUNDING PREFERENCE:
  Leveraged Buyouts
  Acquisitions
INDUSTRY PREFERENCE:
  Diversified
  Manufacturing
  Real Estate
  Services
GEOGRAPHIC PREFERENCE:
  No Preference (U.S.A.)
TYPES OF FUNDS:
  Leasing
  Other
  Minimum: Open
  Maximum: Open

Beacon Partners
71 Strawberry Hill Ave., Suite 614
Stamford, CT 06902
203 348 8858

CONTACT: Leonard Vignoh
TYPE OF FIRM: Investment Banking Firm
  Consulting Firm
FUNDING PREFERENCE:
  Seed Funding
  Start-Up Funding
  First-Round Funding
  Second-Round Funding
  Third-Round Funding
  Fourth-Round Funding
  Later-Stage Funding
  Leveraged Buyouts
  Acquisitions
INDUSTRY PREFERENCE:
  Communications Technology
  Computer Hardware
  Computer Software
  Manufacturing
  Media
  Medical Technology
  Retail
  Services
  Wholesale Distribution
  Franchise
GEOGRAPHIC PREFERENCE:
  Northeast
TYPES OF FUNDS:
  Equity (stock purchases)
  Loans With Equity Kickers
  Minimum: $250,000
  Maximum: several million

Business Development Resources, Inc.
26 Strawberry Hill Ave., Penthouse A
Stamford, CT 06902
203 348 0830

CONTACT: L. Robert Oros
TYPE OF FIRM: New Business/New Product Development
  Specialists

FUNDING PREFERENCE:
  Seed Funding
  Start-Up Funding
INDUSTRY PREFERENCE:
  Diversified
  Consumer Products
GEOGRAPHIC PREFERENCE:
  No Preference (U.S.A.)
TYPES OF FUNDS:
  Equity (stock purchases)
  Time for Percentage of Gross Revenues
  Minimum: Open
  Maximum: Open


Campbell & Associates
P.O. Box 998
Darien, CT 06820
203 656 0555

CONTACT: Douglas Campbell
TYPE OF FIRM: Individual Investor Consulting Firm
FUNDING PREFERENCE:
  Start-Up Funding
  First-Round Funding
INDUSTRY PREFERENCE:
  Services
GEOGRAPHIC PREFERENCE:
  Northeast
TYPES OF FUNDS:
  Equity (stock purchases)
  Bonds With Equity Kickers
  Minimum: $10,000
  Maximum: Open


Capital Impact Corporation
961 Main Street
Bridgeport, CT 06601
203 384 5670

CONTACT: William D. Starbuck, President
TYPE OF FIRM: SBIC
FUNDING PREFERENCE:
  Second-Round Funding
  Third-Round Funding

Fourth-Round Funding
Later-Stage Funding
Leveraged Buyouts
Acquisitions
INDUSTRY PREFERENCE:
Diversified
GEOGRAPHIC PREFERENCE:
Northeast
TYPES OF FUNDS:
Equity (stock purchases)
Loans
Loans With Equity Kickers
Minimum: $100,000
Maximum: $1,500,000


Darcon Corporation
P.O. Box 2461
Darian, CT. 06820
203 656 1008

CONTACT: Robert J. Gustavson
TYPE OF FIRM: Investment Banking Firm
Individual Investor
FUNDING PREFERENCE:
Leveraged Buyouts
Acquisitions
INDUSTRY PREFERENCE:
Manufacturing
GEOGRAPHIC PREFERENCE:
Northeast
Middle Atlantic
Mid-West
TYPES OF FUNDS:
Equity (stock purchases)
Minimum: $50,000
Maximum: $500,000


Food, Drug, Chemical Services
54 Ledge Brook Road
Stamford, CT 06903

CONTACT: Dr. Bob West
TYPE OF FIRM: Consulting Firm

FUNDING PREFERENCE:
  Acquisitions
  Public Offerings
INDUSTRY PREFERENCE:
  Medical Technology
GEOGRAPHIC PREFERENCE:
  Northeast
  Middle Atlantic
  Southeast
TYPES OF FUNDS:
  Equity (stock purchases)
  Other: Services for Equity
  Minimum: $50,000
  Maximum: $250,000


International Plastics Consultants Corp.
1492 High Ridge Rd.
Stamford, CT 06903
203 968 1233

CONTACT: R. Peter Afif
TYPE OF FIRM: Venture Capital Firm
  MESBIC
  Consulting Firm
FUNDING PREFERENCE:
  Second-Round Funding
  Third-Round Funding
  Leveraged Buyouts
  Acquisitions
INDUSTRY PREFERENCE:
  Manufacturing
GEOGRAPHIC PREFERENCE:
  No Preference (U.S.A.)
TYPES OF FUNDS:
  Equity (stock purchases)
  Loans
  Loans With Equity Kickers
  Minimum: $100,000
  Maximum: $500,000


Marketing Sciences, Inc.
2 Whitney Ave.
New Haven, CT 06510
203 789 1717

CONTACT: Dr. Steven E. Permut
TYPE OF FIRM: Consulting Firm
FUNDING PREFERENCE:
  Start-Up Funding
  First-Round Funding
  Later-Stage Funding
  Leveraged Buyouts
  Acquisitions
INDUSTRY PREFERENCE:
  Diversified
  Communications Technology
  Computer Hardware
  Computer Software
  Manufacturing
  Medical Technology
  Services
GEOGRAPHIC PREFERENCE:
  Northeast
TYPES OF FUNDS:
  Combination
  Minimum: Open
  Maximum: Open


More Phillips Hull & Duncan, P.C.
One Lafayette Place
Greenwich, CT 06830
203 629 2611
Telecopier: 203 629 2375
Telex: 490-9968630

CONTACT: J. Bruce Duncan, Esq.
TYPE OF FIRM: Law Firm
FUNDING PREFERENCE:
  Leveraged Buyouts
  Acquisitions
  Public Offerings
INDUSTRY PREFERENCE:
  Medical Technology
  Other High Technologies Not Mentioned
GEOGRAPHIC PREFERENCE:
  Northeast
  Southeast
  Home State: Connecticut

Immediate Area: Greenwich/Fairfield County
Minimum: Open
Maximum: Open


New Park Ventures, Inc.
151 New Park Ave.
Hartford, CT 06106
203 233 2176

CONTACT: David Fuller, President
TYPE OF FIRM: Merchant Bank
FUNDING PREFERENCE:
  Leveraged Buyouts
  Acquisitions
INDUSTRY PREFERENCE:
  Manufacturing
  Wholesale Distribution
GEOGRAPHIC PREFERENCE:
  Home State: Connecticut
  Immediate Area: CT, NY, MA, RI
TYPES OF FUNDS:
  Equity (stock purchases)
  Loans With Equity Kickers
  Bonds
  Bonds With Equity Kickers
  Minimum: $100,000
  Maximum: $5,000,000


North American Ventures, Inc.
800 Connecticut Blvd.
East Hartford, CT 06108
203 528 9021

CONTACT: Laurie N. Porter
TYPE OF FIRM: Venture Capital Firm
FUNDING PREFERENCE:
  Leveraged Buyouts
  Acquisitions
INDUSTRY PREFERENCE:
  Diversified
GEOGRAPHIC PREFERENCE:
  Northeast

TYPES OF FUNDS:
  Loans With Equity Kickers
  Bonds With Equity Kickers
  Minimum: Open
  Maximum: Open


Oak Investment Partners
One Gorham Island
Westport, CT 06880
203 226 8346

CONTACT: S. H. Greenfield; E. F. Glassmeyer
TYPE OF FIRM: Venture Capital Firm
FUNDING PREFERENCE:
  Start-Up Funding
INDUSTRY PREFERENCE:
  Communications Technology
  Computer Software
  Medical Technology
  Retail
  Services
GEOGRAPHIC PREFERENCE:
  No Preference (U.S.A.)
TYPES OF FUNDS:
  Equity (stock purchases)
  Minimum: $500,000
  Maximum: $2,000,000


Oxford Partners
1266 Main Street, Soundview Plaza
Stamford, CT 06902
203 964 0592

CONTACT: Kenneth W. Rind, General Partner
TYPE OF FIRM: Venture Capital Firm
FUNDING PREFERENCE:
  Seed Funding
  Start-Up Funding
  First-Round Funding
  Second-Round Funding
  Third-Round Funding
  Fourth-Round Funding
  Later-Stage Funding

Leveraged Buyouts
Acquisitions
INDUSTRY PREFERENCE:
  Communications Technology
  Computer Hardware
  Computer Software
  Medical Technology
  Other High Technologies Not Mentioned
GEOGRAPHIC PREFERENCE:
  No Preference (U.S.A.)
TYPES OF FUNDS:
  Equity (stock purchases)
  Minimum: $500,000
  Maximum: $1,500,000


Parker Benjamin Inc.
160 Farmington Avenue
Farmington, CT 06032
203 677 5044

CONTACT: Paul M. Ruby
TYPE OF FIRM: Investment Banking Firm
FUNDING PREFERENCE:
  Seed Funding
  Start-Up Funding
  First-Round Funding
  Second-Round Funding
  Third-Round Funding
  Fourth-Round Funding
  Later-Stage Funding
  Leveraged Buyouts
  Acquisitions
INDUSTRY PREFERENCE:
  Diversified
  Communications Technology
  Computer Hardware
  Computer Software
  Manufacturing
  Media
  Medical Technology
  Other High Technologies Not Mentioned
  Real Estate
  Services
GEOGRAPHIC PREFERENCE:
  Northeast

TYPES OF FUNDS:
  Equity (stock purchases)
  Loans
  Loans With Equity Kickers
  Bonds
  Bonds With Equity Kickers
  Leasing
  Minimum: $500,000
  Maximum: $20,000,000


Prime Capital Management Co.
One Landmark Sq.
Stamford, CT 06901
203 964 0642

CONTACT: Joan Ardrey
TYPE OF FIRM: Venture Capital Firm
FUNDING PREFERENCE:
  First-Round Funding
  Second-Round Funding
INDUSTRY PREFERENCE:
  Diversified
  Other High Technologies Not Mentioned
GEOGRAPHIC PREFERENCE:
  Northeast
TYPES OF FUNDS:
  Equity (stock purchases)
  Loans
  Minimum: $300,000
  Maximum: $600,000


R. Mark Van Allen
Bridgeport Innovation Center
955 Connecticut Ave.
Bridgeport, CT 06607
203 336 8864

CONTACT: R. Mark Van Allen
TYPE OF FIRM: Venture Capital Firm Local
  Certified Development Co.
FUNDING PREFERENCE:
  Seed Funding
  Start-Up Funding

INDUSTRY PREFERENCE:
 Diversified
 Manufacturing
 Real Estate
GEOGRAPHIC PREFERENCE:
 Northeast
TYPES OF FUNDS:
 Equity (stock purchases)
 Minimum: $25,000
 Maximum: $50,000


Southport Partners
2425 Post Road, Suite 200
Southport, CT 06490
203 255 1231

CONTACT: Dale E. McIvor
TYPE OF FIRM: Investment Banking Firm
FUNDING PREFERENCE:
 First-Round Funding
 Later-Stage Funding
 Leveraged Buyouts
 Acquisitions
INDUSTRY PREFERENCE:
 Communications Technology
 Computer Hardware
 Computer Software
 Manufacturing
 Media
 Other High Technologies Not Mentioned
 Wholesale Distribution
GEOGRAPHIC PREFERENCE:
 No Preference (U.S.A.)
TYPES OF FUNDS:
 Equity (stock purchases)
 Loans With Equity Kickers
 Minimum: Open
 Maximum: Open


State Street Technologies
One State Street, Ste. 1520
Hartford, CT 06103
203 522 3260

CONTACT: R.K. Brandstedter
TYPE OF FIRM: Individual Investor
FUNDING PREFERENCE:
  Seed Funding
INDUSTRY PREFERENCE:
  Other High Technologies Not Mentioned
GEOGRAPHIC PREFERENCE:
  Northeast
TYPES OF FUNDS:
  Loans With Equity Kickers
  Minimum: $100,000
  Maximum: $1,500,000


VentureLaunch
28 Oak Ledge Lane
Wilton, CT 06897
203 762 3100

CONTACT: David Abraham
TYPE OF FIRM: Consulting Firm
FUNDING PREFERENCE:
  Start-Up Funding
  Leveraged Buyouts
  Acquisitions
INDUSTRY PREFERENCE:
  Alternative Energy
  Communications Technology
  Other High Technologies Not Mentioned (Biotechnology)
GEOGRAPHIC PREFERENCE:
  Northeast
TYPES OF FUNDS:
  Depends on Deal
  Minimum: Open
  Maximum: Open


Venture Partners
P.O. Box 31382
Old Statehouse Station
Hartford, CT 06103
203 828 1616

CONTACT: G. M. Laskowski
TYPE OF FIRM: Investment Banking Firm
  Consulting Firm

FUNDING PREFERENCE:
  Seed Funding
  Start-Up Funding
INDUSTRY PREFERENCE:
  Computer Hardware
  Computer Software
  Medical Technology
GEOGRAPHIC PREFERENCE:
  Northeast
TYPES OF FUNDS:
  Equity (stock purchases)
  Loans
  Minimum: $100,000
  Maximum: $250,000


The Vista Group
36 Grove St.
New Canaan, CT 06840
203 972 3400

CONTACT: Mary Lou Mitovich
TYPE OF FIRM: Venture Capital Firm
FUNDING PREFERENCE:
  Start-Up Funding
  First-Round Funding
  Second-Round Funding
  Later-Stage Funding
  Leveraged Buyouts
INDUSTRY PREFERENCE:
  Diversified
  Communications Technology
  Computer Hardware
  Computer Software
  Medical Technology
  Other High Technologies Not Mentioned
  Retail
GEOGRAPHIC PREFERENCE:
  No Preference (U.S.A.)
TYPES OF FUNDS:
  Equity (stock purchases)
  Minimum: $500,000
  Maximum: $3,000,000

Xerox Venture Capital
800 Long Ridge Road
Stamford, CT 06904
203 968 3383

CONTACT: L. J. Harris
TYPE OF FIRM: Venture Capital Subsidiary or Affiliate of
  Operating Co.
FUNDING PREFERENCE:
  Start-Up Funding
  First-Round Funding
INDUSTRY PREFERENCE:
  Communications Technology
  Computer Hardware
  Computer Software
  Other High Technologies Not Mentioned
GEOGRAPHIC PREFERENCE:
  No Preference (U.S.A.)
TYPES OF FUNDS:
  Equity (stock purchases)
  Minimum: $250,000
  Maximum: $1,000,000


*COLORADO*


Hill, Kirby & Washing
885 Arapahoe Ave.
Boulder, CO 80302
303 442 5151

CONTACT: John Hill, Paul Kirby, Tom Washing
TYPE OF FIRM: Venture Capital Firm
FUNDING PREFERENCE:
  Seed Funding
  Start-Up Funding
  First-Round Funding
INDUSTRY PREFERENCE:
  Communications Technology
  Computer Hardware
  Computer Software
  Medical Technology
  Other High Technologies Not Mentioned

GEOGRAPHIC PREFERENCE:
  Rocky Mountain States
  Northwest
  Far West
  Southwest
TYPES OF FUNDS:
  Equity (stock purchases)
  Minimum: $500,000
  Maximum: $2,000,000


Stephenson Merchant Banking
100 Garfield St., Suite 400
Denver, CO 80206
303 355 6000

CONTACT: E. Preston Sumner, Jr.
TYPE OF FIRM: Venture Capital Firm
FUNDING PREFERENCE:
  Leveraged Buyouts
INDUSTRY PREFERENCE:
  Diversified
GEOGRAPHIC PREFERENCE:
  Rocky Mountain States
  Far West
  Southwest
TYPES OF FUNDS:
  Equity (stock purchases)
  Minimum: $500,000
  Maximum: $1,500,000


*DISTRICT OF COLUMBIA*


Allied Capital Corporation
1666 K St., N.W., #901
Washington, DC 20006
202 331 1112

CONTACT: David Gladstone
TYPE OF FIRM: Venture Capital Firm
  SBIC
  MESBIC

FUNDING PREFERENCE:
  Second-Round Funding
  Third-Round Funding
  Fourth-Round Funding
  Later-Stage Funding
  Leveraged Buyouts
INDUSTRY PREFERENCE:
  Diversified
GEOGRAPHIC PREFERENCE:
  No Preference (U.S.A.)
TYPES OF FUNDS:
  Loans
  Loans With Equity Kickers
  Subordinated Convertible Debentures
  Minimum: $500,000
  Maximum: $3,500,000


American Security Capital Corp.
730 Fifteenth Street, NW (A2/625)
Washington, DC 20013
202 024 4843


CONTACT: Mr. Brian Mercer
TYPE OF FIRM: SBIC
FUNDING PREFERENCE:
  First-Round Funding
  Second-Round Funding
  Third-Round Funding
  Fourth-Found Funding
  Later-Stage Funding
INDUSTRY PREFERENCE:
  Diversified
GEOGRAPHIC PREFERENCE:
  Immediate Area: Within 2 hrs. of office
TYPES OF FUNDS:
  Equity (stock purchases)
  Other: Subordinated Debt
  Minimum: $250,000
  Maximum: Open


Broadcast Capital Fund, Inc.
1771 N St. N.W.
Washington, DC 20036
202 429 5393

CONTACT: John E. Oxenoine, President
TYPE OF FIRM: MESBIC
FUNDING PREFERENCE:
  Start-Up Funding
  Leveraged Buyouts
  Acquisitions
INDUSTRY PREFERENCE:
  Media—Broadcasting Only
GEOGRAPHIC PREFERENCE:
  No Preference (U.S.A.)
TYPES OF FUNDS:
  Loans With Equity Kickers
  Minimum: $200,000
  Maximum: $900,000


Consumers United Capital Corporation
2100 M Street, N.W. Suite 207
Washington, DC 20036
202 872 5262

CONTACT: Esther M. Carr-Davis, President
TYPE OF FIRM: MESBIC
FUNDING PREFERENCE:
  Start-Up Funding
  First-Round Funding
INDUSTRY PREFERENCE:
  Diversified
  Retail
  Services
  Wholesale Distribution
GEOGRAPHIC PREFERENCE:
  No Preference (U.S.A.)
TYPES OF FUNDS:
  Equity (stock purchases)
  Loans
  Loans With Equity Kickers
  Minimum: $10,000
  Maximum: $50,000


DC Bancorp Venture Capital Co.
1801 K St. N.W.
Washington, DC 20006
202 955 6970

CONTACT: A. A. Weissburg

TYPE OF FIRM: Venture Capital Firm
  SBIC
FUNDING PREFERENCE:
  First-Round Funding
  Second-Round Funding
INDUSTRY PREFERENCE:
  Diversified
GEOGRAPHIC PREFERENCE:
  Middle Atlantic
TYPES OF FUNDS:
  Equity (stock purchases)
  Loans With Equity Kickers
  Minimum: $100,000
  Maximum: $500,000


*FLORIDA*


Caribank Capital Corp./Caribank Venture Corp.
255 E. Dania Beach Blvd.
Dania, Florida 33004
305 925 2211

CONTACT: Michael E. Chaney, President, or Elaine E. Healy,
Vice President
TYPE OF FIRM: Venture Capital Firm
  SBIC
FUNDING PREFERENCE:
  Second-Round Funding
  Third-Round Funding
INDUSTRY PREFERENCE:
  Diversified
GEOGRAPHIC PREFERENCE:
  No Preference (U.S.A.)
TYPES OF FUNDS:
  Equity (stock purchases)
  Bonds With Equity Kickers
  Minimum: $300,000
  Maximum: $500,000


Interstate Capital Corporation
701 E. Camino Real—Suite 9A
Boca Raton, FL 33432
305 395 8535

CONTACT: William McConnell, Jr.
TYPE OF FIRM: Venture Capital Firm
FUNDING PREFERENCE:
  Start-Up Funding
  First-Round Funding
  Second-Round Funding
FUNDING PREFERENCE:
  Diversified
  Medical Technology
  Other High Technologies Not Mentioned
GEOGRAPHIC PREFERENCE:
  Northeast
  Southeast
TYPES OF FUNDS:
  Equity (stock purchases)
  Loans
  Loans With Equity Kickers
  Minimum: $50,000
  Maximum: $500,000


Pro-Med Capital, Inc.
1380 Miami Gardens Drive, N.E., #225
North Miami Beach, FL 33179
305 949 5900

CONTACT: Lance R. Rosemore
TYPE OF FIRM: SBIC
    MESBIC
FUNDING PREFERENCE:
  Second-Round Funding
INDUSTRY PREFERENCE:
  Diversified
GEOGRAPHIC PREFERENCE:
  No Preference (U.S.A.)
TYPES OF FUNDS:
  Loans
  Minimum: $50,000
  Maximum: $1,000,000


South Atlantic Venture Fund, Limited Partnership
614 West Bay Street, Ste. 200
Tampa, Florida 33606-2704
813 253 2500

CONTACT: Donald W. Burton, Richard J. Brandewie
TYPE OF FIRM: Venture Capital Firm
FUNDING PREFERENCE:
  First-Round Funding
  Second-Round Funding
  Third-Round Funding
  Fourth-Round Funding
  Later-Stage Funding
  Leveraged Buyouts
INDUSTRY PREFERENCE:
  Communications Technology
  Manufacturing
  Medical Technology
  Other High Technologies Not Mentioned
  Retail
  Services
GEOGRAPHIC PREFERENCE:
  Southeast
TYPES OF FUNDS:
  Equity (stock purchases)
  Minimum: $250,000
  Maximum: $1,000,000


Universal Financial Services, Inc.
3550 Biscayne Blvd. #702
Miami, FL 33137
305 573 1496


CONTACT: Norman N. Zipkin
TYPE OF FIRM: MESBIC
FUNDING PREFERENCE:
  Start-Up Funding
  Later-Stage Funding
INDUSTRY PREFERENCE:
  Real Estate
  Services
GEOGRAPHIC PREFERENCE:
  Northeast
  Middle Atlantic
  Southeast
TYPES OF FUNDS:
  Loans
  Loans With Equity Kickers
  Minimum: $25,000
  Maximum: $150,000

*HAWAII*

Bancorp Hawaii Small Business Investment Co., Inc.
P.O. Box 2900 (111 So. King St., Honolulu 96813)
Honolulu, HI 96846
808 537 8557

CONTACT: Thomas T. Triggs
TYPE OF FIRM: SBIC
FUNDING PREFERENCE:
  First-Round Funding
  Second-Round Funding
  Third-Round Funding
  Fourth-Round Funding
  Later-Stage Funding
  Leveraged Buyouts
INDUSTRY PREFERENCE:
  Diversified
GEOGRAPHIC PREFERENCE:
  Northwest
  Far West
  Hawaii
TYPES OF FUNDS:
  Equity (stock purchases)
  Loans With Equity Kickers
  Minimum: $100,000
  Maximum: $300,000

*ILLINOIS*

Allstate Insurance Co.
Venture Capital Div. E-2
Allstate Plaza
Northbrook, IL 60062
312 402 5681

CONTACT: Robert L. Lestina
TYPE OF FIRM: Venture Capital Firm
FUNDING PREFERENCE:
  Seed Funding
  Start-Up Funding
  First-Round Funding
  Second-Round Funding

Third-Round Funding
Fourth-Round Funding
Later-Stage Funding
Leveraged Buyouts
INDUSTRY PREFERENCE:
Diversified
Communications Technology
Manufacturing
Media
Medical Technology
Other Technologies Not Mentioned
Retail
Services
GEOGRAPHIC PREFERENCE:
No Preference (U.S.A.)
TYPES OF FUNDS:
Equity (stock purchases)
Bonds With Equity Kickers
Minimum: $500,000
Maximum: $10,000,000


Caterpillar Venture Capital, Inc.
100 N.E. Adams St.
Peoria, IL 61629-4390
309 675 5503

CONTACT: William B. Heming
TYPE OF FIRM: Corporate Venture Capital Investor
FUNDING PREFERENCE:
Start-Up Funding
First-Round Funding
Second-Round Funding
Third-Round Funding
Fourth-Round Funding
INDUSTRY PREFERENCE:
Manufacturing
Other High Technologies Not Mentioned
GEOGRAPHIC PREFERENCE:
No Preference (U.S.A.)
TYPES OF FUNDS:
Equity (stock purchases)
Loans
Loans With Equity Kickers
Minimum: $500,000
Maximum: $2,000,000

Continental Illinois Venture Corporation
Continental Illinois Equity Corporation
231 South LaSalle Street
Chicago, IL 60697
312 828 8023

CONTACT: John L. Hines
TYPE OF FIRM: Venture Capital Firm
  SBIC
FUNDING PREFERENCE:
  Start-Up Funding
  First-Round Funding
  Second-Round Funding
  Third-Round Funding
  Leveraged Buyouts
INDUSTRY PREFERENCE:
  Communications Technology
  Manufacturing
  Medical Technology
  Other Technologies Not Mentioned
  Retail
  Services
GEOGRAPHIC PREFERENCE:
  No Preference (U.S.A.)
TYPES OF FUNDS:
  Equity (stock purchases)
  Minimum: $500,000
  Maximum: $10,000,000

IEG Venture Management, Inc.
401 North Michigan Ave.—Ste. 2020
Chicago, IL 60611
312 644 0890

CONTACT: Frank Blair or Marian Zamlynski
TYPE OF FIRM: Venture Capital Firm
FUNDING PREFERENCE:
  Start-Up Funding
INDUSTRY PREFERENCE:
  Diversified
GEOGRAPHIC PREFERENCE:
  Mid-West

TYPES OF FUNDS:
  Equity (stock purchases)
  Minimum: $200,000
  Maximum: $500,000


Mesirow Venture Capital, Inc.
135 S. LaSalle Street, Ste. 3910
Chicago, IL 60603
312 443 5757

CONTACT: James C. Tyree
TYPE OF FIRM: Venture Capital Firm
  SBIC
FUNDING PREFERENCE:
  Later-Stage Funding
  Leveraged Buyouts
  Acquisitions
INDUSTRY PREFERENCE:
  Diversified
  Manufacturing
  Medical Technology
  Retail
  Wholesale Distribution
  Franchise
GEOGRAPHIC PREFERENCE:
  No Preference (U.S.A.)
TYPES OF FUNDS:
  Equity (stock purchases)
  Loans With Equity Kickers
  Bonds With Equity Kickers
  Minimum: $1,000,000
  Maximum: $10,000,000


William Blair Venture Partners
135 South LaSalle St.
Chicago, IL 60603
312 853 8250

CONTACT: Gregg Newmark
TYPE OF FIRM: Venture Capital Firm
FUNDING PREFERENCE:
  Start-Up Funding
  First-Round Funding
  Second-Round Funding

Third-Round Funding
Leveraged Buyouts
INDUSTRY PREFERENCE:
Diversified
GEOGRAPHIC PREFERENCE:
No Preference (U.S.A.)
TYPES OF FUNDS:
Equity (stock purchases)
Minimum: $1,000,000
Maximum: $3,000,000


*INDIANA*


Corporation for Innovation Development
One North Capitol Ave., Suite 520
Indianapolis, IN 46204
317 635 7325

CONTACT: Mr. Marion C. Dietrich, Mr. M. Archie Leslie,
Mr. Donald K. Taylor
TYPE OF FIRM: Venture Capital Firm (Private)
FUNDING PREFERENCE:
First-Round Funding
Second-Round Funding
Third-Round Funding
Later-Stage Funding
Leveraged Buyouts
Acquisitions
INDUSTRY PREFERENCE:
Communications Technology
Computer Hardware
Computer Software
Manufacturing
Medical Technology
Retail
Services
Wholesale Distribution
GEOGRAPHIC PREFERENCE:
Home State: Indiana
TYPES OF FUNDS:
Equity (stock purchases)
Loans With Equity Kickers
Minimum: $250,000
Maximum: $1,000,000

White River Capital Corporation
432 Washington Street, P.O. Box 929
Columbus, IN 47202
812 376 1759

CONTACT: Bradley J. Kime, Vice President
TYPE OF FIRM: SBIC
FUNDING PREFERENCE:
  Later-Stage Funding
  Leveraged Buyouts
INDUSTRY PREFERENCE:
  Diversified
GEOGRAPHIC PREFERENCE:
  Mid-West
TYPES OF FUNDS:
  Loans With Equity Kickers
  Minimum: $100,000
  Maximum: $200,000


*IOWA*


InvestAmerica Venture Group, Inc.
800 American Bldg.
Cedar Rapids, IA 52401
319 363 8249

CONTACT: David Schroder
TYPE OF FIRM: Venture Capital Firm
FUNDING PREFERENCE:
  First-Round Funding
  Second-Round Funding
  Leveraged Buyouts
INDUSTRY PREFERENCE:
  Diversified
GEOGRAPHIC PREFERENCE:
  Mid-West
TYPES OF FUNDS:
  Equity (stock purchases)
  Loans With Equity Kickers
  Minimum: $200,000
  Maximum: $1,000,000

*KENTUCKY*


Kentucky Highlands Investment Corporation
P.O. Box 628
London, KY 40741
606 864 5175

CONTACT: Brenda McDaniel
TYPE OF FIRM: Venture Capital Firm
  SBIC
  Consulting Firm
FUNDING PREFERENCE:
  Start-Up Funding
  Later-Stage Funding
  Leveraged Buyouts
INDUSTRY PREFERENCE:
  Diversified
  Communications Technology
  Manufacturing
  Services
GEOGRAPHIC PREFERENCE:
  Home State: Kentucky
  Immediate Area: Eastern Kentucky
TYPES OF FUNDS:
  Equity (stock purchases)
  Loans
  Loans With Equity Kickers
  Leasing
  Minimum: $250,000
  Maximum: $750,000


*LOUISIANA*


First Southern Capital Corporation
6161 Perkins Rd., Suite 1D (PO Box 14418, zip: 70898)
Baton Rouge, LA 70808
504 769 3004

CONTACT: Mr. Charest Thibaut, Jr.
TYPE OF FIRM: SBIC
FUNDING PREFERENCE:
  Start-Up Funding

INDUSTRY PREFERENCE:
  Diversified
GEOGRAPHIC PREFERENCE:
  Southeast
TYPES OF FUNDS:
  Equity (stock purchases)
  Loans
  Minimum: $50,000
  Maximum: $250,000


SCDF Investment Corporation
P.O. Box 3885/1006 Surrey Street
Lafayette, Louisiana 70501
318 232-9206

CONTACT: Clayton Williams
TYPE OF FIRM: MESBIC
FUNDING PREFERENCE:
  Second-Round Funding
INDUSTRY PREFERENCE:
  Diversified
  Computer Software
  Manufacturing
  Other High Technologies Not Mentioned
  Services
  Wholesale Distribution
  Franchise
GEOGRAPHIC PREFERENCE:
  Southeast
TYPES OF FUNDS:
  Equity (stock purchases)
  Loans
  Loans With Equity Kickers
  Minimum: Open
  Maximum: Open


*MARYLAND*


Broventure Capital Management
16 W. Madison St.
Baltimore, MD 21201
301 727 4520

CONTACT: William Gust

TYPE OF FIRM: Venture Capital Firm
FUNDING PREFERENCE:
  Seed Funding
  Start-Up Funding
  First-Round Funding
INDUSTRY PREFERENCE:
  Communications Technology
  Computer Hardware
  Computer Software
  Medical Technology
  Other High Technologies Not Mentioned
GEOGRAPHIC PREFERENCE:
  Northeast
  Middle Atlantic
  Southeast
  Far West
TYPES OF FUNDS:
  Equity (stock purchases)
  Loans With Equity Kickers
  Minimum: $500,000
  Maximum: $1,000,000


New Enterprise Associates
1119 St. Paul St.
Baltimore, MD 21202
301 244 0115

CONTACT: Nora Zietz
TYPE OF FIRM: Venture Capital Firm
FUNDING PREFERENCE:
  Seed Funding
  Start-Up Funding
  First-Round Funding
INDUSTRY PREFERENCE:
  Diversified
  Communications Technology
  Computer Hardware
  Computer Software
  Medical Technology
  Other High Technologies Not Mentioned
  Retail
GEOGRAPHIC PREFERENCE:
  No Preference (U.S.A.)
TYPES OF FUNDS:
  Equity (stock purchases)

Minimum: $300,000
Maximum: $2,000,000


*MASSACHUSETTS*

Aegis Funds
One Cranberry Hill
Lexington, MA 02173
618 862 0200

CONTACT: Clifton C. Smith
TYPE OF FIRM: Venture Capital Firm
FUNDING PREFERENCE:
  Seed Funding
  Start-Up Funding
INDUSTRY PREFERENCE:
  Diversified
GEOGRAPHIC PREFERENCE:
  Immediate Area: 75 miles of Boston
TYPES OF FUNDS:
  Equity (stock purchases)
  Minimum: $300,000
  Maximum: $1,500,000


BancBoston Ventures (Subsidiary of Bank of Boston)
100 Federal St.
Boston, MA 02110
617 434 2442

CONTACT: Jeffrey Wilson
TYPE OF FIRM: SBIC
FUNDING PREFERENCE:
  Second-Round Funding
  Third-Round Funding
  Fourth-Round Funding
  Later-Stage Funding
INDUSTRY PREFERENCE:
  Diversified
GEOGRAPHIC PREFERENCE:
  No Preference (U.S.A.)
TYPES OF FUNDS:
  Equity (stock purchases)
  Minimum: $250,000
  Maximum: $2,000,000

Boston Capital Ventures
45 School Street
Boston, MA 02108
617 227 6550

CONTACT: A. Dana Callon, Jr.
TYPE OF FIRM: Venture Capital Firm
FUNDING PREFERENCE:
  Start-Up Funding
  First-Round Funding
  Second-Round Funding
  Third-Round Funding
  Later-Stage Funding
  Leveraged Buyouts
  Acquisitions
INDUSTRY PREFERENCE:
  Diversified
GEOGRAPHIC PREFERENCE:
  Northeast
TYPES OF FUNDS:
  Equity (stock purchases)
  Loans With Equity Kickers
  Minimum: $250,000
  Maximum: $2,000,000


Burr, Egan, Deleage & Co.
One Post Office Square, Suite 3800
Boston, MA 02109
617 482 8020

CONTACT: William P. Egan
TYPE OF FIRM: Venture Capital Firm
FUNDING PREFERENCE:
  Start-Up Funding
  First-Round Funding
  Second-Round Funding
  Third-Round Funding
  Fourth-Round Funding
  Later-Stage Funding
  Leveraged Buyouts
  Acquisitions
INDUSTRY PREFERENCE:
  Diversified
  Communications Technology
  Computer Hardware

Computer Software
Manufacturing
Media
Medical Technology
Other High Technologies Not Mentioned
GEOGRAPHIC PREFERENCE:
No Preference (U.S.A.)
TYPES OF FUNDS:
Equity (stock purchases)
Loans
Loans With Equity Kickers
Minimum: $1,500,000
Maximum: $5,000,000


Commonwealth Partners Limited Partnership
881 Commonwealth Ave.
Boston, MA 02215
617 353 4550

CONTACT: Charles W. Smith
TYPE OF FIRM: Venture Capital Firm
FUNDING PREFERENCE:
Seed Funding
Start-Up Funding
INDUSTRY PREFERENCE:
Communications Technology
Medical Technology
Other High Technologies Not Mentioned
GEOGRAPHIC PREFERENCE:
Northeast
TYPES OF FUNDS:
Equity (stock purchases)
Loans With Equity Kickers
Minimum: $50,000
Maximum: $150,000


Eastech Management Company, Inc.
One Liberty Street
Boston, MA 02109
617 338 0200

CONTACT: Michael H. Shanahan
TYPE OF FIRM: Venture Capital Firm

FUNDING PREFERENCE:
  Start-Up Funding
  First-Round Funding
INDUSTRY PREFERENCE:
  Computer Hardware
  Computer Software
GEOGRAPHIC PREFERENCE:
  Northeast
TYPES OF FUNDS:
  Equity (stock purchases)
  Minimum: $300,000
  Maximum: $900,000


Equitec
33 Bedford Street
Lexington, MA 02173
617 863 8700

TYPE OF FIRM: Venture Capital Firm
  Venture Leasing Firm
FUNDING PREFERENCE:
  Seed Funding
  Start-Up Funding
  First-Round Funding
  Second-Round Funding
  Third-Round Funding
  Fourth-Round Funding
  Later-Stage Funding
  Leveraged Buyouts
INDUSTRY PREFERENCE:
  Diversified
  Alternative Energy
  Communications Technology
  Computer Hardware
  Computer Software
  Manufacturing
  Media
  Medical Technology
  Other High Technologies Not Mentioned
GEOGRAPHIC PREFERENCE:
  No Preference (U.S.A.)
TYPES OF FUNDS:
  Loans With Equity Kickers
  Leasing With Equity Kickers

Minimum: $250,000
Maximum: $3,000,000


Matrix Partners
One Post Office Square
Boston, MA 02109
617 482 7735


CONTACT: Timothy A. Barrows
TYPE OF FIRM: Venture Capital Firm
FUNDING PREFERENCE:
  Start-Up Funding
  First-Round Funding
  Second-Round Funding
  Third-Round Funding
  Leveraged Buyouts
INDUSTRY PREFERENCE:
  Communications Technology
  Computer Hardware
  Computer Software
  Manufacturing
  Media
  Medical Technology
  Other High Technologies Not Mentioned
  Retail
  Services
  Wholesale Distribution
GEOGRAPHIC PREFERENCE:
  Northeast
  Middle Atlantic
  Southeast
  Mid-West
  Rocky Mountain States
  Northwest
  Far West
  Southwest
TYPES OF FUNDS:
  Equity (stock purchases)
  Minimum: $750,000
  Maximum: $4,000,000


Palmer
300 Unicorn Park Drive
Woburn, MA 01801
617 933 5445

CONTACT: Michael T. Fitzgerald
TYPE OF FIRM: Venture Capital Firm
FUNDING PREFERENCE:
  Seed Funding
  Start-Up Funding
  First-Round Funding
INDUSTRY PREFERENCE:
  Diversified
GEOGRAPHIC PREFERENCE:
  No Preference (U.S.A.)
  Also International
TYPES OF FUNDS:
  Equity (stock purchases)
  Loans With Equity Kickers
  Minimum: $250,000
  Maximum: $1,000,000


Shawmut National Ventures Corporation
One Federal Street, 30th Floor
Boston, MA 02211
617 556 4700


CONTACT: Steven J. Lee, President & Director
TYPE OF FIRM: Venture Capital Firm
  SBIC
  Part of a $26 billion bank holding company
FUNDING PREFERENCE:
  Start-Up Funding
  First-Round Funding
  Second-Round Funding
  Leveraged Buyouts
INDUSTRY PREFERENCE:
  Diversified
  Alternative Energy
  Communications Technology
  Manufacturing
  Medical Technology
  Other High Technologies Not Mentioned
  Retail
  Wholesale Distribution
GEOGRAPHIC PREFERENCE:
  No Preference (U.S.A.)
TYPES OF FUNDS:
  Equity (stock purchases)
  Loans With Equity Kickers
  Minimum: $500,000
  Maximum: $2,000,000

Sigma Partners
342 Green St.
Northboro, MA 01532
617  393 7396

CONTACT: Gardner Hendrie
TYPE OF FIRM: Venture Capital Firm
FUNDING PREFERENCE:
  Seed Funding
  Start-Up Funding
  First-Round Funding
  Second-Round Funding
INDUSTRY PREFERENCE:
  Communications Technology
  Computer Hardware
  Computer Software
  Medical Technology
  Other High Technologies Not Mentioned
GEOGRAPHIC PREFERENCE:
  Northeast
  Far West
TYPES OF FUNDS:
  Equity (stock purchases)
  Minimum: $500,000
  Maximum: $2,000,000


Vimac Corp.
12 Arlington St.
Boston, MA 02116
617 267 2785

CONTACT: Max J. Steinmann
TYPE OF FIRM: Venture Capital Firm
FUNDING PREFERENCE:
  Seed Funding
INDUSTRY PREFERENCE:
  Computer Hardware
  Computer Software
GEOGRAPHIC PREFERENCE:
  Northeast
TYPES OF FUNDS:
  Equity (stock purchases)
  Minimum: $100,000
  Maximum: $250,000

*MICHIGAN*


MBW Management, Inc.
4251 Plymouth Road, P.O. Box 986
Ann Arbor, MA 48106-0986
313 747 9401

CONTACT: Ian R. N. Bund
TYPE OF FIRM: Venture Capital Firm
FUNDING PREFERENCE:
  Start-Up Funding
  First-Round Funding
  Second-Round Funding
  Third-Round Funding
  Fourth-Round Funding
  Later-Stage Funding
  Leveraged Buyouts
  Acquisitions
INDUSTRY PREFERENCE:
  Diversified
  Communications Technology
  Computer Hardware
  Computer Software
  Manufacturing
  Media
  Medical Technology
  Other High Technologies Not Mentioned
GEOGRAPHIC PREFERENCE:
  No Preference (U.S.A.)
TYPES OF FUNDS:
  Equity (stock purchases)
  Loans With Equity Kickers
  Minimum: $500,000
  Maximum: $2,000,000


Motor Enterprise, Inc.
3044 W. Grand Blvd.—Rm. 15-134
Detroit, MI 48202
313 556 4273

CONTACT: Mr. James Kobus, Manager
TYPE OF FIRM: MESBIC

FUNDING PREFERENCE:
  First-Round Funding
  Second-Round Funding
INDUSTRY PREFERENCE:
  Diversified
  Manufacturing
GEOGRAPHIC PREFERENCE:
  Mid-West
TYPES OF FUNDS:
  Loans
  Minimum: $100,000
  Maximum: $1,000,000


*MINNESOTA*


Cherry Tree Ventures
3800 West 80th St., Suite 1400
Minneapolis, MI 55431
612 893 9012

CONTACT: John Bergstrom, Mark Derus
TYPE OF FIRM: Venture Capital Firm
FUNDING PREFERENCE:
  Start-Up Funding
  First-Round Funding
  Second-Round Funding
  Third-Round Funding
  Leveraged Buyouts
INDUSTRY PREFERENCE:
  Diversified
GEOGRAPHIC PREFERENCE:
  Mid-West
  Home State: Minnesota
TYPES OF FUNDS:
  Equity (stock purchases)
  Minimum: $500,000
  Maximum: $1,500,000


Norwest Growth Fund, Inc.
2800 Piper Jaffray Tower
222 South Ninth Street
Minneapolis, MN 55402-3389
612 372 8770
612 372 0950 (FAX)

CONTACT: Ernie Parizeau
TYPE OF FIRM: Venture Capital Firm
FUNDING PREFERENCE:
   Start-Up Funding
   First-Round Funding
   Second-Round Funding
   Third-Round Funding
   Fourth-Round Funding
   Later-Stage Funding
   Leveraged Buyouts
   Acquisitions
INDUSTRY PREFERENCE:
   Diversified
   Communications Technology
   Computer Hardware
   Computer Software
   Manufacturing
   Medical Technology
   Other High Technologies Not Mentioned
   Retail
   Franchise
GEOGRAPHIC PREFERENCE:
   Mid-West
   Rocky Mountain States
   Northwest
   Far West
   Southwest
TYPES OF FUNDS:
   Equity (stock purchases)
   Loans With Equity Kickers
   Minimum: $1,000,000
   Maximum: VC: $6,000,000   LBO: $15,000,000


Pathfinder Venture Capital Funds
7300 Metro Blvd.—Suite 585
Minneapolis, MN 55435
612 835 1121

CONTACT: Mr. A. J. Greenshields
TYPE OF FIRM: Venture Capital Firm
FUNDING PREFERENCE:
   Seed Funding
   Start-Up Funding
   First-Round Funding
   Second-Round Funding

Third-Round Funding
Fourth-Round Funding
Later-Stage Funding
Leveraged Buyouts
INDUSTRY PREFERENCE:
Communications Technology
Computer Hardware
Computer Software
Medical Technology
Other High Technologies Not Mentioned
GEOGRAPHIC PREFERENCE:
No Preference (U.S.A.)
TYPES OF FUNDS:
Equity (stock purchases)
Minimum: $200,000
Maximum: $2,000,000 First Round
$3,000,000 Total


Piper, Jaffray & Hopwood Incorporated
222 South 9th Street
Minneapolis, MN 55402
612 342 6314

CONTACT: Frank B. Bennett
TYPE OF FIRM: Venture Capital Firm
FUNDING PREFERENCE:
Start-Up Funding
First-Round Funding
Second-Round Funding
Leveraged Buyouts
Public Offerings
INDUSTRY PREFERENCE:
Diversified
GEOGRAPHIC PREFERENCE:
No Preference (U.S.A.)
TYPES OF FUNDS:
Equity (stock purchases)
Loans With Equity Kickers
Minimum: $250,000
Maximum: $1,000,000


Threshold Ventures, Inc.
Suite 200, 430 Oak Grove St.
Minneapolis, MN 55403
612 874 7199

CONTACT: John L. Shannon, Jr.
TYPE OF FIRM: SBIC
FUNDING PREFERENCE:
  Later-Stage Funding
INDUSTRY PREFERENCE:
  Diversified
GEOGRAPHIC PREFERENCE:
  Mid-West
TYPES OF FUNDS:
  Equity (stock purchases)
  Loans With Equity Kickers
  Bonds With Equity Kickers
  Minimum: $50,000
  Maximum: $250,000


*MISSOURI*


Capital For Business, Inc.
11 S. Meramee Ave.—Suite 800
St. Louis, MO 63105
314 854 7427

CONTACT: Timothy P. Nolan
TYPE OF FIRM: Venture Capital Firm
  SBIC
FUNDING PREFERENCE:
  First-Round Funding
  Second-Round Funding
  Later-Stage Funding
  Leveraged Buyouts
  Acquisitions
INDUSTRY PREFERENCE:
  Manufacturing
  Medical Technology
  Services
GEOGRAPHIC PREFERENCE:
  No Preference (U.S.A.)
TYPES OF FUNDS:
  Equity (stock purchases)
  Loans With Equity Kickers
  Minimum: $300,000
  Maximum: $1,000,000

United Missouri Capital Corporation
1010 Grand Ave., Kansas City, MO 64196
PO Box 419226, KCMO 64141-9946
816 556 7333

CONTACT: Joseph M. Kessinger
TYPE OF FIRM: Venture Capital Firm
  SBIC
FUNDING PREFERENCE:
  Second-Round Funding
  Third-Round Funding
  Fourth-Round Funding
  Later-Stage Funding
  Leveraged Buyouts
  Acquisitions
INDUSTRY PREFERENCE:
  Diversified
GEOGRAPHIC PREFERENCE:
  Home State: Missouri/Kansas
TYPES OF FUNDS:
  Equity (stock purchases)
  Loans With Equity Kickers
  Bonds With Equity Kickers
  Minimum: $150,000
  Maximum: $1,500,000


*MONTANA*


Development Corporation of Montana
P.O. Box 916
Helena, MT 59624
406 442 3850

CONTACT: Deanne Degnan
TYPE OF FIRM: Venture Capital Firm
FUNDING PREFERENCE:
  Expansion
  Start-Up Funding
  Leveraged Buyouts
INDUSTRY PREFERENCE:
  Diversified
GEOGRAPHIC PREFERENCE:
  Home State: Montana

TYPES OF FUNDS:
  Equity (stock purchases)
  Loans
  Loans With Equity Kickers
  Minimum: $50,000
  Maximum: $100,000


*NEW HAMPSHIRE*


Granite State Capital, Inc.
P.O. Box 6564, 7 Islington St.
Portsmouth, NH 03801
603 436 5044


CONTACT: Richard S. Carey, Treasurer
TYPE OF FIRM: SBIC
FUNDING PREFERENCE:
  Start-Up Funding
  First-Round Funding
  Leveraged Buyouts
INDUSTRY PREFERENCE:
  Communications Technology
  Computer Hardware
  Computer Software
  Manufacturing
  Franchise
GEOGRAPHIC PREFERENCE:
  Northeast
TYPES OF FUNDS:
  Equity (stock purchases)
  Loans With Equity Kickers
  Bonds With Equity Kickers
  Minimum: $50,000
  Maximum: $200,000


*NEW JERSEY*


DSV Partners
221 Nassau Street
Princeton, NJ 08542
609 924 6420

CONTACT: Morton Collins
TYPE OF FIRM: Venture Capital Firm
FUNDING PREFERENCE:
  Seed Funding
  Start-Up Funding
  First-Round Funding
  Second-Round Funding
INDUSTRY PREFERENCE:
  Alternative Energy
  Communications Technology
  Computer Hardware
  Computer Software
  Medical Technology
  Other High Technologies Not Mentioned
GEOGRAPHIC PREFERENCE:
  No Preference (U.S.A.)
TYPES OF FUNDS:
  Equity (stock purchases)
  Loans With Equity Kickers
  Bonds With Equity Kickers
  Minimum: $250,000
  Maximum: $750,000—$1,250,000

MBW Management Inc.
365 South St.
Mortistown, NJ 07960
201 285 5533

CONTACT: Robert E. Savage
TYPE OF FIRM: Venture Capital Firm
FUNDING PREFERENCE:
  Start-Up Funding
  Leveraged Buyouts
INDUSTRY PREFERENCE:
  Diversified
GEOGRAPHIC PREFERENCE:
  No Preference  (U.S.A.)
TYPES OF FUNDS:
  Equity (stock purchases)
  Loans With Equity Kickers
  Minimum: $250,000
  Maximum: $2,000,000

*NEW MEXICO*

Albuquerque Small Business Investment Co.
P.O. Box 487
Albuquerque, NM 87102
505 247 0145

CONTACT: Albert T. Ussery
TYPE OF FIRM: SBIC
FUNDING PREFERENCE:
  Leveraged Buyouts
  Second-Round Funding
INDUSTRY PREFERENCE:
  Diversified
GEOGRAPHIC PREFERENCE:
  Immediate Area
  Home State: New Mexico
  Southwest
  Rocky Mountain States
TYPES OF FUNDS:
  Loans With Equity Kickers
  Minimum: $50,000
  Maximum: $100,000

Meadows Ventures
1650 University Blvd., N.E., Suite 500
Albuquerque, NM 87102
505 768 6248

CONTACT: John Farah, Beth Petronis
TYPE OF FIRM: Venture Capital Firm
FUNDING PREFERENCE:
  Start-Up Funding
  First-Round Funding
  Second-Round Funding
  Third-Round Funding
INDUSTRY PREFERENCE:
  Diversified
  Communications Technology
  Computer Hardware
  Computer Software
  Medical Technology
  Other High Technologies Not Mentioned

GEOGRAPHIC PREFERENCE:
  No Preference (U.S.A.)
TYPES OF FUNDS:
  Equity (stock purchases)
  Minimum: $250,000
  Maximum: $2,000,000


*NEW YORK*


Bankers Trust Company
280 Park Ave.
New York, NY 10019
212 850 2906

CONTACT: Peter Santry
TYPE OF FIRM: Investment Banking Firm
FUNDING PREFERENCE:
  Second-Round Funding
  Later-Stage Funding
  Leveraged Buyouts
INDUSTRY PREFERENCE:
  Diversified
  Manufacturing
  Retail
GEOGRAPHIC PREFERENCE:
  No Preference (U.S.A.)
TYPES OF FUNDS:
  Equity (stock purchases)
  Loans
  Loans With Equity Kickers
  Minimum: $5,000,000
  Maximum: Open


Bradford Ventures Ltd.
1212 Avenue of the Americas
New York, NY 10036
212 221 4620

CONTACT: John L. Pouschine
TYPE OF FIRM: Venture Capital Firm
FUNDING PREFERENCE:
  Leveraged Buyouts
  Acquisitions

INDUSTRY PREFERENCE:
 Diversified
 Manufacturing
 Media
 Wholesale Distribution
GEOGRAPHIC PREFERENCE:
 Northeast
 Middle Atlantic
 Southeast
 Mid-West
TYPES OF FUNDS:
 Equity (stock purchases)
 Minimum: $2,000,000
 Maximum: $10,000,000


BT Capital Corporation
280 Park Avenue
New York, NY 10017
212 850 1916


CONTACT: James G. Hellmuth
TYPE OF FIRM: SBIC
FUNDING PREFERENCE:
 Later-Stage Funding
 Leveraged Buyouts
INDUSTRY PREFERENCE:
 Diversified
 Manufacturing
 Retail
GEOGRAPHIC PREFERENCE:
 No Preference (U.S.A.)
TYPES OF FUNDS:
 Loans With Equity Kickers
 Minimum: $1,000,000
 Maximum: $15,000,000


CMNY Capital L.P.
77 Water Street
New York, NY 10005
212 437 7133


CONTACT: Howard Davidoff
TYPE OF FIRM: SBIC
FUNDING PREFERENCE:
 First-Round Funding

Second-Round Funding
Third-Round Funding
Leveraged Buyouts
INDUSTRY PREFERENCE:
Diversified
GEOGRAPHIC PREFERENCE:
No Preference (U.S.A.)
TYPES OF FUNDS:
Equity (stock purchases)
Loans With Equity Kickers
Minimum: $200,000
Maximum: $2,000,000


CW Group, Inc.
1041 3rd Ave.
New York, NY 10021
212 308 5266

CONTACT: Barry Weinberg
TYPE OF FIRM: Venture Capital Firm
FUNDING PREFERENCE:
Seed Funding
Start-Up Funding
First-Round Funding
INDUSTRY PREFERENCE:
Medical Technology
GEOGRAPHIC PREFERENCE:
No Preference (U.S.A.)
TYPES OF FUNDS:
Equity (stock purchases)
Minimum: $100,000
Maximum: $3,000,000


DeMuth, Folger & Terhune
1 Exchange Plaza at 55 Broadway
New York, NY 10006
212 509 5580

CONTACT: D.F. DeMuth
TYPE OF FIRM: Venture Capital Firm
Investment Banking Firm
FUNDING PREFERENCE:
Start-Up Funding
First-Round Funding

Second-Round Funding
Leveraged Buyouts
Acquisitions
INDUSTRY PREFERENCE:
Communications Technology
Computer Hardware
Computer Software
Medical Technology
Other High Technologies Not Mentioned
Services
GEOGRAPHIC PREFERENCE:
No Preference (U.S.A.)
TYPES OF FUNDS:
Equity (stock purchases)
Bonds With Equity Kickers
Minimum: $300,000
Maximum: $6,000,000


Edwards Capital Company
215 Lexington Ave.
New York, NY 10016
212 686 2568

CONTACT: G. Snyder
TYPE OF FIRM: Venture Capital Firm
    SBIC
FUNDING PREFERENCE:
Start-Up Funding
Public Offerings
INDUSTRY PREFERENCE:
Real Estate
Transportation–Taxi Medallions
GEOGRAPHIC PREFERENCE:
Home State: New York
Immediate Area: New York City
TYPES OF FUNDS:
Loans
Minimum: $10,000
Maximum: $180,000


Erlanger Associates
277 Park Ave.
New York, NY 10172
212 935 1508

CONTACT: Dick Erlanger
TYPE OF FIRM: Investment Banking Firm
  Exec. Search for LBO, Venture & Turnarounds only
FUNDING PREFERENCE:
  Second-Round Funding
  Third-Round Funding
  Fourth-Round Funding
  Later-Stage Funding
  Leveraged Buyouts
  Acquisitions
INDUSTRY PREFERENCE:
  Computer Hardware
  Computer Software
  Manufacturing
GEOGRAPHIC PREFERENCE:
  No Preference (U.S.A.)
TYPES OF FUNDS:
  Equity (stock purchases)
  Minimum: $5,000,000
  Maximum: $100,000,000


Euclid Partners Corporation
50 Rockefeller Plaza, Suite 1022
New York, NY 10020
212 489 1770


CONTACT: Frederick Wilson
TYPE OF FIRM: Venture Capital Firm
FUNDING PREFERENCE:
  First-Round Funding
INDUSTRY PREFERENCE:
  Communications Technology
  Computer Hardware
  Computer Software
  Medical Technology
GEOGRAPHIC PREFERENCE:
  No Preference (U.S.A.)
TYPES OF FUNDS:
  Equity (stock purchases)
  Minimum: $500,000
  Maximum: $1,000,000


Fundex Capital Corporation
525 Northern Boulevard
Great Neck, NY 11021
516 466 8550

CONTACT: Howard Sommer
TYPE OF FIRM: SBIC
FUNDING PREFERENCE:
  First-Round Funding
  Second-Round Funding
  Third-Round Funding
  Fourth-Round Funding
  Later-Stage Funding
  Leveraged Buyouts
  Acquisitions
INDUSTRY PREFERENCE:
  Diversified
GEOGRAPHIC PREFERENCE:
  Northeast
TYPES OF FUNDS:
  Loans
  Loans With Equity Kickers
  Minimum: $50,000
  Maximum: $1,000,000


Irving Capital Corporation
1290 Avenue of the Americas, 29th Floor
New York, NY 10104
212 408 4800

CONTACT: Kathleen Snyder
TYPE OF FIRM: Venture Capital Firm
FUNDING PREFERENCE:
  Third-Round Funding
  Fourth-Round Funding
  Later-Stage Funding
  Leveraged Buyouts
  Acquisitions
INDUSTRY PREFERENCE:
  Diversified
GEOGRAPHIC PREFERENCE:
  No Preference (U.S.A.)
TYPES OF FUNDS:
  Equity (stock purchases)
  Bonds With Equity Kickers
  Minimum: $500,000
  Maximum: $5,000,000

J.H. Whitney & Co.
630 Fifth Ave.
New York, NY
212 757 0500

CONTACT: Any Partner
TYPE OF FIRM: Venture Capital Firm
FUNDING PREFERENCE:
  Start-Up Funding
  First-Round Funding
  Leveraged Buyouts
INDUSTRY PREFERENCE:
  Diversified
GEOGRAPHIC PREFERENCE:
  No Preference (U.S.A.)
TYPES OF FUNDS:
  Equity (stock purchases)
  Minimum: $2,000,000
  Maximum: $5,000,000


Lambda Funds/Drexel Burnham Lambert
55 Broad St.
New York, NY 10004
212 480 6018

CONTACT: Alexandra Mahnkey
TYPE OF FIRM: Venture Capital Firm
  Investment Banking Firm
FUNDING PREFERENCE:
  Second-Round Funding
  Third-Round Funding
  Fourth-Round Funding
  Later-Stage Funding
  Leveraged Buyouts
INDUSTRY PREFERENCE:
  Diversified
GEOGRAPHIC PREFERENCE:
  No Preference (U.S.A.)
TYPES OF FUNDS:
  Equity (stock purchases)
  Minimum: $500,000
  Maximum: $1,000,000

Merrill Lynch R & D Management Inc.
World Financial Center, North Tower (18th Floor)
New York, NY 10128
212 449 3632


CONTACT: Richard G. Minicus
TYPE OF FIRM: Venture Capital Firm
FUNDING PREFERENCE:
  Start-Up Funding
  First-Round Funding
  Second-Round Funding
  Third-Round Funding
INDUSTRY PREFERENCE:
  Communications Technology
  Computer Hardware
  Computer Software
  Medical Technology
  Other High Technologies Not Mentioned
    (Biotechnology, Agricultural technology)
GEOGRAPHIC PREFERENCE:
  No Preference (U.S.A.)
TYPES OF FUNDS:
  Equity (stock purchases)
  Research and Development Limited Partnerships
  Minimum: $500,000
  Maximum: $7,000,000


NatWest USA Capital Corporation
175 Water Street
New York, NY 10038
212 602 1200


CONTACT: Orville G. Aarons, Senior Vice-President and Gen-
eral Manager
TYPE OF FIRM: SBIC
FUNDING PREFERENCE:
  Later-Stage Funding
  Leveraged Buyouts
  Acquisitions
  Public Offerings
INDUSTRY PREFERENCE:
  Diversified
  Alternative Energy
  Manufacturing
  Media

GEOGRAPHIC PREFERENCE:
  No Preference (U.S.A.)
TYPES OF FUNDS:
  Equity (stock purchases)
  Loans With Equity Kickers
  Minimum: $1,000,000
  Maximum: $3,000,000


North Street Capital Corp.
250 North St.—RA-65
White Plains, NY 10625
914 335 7901

CONTACT: Ralph L. McNeal, Sr., Pres.
TYPE OF FIRM: MESBIC
FUNDING PREFERENCE:
  Start-Up Funding
  First-Round Funding
  Second-Round Funding
  Third-Round Funding
  Fourth-Round Funding
  Later-Stage Funding
  Leveraged Buyouts
  Acquisitions
INDUSTRY PREFERENCE:
  Diversified
GEOGRAPHIC PREFERENCE:
  No Preference (U.S.A.)
TYPES OF FUNDS:
  Equity (stock purchases)
  Loans With Equity Kickers
  Minimum: $500,000
  Maximum: $1,200,000


Rothschild Ventures
One Rockefeller Plaza
New York, NY 10020
212 757 6000

CONTACT: Jess L. Belser, President
TYPE OF FIRM: Venture Capital Firm
FUNDING PREFERENCE:
  Seed Funding
  Start-Up Funding

First-Round Funding
Second-Round Funding
Third-Round Funding
INDUSTRY PREFERENCE:
Diversified
Communications Technology
Computer Hardware
Computer Software
Manufacturing
Media
Medical Technology
Other High Technologies Not Mentioned
Retail
Services
Wholesale Distribution
GEOGRAPHIC PREFERENCE:
No Preference (U.S.A.)
TYPES OF FUNDS:
Equity (stock purchases)
Minimum: $500,000
Maximum: $2,000,000


Tessler & Cloherty, Inc.
155 Main St.
Coldspring, NY 10516
914 265 4244

CONTACT: Daniel Tessler
TYPE OF FIRM: Venture Capital Firm
FUNDING PREFERENCE:
Start-Up Funding
First-Round Funding
Second-Round Funding
Leveraged Buyoyts
INDUSTRY PREFERENCE:
Diversified
GEOGRAPHIC PREFERENCE:
No Preference (U.S.A.)
Minimum: $250,000
Maximum: $1,000,000


Transportation Capital Corp.
60 East 42nd St.
New York, NY 10165
212 697 4885

CONTACT: Melvin Hirsch
TYPE OF FIRM: MESBIC
FUNDING PREFERENCE:
  Start-Up Funding
  First-Round Funding
  Leveraged Buyouts
INDUSTRY PREFERENCE:
  Manufacturing
  Franchise
  Transportations
GEOGRAPHIC PREFERENCE:
  No Preference (U.S.A.)
TYPES OF FUNDS:
  Loans
  Loans With Equity Kickers
  Minimum: $20,000
  Maximum: $2,000,000


Vega Capital Corp.
720 White Plains Road
Scarsdale, NY 10583
914 472 8550

CONTACT: Ronald A. Linden
TYPE OF FIRM: SBIC
FUNDING PREFERENCE:
  Second-Round Funding
  Third-Round Funding
  Fourth-Round Funding
  Later-Stage Funding
  Leveraged Buyouts
  Acquisitions
INDUSTRY PREFERENCE:
  Diversified
  Manufacturing
  Medical Technology
  Services
  Wholesale Distribution
GEOGRAPHIC PREFERENCE:
  Northeast
  Middle Atlantic
  Southeast
TYPES OF FUNDS:
  Loans
  Loans With Equity Kickers

Minimum: $100,000
Maximum: $2,500,000

Venture Opportunities Corp.
110 E. 59th St., 29th Floor
New York, NY 10022
212 832 3737

CONTACT: A. Fred March, President
TYPE OF FIRM: MESBIC
FUNDING PREFERENCE:
  Second-Round Funding
  Later-Stage Funding
  Leveraged Buyouts
  Acquisitions
  Public Offerings
INDUSTRY PREFERENCE:
  Diversified
GEOGRAPHIC PREFERENCE:
  Northeast
  Middle Atlantic
  Southeast
TYPES OF FUNDS:
  Loans With Equity Kickers
  Bonds With Equity Kickers
  Minimum: $100,000
  Maximum: $300,000

Vescon Management, Inc.
301 West 53rd St.
New York, NY 10019

CONTACT: Irvin Barash
TYPE OF FIRM: Venture Capital Firm
FUNDING PREFERENCE:
  Start-Up Funding
  Leveraged Buyouts
  Acquisitions
INDUSTRY PREFERENCE:
  Manufacturing
  Other High Technologies Not Mentioned
GEOGRAPHIC PREFERENCE:
  No Preference (U.S.A.)
TYPES OF FUNDS:
  Equity (stock purchases)

Minimum: $250,000
Maximum: $1,000,000

*OHIO*

Center City MESBIC, Inc.
40 South Main St., Ste. 72
Dayton, OH 45402
513 461 6164

CONTACT: Michael A. Robinson, President
TYPE OF FIRM: MESBIC
FUNDING PREFERENCE:
  Start-Up Funding
  First-Round Funding
  Second-Round Funding
  Third-Round Funding
  Fourth-Round Funding
  Later-Stage Funding
  Leveraged Buyouts
  Acquisitions
INDUSTRY PREFERENCE:
  Diversified
GEOGRAPHIC PREFERENCE:
  Home State: Ohio
TYPES OF FUNDS:
  Equity (stock purchases)
  Loans
  Loans With Equity Kickers
  Bonds
  Bonds With Equity Kickers
  Minimum: $25,000
  Maximum: $150,000

Rubber City Capital Corporation
1144 East Market Street—D/670
Akron, OH 44316-0001
216 796 9167

CONTACT: T. V. Harrington, Manager
TYPE OF FIRM: MESBIC
FUNDING PREFERENCE:
  Start-Up Funding

INDUSTRY PREFERENCE:
  Retail
  Franchise
GEOGRAPHIC PREFERENCE:
  No Preference (U.S.A.)
TYPES OF FUNDS:
  Loans
  Minimum: Open
  Maximum: Open


*OKLAHOMA*


Western Venture Capital Corp.
4880 S. Lewis
Tulsa, OK 74105
918 749 7000


CONTACT: Mr. William B. Baker
TYPE OF FIRM: SBIC
FUNDING PREFERENCE:
  Later-Stage Funding
  Leveraged Buyouts
  Acquisitions
INDUSTRY PREFERENCE:
  Alternative Energy
  Conventional Energy (oil, natural gas, and coal)
  Communications Technology
  Manufacturing
  Medical Technology
GEOGRAPHIC PREFERENCE:
  No Preference (U.S.A.)
TYPES OF FUNDS:
  Equity (stock purchases)
  Loans
  Loans With Equity Kickers
  Minimum: $250,000
  Maximum: $2,000,000


*OREGON*


InterVen II, L.P.
227 S.W. Pine St., Suite 200
Portland, OR 97204
503 223 4334

CONTACT: Kerra Larson
TYPE OF FIRM: Venture Capital Firm
FUNDING PREFERENCE:
  Seed Funding
  Start-Up Funding
  First-Round Funding
  Second-Round Funding
  Third-Round Funding
  Leveraged Buyouts
  Acquisitions
INDUSTRY PREFERENCE:
  Diversified
GEOGRAPHIC PREFERENCE:
  Northwest
  Immediate Area: Southern California
TYPES OF FUNDS:
  Equity (stock purchases)
  Minimum: $750,000
  Maximum: $5,000,000


Norwest Growth Fund, Inc.
1300 Southwest Fifth Ave., Suite 3018
Portland, OR 97201-5683
503 233 6622
503 223 7210 (FAX)

CONTACT: Michael Cohen
TYPE OF FIRM: Venture Capital Firm
FUNDING PREFERENCE:
  Start-Up Funding
  First-Round Funding
  Second-Round Funding
  Third-Round Funding
  Fourth-Round Funding
  Later-Stage Funding
  Leveraged Buyouts
  Acquisitions
INDUSTRY PREFERENCE:
  Diversified
  Communications Technology
  Computer Hardware
  Computer Software
  Manufacturing
  Medical Technology
  Other High Technologies Not Mentioned

Retail
Franchise
GEOGRAPHIC PREFERENCE:
Mid-West
Rocky Mountain States
Northwest
Far West
Southwest
TYPES OF FUNDS:
Equity (stock purchases)
Loans With Equity Kickers
Bonds With Equity Kickers
Minimum: $1,000,000
Maximum: VC: $6,000,000   LBO: $15,000,000

*PENNSYLVANIA*

Capital Corporation of America
225 S. 15th St.—#920
Philadelphia, PA 19102
215 732 1666

CONTACT: Martin Newman, Pres.
TYPE OF FIRM: SBIC
FUNDING PREFERENCE:
First-Round Funding
Second-Round Funding
INDUSTRY PREFERENCE:
Communications Technology
Computer Hardware
Computer Software
Manufacturing
Medical Technology
GEOGRAPHIC PREFERENCE:
No Preference (U.S.A.)
TYPES OF FUNDS:
Loans With Equity Kickers
Minimum: $50,000
Maximum: $300,000

Enterprise Venture Capital Corporation of Pennsylvania
227 Franklin St., Ste. 215
Johnstown, PA 15901
814 535 7597

CONTACT: Donald W. Cowie, Vice President
TYPE OF FIRM: SBIC
FUNDING PREFERENCE:
  Start-Up Funding
  First-Round Funding
  Second-Round Funding
INDUSTRY PREFERENCE:
  Diversified
GEOGRAPHIC PREFERENCE:
  Home State: Pennsylvania
  Immediate Area: Cambria/Somerset Co. Region
TYPES OF FUNDS:
  Equity (stock purchases)
  Loans
  Loans With Equity Kickers
  Minimum: $20,000
  Maximum: $100,000


Genesis Seed Fund, Ltd.
Ste. 105, 3 Great Valley Parkway
Malvern, PA 19355
215 640 1447

CONTACT: Thomas A. Penn
TYPE OF FIRM: Venture Capital Firm
FUNDING PREFERENCE:
  Seed Funding
  Start-Up Funding
  First-Round Funding
INDUSTRY PREFERENCE:
  Diversified
  Communications Technology
  Computer Hardware
  Computer Software
  Manufacturing
  Media
  Medical Technology
  Other High Technologies Not Mentioned
  Services
GEOGRAPHIC PREFERENCE:
  Middle Atlantic
TYPES OF FUNDS:
  Equity (stock purchases)
  Minimum: $250,000
  Maximum: $500,000

Philadelphia Ventures/Century IV Partners
1760 Market St.
Philadelphia, PA 19103
215 751 9444

CONTACT: Thomas R. Morse
TYPE OF FIRM: Venture Capital Firm
FUNDING PREFERENCE:
  Seed Funding
  Start-Up Funding
  First-Round Funding
  Second-Round Funding
  Third-Round Funding
INDUSTRY PREFERENCE:
  Diversified
  Communications Technology
  Computer Hardware
  Computer Software
  Manufacturing
  Media
  Medical Technology
  Other High Technologies Not Mentioned
  Retail
  Services
GEOGRAPHIC PREFERENCE:
  No Preference (U.S.A.)
TYPES OF FUNDS:
  Equity (stock purchases)
  Minimum: $750,000
  Maximum: $2,500,000


*PUERTO RICO*


Venture Capital P.R., Inc.
Edificio Hideca Altos
Calle Caribe #58
Condado, PR 00907

TYPE OF FIRM: MESBIC
FUNDING PREFERENCE:
  Seed Funding
INDUSTRY PREFERENCE:
  Diversified
  Real Estate
  Franchise

GEOGRAPHIC PREFERENCE:
  Home State: Puerto Rico
TYPES OF FUNDS:
  Equity (stock purchases)
  Loans With Equity Kickers
  Minimum: $50,000
  Maximum: $200,000


*TENNESSEE*


International Paper Capital Formation, Inc.
6400 Poplar Ave., Room 10-74
Memphis, TN 38119
901 763 6282

CONTACT: John C. Herman, Vice Pres./Controller
TYPE OF FIRM: MESBIC
FUNDING PREFERENCE:
  Second-Round Funding
INDUSTRY PREFERENCE:
  Manufacturing
GEOGRAPHIC PREFERENCE:
  No Preference (U.S.A.)
TYPES OF FUNDS:
  Loans
  Minimum: $25,000
  Maximum: $300,000


Valley Capital Corporation
Suite 806, Krystal Building
100 West M. L. King Blvd.
Chattanooga, TN 37402
615 265 1557

CONTACT: Faye Donato
TYPE OF FIRM: MESBIC
FUNDING PREFERENCE:
  Second-Round Funding
  Leveraged Buyouts
  Acquisitions
INDUSTRY PREFERENCE:
  Diversified

GEOGRAPHIC PREFERENCE:
  Southeast
TYPES OF FUNDS:
  Loans
  Loans With Equity Kickers
  Minimum: $50,000
  Maximum: $150,000


*TEXAS*


Acorn Ventures, Inc.
2401 Fountainview, Ste. 950
Houston, TX 77057
713 977 7421

TYPE OF FIRM: Venture Capital Firm
FUNDING PREFERENCE:
  Seed Funding
  Start-Up Funding
  First-Round Funding
  Second-Round Funding
  Third-Round Funding
INDUSTRY PREFERENCE:
  Diversified
GEOGRAPHIC PREFERENCE:
  Southwest
TYPES OF FUNDS:
  Equity (stock purchases)
  Loans
  Minimum: $250,000
  Minimum: $1,500,000


Brittany Capital Company
2424 LTV Tower
Dallas, TX 75201
214 954 1515

CONTACT: Steven S. Peden, Genl. Partner
TYPE OF FIRM: SBIC
FUNDING PREFERENCE:
  Start-Up Funding
  First-Round Funding
  Public Offerings

INDUSTRY PREFERENCE:
  Diversified
GEOGRAPHIC PREFERENCE:
  No Preference (U.S.A.)
TYPES OF FUNDS:
  Loans With Equity Kickers
  Equity (stock purchases)
  Minimum: $100,000
  Maximum: $175,000


MESBIC Financial Corporation of Dallas
Allied Bank Plaza, Suite 814
12655 N. Central Expressway
Dallas, TX 75243
214 991 1597

CONTACT: Ira P. Harrison
TYPE OF FIRM: MESBIC
FUNDING PREFERENCE:
  First-Round Funding
  Second-Round Funding
INDUSTRY PREFERENCE:
  Diversified
GEOGRAPHIC PREFERENCE:
  Southwest
TYPES OF FUNDS:
  Loans With Equity Kickers
  Minimum: $100,000
  Maximum: $300,000


Criterion Venture Partners
1000 Louisiana, Suite 6200
Houston, TX 77002
713 751 2400

CONTACT: David Wicks, Scott Albert, David Hull
TYPE OF FIRM: Venture Capital Firm
FUNDING PREFERENCE:
  Start-Up Funding
  First-Round Funding
  Second-Round Funding
  Leveraged Buyouts

INDUSTRY PREFERENCE:
  Diversified
  Communications Technology
  Computer Hardware
  Computer Software
  Medical Technology
  Other High Technologies Not Mentioned
GEOGRAPHIC PREFERENCE:
  Southwest
TYPES OF FUNDS:
  Equity (stock purchases)
  Minimum: $500,000
  Maximum: $1,000,000


Curtin & Co., Inc.
1200 Travis, Suite 2050
Houston, TX 77002
713 658 9806

CONTACT: Charles A. Armbrust
TYPE OF FIRM: Venture Capital Firm
FUNDING PREFERENCE:
  Start-Up Funding
  First-Round Funding
  Second-Round Funding
INDUSTRY PREFERENCE:
  Diversified
  Communications Technology
  Computer Hardware
  Computer Software
  Manufacturing
  Medical Technology
GEOGRAPHIC PREFERENCE:
  Southwest
  Home State: Texas
TYPES OF FUNDS:
  Equity (stock purchases)
  Minimum: $500,000
  Maximum: $5,000,000


MESBIC Financial Corporation of Houston
811 Rusk, Ste. 201
Houston, TX 77002
713 228 8321

CONTACT: Mr. Lynn Miller, President
TYPE OF FIRM: MESBIC
FUNDING PREFERENCE:
  Second-Round Funding
  Third-Round Funding
  Fourth-Round Funding
  Leveraged Buyouts
INDUSTRY PREFERENCE:
  Diversified
GEOGRAPHIC PREFERENCE:
  Immediate Area: Houston Market Area
TYPES OF FUNDS:
  Loans
  Loans With Equity Kickers
  Loans with Interest Overrides
  Minimum: $25,000
  Maximum: $250,000


MSI Capital Corporation
6510 Abrams Road, Suite 650
Dallas, TX 75231
214 341 1553


CONTACT: Nick Stanfield
TYPE OF FIRM: Venture Capital Firm
  Investment Banking Firm
FUNDING PREFERENCE:
  Start-Up Funding
  First-Round Funding
  Leveraged Buyouts
INDUSTRY PREFERENCE:
  Diversified
GEOGRAPHIC PREFERENCE:
  Home State: Texas
TYPES OF FUNDS:
  Equity (stock purchases)
  Bonds With Equity Kickers
  Minimum: $100,000
  Maximum: $1,000,000


Republic Venture Group, Inc.
P.O. Box 83100
Dallas, TX 75283-0600
214 922 3500

CONTACT: Robert H. Wellborn
TYPE OF FIRM: Venture Capital Firm
  SBIC
FUNDING PREFERENCE:
  Second-Round Funding
  Third-Round Funding
  Fourth-Round Funding
  Leveraged Buyouts
INDUSTRY PREFERENCE:
  Diversified
  Communications Technology
  Computer Hardware
  Computer Software
  Manufacturing
  Media
  Medical Technology
  Other High Technologies Not Mentioned
  Retail
  Services
  Wholesale Distribution
GEOGRAPHIC PREFERENCE:
  No Preference (U.S.A.)
TYPES OF FUNDS:
  Equity (stock purchases)
  Minimum: $500,000
  Maximum: $2,000,000


San Antonio Venture Group
2300 West Commerce St.
San Antonio, TX 78209
512 223 3633

CONTACT: Tom Woodley
TYPE OF FIRM: SBIC
FUNDING PREFERENCE:
  Second-Round Funding
INDUSTRY PREFERENCE:
  Diversified
GEOGRAPHIC PREFERENCE:
  Immediate Area
TYPES OF FUNDS:
  Loans With Equity Kickers
  Minimum: Open
  Maximum: $200,000

*VIRGINIA*

Atlantic Venture Partners
P.O. Box 1493
Richmond, VA 23212
804 644 5496

CONTACT: Robert H. Pratt
TYPE OF FIRM: Venture Capital Firm
FUNDING PREFERENCE:
  Start-Up Funding
  First-Round Funding
  Second-Round Funding
  Leveraged Buyouts
  Acquisitions
INDUSTRY PREFERENCE:
  Diversified
GEOGRAPHIC PREFERENCE:
  Southeast
TYPES OF FUNDS:
  Equity (stock purchases)
  Loans With Equity Kickers
  Minimum: $300,000
  Maximum: $1,000,000


Basic Investment Corp.
6723 Whittier Ave., Off. 201
McLean, VA 22101
703 356 4300

CONTACT: Ed Sandler
TYPE OF FIRM: MESBIC
FUNDING PREFERENCE:
  Start-Up Funding
INDUSTRY PREFERENCE:
  Franchise
GEOGRAPHIC PREFERENCE:
  Northeast
  Southeast
TYPES OF FUNDS:
  Loans
  Loans With Equity Kickers
  Minimum: $15,000
  Maximum: $75,000

Hillcrest Group
9 S. 12th St.
Richmond, VA 23219
804 643 7358

CONTACT: A. Hogel Ewing, General Partner
TYPE OF FIRM: SBIC
FUNDING PREFERENCE:
  Start-Up Funding
  First-Round Funding
  Second-Round Funding
  Third-Round Funding
  Fourth-Round Funding
  Later-Stage Funding
  Leveraged Buyouts
  Acquisitions
INDUSTRY PREFERENCE:
  Diversified
GEOGRAPHIC PREFERENCE:
  Middle Atlantic
  Southeast
TYPES OF FUNDS:
  Equity (stock purchases)
  Loans With Equity Kickers
  Bonds With Equity Kickers
  Minimum: $500,000
  Maximum: $1,000,000


Souran Funding Corporation
6th Floor Souran Center
One Commercial Plaza
Norfolk, VA 23510
804 441 4041

CONTACT: David A. King, Jr., Allen Kendle
TYPE OF FIRM: SBIC
FUNDING PREFERENCE:
  Second-Round Funding
  Third-Round Funding
  Fourth-Round Funding
  Later-Stage Funding
  Leveraged Buyouts
  Acquisitions
INDUSTRY PREFERENCE:
  Diversified

GEOGRAPHIC PREFERENCE:
  Middle Atlantic
  Southeast
TYPES OF FUNDS:
  Equity (stock purchases)
  Loans With Equity Kickers
  Bonds With Equity Kickers
  Minimum: $250,000
  Maximum: $1,000,000


*WASHINGTON*


Walden Investors
901 14th Place N.E.
Bellevue, WA 98007

CONTACT: Theodore M. Wight, General Partner
TYPE OF FIRM: Venture Capital Firm
FUNDING PREFERENCE:
  Seed Funding
  Start-Up Funding
  First-Round Funding
INDUSTRY PREFERENCE:
  Diversified
GEOGRAPHIC PREFERENCE:
  Northwest
  Far West
TYPES OF FUNDS:
  Equity (stock purchases)
  Minimum: $500,000
  Maximum: $1,500,000


*WEST VIRGINIA*


GASP Ventures, Inc.
P.O. Box 4005
Charleston, WV 25364
304 925 4086

CONTACT: James L. Teed
TYPE OF FIRM: Venture Capital Firm
  State Development Company

FUNDING PREFERENCE:
Start-Up Funding
INDUSTRY PREFERENCE:
Diversified
Communications Technology
Computer Hardware
Computer Software
Manufacturing
GEOGRAPHIC PREFERENCE:
Home State: West Virginia
TYPES OF FUNDS:
Loans With Equity Kickers
Minimum: $50,000
Maximum: $300,000


Ohio Valley Venture Capital Corp.
P.O. Box 1029
Wheeling, WV 26003
304 232 7722

CONTACT: Terry Burkhart
TYPE OF FIRM: Venture Capital Firm
Local or Certified Development Co.
FUNDING PREFERENCE:
Seed Funding
Start-Up Funding
First-Round Funding
Second-Round Funding
Third-Round Funding
Fourth-Round Funding
Later-Stage Funding
Leveraged Buyouts
Acquisitions
Public Offerings
INDUSTRY PREFERENCE:
Diversified
Manufacturing
GEOGRAPHIC PREFERENCE:
Immediate Area: Greater Wheeling, WV
TYPES OF FUNDS:
Equity (stock purchases)
Loans
Leasing
Minimum: $25,000
Maximum: $500,000

Roundtable Venture Fund
1119 Charleston National Plaza
Charleston, WV 25301
304 357 0850

CONTACT: Donald L. Davis
TYPE OF FIRM: Venture Capital Firm
FUNDING PREFERENCE:
  First-Round Funding
INDUSTRY PREFERENCE:
  Diversified
GEOGRAPHIC PREFERENCE:
  Home State: West Virginia
TYPES OF FUNDS:
  Equity (stock purchases)
  Loans
  Loans With Equity Kickers
  Minimum: $50,000
  Maximum: $250,000


*WISCONSIN*


Bando McGlocklin Capital Corporation
13555 Bishops Court, Suite 205
Brookfield, WI 53005
414 784 9010

CONTACT: Kent Eliason, Vice President
TYPE OF FIRM: SBIC
FUNDING PREFERENCE:
  Later-Stage Funding
  Leveraged Buyouts
INDUSTRY PREFERENCE:
  Manufacturing
  Services
  Wholesale Distribution
GEOGRAPHIC PREFERENCE:
  Immediate Area: Southeast Wisconsin
TYPES OF FUNDS:
  Loans—No Equity
  Minimum: $100,000
  Maximum: $1,500,000

Future Value Ventures, Inc.
622 N. Water St., Suite 500
Milwaukee, WI 53202
414 278 0377

CONTACT: William Beckett
TYPE OF FIRM: MESBIC
FUNDING PREFERENCE:
  Start-Up Funding
  First-Round Funding
  Leveraged Buyouts
  Acquisitions
INDUSTRY PREFERENCE:
  Diversified
GEOGRAPHIC PREFERENCE:
  No Preference (U.S.A.)
  Mid-West
TYPES OF FUNDS:
  Loans With Equity Kickers
  Minimum: $100,000
  Maximum: $300,000


Venture Investors of Wisconsin
100 State Street
Madison, WI 53703
608 256 8185

CONTACT: Roger Ganser
TYPE OF FIRM: Venture Capital Firm
FUNDING PREFERENCE:
  Seed Funding
  Start-Up Funding
  First-Round Funding
  Second-Round Funding
  Third-Round Funding
  Fourth-Round Funding
  Later-Stage Funding
  Leveraged Buyouts
  Acquisitions
  Public Offerings
INDUSTRY PREFERENCE:
  Diversified
GEOGRAPHIC PREFERENCE:
  Mid-West
  Prefer Home State

TYPES OF FUNDS:
  Equity (stock purchases)
  Minimum: $50,000
  Maximum: $500,000

*CANADA*

Grayrock Shared Ventures Ltd.
150 King Street West, Ste. 1212
Sun Life Tower
Toronto, Ontario M5H 1J9
416 979 7677

CONTACT: C. Truax, V.P., Administration
TYPE OF FIRM: Venture Capital Firm
FUNDING PREFERENCE:
  Seed Funding
  Start-Up Funding
  First-Round Funding
  Second-Round Funding
  Later-Stage Buyouts
INDUSTRY PREFERENCE:
  Communications Technology
  Manufacturing
  Medical Technology
  Other High Technologies Not Mentioned
  Retail
  Services
  Franchise

GEOGRAPHIC PREFERENCE:
  Northeast
  Southwest
  Immediate Area: Canada
TYPES OF FUNDS:
  Equity (stock purchases)
  Bonds With Equity Kickers
  Minimum: $500,000
  Maximum: $1,000,000

# UNDERWRITING FIRMS

Underwriting firms assist growth-oriented companies that seek funds for expansion purposes or start-up. Some of these funding organizations specialize in small businesses and are listed here. They will help an enterprise sell equity ownership or debt in order to raise funds if the proposition in question has merit in their opinion. Underwriting companies were discussed in Chapter VI.

Advanced Securities and Investments
(303) 779-8811

Alliance Securities
(801) 355-2048

Allied Capital
(800) 628-8094
(303) 790-2480

Alta Investment Co.
(303) 573-7244

Blinder Robinson
(303) 733-8200

Bradley Martin & Appel
(800) 367-7406

Brennan Ross Securities
(800) 237-8723
(303) 220-1451

Brocks Weinger
(212) 837-7414

Brownstone Smith
(305) 771-1211
(800) 626-0359

Capital Securities Group
(303) 493-0563

Castle Securities
(516) 379-3211

Concord Brokerage
(212) 406-3177

Covey & Co.
(801) 521-3830

Cromwell Knight
(305) 481-1797

Dillon Securities
(800) 541-0857
(509) 838-6455

Douglas Breman
(515) 484-5444

Dunhill Investments
(800) 824-1517
(303) 694-0088

Evan Ryan Securities
(303) 321-3336

First Eagle
(800) 525-4348
(303) 694-0088

First Philadelphia
(212) 943-5442

Fitzgerald Talman
(303) 793-0523

General Bond
(303) 733-8437

Gilbert Marshall & Co.
(303) 352-0032

G. S. George
(509) 747-4114

J. J. Kreiger
(212) 608-2844

Johnson & Bowles Co.
(801) 364-1900

K. A. Knapp
(800) 638-8094
(616) 363-6970

Kimbridge & Co.
(800) 328-8322

Kober Financial
(303) 793-3070

Main Street Securities
(801) 531-7447
(800) 426-3076

Malone & Associates
(800) 288-7700
(303) 288-7700

Monarch Funding
(212) 406-4047

Mostel & Taylor
(212) 308-3700

P. B. James
(800) 423-6806
(801) 261-5858

P. B. Jameson
(801) 521-3830

P. K. Hickney
(212) 692-9460

R. A. Johnson
(801) 531-0324

Richfield Securities
(303) 721-7627

Sheridan Securities
(303) 721-7627

Tri-Bradley Investment
(303) 770-7752
(800) 843-6504

USA Capital Management Group
(800) 872-1161
(702) 734-8721

Wakefield Financial
(212) 406-1089

Western Capital Corporation
(801) 532-0230

## Government Sources

### STATE FUNDING PROGRAMS

State governments have realized the importance of a viable business sector to their respective economies. Consequently, many states maintain funding programs, varying in depth and effectiveness, directed to the small business community. Below are the names and addresses of these programs.

*ALABAMA*
Southern Development Council
Alabama Development Office
State Capitol
Montgomery, AL 36130
(205) 263-0048

Industrial Financing Division
135 South Union Street
Montgomery, AL 36130
(205) 264-5441

*ALASKA*
Department of Commerce and Economic Development
Alaska Business Development Center, Inc.
143 E. Ninth Avenue, #250
Anchorage, AK 99501
(907) 279-7427

Alaska Industrial Development Authority
1577 C Street, Suite 304
Anchorage, AK 99501
(907) 274-1651

Division of Investment
P.O. Box D, Suite 740
Juneau, AK 99811
(907) 562-3779
   or
3601 C Street, Suite 740
Anchorage, AK 99503
(907) 465-2510

*ARIZONA*
Development Finance
Department of Commerce
1700 W. Washington, 4th Floor
Phoenix, AZ 85007
(602) 255-5705

Arizona Enterprise Development Corp.
1700 West Washington St., 4th Floor
Phoenix, AZ 85007
(602) 255-5371

*ARKANSAS*
Arkansas Science & Technology Authority
100 Main St., #450
Little Rock, AR 72201
(501) 371-3554

Arkansas Industrial Development Commission
1 State Capitol Mall
Little Rock, AR 72201
(501) 371-7786

*CALIFORNIA*
Office of Small Business
Department of Commerce
1121 L Street, 6th Floor
Sacramento, CA 95814
(916) 445-6545

Loans Guarantee & Direct Loan Program
Office of Local Development
1121 L Street, Suite 600
Sacramento, CA 95814
(916) 322-1398

California Industrial Development
Financing Advisory Commission
9800 South Sepulveda, Suite 820
Los Angeles, CA 90045
(213) 620-2362

SAFE-BIDCO
1014 2nd Street, 3rd Floor
Sacramento, CA 95814
(916) 442-3321

California Pollution Control
Financing Authority
915 Capitol Mall, Room 280
Sacramento, CA 95814
(916) 445-9597

Alternative Energy Source
Financing Authority
915 Capitol Mall, Room 280
Sacramento, CA 95814
(916) 445-9597

*COLORADO*
Division of Commerce and Development
1313 Sherman St., #523
Denver, CO 80203
(303) 866-2205

Housing and Finance Authority
777 Pearl Street
Denver, CO 80203
(303) 861-8962

*CONNECTICUT*
Connecticut Product Development Corp.
93 Oak Street
Hartford, CT 06106
(203) 566-2920

Connecticut Development Authority
217 Washington Street
Hartford, CT 06106
(203) 522-3730

*DELAWARE*
Delaware Development Office
99 Kings Hwy., P.O. Box 1401
Dover, DE 19901
(302) 736-4271

*DISTRICT OF COLUMBIA*
Economic Development Finance Corporation
Office of Business & Economic Development
1111 E. St. N.W., 7th Floor
Washington, DC 20004
(202) 727-6600

*FLORIDA*
Bureau of Business Assistance
Department of Commerce
107 W. Gaines St.
Tallahassee, FL 32399-2000
(904) 487-1314

Florida Department of Commerce
410 Fletcher Building
Tallahassee, FL 32301-8132
(904) 487-0463

*GEORGIA*
International Program for Adv. Technology
Development Center
Georgia Institute of Technology
430 10th St. N.W., #N-116

Atlanta, GA 30318
(404) 894-3575

Department of Community Affairs
40 Marietta St., N.W.
Atlanta, GA 30303
(404) 656-6200

*HAWAII*
Small Business Information Service
c/o Dept. of Planning & Economic Development
240 S. King St., #724
Honolulu, HI 98613
(808) 548-7645

Financial Assistance Branch
Department of Planning & Economic Development
250 South King Street
Honolulu, HI 96813
(808) 548-4616

*IDAHO*
Treasure Valley Certif. Development Corp.
Department of Planning & Development
7270 Potomac Drive
Boise, ID 83704
(208) 322-7033

Division of Community Development
Department of Commerce
State Capitol
Boise, ID 83720
(208) 334-9499

Economic Development and Data
Department of Commerce
Statehouse, Room 108
Boise, ID 83720
(208) 334-4719

*ILLINOIS*
Small Business Finance
Department of Commerce & Community Affairs
620 E. Adams St., 5th Floor
Springfield, IL 62701
(217) 785-2708

Business Innovation Fund & Equity Investment Fund
Small Business Assistance Bureau
Department of Commerce & Community Affairs
620 E. Adams St., 5th Floor
Springfield, IL 62701
(312) 917-2387

Division of Economic Development and Management Assistance
Dept. of Commerce & Community Affairs
620 E. Adams St., 5th Floor
Springfield, IL 62701
(217) 785-6151

Governor's Commission on Science and Technology
State of Illinois
Department of Commerce & Community Affairs
100 West Randolph St., Suite 3-400
Chicago, IL 60601
(312) 917-7179

*INDIANA*
Institute for New Business Ventures
1 N. Capitol, #420
Indianapolis, IN 46204-2248
(317) 634-8418

Corporation for Innovation Development
1 N. Capitol, #520
Indianapolis, IN 46204-2248
(317) 635-7325

Division of Business Expansion
Department of Commerce
1 N. Capitol, #700
Indianapolis, IN 46204-2248
(317) 232-5296

Corporation of Science & Technology
1 N. Capitol, 9th Floor
Indianapolis, IN 46204-2248
(317) 635-3058

Business & Financial Services Division
Indiana Department of Commerce
1 N. Capitol Ave., Suite 700

Indianapolis, IN 46204
(317) 232-8782

Indiana Statewide Cert. Development Corp.
2506 Willowbrook Parkway, Suite 110
Indianapolis, IN 46205
(317) 253-6166

*IOWA*
Iowa Product Development Corporation
Department of Economic Development
200 E. Grand Avenue
Des Moines, IA 50309
(515) 281-7636

Department of Economic Development
Dept. of Business Grants & Loans
200 E. Grand Avenue
Des Moines, IA 50309
(515) 281-3635

Department of Economic Development
Bureau of Technology and Innovation
200 E. Grand Avenue
Des Moines, IA 50309
(515) 281-5459

Iowa Business Development Credit Corp.
Iowa Business Growth Company
901 Insurance Exchange Building
Des Moines, IA 50309
(515) 282-2164

*KANSAS*
Kansas Technology Enterprise Corp.
Department of Commerce
400 W. 8th St., 5th Floor
Topeka, KS 66603
(913) 296-4490

Existing Industry Division
Department of Commerce
400 W. 8th St., 5th Floor
Topeka, KS 66603
(913) 296-2932

Kansas Association of Certified Development Companies
407 S. Main St., Box 8776
Pratt, KS 67124
(316) 672-9421

Kansas Development Credit Corporation
Bank IV Tower, Suite 1030, #1
Town Site Plaza
Topeka, KS 66603
(913) 235-3437

*KENTUCKY*
Small Business Division
Kentucky Commerce Cabinet
Capital Plaza Tower, 22nd Floor
Frankfort, KY 40601
(502) 564-4252

Small Business Division
Kentucky Commerce Cabinet
Capital Plaza Tower, 22nd Floor
Frankfort, KY 40601
(502) 564-4252

Business Investor Network
Office of Economic Development
515 W. Market St., #650
Louisville, KY 40202
(502) 587-3051

Kentucky Development Finance Authority
Capital Plaza Tower, 24th Floor
Frankfort, KY 40601
(502) 564-4554

Area Dev. Districts Program
Department of Local Government
Capital Plaza Tower, 2nd Floor
Frankfort, KY 40601
(502) 564-2382

*LOUISIANA*
Department of Commerce
Office of Commerce & Industry
P.O. Box 94185

Baton Rouge, LA 70804-9185
(504) 342-5361

Louisiana Small Business Equity Corp.
P.O. Box 14942
Baton Rouge, LA 70898-4942
(504) 925-4112

*MAINE*
Finance Authority of Maine
Western Avenue
Augusta, ME 04330
(207) 623-3263

Maine Capital Corporation
70 Center Street
Portland, ME 04101
(207) 772-1001

*MARYLAND*
Industrial Development Finance Authority
World Trade Center, 7th Floor
401 E. Pratt Street
Baltimore, MD 21202
(301) 333-1832

Small Business Development
Financing Authority, 7th Floor
401 E. Pratt Street
Baltimore, MD 21202
(301) 333-4270

Office of Business & Industrial Development
Md. Dept. of Economic & Community Development
45 Calvert Street
Annapolis, MD 21401
(301) 269-3514

*MASSACHUSETTS*
Office of Financial Assistance
Dept. of Commerce & Development
100 Cambridge St.
Boston, MA 02202
(617) 727-3048

Massachusetts Technology Development Corp.
84 State Street, #500
Boston, MA 02109
(617) 723-4920

Industrial Services Program
Massachusetts Production Development Corp.
12 Marshall Street
Boston, MA 02108
(617) 727-8186

Massachusetts Industrial Finance Agency
400 Atlantic Avenue
Boston, MA 02110
(617) 451-2477

Massachusetts Capital Resources
545 Boylston Street
Boston, MA 02116
(617) 536-3900

Massachusetts Business Development Corp.
1 Liberty Square
Boston, MA 01902
(617) 350-8877

Massachusetts Community Dev. Finance Corp.
131 State Street, #600
Boston, MA 02109
(617) 742-0366

Massachusetts Government Land Banks
6 Beacon Street, #900
Boston, MA 02108
(617) 727-8257

*MICHIGAN*
Strategic Funds
Law Building
P.O. Box 30234
Lansing, MI 48909
(517) 373-6378

Michigan Investment Division
Department of the Treasury

Treasury Building
Lansing, MI 48922
(517) 373-4330

Michigan Product Development Corp.
23935 Research Drive
Farmington Hill, MI 48024
(313) 451-0180

*MINNESOTA*
Economic Development Authority
150 E. Kellogg Blvd.
St. Paul, MN 55101
(612) 296-6616

Financial Management Division
Minnesota Dept. of Energy and Economic Development
900 American Center Building
150 E. Kellogg Boulevard
St. Paul, MN 55101
(612) 297-3547

*MISSISSIPPI*
Research and Development Center
3825 Ridgewood Road
Jackson, MS 39211
(601) 982-6513

Rural Missouri Incorporated
1108 Missouri Boulevard
Jefferson City, Missouri 65101
(314) 635-0136

Department of Economic Development
P.O. Box 849
Jackson, MS 39205
(601) 359-3437

*MISSOURI*
High Technology Program
Higher Education Applied Projects Fund and Seed Capital Tax Credits
Department of Economic Development
P.O. Box 118
Jefferson City, MO 65102
(314) 751-3906

Finance Program
Missouri Industrial Development Board
Department of Economic Development
P.O. Box 118
Jefferson City, MO 65102
(314) 751-0717

Missouri Agriculture and Small Business Development Authority
P.O. Box 630
Jefferson City, MO 65102
(314) 751-3359

*MONTANA*
Montana Science and Technical Alliance
Department of Commerce
1424 Ninth Street
Helena, MT 59620
(406) 444-3707

Development Corp. of Montana
Department of Commerce
1424 Ninth Street
Helena, MT 59620
(406) 422-3850

Economic Development Board
Department of Commerce
Lee Metcalf Building
1520 E. Sixth Avenue
Helena, MT 59620
(406) 444-2090

Bond Program Manager
Montana Economic Development Board
Helena, MT 59620
(406) 444-2090

*NEBRASKA*
Research and Development Authority
NBC Center, #646
Omaha, NE 68508
(402) 475-5109

Nebraska Venture Group
University of Nebraska at Omaha

Omaha, NE 68162
(402) 554-2521

Nebraska Investment Finance Authority
1033 O Street, #304
Lincoln, NE 68509
(402) 477-4406

Small Business Division
Department of Economic Development
301 Centennial Mall South
P.O. Box 94666
Lincoln, NE 68509
(402) 471-3765

Business Development Corporation of Nebraska
Stuart Building, Suite 1044
Lincoln, NE 68508
(402) 474-3855

*NEVADA*
Nevada State Development Corporation
350 S. Center St., #310
Reno, NV 89501
(702) 323-3625

Nevada Office of Community Services
Small Business Revitalization Program
1100 E. William, #117
Carson City, NV 89710
(702) 885-4602

Nevada Financial Development Corporation
One East Liberty Street, Suite 602
Reno, NV 89501
(702) 323-3033

*NEW HAMPSHIRE*
Industrial Development Authority
4 Park Street
Concord, NH 03301
(603) 271-2391

New Hampshire Business Development Corp.
10 Fort Eddy Road
Concord, NH 03301
(603) 224-1432

*NEW JERSEY*
Comm. on Science and Technology
122 W. State St., CN-832
Trenton, NJ 08625
(609) 984-1671

N.J. Development Authority for Small
   Business & Women & Minority Businesses
c/o Department of Commerce & Economic Dev.
1 West State Street, CN-835
Trenton, NJ 08625
(609) 984-4442

Economic Development Authority
Capital Place One, CN-990
Trenton, NJ 08625
(609) 292-0192

Urban Programs
Department of Commerce & Economic Development
1 West State Street, CN-829
Trenton, NJ 08625
(609) 292-2765

Office of Small Business Assistance
Department of Commerce & Economic Development
1 West State Street, CN-835
Trenton, NJ 08625
(609) 984-4442

Corporation for Business Assistance in NJ
Capital Place One, CN-990
Trenton, NJ 08625
(609) 633-7737

*NEW MEXICO*
New Mexico Business Development Corporation
6001 Marble N.E., #6
Albuquerque, NM 87110
(505) 268-1316

Economic Development & Tourism Department
State of New Mexico
Joseph M. Montoya Building
1100 Saint Francis Drive
Santa Fe, NM 87503
(505) 827-0305

*NEW YORK*
Corp. for Innovation Development Program
State Science & Technical Foundation
99 Washington Ave., #1730
Albany, NY 12210
(518) 473-9471

Job Development Authority
605 Third Avenue
New York, NY 10158
(212) 818-1700

State Urban Development Corporation
1515 Broadway
New York, NY 10036
(212) 930-0334

Empire State Certified Development Corp.
41 State Street
Albany, NY 12207
(518) 463-2268

New York State Science and Technology Foundation
99 Washington Avenue, Suite 1730
Albany, NY 12210
(518) 474-4349

*NORTH CAROLINA*
Small Business Administrator
Department of Commerce
430 N. Salisbury Street
Raleigh, NC 27611
(919) 733-7980

Industrial Financing (for manufacturing)
Department of Commerce
430 N. Salisbury Street
Raleigh, NC 27695
(919) 733-5297

*NORTH DAKOTA*
Economic Development Commission
Liberty Memorial Building
Bismarck, ND 58505
(701) 224-2810

Bank of North Dakota
P.O. Box 5509
Bismarck, ND 58502
(701) 224-5600

North Dakota State Development Credit Corp.
P.O. Box 1212
Bismarck, ND 58502
(701) 223-2288

*OHIO*
Edison Seed Development Fund
Department of Development
65 E. State Street, #200
Columbus, OH 43266-0330
(614) 466-5867

Business Development & Economic Financing
Direct-Loan Program
Department of Development
P.O. Box 1001
Columbus, OH 43266-0101
(614) 466-2317

Small & Developing Business
Department of Development
P.O. Box 1001
Columbus, OH 43266-0101
(614) 466-5700

Construction Contract Bond Assistance Prog.
P.O. Box 1001
Columbus, OH 43266-0101

*OKLAHOMA*
Oklahoma Industrial Finance Authority
205 N.W. 63rd St., #260
Oklahoma City, OK 73116
(405) 521-2182

Oklahoma Industries Authority
3 Santa Fe Plaza
Oklahoma City, OK 73102
(405) 232-9921

Department of Economic Development
5 Broadway Executive Park, Suite 200
6601 Broadway Extension
Oklahoma City, OK 73116-8214
(405) 521-2401

*OREGON*
Oregon Resources & Technology Development Corporation
1 Lincoln Center, #430
10300 S.W. Greenburg Road
Portland, OR 97223
(503) 246-4844

Economic Development Department
595 Cottage St. N.E.
Salem, OR 97310
(503) 378-3732

*PENNSYLVANIA*
Minority Business Development Authority
Department of Commerce
486 Forum Building
Harrisburg, PA 17120
(717) 783-1127

State Bureau of Economic Assistance
Department of Commerce
405 Forum Building
Harrisburg, PA 17120
(717) 787-1909

Ben Franklin Partnership
Pennsylvania Department of Commerce
Forum Building, Room 463
Harrisburg, PA 17120
(717) 787-4147

*PUERTO RICO*
Government Development Bank
Minillas Government Center
P.O. Box 42001
San Juan, Puerto Rico 00940
(809) 726-2525 or 726-4675

Puerto Rico Development Fund
Minillas Government Center

P.O. Box 42001
San Juan, Puerto Rico 00940
(809) 726-2525


*RHODE ISLAND*
Financial Services Division
Department of Economic Development
7 Jackson Walkway
Providence, RI 02903
(401) 277-2601

Rhode Island Industrial Building Authority
Department of Economic Development
7 Jackson Walkway
Providence, RI 02903
(401) 277-2601

Revolving Loan Fund
Department of Economic Development
7 Jackson Walkway
Providence, RI 02903
(401) 277-2601

Rhode Island Business Investment Fund
General Treasurer's Office
State House
Providence, RI 02903
(401) 277-6522

Ocean State Business Development Authority
7 Jackson Walkway
Providence, RI 02903
(401) 277-2601


*SOUTH CAROLINA*
State Development Board
1111 Executive Center Drive
Columbia, SC 29210
(803) 734-1400

Jobs & Economic Development Authority
1203 Gervais Street
Columbia, SC 29201
(803) 734-1345

*SOUTH DAKOTA*
Financial Resources
Governor's Office of Economic Development
Capital Lake Plaza Building
711 Wells
Pierre, SD 57501
(605) 773-5032

South Dakota Department of State Development
711 Wells Avenue
Pierre, SD 57501
(800) 843-8000 (toll-free—out of state)
(800) 952-3625 (in state)

South Dakota Housing Development Authority
P.O. Box 1237
Pierre, SD 57501
(605) 773-3181

Division of Industries & Agricultural Development
South Dakota Department of State Development
711 Wells Avenue
Pierre, SD 57501
(605) 773-5032
(800) 843-8000 (Toll-free)
(800) 952-3625 (In-State)

*TENNESSEE*
Department of Economic & Community Development
Rachel Jackson Building, 8th Floor
320 Sixth Avenue North
Nashville, TN 37219
(615) 741-1888

*TEXAS*
Texas Economic Development Commission
Box 12728 Capitol Station
Austin, TX 78711
(512) 472-5059

*UTAH*
Utah Innovation Foundation
417 Wakara Wy., #195
Salt Lake City, UT 84108-2520
(801) 584-2520

Utah Technological Finance Corp.
419 Wakara Wy., #150
Salt Lake City, UT 84108

Deseret Certified Development Co.
4885 S. 900 East, #304
Salt Lake City, UT 84117
(801) 266-0443

Utah Business Finance Program
Room 6150, State Office building
Salt Lake City, UT 84114
(801) 533-5325

Provo Central Utah Certified Development Company
152 West Center
Provo, UT 84601
(801) 374-1025 or 375-1822

Historic 25th Street Certified Development Company
2450 Washington Boulevard, 6th Floor
Ogden, UT 84401
(801) 399-8397

*VERMONT*
Department of Development
Ag. of Development & Community Affairs
109 State Street
Montpelier, VT 05602
(802) 828-3221

Vermont Industrial Development Authority
58 E. State Street
Montpelier, VT 05602
(802) 223-7226

State Economic Opportunity Office
Waterbury Complex
103 South Main Street
Waterbury, VT 05676
(802) 241-2450

*VIRGINIA*
Virginia Small Business Financing Authority
Office of Small Business & Financial Services

Department of Economic Development
1000 Washington Building
Richmond, VA 23219
(804) 786-3791

*WASHINGTON*
Department of Trade & Economic Development
101 General Administration Building, AX-13
Olympia, WA 98504
(800) 237-1233

Department of Community Development
Ninth & Columbia Building
Olympia, WA 98504
(800) 562-5677
(206) 753-2220

Department of Trade & Economic Development
Community Economic Revitalization Board
101 General Administration Building, AX-13
Olympia, WA 98504
(206) 586-1667

Industrial Revenue Bond Program
Department of Trade & Economic Development
101 General Administration Building, AX-13
Olympia, WA 98504
(206) 586-1667

Community Development Finance Program
Dept. of Community Development
101 General Administration Building, AX-13
Olympia, WA 98504
(800) 562-5677
(206) 586-2274

Development Loan Fund Program
Dept. of Community Development
101 General Administration Building, AX-13
Olympia, WA 98504
(206) 586-8976

*WEST VIRGINIA*
Small Business Development Center Division
Govenor's Office of Community and Industrial Development
State Capitol Complex

Charleston, WV 25305
(304) 348-2960

Economic Development Authority
Governor's Office of Community and Industrial Development
State Capitol Complex
Charleston, WV 25305
(304) 348-3650

West Virginia Certified Development Corp.
1900 Washington Street E
Building 6, Room 525
Charleston, WV 25305
(304) 348-3650

TEDDI Program
Treasurer of States Office
State Capitol Building, Room E147
Charleston, WV 25303
(304) 346-2623

West Virginia Industrial and Trade Jobs
   Development Corporation
Governor's Office
Financial Strategist, M-146
State Capitol
Charleston, WV 25305
(304) 348-0400

*WISCONSIN*
Technology Development Fund
Department of Development
P.O. Box 7970
Madison, WI 53707
(608) 266-5363

Business Development Bond Programs
Housing and Economic Development Authority
P.O. Box 1728
Madison, WI 53701-1728
(800) 362-2767
(608) 266-0191

Linked Deposit Loan Program
Housing & Economic Development Authority
P.O. Box 1728

Madison, WI 53701-1728
(800) 362-2767
(608) 266-2297

Wisconsin Business Development Finance Corp.
P.O. Box 2717
Madison, WI 53701-2717
(608) 258-8830

Seed Capital Fund
Wisconsin Housing & Economic Development Authority
First Wisconsin Building
1 South Pinckey, Suite 500
Madison, WI 53703
(608) 266-7884

Wisconsin Community Capital (WCC)
Wisconsin Community Development Authority
14 West Mifflin Street, Suite 312
Madison, WI 53703
(608) 266-0590

*WYOMING*
Economic Development & Stabilization Board
Herschler Building
122 W. 25th Street
Cheyenne, WY 8002
(307) 777-7284

Wyoming Development Corporation
P.O. Box 3599
Casper, WY 82602
(307) 234-5351

*VIRGIN ISLANDS*
Small Business Development Agency
P.O. Box 2085
St. Thomas, U.S. VI 00801
(809) 774-8784


## U.S. GOVERNMENT FUNDING PROGRAMS

This section contains information on U.S. Government funding programs directed to small businesses. These sources represent an expansion of programs mentioned in Chapter VI.

AGRICULTURAL STABILIZATION AND CONSERVATION SERVICE

## COMMODITY LOANS AND PURCHASES
OBJECTIVES: To improve and stabilize farm income, to assist in bringing about a better balance between supply and demand of the commodities, and to assist farmers in the orderly marketing of their crops.

TYPES OF ASSISTANCE: Direct Payments with Unrestricted Use; Direct Loans. range not available. Loans: $50 to $76,000,000; $13,771.

CONTACT: Agriculture Stabilization and Conservation Service, U.S. Department of Agriculture, P.O. Box 2415, Washington, D.C. 20013. (202) 477-5074.

## COTTON PRODUCTION STABILIZATION
OBJECTIVES: To assure adequate production for domestic and foreign demand for fiber, to protect income for farmers, to hold down Federal costs, to enhance the competitiveness of U.S. cotton for domestic mill use and export, and to conserve our natural resources.

TYPES OF ASSISTANCE: Direct Payments with Unrestricted Use.

RANGE AND AVERAGE OF FINANCIAL ASSISTANCE: $3 to $50,000 per person.

CONTACT: Commodity Analysis Division, Agricultural Stabilization and Conservation Service, P.O. Box 2415, U.S. Department of Agriculture, Washington, D.C. 20013. (202) 447-6734.

## DAILY INDEMNITY PROGRAM
OBJECTIVES: To protect dairy farmers and manufacturers of dairy products who are directed to remove their milk, milk cows or dairy products from commercial markets because of contamination with residues of pesticides resulting from no misaction on the part of the dairy farmer or the manufacturer of the dairy product. Dairy farmers can also be indemnified because of contamination with chemicals or toxic substances, nuclear radiation or fallout.

TYPES OF ASSISTANCE: Direct Payments with Unrestricted Use.

RANGE AND AVERAGE OF FINANCIAL ASSISTANCE: $88 to $95,000; $40,000.

CONTACT: Emergency Operations and Livestock Division, Agricultural Stabilization and Conservation Service, Department of Agriculture, P.O. Box 2415, Washington, D.C. 20013. (202) 447-7673.

## EMERGENCY CONSERVATION PROGRAM
OBJECTIVES: To enable farmers to perform emergency conservation measures to control wind erosion, floods, hurricanes, or other natural disasters and to carry out emergency water conservation or water enhancing measures during periods of severe drought.

TYPES OF ASSISTANCE: Direct Payments for Specified Use.

RANGE AND AVERAGE OF FINANCIAL ASSISTANCE: $3 to $64,000; $1,780.

CONTACT:   Conservation and Environmental Protection Division, Agricultural Stabilization and Conservation Service, Department of Agriculture, P.O. Box 2415, Washington, D.C. 20013. (202) 447-6221.

## FEED GRAIN PRODUCTION STABILIZATION

OBJECTIVES:   To assure adequate production for domestic and foreign demand, to protect income for farmers, to hold down Federal costs, to enhance the competitiveness of United States exports, and to conserve our natural resources.

TYPES OF ASSISTANCE:   Direct Payments with Unrestricted Use.

RANGE AND AVERAGE OF FINANCIAL ASSISTANCE:   $3 to $50,000 per person.

CONTACT:   Commodity Analysis Division, Agricultural Stabilization and Conservation Service, Department of Agriculture, P.O. Box 2415, Washington, D.C. 20013 (202) 447-4417.

## STORAGE FACILITIES AND EQUIPMENT LOANS

OBJECTIVES:   To complement the commodity loan and grain reserve programs by providing financing for needed on farm storage facilities, thereby affording farmers the opportunity for orderly marketing of their crops.

TYPES OF ASSISTANCE:   Direct Loans.

RANGE AND AVERAGE OF FINANCIAL ASSISTANCE:   To be calculated.

CONTACT:   Cotton, Grain and Rice Price Support Division, Agricultural Stabilization and Conservation Service, Department of Agriculture, P.O. Box 2415, Washington, D.C. 20013. (202) 447-8374.

## WHEAT PRODUCTION STABILIZATION

OBJECTIVES:   To assure adequate production for domestic and foreign demand, to protect income for farmers, to hold down Federal costs, to enhance the competitiveness of U.S. exports, and to conserve our natural resources.

TYPES OF ASSISTANCE:   Direct Payments with Unrestricted Use.

RANGE AND AVERAGE OF FINANCIAL ASSISTANCE:   As of October 31, 1986, the average deficiency payment per producer for the 1985 crop was $3,725 and the average diversion payment per producer was $1,222. (Feed grain, wheat, cotton and rice deficiency and diversion payments, in total, may not exceed $50,000 to any one person for the 1986 through 1990 crop years.)

CONTACT:   Commodity Analysis Division, Agricultural Stabilization and Conservation Service, Department of Agriculture, P.O. Box 2415, Washington, D.C. 20013. (202) 447-4146.

## NATIONAL WOOL ACT PAYMENTS

OBJECTIVES:   To encourage increased domestic production of wool at prices fair to both producers and consumers in a way that has the least adverse effect on domestic and foreign trade and to encourage producers to improve the quality and marketing of their wool and mohair.

TYPES OF ASSISTANCE:   Direct Payments with Unrestricted Use.

RANGE AND AVERAGE OF FINANCIAL ASSISTANCE: Wool $5 to $336,761; Mohair $5 to $162,607. In fiscal year 1986, the average wool payment was $1,081 and the average mohair payment was $930.

CONTACT: Commodity Analysis Division, Agricultural Stabilization and Conservation Service, Department of Agriculture, P.O. Box 2415, Washington, D.C. 20013. (202) 475-4645.

*WATER BANK PROGRAM*

OBJECTIVES: To conserve surface waters; preserve and improve the Nation's Wetlands; increase migratory waterfowl habitat in nesting, breeding and feeding areas in the U.S.; and secure environmental benefits for the Nation.

TYPES OF ASSISTANCE: Direct Payments for Specified Use.

RANGE AND AVERAGE OF FINANCIAL ASSISTANCE: From $8 to $65 per acre; $15.69.

CONTACT: Conservation and Environmental Protection Division, Agricultural Stabilization and Conservation Service, Department of Agriculture, P.O. Box 2415, Washington, D.C. 20013. (202) 447-6221.

*AGRICULTURAL CONSERVATION PROGRAM*

OBJECTIVES: Control of erosion and sedimentation, encourage voluntary compliance with Federal and State requirements to solve point and nonpoint source pollution, improve water quality, encourage energy conservation measures, and assure a continued supply of necessary food and fiber for a strong and healthy people and economy. The program will be directed toward the solution of critical soil, water, energy, woodland, and pollution abatement problems on farms and ranches.

TYPES OF ASSISTANCE: Direct Payments for Specified Use.

RANGE AND AVERAGE OF FINANCIAL ASSISTANCE: $3 to $3,500; $990.

CONTACT: Conservation and Environmental Protection Division, Agricultural Stabilization and Conservation Service, Department of Agriculture, P.O. Box 2415, Washington, D.C. 20013. (202) 447-6221.

*FORESTRY INCENTIVES PROGRAM*

OBJECTIVES: To bring private non-industrial forest land under intensified management; to increase timber production; to assure adequate supplies of timber; and to enhance other forest resources through a combination of public and private investments on the most productive sites on eligible individual or consolidated ownerships of efficient size and operation.

TYPES OF ASSISTANCE: Direct Payments for Specified Use.

RANGE AND AVERAGE OF FINANCIAL ASSISTANCE: $3 to $10,000 per year; $1,600.

CONTACT: Conservation and Environmental Protection Division, Agricultural Stabilization and Conservation Service, Department of Agriculture, P.O. Box 2415, Washington, D.C. 20013. (202) 382-9036.

*RICE PRODUCTION STABILIZATION*
   OBJECTIVES: To assure adequate production for domestic and foreign
   demand to protect income for farmers, to hold down Federal costs, to enhance
   the competitiveness of U.S. exports, and to conserve our natural resources.
   TYPES OF ASSISTANCE: Direct Payments with Unrestricted Use.
   RANGE AND AVERAGE OF FINANCIAL ASSISTANCE: $3 to $50,000 per
   person.
   CONTACT: Commodity Analysis Division, Agricultural Stabilization and Con-
   servation Service, Department of Agriculture, P.O. Box 2415, Washington,
   D.C. 20013. (202) 447-5954.

*GRAIN RESERVE PROGRAM*
   OBJECTIVES: To insulate sufficient quantities of grain from the market to
   increase prices to farmers. To improve and stabilize farm income and to assist
   farmers in the orderly marketing of their crops.
   TYPES OF ASSISTANCE: Direct Payments with Unrestricted Use.
   RANGE AND AVERAGE OF FINANCIAL ASSISTANCE: $25 to $79,500;
   $1,300.
   CONTACT: Cotton, Grain and Rice Price Support Division, Agricultural Stabilization and Conservation Service, Department of Agriculture, P.O. Box
   2415, Washington, D.C. 20013. (202) 382-9886.

*RURAL CLEAN WATER PROGRAM*
   OBJECTIVES: (1) To achieve improved water quality in the most cost-effective
   manner possible in keeping with the provisions of adequate supplies of food,
   fiber, and a quality environment, and (2) to develop and test programs, policies, and procedures for the control of agricultural nonpoint source pollution.
   TYPES OF ASSISTANCE: Direct Payments for Specified Use.
   RANGE AND AVERAGE OF FINANCIAL ASSISTANCE: Maximum payment limited to $50,000 per individual for life of contract.
   CONTACT: Conservation and Environmental Protection Division, Agricultural
   Stabilization and Conservation Service, Department of Agriculture, P.O. Box
   2415, Washington, D.C. 20013. (202) 447-6221.

*CONSERVATION RESERVE PROGRAM*
   OBJECTIVES: To protect the nation's long-term capability to produce food and
   fiber; to reduce soil erosion; to reduce sedimentation; to improve water qual-
   ity; to create a better habitat for fish and wildlife; to curb production of
   surplus commodities; and to provide some needed income support for farmers.
   TYPES OF ASSISTANCE: Direct Payments for Specified Use.
   RANGE AND AVERAGE OF FINANCIAL ASSISTANCE: $50 to $50,000;
   $4,000.
   CONTACT: Conservation and Environmental Protection Division, Agricultural
   Stabilization and Conservation Service, Department of Agriculture, P.O. Box
   2415, Washington, D.C. 20013. (202) 447-6221.

## BUREAU OF INDIAN AFFAIRS

*INDIAN LOANS—ECONOMIC DEVELOPMENT*
  OBJECTIVES:  To provide assistance to Indians, Alaska Natives, tribes, and
    Indian organizations to obtain financing from private and governmental sources
    which serve other citizens. When otherwise unavailable, financial assistance
    through the Bureau is provided eligible applicants for any purpose that will
    promote the economic development of a Federal Indian Reservation.
  TYPES OF ASSISTANCE:  Direct Loans; Guaranteed/Insured Loans; Provi-
    sion of Specialized Services.
  RANGE AND AVERAGE OF FINANCIAL ASSISTANCE:   $1,000 to over
    $1,000,000; $100,000.
  CONTACT:  Director, Office of Indian Services, Bureau of Indian Affairs, 18th
    and C Streets, N.W., Rm 4600, Washington, D.C. 20245. (202) 343-3657.

*TRAINING AND TECHNICAL ASSISTANCE—INDIAN TRIBAL GOVERNMENTS*
  OBJECTIVES:  To aid Indian Tribes to exercise self-determination in accord
    with Public Law 93-638.
  TYPES OF ASSISTANCE:  Project Grants (Contracts); Advisory Services and
    Counseling; Provision of Specialized Services; Training.
  RANGE AND AVERAGE OF FINANCIAL ASSISTANCE:   Varies with needs
    of individual tribes and availability of funds.
  CONTACT:  Division Chief, Office of Indian Services, Code 480 Division of
    Self Determination Services, 1951 Constitution Avenue, N.W., Washington,
    D.C. 20240. (202) 343-4796.

## DEPARTMENT OF ENERGY

*ENERGY-RELATED INVENTIONS*
  OBJECTIVES:  To encourage innovation in developing non-nuclear energy
    technology by providing assistance to individual and small business companies
    in the development of promising energy-related inventions.
  TYPES OF ASSISTANCE:  Project Grants; Use of Property, Facilities and
    Equipment; Advisory Services and Counseling; Dissemination of Technical
    Information.
  RANGE AND AVERAGE OF FINANCIAL ASSISTANCE:   Past awards aver-
    age $65,000.
  CONTACT:  Director, NBS Office of Energy-Related Inventions, National
    Bureau of Standards, Gaithersburg, MD 20899, (301) 975-5500; or Director,
    Energy-Related Inventions Program (CE-12), 1000 Independence Avenue, SW,
    Washington, D.C. 20585. (202) 586-1478.

*BASIC ENERGY SCIENCES, HIGH ENERGY AND NUCLEAR PHYSICS, MAG-
NETIC FUSION ENERGY, HEALTH AND ENVIRONMENTAL RESEARCH, PRO-
GRAM ANALYSIS AND FIELD OPERATIONS MANAGEMENT*

OBJECTIVES: To provide financial support for fundamental research in the basic sciences and advanced technology concepts and assessments in fields related to energy.

TYPES OF ASSISTANCE: Project Grants (Contracts).

RANGE AND AVERAGE OF FINANCIAL ASSISTANCE: $10,000 to $2,000,000; $100,000/$200,000.

CONTACT: Division of Acquisition and Assistance Management, Office of Energy Research, Department of Energy, Mail Stop G-256, Washington, D.C. 20545. (301) 353-4946.

*COAL LOAN GUARANTEES*

OBJECTIVES: To encourage and assist small and medium sized coal producers to increase production of underground low sulfur coal, to reduce the sulfur content of raw coal through coal preparation, and to enhance competition in the coal industry.

TYPES OF ASSISTANCE: Guaranteed/Insured Loans.

RANGE AND AVERAGE OF FINANCIAL ASSISTANCE: No minimum, but up to $30 million per applicant and all affiliates. Average of $1.1 million.

CONTACT: Project Manager, Coal Loan Guarantee Program, Department of Energy, Room C-156, Germantown, MD 20545. (301) 353-4348 or (301) 353-2603.

*OFFICE OF MINORITY ECONOMIC IMPACT LOANS*

OBJECTIVES: To provide direct loans to minority business enterprises (MBE) to assist them in financing bid or proposal preparation costs they would incur in pursuing Department of Energy work, enabling such MBE's to participate in Department of Energy research, development, demonstration and contract activities.

TYPES OF ASSISTANCE: Direct Loans

RANGE AND AVERAGE OF FINANCIAL ASSISTANCE: $1,000 to $25,000; $5,000.

CONTACT: Office of Minority Economic Impact, MI-3.2, Department of Energy, Forrestal Building, Room 5B-110, Washington, D.C. 20585.

*NUCLEAR WASTE DISPOSAL SITING*

OBJECTIVES: To provide for the development of repositories for the disposal of high level radioactive waste and spent nuclear fuel.

TYPES OF ASSISTANCE: Project Grants; Project Grants (Cooperative Agreements).

RANGE AND AVERAGE OF FINANCIAL ASSISTANCE: $200,000 to $8,000,000, depending on program phase.

CONTACT: Office of Civilian Radioactive Nuclear Waste Management. (202) 586-9692.

*INDUSTRIAL ENERGY CONSERVATION*

OBJECTIVES: To increase industrial energy use efficiency and to promote the substitution of abundant, preferably renewable fuels for scarce fuels in the industrial sector. The primary objective of this program is to perform research and development of high risk technologies and assist in the transfer of energy efficient technologies and practices. Assistance may be used in support of industrial research and development as well as technical reports, conferences, guidebooks or other means of disseminating information relating to energy conservation.

TYPES OF ASSISTANCE:    Project Grants (Cooperative Agreements).

RANGE AND AVERAGE OF FINANCIAL ASSISTANCE:    $10,000 to $5,000,000; $1,400,000.

CONTACT:    Office of Industrial Program, CE-14, Department of Energy, Washington, D.C. 20585. (202) 586-9495.

## RENEWABLE ENERGY RESEARCH AND DEVELOPMENT

OBJECTIVES:    To conduct a balanced, long-term research effort in the following energy technologies; solar buildings, photovoltaics, solar thermal, biomass, alcohol fuels, urban waste, wind, ocean, geothermal and small scale hydropower. Grants will be offered to develop and transfer to the nonfederal sector various renewable energy technologies.

TYPES OF ASSISTANCE:    Project Grants

RANGE AND AVERAGE OF FINANCIAL ASSISTANCE:    From $118,000 to $183,000.

CONTACT:    Renewable Energy—Research and Technology Integration, Department of Energy, Washington, D.C. 20585. (202) 586-9282.

### ECONOMIC DEVELOPMENT ADMINISTRATION

## ECONOMIC DEVELOPMENT—BUSINESS DEVELOPMENT ASSISTANCE

OBJECTIVES:    To sustain industrial and commercial viability in designated areas by providing financial assistance to businesses that create or retain permanent jobs, expand or establish plants in redevelopment areas for projects where financial assistance is not available from other sources, on terms and conditions that would permit accomplishment of the project and further economic development in the area.

TYPES OF ASSISTANCE:    Loan Guarantees/Grants

RANGE AND AVERAGE OF FINANCIAL ASSISTANCE:    $500,000 to $111,100,000; $2,000,000.

CONTACT:    Economic Development Administration, Room H7844, Herbert C. Hoover Building, Department of Commerce, Washington, D.C. 20230. (202) 377-5067.

## SPECIAL ECONOMIC DEVELOPMENT AND ADJUSTMENT ASSISTANCE PROGRAM—SUDDEN AND SEVERE ECONOMIC DISLOCATION AND LONG-TERM ECONOMIC DETERIORATION

OBJECTIVES:    To assist State and local areas develop and/or implement strategies designed either to arrest and reverse problems associated with sudden and severe economic dislocation such as plant closings (SSED), or an erosion and long-term decline in the area's economy (LTED).

TYPES OF ASSISTANCE: Project Grants
RANGE AND AVERAGE OF FINANCIAL ASSISTANCE: No specific minimum or maximum size.
CONTACT: Director, Economic Adjustment Division, Economic Development Administration, Room H7217, Herbert C. Hoover Building, Department of Commerce, Washington, D.C. 20230. (202) 337-2659.

## FARMERS HOME ADMINISTRATION

### EMERGENCY LOANS
OBJECTIVES: To assist family farmers, ranchers and aquaculture operators with loans to cover losses resulting from major and/or natural disasters; which can be used for annual farm operating expenses; and, for other essential needs necessary to return disaster victims' farming operation(s) to a financially sound basis in order that they will be able to return to private sources of credit as soon as possible.
TYPES OF ASSISTANCE: Guaranteed/Insured Loans.
RANGE AND AVERAGE OF FINANCIAL ASSISTANCE: $500 to $6,000,000. $35,000 average size for fiscal year 1986; estimate $40,000 average size for fiscal year 1987.
CONTACT: Administrator, Farmers Home Administration, Department of Agriculture, Washington, D.C. 20013. (202) 382-1632.

### FARM LABOR HOUSING LOANS AND GRANTS
OBJECTIVES: To provide decent, safe, and sanitary low-rent housing and related facilities for domestic farm laborers.
TYPES OF ASSISTANCE: Project Grants, Guaranteed/Insured Loans.
RANGE AND AVERAGE OF FINANCIAL ASSISTANCE: Initial Grants $135,000 to $2,300,000; $1,104,120. Initial loans to individuals $20,000 to $200,000; $34,500. Initial loans to organizations $165,000 to $670,000; $292,753.
CONTACT: Multi-Family Housing Processing Division, Farmers Home Administration, Department of Agriculture, Washington, D.C. 20250. (202) 382-1604.

### FARM OPERATING LOANS
OBJECTIVES: To enable operators of not larger than family farms through the extension of credit and supervisory assistance, to make efficient use of their land, labor, and other resources.
TYPES OF ASSISTANCE: Guaranteed/Insured Loans.
RANGE AND AVERAGE OF FINANCIAL ASSISTANCE: Insured loans up to $200,000; guaranteed loans up to $400,000; Insured averaged $47,000 and the guaranteed averaged $114,000 for FY 1985. For FY 1986, the estimated average insured loan is $44,500 and the average guaranteed loan is $92,500.
CONTACT: Director, Farm Real Estate and Production Division, Farmers Home Administration, Department of Agriculture, Washington, D.C. 20250. (202) 447-4572.

*FARM OWNERSHIP LOANS*

OBJECTIVES: To assist eligible farmers and ranchers, including farming cooperatives, partnerships, joint operators and corporations through the extension of credit and supervisory assistance; to become owner-operators of not larger than family farms; to make efficient use of the land, labor and other resources; to carry on sound and successful operations on the farm; and to enable farm families to have a reasonable standard of living.

TYPES OF ASSISTANCE: Guaranteed/Insured Loans

RANGE AND AVERAGE OF FINANCIAL ASSISTANCE: Insured $200,000, guaranteed $300,000. Average insured $92,000, guaranteed $151,800.

CONTACT: Administrator, Farmers Home Administration, Department of Agriculture, Washington, D.C. 20250. (202) 447-7967.

*RURAL RENTAL HOUSING LOANS*

OBJECTIVES: To provide economically designed and constructed rental and cooperative housing and related facilities suited for independent living for rural residents.

TYPES OF ASSISTANCE: Guaranteed/Insured Loans

RANGE AND AVERAGE OF FINANCIAL ASSISTANCE: Initial insured loans to individuals, $60,000 to $450,000; $250,000. Initial insured loans to organizations, $75,000 to $2,000,000; $750,000.

CONTACT: Administrator, Farmers Home Administration, Department of Agriculture, Washington, D.C. 20250. (202) 382-1604.

*SOIL AND WATER LOANS*

OBJECTIVES: To facilitate improvement, protection, and proper use of farmland by providing adequate financing and supervisory assistance for soil conservation; water development, conservation and use; forestation; drainage of farmland; the establishment and improvement of permanent pasture; the development of pollution abatement and control facilities on farms; develop energy conserving measures and other related conservation measures.

TYPES OF ASSISTANCE: Guaranteed/Insured Loans

RANGE AND AVERAGE OF FINANCIAL ASSISTANCE: $4,000 to $101,000; $19,000.

CONTACT: Administrator, Farmers Home Administration, Department of Agriculture, Washington, D.C. 20250. (202) 447-7967.

*INDIAN TRIBES AND TRIBAL CORPORATION LOANS*

OBJECTIVES: To enable tribes and tribal corporations to mortgage lands as security for loans from the Farmers Home Administration to buy additional land within the reservation.

TYPES OF ASSISTANCE: Guaranteed/Insured Loans.

RANGE AND AVERAGE OF FINANCIAL ASSISTANCE: $450,000 to $956,000; $703,000.

CONTACT: Administrator, Farmers Home Administration, Department of Agriculture, Washington, D.C. 20250. (202) 447-7967.

*BUSINESS AND INDUSTRIAL LOANS*

OBJECTIVES:   To assist public, private, and cooperative organizations (profit or nonprofit), Indian tribes or individuals in rural areas to obtain quality loans for the purpose of improving, developing or financing business, industry, and employment and improving the economic and environmental climate in rural communities including pollution abatement and control.

TYPES OF ASSISTANCE:   Guaranteed/Insured Loans

RANGE AND AVERAGE OF FINANCIAL ASSISTANCE: $310,000 to $7,500,000; $1,250,000 (average size).

CONTACT:   Administrator, Farmers Home Administration, Department of Agriculture, Washington, D.C. 20250. (202) 447-7967.

## MARITIME ADMINISTRATION

*CONSTRUCTION—DIFFERENTIAL SUBSIDIES*

OBJECTIVES:   To promote the development and maintenance of the U.S. Merchant Marine by granting financial aid to equalize cost of construction of a new ship in a U.S. shipyard with the cost of constructing the same ship in a foreign shipyard.

TYPES OF ASSISTANCE:   Direct Payments for Specified Use.

RANGE AND AVERAGE OF FINANCIAL ASSISTANCE:   In fiscal year 1981, 3 new buildings and 21 reconstructions were subsidized. The average subsidy per reconstruction in fiscal year 1981 was approximately $3,182,000. (More recent data unavailable.) Historically, subsidy for reconstruction of a vessel has ranged from under $60,000 to almost $7,850,000.

CONTACT:   Associate Administrator for Maritime Aids, Maritime Administration, Department of Transportation, 400 Seventh Street, S.W., Washington, D.C. 20590. (202) 366-0364.

*FEDERAL SHIP FINANCING GUARANTEES*

OBJECTIVES:   To promote construction and reconstruction of ships in the foreign and domestic commerce of the United States by providing Government guarantees of obligations so as to make commercial credit more readily available.

TYPES OF ASSISTANCE:   Guaranteed/Insured Loans

RANGE AND AVERAGE OF FINANCIAL ASSISTANCE:   $1,716,000 to $94,883,000. Average is not entered because it would not be typical of the breadth of the program.

CONTACT:   Associate Administrator for Maritime Aids, Maritime Administration, Department of Transportation, Washington, D.C. 20590. (202) 366-5744.

*OPERATING—DIFFERENTIAL SUBSIDIES*

OBJECTIVES:   To promote development and maintenance of the U.S. Merchant Marine by granting financial aid to equalize cost of operating a U.S. flag ship with the cost of operating a competitive foreign flag ship.

TYPES OF ASSISTANCE:   Direct Payments for Specified Use.

RANGE AND AVERAGE OF FINANCIAL ASSISTANCE: Depending upon the type of service vessel and trade, the per day subsidy payments per ship normally range from about $5,500 to $13,500 with $9,600 as an average.

CONTACT: Associate Administrator for Maritime Aids, Maritime Administration, Department of Transportation, 400 Seventh Street, S.W., Washington, D.C. 20590. (202) 366-0364.

## CAPITAL CONSTRUCTION FUND

OBJECTIVES: To provide for replacement vessels, additional vessels or reconstructed vessels, built and documented under the laws of the United States for operation in the United States foreign, Great Lakes or noncontiguous domestic trades.

TYPES OF ASSISTANCE: Direct Payments for Specified Use.

RANGE AND AVERAGE OF FINANCIAL ASSISTANCE: Applicant receives tax benefits for depositing assets in accordance with the program.

CONTACT: Associate Administrator for Maritime Aids, Maritime Administration, Department of Transportation, Washington, D.C. 20590. (202) 366-0364.

## NATIONAL OCEANIC AND ATMOSPHERIC ADMINISTRATION

## FISHERMEN'S CONTINGENCY FUND

OBJECTIVES: To compensate U.S. commercial fishermen for damage/loss of fishing gear and 50 percent of resulting economic loss due to oil and gas related activities in any area of the Outer Continental Shelf.

TYPES OF ASSISTANCE: Direct Payments with Unrestricted Use.

RANGE AND AVERAGE OF FINANCIAL ASSISTANCE: Range $500 to $25,000; Average $3,883.

CONTACT: Chief, Financial Services Division, National Marine Fisheries Service, 1825 Connecticut Ave., N.W., Washington, D.C. 20235. (202) 673-5421.

## FISHING VESSEL AND GEAR DAMAGE COMPENSATION FUND

OBJECTIVES: To compensate U.S. fishermen for the loss, damage, or destruction of their vessels by foreign fishing vessels and their gear by any vessel.

TYPES OF ASSISTANCE: Direct Payments with Unrestricted Use

RANGE AND AVERAGE OF FINANCIAL ASSISTANCE: $600 to $15,000.

CONTACT: Chief, Financial Services Division, Atten: National Marine Fisheries Service, Department of Commerce, 1825 Connecticut Avenue, N.W., Washington, D.C. 20235. (202) 673-5421.

## FISHING VESSEL OBLIGATION GUARANTEES

OBJECTIVES: To provide government guarantees of private loans to finance or upgrade U.S. fishing vessels or shoreside facilities.

TYPES OF ASSISTANCE: Guaranteed/Insured Loans.

RANGE AND AVERAGE OF FINANCIAL ASSISTANCE: $100,000 to $10,000,000; $500,000.

CONTACT:   Chief, Financial Services Division, National Marine Fisheries Service, Department of Commerce, 1825 Connecticut Ave., N.W., Washington, D.C. 20235. (202) 673-5424.

### FISHERIES DEVELOPMENT AND UTILIZATION RESEARCH AND DEVELOPMENT GRANTS AND COOPERATIVE AGREEMENTS

OBJECTIVES:   To foster the development and strengthening of the fishing industry of the United States and increase the supply of wholesome, nutritious fish and fish products available to consumers.

TYPES OF ASSISTANCE:   Project Grants.

RANGE AND AVERAGE OF FINANCIAL ASSISTANCE:   $5,000 to $2,500,000; $10,000.

CONTACT:   Office of Industry Services, National Marine Fisheries Service, National Oceanic and Atmospheric Administration, Department of Commerce, Washington, D.C. 20235.  (202) 673-5497.

## NATIONAL SCIENCE FOUNDATION

### BIOLOGICAL, BEHAVIORAL, AND SOCIAL SCIENCES

OBJECTIVES:   To promote the progress of science and thereby insure the continued scientific strength of the Nation; to increase the store of scientific knowledge and enhance understanding of major problems confronting the Nation. Most of the research supported is basic in character. The program includes support of research project grants in the following disciplines: cellular and molecular biosciences, behavioral and neural sciences, biotic systems and resources, and social and economic science. Support is also provided for research workshops, symposia and conferences, and for the purchase of scientific equipment. In addition, awards are made to improve the quality of doctoral dissertations in behavioral, neural, and social sciences and in research on bionic systems and resources; and for postdoctoral fellowships in plant and environmental biology.

TYPES OF ASSISTANCE:   Project Grants.

RANGE AND AVERAGE OF FINANCIAL ASSISTANCE:   $5,000 to $1,000,000; $64,364.

CONTACT:   Assistant Director, Biological, Behavioral, and Social Sciences, National Science Foundation, 1800 G Street N.W., Washington, D.C. 20550. (202) 357-9854.

### SCIENTIFIC, TECHNOLOGICAL, AND INTERNATIONAL AFFAIRS

OBJECTIVES:   To provide opportunities for small high-technology business firms to participate in NSF-supported research; promote healthy international relationships and enhance the work of U.S. researchers by facilitating cooperative activities with foreign scientists and institutions; study policy issues related to science and technology, and provide information and analysis for public policies designed to improve the vigor of the Nation's scientific enterprise and its service to society; collect, analyze, and disseminate data to illuminate the status of the nation's science and engineering resources; and extend greater research opportunities to all segments of the scientific community, with special emphasis on participation of women and minority investigators and research faculty from predominately undergraduate institutions. Objectives are pursued through International Cooperative Scientific Activities; programs for Industrial Science and Technological Innovation; Policy Research and Analysis; Science Resources Studies; and Research Initiation and Improvement.

TYPES OF ASSISTANCE: Project Grants.

RANGE AND AVERAGE OF FINANCIAL ASSISTANCE: $1,000 to $800,000; $65,000. International travel awards utilizing U.S.-owned local foreign currencies average $2,700.

CONTACT: Assistant Director, Directorate for Scientific, Technological and International Affairs, National Science Foundation, 1800 G St. N.W., Washington, D.C. 10550. (202) 357-7631.

### RESEARCH, STUDIES, AND PROGRAM ASSESSMENT

OBJECTIVES: To serve a major role in policy formulation, to improve and strengthen science and engineering education in the U.S., and to provide support for leadership efforts of the Foundation in science and engineering education activities. These objectives are accomplished through the collection, analyses, evaluation, and dissemination of information on the condition of education in mathematics, science, and technology.

TYPES OF ASSISTANCE: Project Grants.

RANGE AND AVERAGE OF FINANCIAL ASSISTANCE: $10,000 to $1,516,000; $135,000.

CONTACT: Office of Studies and Program Assessment, National Science Foundation, 1800 G Street, N.W., Washington, D.C. 20550. (202) 357-7425.

### COMPUTER AND INFORMATION SCIENCE AND ENGINEERING

OBJECTIVES: To support research improving the fundamental understanding of computer and information processing, to enhance the training and education of scientists and engineers who contribute to and exploit that understanding, and to provide access to very advanced computing and networking capabilities.

TYPES OF ASSISTANCE: Project Grants.

RANGE AND AVERAGE OF FINANCIAL ASSISTANCE: $15,000 to $9,000,000; $160,000.

CONTACT: Assistant Director, Computer and Information Science and Engineering, National Science Foundation, 1800 G Street, N.W., Room 306, Washington, D.C. 20550. (202) 357-7936.

## OFFICE OF HUMAN DEVELOPMENT SERVICES

### NATIVE AMERICAN PROGRAMS—RESEARCH, DEMONSTRATION, AND EVALUATION

OBJECTIVES: To promote social and economic self-sufficiency for American Indians, Native Hawaiians, and Native Alaskans.

TYPES OF ASSISTANCE: Project Grants (Contracts).

RANGE AND AVERAGE OF FINANCIAL ASSISTANCE: $10,000 to $170,000; $60,000.

CONTACT: Administration for Native Americans, Department of Health and Human Services, Room 5300, 330 Independence Avenue, S.W., Washington, D.C. 20201. Contact Director, Planning and Support Division. (202) 245-7714.

## OVERSEAS PRIVATE INVESTMENT CORPORATION

*FOREIGN INVESTMENT GUARANTEES*

OBJECTIVES: To guarantee loans and other investments made by eligible investors in friendly developing countries and areas.

TYPES OF ASSISTANCE: Guaranteed/Insured Loans

RANGE AND AVERAGE OF FINANCIAL ASSISTANCE: $225,000 to $26,500,000; $10,500,000.

CONTACT: Information Officer, Overseas Private Investment Corporation, Washington, D.C. 20527. (202) 457-7093.

*DIRECT INVESTMENT LOANS*

OBJECTIVES: To make loans for projects in developing countries sponsored by or significantly involving U.S. small business or cooperatives.

TYPES OF ASSISTANCE: Direct Loans

RANGE AND AVERAGE OF FINANCIAL ASSISTANCE: $100,000 to $4,000,000; $971,428.

CONTACT: Information Officer, Overseas Private Investment Corporation, Washington, D.C. 20527. (202) 457-7093.

## SMALL BUSINESS ADMINISTRATION

*ECONOMIC INJURY DISASTER LOANS*

OBJECTIVES: To assist business concerns suffering economic injury as a result of certain Presidential, SBA, and/or Department of Agriculture disaster declarations.

TYPES OF ASSISTANCE: Direct Loans; Guaranteed/Insured Loans (including Immediate Participation Loans).

RANGE AND AVERAGE OF FINANCIAL ASSISTANCE: Direct Loans: Up to $500,000; $72,779.

CONTACT: Disaster Assistance Division, Small Business Administration, 1441 L Street, N.W., Washington, D.C. 20416 (202) 653-6879.

*LOANS FOR SMALL BUSINESSES*

OBJECTIVES: To provide loans to small businesses owned by low-income persons or located in areas of high unemployment.

TYPES OF ASSISTANCE: Direct Loans; Guaranteed/Insured Loans (including Immediate Participation Loans); Advisory Services and Counseling.

RANGE AND AVERAGE OF FINANCIAL ASSISTANCE: Direct Loans: up to $150,000; $56,489. Guarantee Loans: Up to $500,000; $117,524.

CONTACT: Director, Office of Business Loans, Small Business Administration, 1441 L Street, N.W., Washington, D.C. 20416. (202) 653-6570.

## PHYSICAL DISASTER LOANS

OBJECTIVES: To provide loans to the victims of designated physical-type disasters for uninsured losses.

TYPES OF ASSISTANCE: Direct Loans; Guaranteed/Insured Loans (including Immediate Participation Loans).

RANGE AND AVERAGE OF FINANCIAL ASSISTANCE: Direct home loans $120,000 limit plus $60,000 additional in some special cases to refinance existing liens. Direct business loans $500,000 but additional amounts are available for major source of employment. Additional amounts are also available for major source of employment. Additional amounts are also available as guarantee loans made by financial institutions.

CONTACT: Disaster Assistance Division, Small Business Administration, 1441 L Street, N.W., Washington, D.C. 20416. (202) 653-6879.

## SMALL BUSINESS LOANS

OBJECTIVES: To provide direct and guaranteed loans to small businesses which are unable to obtain financing in the private credit marketplace, including agricultural enterprises, but can demonstrate an ability to repay loans granted.

TYPES OF ASSISTANCE: Direct Loans; Guaranteed/Insured Loans (including Immediate Participation Loans).

RANGE AND AVERAGE OF FINANCIAL ASSISTANCE: Direct Loans: Up to $150,000; $59,616. Guarantee Loans: Up to $500,000; $150,127.

CONTACT: Director, Office of Business Loans, Small Business Administration, 1441 L Street, N.W., Washington, D.C. 20416. (202) 653-6570.

## BOND GUARANTEES FOR SURETY COMPANIES

OBJECTIVES: To guarantee surety bonds issued by commercial surety companies for small contractors unable to obtain a bond without a guarantee. Guarantees are for 80 percent of the total amount of the bond.

TYPES OF ASSISTANCE: Guaranteed/Insured Loans (including Guaranteed Surety Bonds).

RANGE AND AVERAGE OF FINANCIAL ASSISTANCE: Size range of contracts awarded and bonded, $2,000 to $1,000,000; $100,000.

CONTACT: Director, Office of Surety Guarantees, Small Business Administration, 4040 North Fairfax Drive, Arlington, VA 22203. (703) 235-2900.

## HANDICAPPED ASSISTANCE LOANS

OBJECTIVES: To provide loans and loan guaranties for nonprofit sheltered workshops and other similar organizations that produce goods and services; and to assist in the establishment, acquisition, or operation of a small business owned by handicapped individuals.

TYPES OF ASSISTANCE: Direct Loans, Guaranteed/Insured Loans (including Immediate Participation Loans).

RANGE AND AVERAGE OF FINANCIAL ASSISTANCE: $500 to $500,000; $95,305, (Direct); $15,000 to $500,000; $166,820. (Guarantee).

CONTACT: Director, Office of Business Loans, Small Business Administration, 1441 L St., N.W., Washington, D.C. 20416. (202) 653-6570.

*SMALL BUSINESS ENERGY LOANS*

OBJECTIVES: To provide loans to small business concerns to finance plant construction, expansion, conversion, or startup; and the acquisition of equipment facilities, machinery supplies or materials to enable such concerns to manufacture, design, market, install or service energy measures.

TYPES OF ASSISTANCE: Direct Loans, Guaranteed/Insured Loans (including Immediate Participation Loans).

RANGE AND AVERAGE OF FINANCIAL ASSISTANCE: Direct loans: Up to $350,000. (Administrative limit is $150,000.) Guarantee loans: Up to $500,000.

CONTACT: Director, Office of Business Loans, Small Business Administration, 1441 L St., N.W., Washington, D.C. 20416. (202) 653-6570.

*SMALL BUSINESS POLLUTION CONTROL FINANCING GUARANTEE*

OBJECTIVES: To provide loans to small businesses to help finance pollution control requirements.

TYPES OF ASSISTANCE: Guaranteed/Insured Loans

RANGE AND AVERAGE OF FINANCIAL ASSISTANCE: $5,000,000; Average approximately $1,300,000.

CONTACT: Director, Pollution Control Financing Staff, Small Business Administrator, 1441 L Street, N.W., Room 808, Washington, D.C. 20416.

*VETERANS LOAN PROGRAM*

OBJECTIVES: To provide loans to small businesses owned by Vietnam-era and disabled veterans.

TYPES OF ASSISTANCE: Direct Loans.

RANGE AND AVERAGE OF FINANCIAL ASSISTANCE: $1,000 to $150,000; $59,960. Guarantee up to $500,000.

CONTACT: Director, Office of Business Loans, Small Business Administration, 1441 L St., N.W., Washington, D.C. 20416. (202) 653-6570.

## CERTIFIED DEVELOPMENT COMPANIES

Certified development companies (CDC) specialize in providing capital to small firms located within specific local or regional areas. They generally prefer asset-based lending deals. CDCs were mentioned in Chapter VI.

Region I (CT, MA, ME, NH, RI, VT)
Region II (NJ, NY Puerto Rico)
Region III (District of Columbia, DE, MD, PA, VA, WV)
Region IV (AL, FL, GA, KY, MS, NC, SC, TN)
Region V (IL, IN, MI MN, OH, WI)
Region VI (AR, LA, NM, OK, TX)
Region VII (IA, KS, MO, NE)
Region VIII (CO, MT, ND, SD, UT, WY)
Region IX (AZ, CA, Guam, HI, NV)
Region X (AK, ID, OR, WA)

REGION: I
Androscoggin Valley Council of Governments
70 Court Street
Auburn, ME 04210
(207) 783-9186
AREA OF OPERATION: Counties of Androscoggin, Franklin and Oxford

REGION: I
Bay Colony Development Corporation
128 Technology Drive
Waltham, MA 02154
(617) 891-3594
AREA OF OPERATION: Through Mass. except Dukes and Nantucket Counties

REGION: I
Bennington County Industrial Corporation
Water Street, Box 357
North Bennington, VT 05257
(802) 442-8975
AREA OF OPERATION: Bennington County

REGION: I
Boston Local Development Corporation
38 Chauncey Street
Boston, MA 02111
(617) 725-3304
AREA OF OPERATION: City of Boston

REGION: I
Brattleboro Development Credit Corporation
5 Grove Street
P.O. Box 1177

Brattleboro, VT 05301
(802) 257-7731
AREA OF OPERATION: Windham and Windsor Counties

REGION: I
Bridgeport Economic Development Corporation
180 Fairfield Avenue
Bridgeport, CT 06601
(203) 355-3800
AREA OF OPERATION: City of Bridgeport

REGION: I
Bristol County Chamber Local Development Corporation
654 Metacom Avenue
P.O. Box 250
Warren, RI 02885
(401) 245-0751
AREA OF OPERATION: Bristol County, RI

REGION: I
Bristol Industrial Development Corporation
57 North Main Street
Bristol, CT 06010
(203) 589-4111
AREA OF OPERATION: Harford County

REGION: I
Brockton Regional Economic Development Corporation
One Legion Parkway
Brockton, MA 02401
(617) 586-0503
AREA OF OPERATION: Designated area of the Brockton Regional Chamber of
    Commerce

REGION: I
Cambridge Economic Development Corporation
859 Massachusetts Avenue
Cambridge, MA 02139
(617) 876-4100
AREA OF OPERATION: City of Cambridge

REGION: I
Cape Cod Economic Development Corporation
165A Route 3A
Box 304
Buzzards Bay, MA 02523

(617) 888-6209
AREA OF OPERATION: Barnstable, Dukes, and Nantucket Counties

REGION: I
Central Vermont Economic Development Corporation
7½ Baily Avenue
Montepelier, VT 05602
(802) 229-0555
AREA OF OPERATION: Washington County plus a part of northern Orange
  County

REGION: I
Coastal Enterprises, Inc.
P.O. Box 268, Middle Street
Wiscasset, ME 04578
(207) 882-7552
AREA OF OPERATION: Eastern Cumberland, Sagadahoc, Lincoln, and
  Knox Counties

REGION: I
Concord Regional Development Corporation
P.O. Box 664
Concord, NH 03301
(603) 228-1872
AREA OF OPERATION: All of Merrimack County

REGION: I
Connecticut Business Development Corporation
217 Washington Street
Hartford, CT 06106
(203) 241-0640
AREA OF OPERATION: Statewide

REGION: I
Cynosure, Inc.
7 Burlington Square
P.O. Box 786
Burlington, VT 05402
(802) 862-5726
AREA OF OPERATION: Greater Burlington Area

REGION: I
East Boston Local Development Corporation
72 Marginal Street
6th Floor
East Boston, MA 02128

364

(617) 569-7174
AREA OF OPERATION: East Boston and its North Shore Environs of Chelsea,
  Revere and Winthrop

REGION: I
Eastern Main Development District
10 Franklin Street
Bangor, ME 04401
(207) 942-6389
AREA OF OPERATION: Six Counties in Eastern Maine

REGION: I
Essex County Economic Development Corporation
36 Federal Street
Room 210
Salem, MA 01970
(617) 741-0201
AREA OF OPERATION: Essex County

REGION: I
Franklin County Industrial Development Corporation
2 Federal Street
St. Albans, VT 05478
(802) 524-2194
AREA OF OPERATION: Complete County of Franklin

REGION: I
Granite State Economic Development Corporation
126 Daniel Street
P.O. Box 1491
Portsmouth, NH 03801
(603) 436-0009
AREA OF OPERATION: Statewide

REGION: I
Greater Hartford Business Development Center, Inc.
c/o HEDCO
15 Lewis Street
Hartford, CT 06103
(203) 527-1301
AREA OF OPERATION: County of Hartford

REGION: I
Greater Peabody Economic Development Corporation
47 Lowell Street
Peabody, MA 01960

(617) 531-0384
AREA OF OPERATION: Peabody and contiguous communities

REGION: I
Housatonic Industrial Development Corporation
57 North Street
Suite 407
Danbury, CT 06810
(203) 743-0306
AREA OF OPERATION: West of Connecticut River

REGION: I
Lewiston Development Corporation
95 Park Street
Lewiston, ME 04240
(207) 783-3505
AREA OF OPERATION: City of Lewiston

REGION: I
Lowell Development and Financial Corporation
100 Merrimack Street
Lowell, MA 01852
(617) 459-9899
AREA OF OPERATION: City of Lowell

REGION: I
Lynn Capital Investment Corporation
598 Essex Street
Lynn, MA 01901
(617) 592-2361
AREA OF OPERATION: City of Lynn

REGION: I
Maine Development Foundation
One Memorial Circle
Box #4
Augusta, ME 04330
(207) 622-6345
AREA OF OPERATION: Statewide

REGION: I
Massachusetts Certified Development Corporation
One Liberty Square
Boston, MA 02109
(617) 350-8877
AREA OF OPERATION: Statewide

REGION: I
Meriden Economic Development Corporation
43½ Colony Street
Meriden, CT 06450
(203) 237-5573
AREA OF OPERATION: The communities of Meriden, Berlin, Cheshire, Durham, Middletown, Middlefield, Southington and Wallingford

REGION: I
New Haven Community Investment Corporation, LDC
770 Chapel Street
#B31
New Haven, CT 06510-3101
(203) 787-6023
AREA OF OPERATION: New Haven County

REGION: I
Newport County Certified Development Company, Inc.
c/o Chamber of Commerce
10 America's Cup Avenue
Newport, RI 02840
(401) 847-8484
AREA OF OPERATION: County of Newport

REGION: I
Northeast Kingdom Development Corporation, Inc.
44 Main Street
St. Johnsbury, VT 05819
(802) 633-2362
AREA OF OPERATION: Caledonia, Essex, and Orleans Counties

REGION: I
Northern Community Investment Corporation
20 Main Street
St. Johnsbury, VT 05819
(802) 748-5101
AREA OF OPERATION: Caledonia, Essex and Orleans Counties in Vermont; also, Coos, Carroll and Grafton in New Hampshire

REGION: I
Northern Regional Planning Commission
Main Street
P.O. Box 779
Caribou, ME 04736
(207) 498-8736
AREA OF OPERATION: Aroostock, Pescatguis (six townships) and Washington (one Community) counties

REGION: I
Ocean State Business Development Authority
St. RI, Dept. of Economic Development
Seven Jackson Walkway
Providence, RI 02903
(401) 277-2601
AREA OF OPERATION: Counties of Providence, Kent, Washington and Newport

REGION: I
Pawtucket Local Commercial and Industrial Development Corp.
200 Main Street
Pawtucket, RI 02860
(401) 724-5201
AREA OF OPERATION: City of Pawtucket and environs

REGION: I
Pittsfield Economic Revitalization Corporation
City Hall, Room 225
Pittsfield, MA 01201
(413) 499-1100
AREA OF OPERATION: County of Berkshire

REGION: I
Plymouth Industrial Development Corporation
130 Court Street
P.O. Box 321
Plymouth, MA 02361
(617) 746-1050
AREA OF OPERATION: Plymouth, Kingston and Plympton

REGION: I
Providence Industrial Development Corporation
Commerce Center
30 Exchange Terrace
Providence, RI 02903
(401) 273-8050
AREA OF OPERATION: City of Providence

REGION: I
Riverside Development Corporation
42 North East Street
Holyoke, MA 01040
(413) 533-7102
AREA OF OPERATION: City of Holyoke

REGION: I
Somerville Local Development Corporation

City Hall
93 Highland Avenue
Somerville, MA 02143
(617) 666-5980
AREA OF OPERATION: Citywide Somerville

REGION: I
South Eastern Economic Development Corporation
88 Broadway
Taunton, MA 02780
(617) 822-1020
AREA OF OPERATION: Bristol County except Easton, portion of Plymouth
   County, Plainville in Norfolk County (Southeastern Pl. & Ec. Dev. Dist.)

REGION: I
South Shore Economic Development Corporation
36 Miller Stile Road
Quincy, MA 02169
(617) 479-1111
AREA OF OPERATION: Plymouth and Norfolk Counties

REGION: I
Vermont 503 Corporation
East 68—East State Street
Montpelier, VT 05602
(802) 828-2385
AREA OF OPERATION: Statewide

REGION: I
Western Massachusetts Small Business Assistance, Inc.
By Bank Tower—Suite 1800
1500 Main Street
Springfield, MA 01115
(413) 734-3124
AREA OF OPERATION: Counties of Hampden, Hampshire and Franklin

REGION: I
Worcester Business Development Corporation
350 Mechanics Tower
100 Front Street
Worcester, MA 01608
(617) 753-2924
AREA OF OPERATION: Worcester County and its contiguous areas

REGION: II
Advancer Local Development Corporation
Del Parque St. #352
Suite 202
Santurce, PR 00912
(809) 721-6797
AREA OF OPERATION: Island of Puerto Rico, except for Municipality of Las
  Marias

REGION: II
Albany Local Development Corporation
City Hall—4th Floor
Albany, NY 12207
(518) 434-5133
AREA OF OPERATION: City of Albany

REGION: II
Buffalo Enterprise Development Corporation
920 City Hall
Buffalo, NY 14202
(716) 855-5017
AREA OF OPERATION: City of Buffalo

REGION: II
Burlington County 503 Development Corporation
49 Rancocas Road
Mt. Holly, NJ 08060
(609) 265-5055
AREA OF OPERATION: County of Burlington

REGION: II
Camden Local Development Company
101 North Seventh Street
Suite 201
Camden, NJ 08102
(609) 963-8230
AREA OF OPERATION: City of Camden

REGION: II
Corporation para el Fomento Economico de la Ciudad Capital
Municipal Building—15th Floor
Chardon Avenue
Hato Rey, PR 00919

(809)
AREA OF OPERATION: Municipality of San Juan

REGION: II
Corporation for Business Assistance in New Jersey
Capital Place One
200 South Warren Street
Trenton, NJ 08625
(609) 292-0187
AREA OF OPERATION: Statewide

REGION: II
Elizabeth Development Company of New Jersey
1045 East Jersey Street
Elizabeth, NJ 07201
(201) 289-0262
AREA OF OPERATION: City of Elizabeth, New Jersey

REGION: II
Empire State Certified Development Corporation
41 State Street
Albany, NY 12207
(518) 463-2268
AREA OF OPERATION: Statewide

REGION: II
Erie Niagara Industrial Development Corporation
107 Delaware Avenue
Buffalo, NY 14202
(716) 849-6685
AREA OF OPERATION: Erie and Niagara Counties

REGION: II
Greater Camden Development Corporation
117 N. Black Horse Pike
Blackwood, NJ 08012
(609) 228-2400
AREA OF OPERATION: Camden County

REGION: II
Greater Lockport Development Corporation
One Locks Plaza
Lockport, NY 14094
(716) 439-6688
AREA OF OPERATION: Citywide Lockport

REGION: II
Greater Rockland Local Development Corporation
1 Blue Hill Plaza
Suite 818
Pearl River, NY 10965
(914) 735-7040
AREA OF OPERATION: Rockland County, New York

REGION: II
Guaynabo Certified Development Company, Inc.
Calle Colton Esquina Jose de Diego (3rd Floor)
Guanyabo, PR 00657
AREA OF OPERATION: Municipality of Guaynabo

REGION: II
Hudson Development Corporation
446 Warren Street
Hudson, NY 12534
(518) 828-3373
AREA OF OPERATION: Columbia County

REGION: II
Jersey City Certified Development Corporation
870 Bergen Avenue
Jersey City, NJ 07306
(201) 292-2899
AREA OF OPERATION: Citywide Jersey City

REGION: II
La Marketing Development Corporation
P.O. Box 331
San Juan, PR 00902
(809) 783-1646
AREA OF OPERATION: The Commonwealth of Puerto Rico except the
  Municipalities of Vieques and Culebra

REGION: II
Long Island Development Corporation
265 Glen Cove Road
Carle Place, NY 11514
(516) 741-5690
AREA OF OPERATION: Counties of Nassau, Suffolk and environs

REGION: II
Metropolitan Business Assistance, LTD

c/o Finance Services Corp.
17 John Street—12th Floor
New York, NY 10038
(212) 566-1358
AREA OF OPERATION: 5 Boroughs of New York—Bronx, Brooklyn, Manhattan,
   Queens and Staten Island

REGION: II
Middlesex County Certified Local Development Company
303 George Street
Suite 304
New Brunswick, NJ 08901
(201) 745-4005
AREA OF OPERATION: Middlesex County

REGION: II
Mohawk Valley Certified Development Corporation
26 West Main Street
P.O. Box 69
Mohawk, NY 13407
(315) 866-4671
AREA OF OPERATION: Oneida, Herkimer, Fulton, Montgomery, and Schoharie
   Counties

REGION: II
Monroe County Industrial Development Corporation
55 St. Paul Street
Rochester, NY 14604
(716) 454-2220
AREA OF OPERATION: Monroe County

REGION: II
N. F. C. Development Corporation
745 Main Street
Niagara Falls, NY 14302
(716) 285-3146
AREA OF OPERATION: City of Niagara Falls

REGION: II
Newark Local Development Corporation
744 Broad Street
Suite 2007
Newark, NJ 07102
(201) 643-2790
AREA OF OPERATION: Citywide Newark

REGION: II
North Puerto Rico Local Development Company, Inc.
Banco Popular Center
Suite 815
Hato Rey, PR 00918
(809) 754-7474
AREA OF OPERATION: Island of Puerto Rico


REGION: II
Ocean County Development Corporation
86 East Water Street
Toms River, NJ 08754
(201) 240-5994
AREA OF OPERATION: Ocean County, New Jersey


REGION: II
Onondaga Industrial Development Second Corporation
100 East Onondaga Street
Syracuse, NY 13202
(315) 470-1343
AREA OF OPERATION: County of Onondaga


REGION: II
Operation Oswego County, Inc.
East 2nd and Schuyler Streets
Post Office Box 4067
Oswego, NY 13126
(315) 343-1545
AREA OF OPERATION: Oswego County


REGION: II
Perth Amboy Local Development Corporation
280-A Madison Avenue
Perth Amboy, NJ 08861
(201) 442-7401
AREA OF OPERATION: The City of Perth Amboy


REGION: II
Port Jervis Development Corporation
14–18 Hammond Street
P.O. Box 3105
Port Jervis, NY 12771
(914) 856-6911
AREA OF OPERATION: Citywide in Port Jervis

REGION: II
Rochester Economic Development Corporation
30 Church Street
Rochester, NY 14614
(716) 428-6808
AREA OF OPERATION: City of Rochester

REGION: II
Southern-Tier Enterprise Development Organization, Inc.
445 Broad Street
Salamanca, NY 14779
(716) 945-5538
AREA OF OPERATION: Counties of Allegany, Cattaraugus and Chautauqua

REGION: II
Syracuse Economic Development Corporation
217 Montgomery Street
Syracuse, NY 13202
(315) 473-5501
AREA OF OPERATION: Citywide in Syracuse, NY

REGION: II
Trenton Business Assistance Corporation
319 East State Street
City Hall Annex
Trenton, NY 08608
(609) 989-3507
AREA OF OPERATION: Citywide in Trenton

REGION: II
Union County Economic Development Corporation
399 Westfield Avenue
Elizabeth, NJ 07208
(201) 527-1166
AREA OF OPERATION: Union County, New Jersey

REGION: III
Accomack-Northampton Housing and Redevelopment Corporation
P.O. Box 387
Accomac, VA 23301
(804) 787-2800
AREA OF OPERATION: Accomack and Northampton Counties

REGION: III
Allentown Economic Development Corporation

801 Hamilton Street
Suite 200
Allentown, PA 18105
(215) 435-8890
AREA OF OPERATION: City of Allentown

REGION: III
Altoona Enterprises, Inc.
1212 Twelfth Avenue
Altoona, PA 16601
(814) 944-6113
AREA OF OPERATION: Counties of Blair and Bedford, Pennsylvania

REGION: III
BEDCO Development Corporation
Suite 2400, Charles Center
36 South Charles Street
Baltimore, MD 21201
(301) 837-9305
AREA OF OPERATION: Citywide Baltimore

REGION: III
Berks County Certified Development Company
GBC Building
645 Pennsylvania Street—S 204
Reading, PA 19601
(215) 376-8405
AREA OF OPERATION: Berks County

REGION: III
Blue Ridge Certified Development Corporation
208 Starling Avenue
Martinsville, VA 24112
(703) 632-8188
AREA OF OPERATION: West Piedmont Planning District (Counties of Franklin,
  Henry, Patrick, and Pittsylvania; also Cities of Martinsville and Danville)

REGION: III
Business and Industrial Development Corporation of Kanawha Valley
818 Virginia Street, East
Charleston, VA 25301
(304) 345-0770
AREA OF OPERATION: Kanawha and Putnam Counties

REGION: III
Capital Region Economic Development Corporation
214 Senate Avenue

Suite 605
Camp Hill, PA 17011
(717) 233-4501
AREA OF OPERATION: Dauphin, Cumberland, and Perry Counties

REGION: III
Central Montgomery County Economic Development Corp.
School and Chestnut Streets
Hatfield, PA 19440
(215) 362-0102
AREA OF OPERATION: Central Montgomery County, Pennsylvania

REGION: III
Central Shenandoah Certified Development Company
119 West Frederick Street
P.O. Box 1337
Staunton, VA 24401
(703) 885-5175
AREA OF OPERATION: Counties of Augusta, Bath, Highland, Rockingham and
    Rockbridge and Cities of Buena Vista, Harrisonburg, Lexington, Staunton &
    Waynesboro

REGION: III
Central Virginia Economic Development Corporation
P.O. Box 2526
Lynchburg, VA 24501
(804) 845-3493
AREA OF OPERATION: Counties of Amherst, Appomattox, and Campbell; Cities
    of Bedford and Lynchburg

REGION: III
Chester County Small Business Assistance Corporation (The)
750 Pottstown Pike
Exton, PA 19341
(215) 363-2569
AREA OF OPERATION: Chester County

REGION: III
Crater Development Company
Monument Professional Building
1964 Wakefield Street
Petersburg, VA 23805
(804) 861-1668
AREA OF OPERATION: Cities of Colonial Heights, Emporia, Hopewell & Peters-
    burg; Chesterfield, Dinwiddie, Greensville, Pr. George, Surry & Sussex Counties

REGION: III
Cumberland-Allegany County Industrial Foundation, Inc.
1 Commerce Drive
Cumberland, MD 21502
(301) 777-5968
AREA OF OPERATION: Cumberland-Allegany County

REGION: III
Delaware County Economic Development Center, Inc.
602 E. Baltimore Pike
Media, PA 19063
(215) 565-7575
AREA OF OPERATION: County of Delaware

REGION: III
Delaware Development Corporation
99 Kings Highway
P.O. Box 1401
Dover, DE 19903
(302) 736-4408
AREA OF OPERATION: Statewide

REGION: III
Easton Economic Development Corporation
650 Ferry Street
Easton, PA 18042
(215) 257-0249
AREA OF OPERATION: Northampton County

REGION: III
Economic and Business Development Corp. of Montgomery County, MD
164 Rollins Avenue
Rockville, MD 20852
(301) 984-0999
AREA OF OPERATION: Montgomery County

REGION: III
Erie County Local Development Corporation
Suite 500, City Hall
Erie, PA 16501
(814) 455-0961
AREA OF OPERATION: Citywide Erie

REGION: III
Fairmont Industrial and Credit Corporation

200 Fairmont Avenue
P.O. Box 208
Fairmont, WV 26555
(304) 363-0447
AREA OF OPERATION: Marion County


REGION: III
Growth Funds Development Company
151 South Warner Road
Wayne, PA 19087
(215) 687-4519
AREA OF OPERATION: Delaware, Montgomery and Philadelphia Counties


REGION: III
JEDECO, Inc.
P.O. Box 237
Charles Town, WV 25414
(304) 725-9761
AREA OF OPERATION: Jefferson County


REGION: III
Johnstown Area Regional Industries Cert. Development Corp.
551 Main Street
East Building, Suite 203
Johnstown, PA 15901
(814) 535-8695
AREA OF OPERATION: Cambria and Somerset Counties


REGION: III
Keystone Small Business Assistance Corporation
311 North Broad Street
P.O. Box 407
Lansdale, PA 19446
(215) 368-4880
AREA OF OPERATION: Bucks and Montgomery Counties


REGION: III
Lake County Development Corporation
123 S. Mecklenburg Avenue
P.O. Box 150
South Hill, VA 23970
(804) 447-7101
AREA OF OPERATION: Counties of Brunswick, Mecklenburg and Halifax; Cities
   of South Hill and South Boston

REGION: III
MetroAction, Inc.
P.O. Box 431
Scranton, PA 18501
(717) 342-7713
AREA OF OPERATION: Counties of Lackawanna, Luzerne and Monroe

REGION: III
Mid-Atlantic Certified Development Company (The)
Maryland National Bank Building
10 Light Street, 32nd Floor
Baltimore, MD 21202
(301) 539-2449
AREA OF OPERATION: State of Maryland except Allegany County and City of
  Baltimore

REGION: III
Mid-Ohio Valley Development Corporation
P.O. Box 247
925 Market Street
Parkersburg, WV 26101
(304) 485-3801
AREA OF OPERATION: Tyler, Pleasants, Wood, Ritchie, Wirt, Jackson, Roone,
  and Calhoun Counties

REGION: III
Middle Monongahela Industrial Development Association, Inc.
P.O. Box 491
Donora, PA 15033
(412) 379-5600
AREA OF OPERATION: Middle Monongahela Valley Region

REGION: III
New Castle County Economic Development Corporation
One Commerce Center
Suite 500
Wilmington, DE 19801
(302) 656-5050
AREA OF OPERATION: New Castle County, Delaware

REGION: III
New River Valley Development Corporation
1612 Wadsworth Street
Radford, VA 24143
(703) 639-9314

AREA OF OPERATION: New River Valley Planning District, City of Radford, Counties of Floyd, Giles, Montgomery and Pulaski

REGION: III
Newport News Pulse Development Corporation
2400 Washington Avenue
Newport News, VA 23607
(804) 247-8777
AREA OF OPERATION: Mercury Blvd. Chessie System tracks S. boundaries of prop. fronting S. side 23rd St. and James River

REGION: III
North Central Business Development, Inc.
122 Center Street
Ridgway, PA 15753
(814) 772-6901
AREA OF OPERATION: Cameron, Clearfield, Elk, Jefferson, McKean and Potter Counties

REGION: III
Northern Virginia Local Development Company, Inc.
8300 Boone Boulevard
Suite 450
Vienna, VA 22180
(703) 790-0600
AREA OF OPERATION: Cities: Alexandria, Falls Church, Manassas & M. Park, Fairfax & Winchester; Arlington, Fairfax, Frederick, Loudon, Pr. William, Clarke, Page, Shenandoah, Warren

REGION: III
OVIBDC CDC, Inc.
12th and Chapline Streets
P.O. Box 1029
Wheeling, WV 26003
(304) 232-2772
AREA OF OPERATION: Ohio, Marshall, and Wetzel Counties

REGION: III
PIDC Local Development Corporation
123 South Broad Street
Fidelity Building, 22nd Floor
Philadelphia, PA 19109
(215) 735-5050
AREA OF OPERATION: City and County of Philadelphia

REGION: III
Philadelphia Industrial Loan Fund, Inc.

One East Penn. Sq. Building
Philadelphia, PA 19107
(215) 568-2630
AREA OF OPERATION: City and County of Philadelphia


REGION: III
Piedmont Regional Opportunities
P.O. Box P
Farmville, VA 23901
(804) 392-6105
AREA OF OPERATION: Amelia, Buckingham, Charlotte, Cumberland, Lunen-
    burg, Nottoway, and Prince Edward Counties—Planning District #14


REGION: III
Pittsburgh Countywide Corporation, Inc.
437 Grant Street
Frick Building, Suite 1220
Pittsburgh, PA 15219
(412) 471-1030
AREA OF OPERATION: Allegheny County


REGION: III
Pocono Northeast Enterprise Development Corporation
1151 Oak Street
Pittston, PA 18640
(717) 655-5587
AREA OF OPERATION: Carbon, Lackawanna, Luzerne, Monroe, Pike, Schuylkill
    and Wayne Counties


REGION: III
Portsmouth Certified Development Corporation
801 Crawford Street
Portsmouth, VA 23704
(804) 393-8989
AREA OF OPERATION: City of Portsmouth


REGION: III
Potomac Valley Area Development Corporation
Post Office Box 887
Grant Industrial Park
Petersburg, WV 26847
(304) 257-1221
AREA OF OPERATION: Grant, Hapshire, Hardy, Mineral, and Pendleton Coun-
    ties


REGION: III
Prince George's County Financial Services Corporation

9200 Basil Court
Suite 200
Landover, MD 20785
(301) 386-5600
AREA OF OPERATION: Prince George's County, Maryland

REGION: III
Quaker State Certified Development Company, Inc.
230 South Broad Street
Philadelphia, PA 19102
(215) 735-3843
AREA OF OPERATION: Philadelphia, Montgomery, Bucks, Delaware, and Chester Counties

REGION: III
Rappahannock Economic Development Corporation
904 Princess Ann Street
P.O. Box 863
Fredericksburg, VA 22401
(703) 373-2897
AREA OF OPERATION: Caroline, King George, Stafford and Spotsylvania Counties and the City of Fredericksburg

REGION: III
Richmond Renaissance Development Corporation
600 East Broad Street
Suite 960
Richmond, VA 23219
(804) 644-0404
AREA OF OPERATION: City of Richmond, Virginia

REGION: III
SEDA-COG Local Development Corporation
R. D. #1
Lewisburg, PA 17837
(717) 524-4491
AREA OF OPERATION: Centre, Clinton, Columbia, Juniata, Lycoming, Mifflin, Montour, Northumberland, Snyder, Union, Perry Counties

REGION: III
Small Enterprise Development Company
1600 Pennsylvania Avenue
York, PA 17404
(717) 846-2970
AREA OF OPERATION: York County, Pennsylvania

REGION: III
Southwestern Pennsylvania Economic Development District
110 Market Street
Pittsburgh, PA 15222
(412) 391-1240
AREA OF OPERATION: Allegheny, Armstrong, Beaver, Butler, Greene, Indiana,
   Fayette, Washington, and Westmoreland Counties

REGION: III
Uniform Region Nine Certified Development Corporation
Biery Building, Suite 406
Franklin, PA 16323
(814) 437-3024
AREA OF OPERATION: Clarion, Crawford, Erie, Forest, Lawrence, Mercer,
   Venango and Warren Counties

REGION: III
Urban Business Development Corporation
201 Granby Mall Building
Suite 1000
Norfolk, VA 23510
(804) 623-2691
AREA OF OPERATION: City of Norfolk

REGION: III
Urban Local Development Corporation
714 Market Street
Sovereign Building—Suite 433
Philadelphia, PA 19106
(215) 561-6600
AREA OF OPERATION: Philadelphia County, PA

REGION: III
Virginia Economic Development Corporation
413 East Market Street
Suite 102
Charlottesville, VA 22901
(804) 972-1720
AREA OF OPERATION: Albemarle, Fluvanna, Greene, Louisa and Nelson Coun-
   ties, and City of Charlottesville

REGION: III
Virginia Peninsula Economic Development Council
610 Thinble Shoals Blvd.
P.O. Box 6000

Newport News, VA 23606
(804) 873-0000
AREA OF OPERATION: VA Peninsula-Counties of Gloucester, James City, York
and Cities of Hampton, Newport News, Poquoson and Williamsburg

REGION: III
Virginia Statewide Development Company, Inc.
1000 Washington Building
Room 1116
Richmond, VA 23219
(804)
AREA OF OPERATION: Statewide

REGION: III
Washington, D.C. Local Development Corporation
1350 "E" Street, N.W.
Room 201
Washington, D.C. 20004
(202) 727-6605
AREA OF OPERATION: Washington, D.C.

REGION: III
West Virginia Certified Development Corporation
State Capitol Complex
Building 6, Room 525
Charleston, WV 25305
(304) 348-3691
AREA OF OPERATION: Statewide

REGION: III
Western Virginia Development Company
145 W. Campbell Avenue
Suite 500
Roanoke, VA 24011
(703) 343-4416
AREA OF OPERATION: Fifth Planning District including Alleghany, Botetourt,
Craig & Roanoke Counties; Cities of Covington, Clifton Forge & Roanoke;
Town of Vinton

REGION: III
Wilmington Local Development Corporation
618 Market Street Mall
Suite 306
Wilmington, DE 19801
(302) 571-9087
AREA OF OPERATION: Citywide Wilmington

REGION: IV
Advancement, Inc.
500 North Walnut Street
Lumberton, NC 28358
(919) 738-4851
AREA OF DEVELOPMENT: Anson, Bladen, Columbus Harnett, Hoke, Moore, Richmond, Robeson, Sampson, and Scotland

REGION: IV
Alabama Community Development Corporation
228 West Valley Avenue
Suite 111
Birmingham, AL 35209
(205) 945-4996
AREA OF DEVELOPMENT: State of Alabama except Sumter, Choctaw and Washington Counties

REGION: IV
Albemarle Development Authority, Inc.
512 South Church Street
P.O. Box 646
Hertford, NC 27944
(919) 426-5755
AREA OF DEVELOPMENT: Camden, Chowan, Currituck, Dare, Gates, Hyde, Pasquotank, Perquimans, Tyrrell, and Washington Counties

REGION: IV
Appalachian Development Corporation
P.O. Box 6668
50 Grand Avenue
Greenville, SC 29606
(803) 242-9733
AREA OF DEVELOPMENT: Anderson, Cherokee, Greenville, Oconee, Pickens and Spartanburg Counties

REGION: IV
Areawide Development Corporation
5616 Kingston Pike
P.O. Box 19806
Knoxville, TN 37919
AREA OF DEVELOPMENT: Scott, Campbell, Claiborne, Anderson, Union, Morgan, Roane, Loudon, Monroe, Blount, Knox, Grainger Hamblen, Jefferson, Cocke, Sevier

REGION: IV
Asheville-Buncombe Development Corporation

P.O. Box 1010
Asheville, NC 28802-1011
(704) 258-0317
AREA OF DEVELOPMENT: The County of Buncombe and its Municipalities

REGION: IV
Atlanta Local Development Company
230 Peachtree Street, N.W.
Suite 1810
Atlanta, GA 30303-1591
(404) 658-7066
AREA OF DEVELOPMENT: Citywide Atlanta

REGION: IV
Barren River Development Council
P.O. Box 154
Bowling Green, KY 42102
(502) 721-2381
AREA OF DEVELOPMENT: Allen, Barren, Butler, Edmonson, Hart, Logan,
   Metcalfe, Monroe, Simpson, Warren Counties, Southcentral Kentucky

REGION: IV
Berkeley Charleston Dorchester Regional Development Corp.
Charleston Business & Technology Ct.
701 East Bay Street, Suit 1-548
Charleston, SC 29403
(803) 723-7267
AREA OF DEVELOPMENT: Berkeley, Charleston and Dorchester Counties
   excluding the City of Charleston

REGION: IV
Buffalo Trace Area Development District, Inc.
327 West Second Street
Maysville, KY 41056
(606) 564-6894
AREA OF DEVELOPMENT: Bracken, Fleming, Lewis, Mason and Robertson Countie

REGION: IV
Business Growth Corporation of Georgia (The)
4000 Cumberland Parkway
Suite 1200A
Atlanta, GA 30339
(404) 434-0273
AREA OF DEVELOPMENT: Statewide

REGION: IV
CSRA Local Development Corporation
2123 Wrightsboro Road
P.O. Box 2800
Augusta, GA 30904
(404) 828-2356
AREA OF DEVELOPMENT: 13 county area in East Central Georgia

REGION: IV
Capital Economic Development Corporation
820 Clay Street
Raleigh, NC 27605
(919) 832-4524
AREA OF DEVELOPMENT: Durham, Wake, and Orange Counties

REGION: IV
Catawba Regional Development Corporation
100 Dave Lyle Blvd.
P.O. Box 682
Rock Hills, SC 29730
(803) 324-3161
AREA OF DEVELOPMENT: Chester, Lancaster, Union and York Counties

REGION: IV
Central Florida Areawide Development Company, Inc.
490 East Davidson Street
Bartow, FL 33830
(813) 533-4146
AREA OF DEVELOPMENT: DeSoto, Hardee, Polk, Highlands & Okeechobee
    Counties

REGION: IV
Central Midlands Development Corporation
Suite 155, Dutch Plaza
800 Dutch Square Boulevard
Columbia, SC 29210
(803) 798-1247
AREA OF DEVELOPMENT: Fairfield, Lexington, Newberry and Richland Coun-
    ties

REGION: IV
Central Mississippi Development Company, Inc.
P.O. Box 4935
Jackson, MS 39216

(601) 981-1511
AREA OF DEVELOPMENT: Copiah, Hinds, Madison, Rankin, Simpson, Warren, and Yazoo Counties

REGION: IV
Centralina Development Corporation, Inc.
P.O. Box 35008
Charlotte, NC 28235
(704) 372-2416
AREA OF DEVELOPMENT: Cabarrus, Gaston, Iredell, Lincoln, Mecklenburg, Rowan, Stanly and Union Counties

REGION: IV
Certified Development Company of Mississippi, Inc.
1201 Walter Sillers Building
Jackson, MS 39205
(601) 359-6710
AREA OF DEVELOPMENT: Statewide

REGION: IV
Certified Development Company of Northeast Georgia, Inc.
305 Research Drive
Athens, GA 30610
(404) 542-7064
AREA OF DEVELOPMENT: Barrow, Clarke, Elbert, Greene, Jackson, Madison, Morgan, Oconee, Oglethorpe and Walton Counties

REGION: IV
Charleston Citywide Local Development Corporation
180 Meeting Street
Suite 310
Charleston, SC 29401
(803) 577-7190
AREA OF DEVELOPMENT: Citywide Charleston

REGION: IV
Charlotte Certified Development Corporation
City Hall
600 East Trade Street
Charlotte, NC 28202
(704) 336-2114
AREA OF DEVELOPMENT: Mecklenburg County

REGION: IV
City of Spartanburg Development Corporation
145 Broad Street

P.O. Box 1749
Spartanburg, SC 29304
(803) 596-2108
AREA OF DEVELOPMENT: City of Spartanburg

REGION: IV
Costal Area District Development Authority, Inc.
P.O. Box 1917
127 F Street
Brunswick, GA 31521
(912) 264-7315
AREA OF DEVELOPMENT: Effingham, Chatham, Bryan, Long, Liberty, McIntosh, Glynn, and Camden Cities, not Savannah City

REGION: IV
Columbus Local Development Corporation
P.O. Box 1340
Columbus, GA 31993
(404) 327-0820
AREA OF DEVELOPMENT: Citywide Columbus, GA

REGION: IV
Commonwealth Small Business Development Corporation
2400 Capital Plaza Tower
Frankfort, KY 40601
(502) 564-4320
AREA OF DEVELOPMENT: Statewide

REGION: IV
Covington First Development Corporation
303 Court Street, Room 805
Covington, KY 41011
(606) 292-2264
AREA OF DEVELOPMENT: Citywide Covington

REGION: IV
Cumberland Area Investment Corporation
1225 Burgess Falls Road
Cookeville, TN 38501
(615) 432-4115
AREA OF DEVELOPMENT: Cannon, Clay, Cumberland, DeKalb, Fentress, Jackson, Macon, Overton, Pickett, Putman, Smith, Van Buren, Warren and White Counties

REGION: IV
Development Corporation of Middle Georgia

600 Grand Building
Mulberry Street
Macon, GA 31201
(912) 751-6160
AREA OF DEVELOPMENT: Bibb, Crawford, Houston, Jones, Monroe, Peach
and Twigg Counties

REGION: IV
Economic Development Corporation of East Kentucky
3000 Louisa Street
Catlettsburg, KY 41129
(606) 739-5191
AREA OF DEVELOPMENT: The FIVCO area consisting of four rural and one
urban area (Boyd, Elliott, Greenup, Carter and Lawrence)

REGION: IV
First Imperial Polk Economic Development Corporation
Post Office Box 1909
Bartow, FL 33830
(813) 533-5190
AREA OF DEVELOPMENT: Polk County

REGION: IV
Florida First Capital Finance Corporation, Inc.
Duncan Fletcher Building
101 East Gaines Street, Room 410
Tallahassee, FL 32399-2000
(904) 487-0466
AREA OF DEVELOPMENT: Statewide

REGION: IV
Fulton County Certified Development Corporation
10 Park Place South
Suite 305
Atlanta, GA 30303
AREA OF DEVELOPMENT: Fulton County

REGION: IV
Gateway Certified Development Company, Inc.
P.O. Box 107
Owingsville, KY 40360
(606) 674-6355
AREA OF DEVELOPMENT: Bath, Montgomery, Menifee, Morgan and Rowan
Counties in Kentucky

REGION: IV
Cumberland Area Investment Corporation

1225 Burgess Falls Road
Cookeville, TN 38501
(615) 432-4115
AREA OF DEVELOPMENT: Cannon, Clay, Cumberland, DeKalb, Fentress, Jackson, Macon, Overton, Pickett, Putman, Smith, Van Buren, Warren and White Counties

REGION: IV
Development Corporation of Middle Georgia
600 Grand Building
Mulberry Street
Macon, GA 31201
(912) 751-6160
AREA OF DEVELOPMENT: Bibb, Crawford, Houston, Jones, Monroe, Peach and Twigg Counties

REGION: IV
Economic Development Corporation of East Kentucky
3000 Louisa Street
Catlettsburg, KY 41129
(606) 739-5191
AREA OF DEVELOPMENT: The FIVCO area consisting of four rural and one urban area (Boyd, Elliott, Greenup, Carter and Lawrence)

REGION: IV
First Imperial Polk Economic Development Corporation
Post Office Box 1909
Bartow, FL 33830
(813) 533-5190
AREA OF DEVELOPMENT: Polk County

REGION: IV
Florida First Capital Finance Corporation, Inc.
Duncan Fletcher Building
101 East Gaines Street, Room 410
Tallahassee, FL 32399-2000
(904) 487-0466
AREA OF DEVELOPMENT: Statewide

REGION: IV
Fulton County Certified Development Corporation
10 Park Place South
Suite 305
Atlanta, GA 30303
(404) 525-6205
AREA OF DEVELOPMENT: Fulton County

REGION: IV
Gateway Certified Development Company, Inc.
P.O. Box 107
Owingsville, KY 40360
(606) 674-6355
AREA OF DEVELOPMENT: Bath, Montgomery, Menifee, Morgan and Rowan
  Counties in Kentucky

REGION: IV
Georgia Mountains Regional Economic Development Corp.
1010 Ridge Road
Gainesville, GA 30501
(404) 532-6541
AREA OF DEVELOPMENT: Banks, Dawson, Fosyth, Franklin, Habersham, Hall,
  Hart, Lumpkin, Rabun, Stephens, Towns, Union and White Counties

REGION: IV
Green River 503 Certified Development Corporation
3860 U.S. Highway 60, West
Owensboro, KY 42301
(502) 926-4433
AREA OF DEVELOPMENT: Daviess, Hancock, Henderson, McLean, Ohio,
  Union and Webster Counties

REGION: IV
Greensville Local Development Corporation
206 South Main Street
P.O. Box 2207
Greensville, SC 29602
(803) 242-1250
AREA OF DEVELOPMENT: City of Greenville

REGION: IV
Gulf-Certco, Inc.
P.O. Box 59
#218 Downtown Building
Gulfport, MS 39502
(601) 864-5657
AREA OF DEVELOPMENT: Corporate limits of Gulfport and ten miles outside
  city limits

REGION: IV
Hattiesburg Area Development Corporation
607 Adeline
P.O. Box 1813
Hattiesburg, MS 39401

(601) 545-8880
AREA OF DEVELOPMENT: Hattiesburg Mississippi area and its environs

REGION: IV
Heart of Georgia Area Development Corporation
501 Oak Street
Eastman, GA 31023
AREA OF DEVELOPMENT: Bleckley, Dodge, Laurens, Montgomery, Pulaski,
   Talfair, Treutlen, Wheeler and Wilcox Counties

REGION: IV
Jacksonville Local Development Company, Inc.
Suite 603, FL Theatre Building
128 E. Forsyth Street
Jacksonville, FL 32202
(904) 630-1914
AREA OF DEVELOPMENT: Citywide Jacksonville, Duval County, FL

REGION: IV
Jefferson County Local Development Corporation
515 West Market Street
Suite 650
Louisville, KY 40202
(502) 587-3051
AREA OF DEVELOPMENT: Jefferson County

REGION: IV
Largo Progress, Inc.
P.O. Box 296
Largo, FL 34294-0296
(813) 586-6639
AREA OF DEVELOPMENT: Largo Planning Boundary

REGION: IV
Lincoln Trail Development Association, Inc.
702 College Street Road
Elizabethtown, KY 42701
(502) 769-2393
AREA OF DEVELOPMENT: Lincoln Trail Area Development District (Counties
   of Breckinridge, Grayson, Hardin, LaRue, Marion, Meade, Nelson, & Washington)

REGION: IV
Louisville Economic Development Corporation
609 West Jefferson Street
2nd Floor

Louisville, KY 40202
(502) 587-3051
AREA OF DEVELOPMENT: City of Louisville, KY

REGION: IV
Lowcountry Regional Development Corporation
P.O. Box 98
I-95 at Point South
Yemassee, SC 29924
(803) 726-5536
AREA OF DEVELOPMENT: Lowcountry Region, including Beaufort, Colleton,
   Hampton and Jasper Counties

REGION: IV
Lower Chattahoochee Development Corporation, Inc.
P.O. Box 1908
Columbus, GA 31902
(404) 322-5571
AREA OF DEVELOPMENT: Chattahoochee, Steward, Randolph, Clay, Quitman,
   Harris and Talbot Counties; Russell County, Alabama

REGION: IV
Lower Savannah Regional Development Corporation
P.O. Box 850
Highway 302 North
Aiken, SC 29801
(803) 649-7985
AREA OF DEVELOPMENT: Aiken, Calhoun, Orangeburg, Bamber, Barnwell and
   Allendale Counties

REGION: IV
Marlboro County Small Business Development Co., Inc.
214 East Market Street
P.O. Box 653
Bennettsville, SC 29512
(803) 479-4046
AREA OF DEVELOPMENT: Marlboro County

REGION: IV
McIntosh Trail Area Development Corporation
P.O. Box Drawer A
Barnesville, GA 30204
(404) 358-3647
AREA OF DEVELOPMENT: Butts, Fayette, Henry, Lamer, Newton, Pike, Spald-
   ing and Upson Counties

REGION: IV
Miami Citywide Development, Inc.
311 N.E.—13th Terrace
Miami, FL 33132
(305) 358-1025
AREA OF DEVELOPMENT: Citywide Miami

REGION: IV
Miami-Dade Business Development Corporation
2929 S.W. 3rd Avenue
Suite 200
Miami, FL 33129
(305) 858-9958
AREA OF DEVELOPMENT: Dade County

REGION: IV
Mid-Cumberland Area Development Corporation
501 Union Street
Suite L-100
Nashville, TN 37219
(615) 244-2646
AREA OF DEVELOPMENT: Cheatham, Davidson, Dickson, Houston, Humphreys, Montgomery, Robertson, Rutherford, Stewart, Sumner, Trousdale, Williamson and Wilson

REGION: IV
Mid-East Certified Development Corporation, Inc.
P.O. Box 1787
Washington, NC 27889
(919) 946-1038
AREA OF DEVELOPMENT: Counties of Beaufort, Bertie, Martin and Hertford

REGION: IV
Middle Flint Area Development Corporation
P.O. Box 6
Ellaville, GA 31806
(912) 937-2561
AREA OF DEVELOPMENT: Crisp, Dooly, Macon, Marion, Schley, Sumter, Taylor and Webster Counties

REGION: IV
Neuse River Development Authority, Inc.
P.O. Box 1717
New Bern, NC 28560
(919) 638-3185

AREA OF DEVELOPMENT: Carteret, Craven, Duplin, Greene, Jones, Lenoir, Onslow, Pamlico, and Wayne Counties

REGION: IV
North Central Florida Areawide Development Company, Inc.
10–300 S.W. 2nd Avenue
Gainesville, FL 32601
(904) 377-7375
AREA OF DEVELOPMENT: Alachua, Bradford, Columbia, Dixie, Gilchrist, Hamilton, Lafayette, Madison, Suwannee, Taylor, and Union Counties

REGION: IV
North Georgia Certified Development Company
503 West Waugh Street
Dalton, GA 30720
(404) 226-1110
AREA OF DEVELOPMENT: Cherokee, Fannin, Gilmer, Murray, Pickens and Whitfield Counties

REGION: IV
Northern Kentucky Area Development District, Inc.
7505 Sussex Drive, Suite 8
Florence, KY 41042
(606) 283-1885
AREA OF DEVELOPMENT: Kenton, Campbell, Boone, Carroll, Gallatin, Grant, Owen and Pendleton Counties

REGION: IV
Northwest Piedmont Development Corporation, Inc.
280 South Liberty Street
Winston-Salem, NC 27101
(919) 722-9348
AREA OF DEVELOPMENT: Davie, Forsyth, Stokes, Surry and Yadkin Counties

REGION: IV
Oconee Area Development Corporation
Heritage Road
P.O. Box 707
Milledgeville, GA 31061
(912) 453-4328
AREA OF DEVELOPMENT: Baldwin, Hancock, Jasper, Johnson, Putman, Washington, and Wilkinson Counties

REGION: IV
Olde Fayetteville Association, Inc.
2504 Raeford Road

Suite B
Fayetteville, NC 28305
(919) 323-1313
AREA OF DEVELOPMENT: Southeastern N.C.—Bladen, Hope, Lee, Moore, Harrnet, Johnston, Sampson, Cumberland, Scotland, and Robeson Counties

REGION: IV
Orlando Neighborhood Improvement Corporation, Inc.
400 South Orange Avenue
Orlando, FL 32801
(305) 849-2522
AREA OF DEVELOPMENT: Orange County

REGION: IV
Pee Dee Regional Development Corporation
P.O. Box 5719
U.S. Highway 52
Florence, SC 29502
(803) 669-3139
AREA OF DEVELOPMENT: Chesterfield, Darlington, Dillon, Florence, Marion and Marlboro Counties

REGION: IV
Pennyrile Area Development District, Inc.
609 Hammond Plaza
Ft. Campbell Boulevard
Hopkinsville, KY 42240
(502) 886-9484
AREA OF DEVELOPMENT: Caldwell, Christian, Crittenden, Hopkins, Livingston, Lyon, Muhlenberg, Todd and Trigg Counties

REGION: IV
Pitt County Dev. Commission Certified Development Company
201 East Second Street
P.O. Box 755
Greenville, NC 27834
(919) 758-1989
AREA OF DEVELOPMENT: Pitt County

REGION: IV
Purchase Area Development District
P.O. Box 588
Highway 45 North
Mayfield, KY 42066
(502) 247-7175
AREA OF DEVELOPMENT: Ballard, Calloway, Carlisle, Fulton, Graves, Hickman, Marshall and McCracken Counties

REGION: IV
Region D Certified Development Corporation, Inc.
P.O. Box 1820—Furman Road
Executive Arts Building, Suite 11
Boone, NC 28607
AREA OF DEVELOPMENT: Alleghany, Ashe, Avery, Mitchell, Watauga,
Wilkes, and Yancey

REGION: IV
Region E Development Corporation
30 Third Street, N.W.
Hickory, NC 28601
AREA OF DEVELOPMENT: Counties of Alexander, Burke, Caldwell and Catawba

REGION: IV
Region K Certified Development Company, Inc.
238 Orange Street
P.O. Box 709
Henderson, NC 27536
(919) 492-2538
AREA OF DEVELOPMENT: Granville, Franklin, Person, Vance
& Warren Counties

REGION: IV
Roanoke-Tar Rivers Regional Certified Dev. Company, Inc.
1309 S. Weslevan Boulevard
P.O. Drawer 2748
Rocky Mount, NC 27802
(919) 446-5775
AREA OF DEVELOPMENT: Edgecombe, Halifax, Nash, Northampton
and Wilson Counties

REGION: IV
Santee-Lynches Regional Development Corporation
115 N. Harvin Street
P.O. Box 1837
Sumter, SC 29150
(803) 775-9215
AREA OF DEVELOPMENT: Clarendon, Kershaw, Lee and Sumter Counties

REGION: IV
Savannah Certified Development Corporation
Gamble Building
6 East By Street
P.O. Box 1027
Savannah, GA 31402

(912) 235-4156
AREA OF DEVELOPMENT: Chatham County


REGION: IV
Smokey Mountain Development Corporation
100 Industrial Park Drive
Waynesville, NC 28786
(704) 488-6511
AREA OF DEVELOPMENT: Madison, Haywood, Grahame, Cherokee, Clay,
   Macon, Jackson, Transylvania, Henderson, and Swain Counties


REGION: IV
South Central Tennessee Business Development Corp.
P.O. Box 1346
815 South Main Street
Columbia, TN 38402
(615) 381-2041
AREA OF DEVELOPMENT: Bedford, Coffee, Franklin, Giles, Hickman,
   Lawrence, Lewis, Lincoln, Marshall, Maury, Moore, Perry, and Wayne Counties


REGION: IV
South Delta Development Company, Inc.
124 South Broadway Street
P.O. Box 1776
Greenville, MS 38702
(601) 378-3831
AREA OF DEVELOPMENT: Bolivar, Humphreys, Issaquena Sharkey, Sunflower
   and Washington Counties


REGION: IV
South Georgia Area Development Corporation
327 W. Savannah Avenue
P.O. Box 1223
Valdosta, GA 31601
(912) 333-5277
AREA OF DEVELOPMENT: Ten-county area in south central Georgia


REGION: IV
Southeast Georgia Development Corporation
P.O. Box 2049
3243 Harris Road
Waycross, GA 31502
(912) 285-6091
AREA OF DEVELOPMENT: Atkinson, Bacon, Brantley, Charlton, Clinch,
   Coffee, Pierce and Ware Counties

REGION: IV
Southeast Local Development Corporation
Civic Forum
1001 Market Street
Chattanooga, TN 37402
(615) 267-7705
AREA OF DEVELOPMENT: 60 mile radius from Hamilton County
  Courthouse (TN)

REGION: IV
Southern Development Council
135 South Union Street
Suite 256
Montgomery, AL 36130
(205) 264-5441
AREA OF DEVELOPMENT: Statewide

REGION: IV
Southern Mississippi Economic Development Company, Inc.
1020 32nd Avenue
Gulfport, MS 39501
(601) 868-2312
AREA OF DEVELOPMENT: Covington, Forrest, George, Greene, Hancock, Har-
  rison, Jackson, Jefferson, Davis, Jones, Lamar, Marion, Pearl River, Perry,
  Stone, Wayne

REGION: IV
Sowega Economic Development Corporation
30 E. Broad Street
P.O. Box 346
Camilla, GA 31730
(912) 336-5617
AREA OF DEVELOPMENT: Baker, Calhoun, Colquitt, Decatur, Dougherty,
  Early, Grady, Lee, Miller, Mitchell, Seminole, Terrell, Thomas, and Worth
  Counties

REGION: IV
St. Petersburg Certified Development Company, Inc.
143—1st Avenue North
Suite 205
St. Petersburg, FL 33701
(813) 823-4311
AREA OF DEVELOPMENT: Citywide St. Petersburg

REGION: IV
Tampa Bay Economic Development Corporation

315 East Kennedy Boulevard
Tampa, FL 33602
(813) 223-8381
AREA OF DEVELOPMENT: Citywide Tampa

REGION: IV
Tarboro Financial Assistance Corporation
112 West Church Street
P.O. Box 220
Tarboro, NC 27886
(919) 823-7194
AREA OF DEVELOPMENT: Township No. 1—Tarboro

REGION: IV
Three Rivers Local Development Company, Inc.
P.O. Drawer B
Pontotoc, MS 38863
(601) 489-2435
AREA OF OPERATION: Calhoun, Chickasaw, Itawamba, Lafayette, Lee, Monroe, Pontotoc, and Union Counties

REGION: IV
United Local Development Corporation
c/o Bank of Mississippi
One MS Plaza, P.O. Box 789
Tupelo, MS 38801
(601) 842-7140
AREA OF OPERATION: Alcorn, Lee, Prentiss, Desota, Itawamba, Monroe, Pontotoc, Union, Chichasaw and Calhoun Counties

REGION: IV
Upper Savannah Development Corporation
P.O. Box 1366
Corner Oak & Main Streets
Greenwood, SC 29648
(803) 229-6627
AREA OF OPERATION: The Upper Savannah Region including Abbeville, Edgefield, Greenwood, Laurens, McCormick, and Saluda Counties

REGION: IV
Urban County Community Development Corporation
200 East Main Street
Lexington, KY 40507
(606) 258-3131
AREA OF OPERATION: Fayette County

REGION: IV
West Tennessee Investment Corporation
125 N. Mid America Mall
Room 419
Memphis, TN 38103
(901) 528-3307
AREA OF OPERATION: 21 Counties in West Tennessee

REGION: IV
Wilmington Industrial Development, Inc.
508 Market Street
P.O. Box 1698
Wilmington, NC 28402
(919) 763-8414
AREA OF OPERATION: City of Wilmington and County of New Hanover

REGION: V
Akron Small Business Development Corporation
166 South High Street
Akron, OH 44308
(216) 375-2133
AREA OF OPERATION: Citywide Akron

REGION: V
Area Investment and Development Corporation, Inc.
400 South Washington Avenue
P.O. Box 969
Green Bay, WI 54305
(414) 432-7225
AREA OF OPERATION: Brown County

REGION: V
Ashtabula County 503 Corporation
25 West Jefferson Street
Jefferson, OH 44047
(216) 570-2040
AREA OF OPERATION: County of Ashtabula

REGION: V
Business Dev. Corporation of South Bend, Mishawaka, St. Joseph County, IN
1200 County-City Building
City of South Bend, Dept. of Dev.
South Bend, IN 46601
(219) 284-9278
AREA OF OPERATION: St. Joseph County

REGION: V
CANDO City-Wide Development Corporation
222 W. Adams Street
Suite 1398
Chicago, IL 60606
(312) 845-9646
AREA OF OPERATION: City of Chicago

REGION: V
Capital Region Business Corporation
913 W. Holmes Road, Suite 201
Lansing, MI 48910
(517) 393-0344
AREA OF OPERATION: Clinton, Eaton and Ingham Counties

REGION: V
Central Upper Peninsula Business Dev. Center, Inc.
2415 24th Avenue South
Escanaba, MI 49829
(906) 786-9234
AREA OF OPERATION: Alger, Schoolcraft, Marquette, Delta, Dickinson, and
  Menominee Counties

REGION: V
Certified Community Development Corporation
P.O. Box 595
210½ Third Street
Sterling, IL 61081
(815) 626-2052
AREA OF OPERATION: Carroll, Ogle, Lee, Whiteside, Bureau and Henry Coun-
  ties

REGION: V
Certified Development Company of Butler County, Inc.
130 High Street
Hamilton, OH 45011
(513) 867-5772
AREA OF OPERATION: Butler County

Certified Development Corporation of Warren County, Inc.
280 W. Central Avenue
Springboro, OH 45066
(513) 932-3126
AREA OF OPERATION: Warren County, Ohio

REGION: V
Champaign County Business Growth Corporation

1303 North Cunningham Avenue
Urbana, IL 61801
(217) 328-3828
AREA OF OPERATION: Champaign County

Chicago Industrial Finance Corporation
8 South Michigan Avenue
Suite 3301
Chicago, IL 60603
(312) 421-7248
AREA OF OPERATION: City of Chicago

REGION: V
Cincinnati Local Development Company
415 West Court Street
Cincinnati, OH 45203
(513) 352-4985
AREA OF OPERATION: Citywide Cincinnati

REGION: V
Citywide Small Business Development Corporation
Miami Valley Tower
40 W. 4th Street—Suite 1400
Dayton, OH 45402
(513) 226-0457
AREA OF OPERATION: City of Dayton and its environs

REGION: V
Clark County Development Corporation
333 N. Limestone Street
Suite 201
Springfield, OH 45501
(513) 325-7621
AREA OF OPERATION: Clark County

REGION: V
Cleveland Area Development Finance Corporation
690 Huntington Building
Cleveland, OH 44115
(216) 241-1166
Cuyahoga, Lake, Geauga, Loran, Medine, Portage and Summit Counties

REGION: V
Cleveland Citywide Development Corporation
601 Lakeside
Room 210

Cleveland, OH 44114
(216) 664-2406
AREA OF OPERATION: City of Cleveland


REGION: V
Columbus Countywide Development Corporation
140 Marconi Blvd.
Marconi Bldg., 8th Floor
Columbus, OH 43215
(614) 222-6171
AREA OF OPERATION: City of Columbus and Counties of Franklin, Union,
    Madison, Delaware, Licking, Fairfield, and Pickaway


REGION: V
Community Development Corporation of Fort Wayne
Department of Economic Development
840 City-County Building
Fort Wayne, IN 46802
(219) 427-1127
AREA OF OPERATION: Allen County


Community Improvement Corporation of Geauga County
8491 Mayfield Road
Chesterland, OH 44026
(216) 729-4393
AREA OF OPERATION: County of Geauga


REGION: V
Coon Rapids Development Company
P.O. Box 33346
Coon Rapids, MN 55433
(612) 574-1656
AREA OF OPERATION: City of Coon Rapids


Detroit Economic Growth Corporation Development Co.
First National Building
Suite 600
Detroit, MI 48226
(313) 963-2940
AREA OF OPERATION: City of Detroit


Downtown Improvement Corporation
4525 Indianapolis Blvd.
East Chicago, IN 46312
(219) 392-8203
AREA OF OPERATION: Lake County

REGION: V
Duluth Business Assistance Corporation
720 Medical Arts Building
Duluth, MN 55802
(218) 727-8549
AREA OF OPERATION: Duluth, MN and Neighboring Municipalities

REGION: V
East Central Michigan Development Corporation
500 Federal Avenue
P.O. Box 930
Saginaw, MI 48606
(571) 752-0200
AREA OF OPERATION: Arenac, Bay, Clare, Gladwin, Gratiot, Huron, Iosco, Isa-
    bella, Midland, Ogemaw, Roscommon Counties

REGION: V
East Toledo Local Development Corporation
222 Main Street
Toledo, OH 43605
(419) 698-2310
AREA OF OPERATION: East Toledo, Ohio

REGION: V
Eastern Minnesota Economic Corporation
100 South Park Street
Mora, MN 55051
(612) 679-4120
AREA OF OPERATION: Chicago, Isanti, Kanabec, Mille Lacs and Pine Counties

REGION: V
Eastern Ohio Development Corporation
100 E. Main Street
St. Clairsville, OH 43950
(614) 695-9678
AREA OF OPERATION: Jefferson, Belmont, Harrison and Monroe Counties in Ohio

REGION: V
Eau Claire County Economic Development Corporation
505 Dewey Street South
Suite 101
Eau Clair, WI 54701-3707
(715) 834-0070
AREA OF OPERATION: Eau Claire County and City of Eau Claire (which is in a
    part of Chippewa County), Wisconsin

REGION: V
Economic Development Corporation of McLean County Area, Inc.
210 South East Street
Bloomington, IL 61701
(309) 829-6344
AREA OF OPERATION: McLean County

Faribault Industrial Corporation
228 Central Avenue
P.O. Box 434
Faribault, MN 55021
(507) 334-9186
AREA OF OPERATION: City of Faribault

REGION: V
Forward Development Corporation
1101 Beach Street
Flint, MI 48502
(313) 257-3010
AREA OF OPERATION: Genesee County

REGION: V
Gary City-Wide Development Corporation
Gary Chamber of Commerce-S#324
Gainer Bank Bldg.
504 Broadway
Gary, IN 46402
(219) 883-9692
AREA OF OPERATION: Citywide Gary

REGION: V
Grand Rapids Local Development Corporation
300 Monroe, N.W.
Grand Rapids, MI 49503
(616) 456-3199
AREA OF OPERATION: Citywide Grand Rapids

REGION: V
Greater Egypt Reg. Planning & Development Commission, Inc.
P.O. Box 3160
Carbondale, IL 62901
(618) 549-3309
AREA OF OPERATION: Franklin, Jackson, Jefferson, Perry, and Williamson
    Counties

REGION: V
Greater Gratiot Development, Inc.
215 E. Center Street
Ithaca, MI 48847
(517) 875-2083
AREA OF OPERATION: Gratiot County

Greater Metropolitan Chicago Development
1 Concourse Plaza
4711 Golf Road, Suite 706
Skokie, IL 60076
(312) 674-2244
AREA OF OPERATION: Cook, Lake, McHenry, Kane, DuPage, Kendall, Will,
  and Grundy Counties

REGION: V
Greater Muskegon Industrial Fund, Inc.
349 West Webster Avenue
Muskegon, MI 49440
(616) 722-2671
AREA OF OPERATION: Muskegon County

Greater North-Pulaski Local Development Corporation
4054 West North Avenue
Chicago, IL 60639
(312) 384-7074
AREA OF OPERATION: Chicago Avenue S., Belmont Ave. N., Western Ave. E.,
  Cicero Ave. W.

REGION: V
Greater Northwest Regional Development Corporation (The)
3668 U.S. Highway #31 South
P.O. Box 605
Traverse City, MI 49685
(616) 946-3604
AREA OF OPERATION: Antrin, Benzie, Charlevoix, Emmet, Grand Traverse,
  Kalkaska, Leelanau, Manistee, Missaukee and Wexford Counties

REGION: V
Greater Southwest Local Development Corporation
6249 Southwestern Avenue
Chicago, IL 60656
(312) 436-1000
AREA OF OPERATION: City of Chicago

Greater West Side Development Corporation
3921 W. Roosevelt Road

Chicago, IL 60624
(312) 421-3942
AREA OF OPERATION:Boundaries of Lake St., Halsted, 22nd St., and Western
  City Limits

REGION: V
Hamilton County Development Company, Inc.
Couth House Annex, Rm. 1000
138 East Court Street
Cincinnati, OH 45202
(513) 632-8292
AREA OF OPERATION: Hamilton County, Ohio (except for City of Cincinnati)

REGION: V
Hammond Development Corporation
Office of Economic Development
649 Conkey Street
Hammond, IN 46324
(219) 853-6508
AREA OF OPERATION: City of Hammond

REGION: V
Illinois Small Business Growth Corporation
620 East Adams
Springfield, IL 62701
(217) 785-2708
AREA OF OPERATION: Statewide

REGION: V
Indiana Statewide Certified Development Corporation
2506 Willowbrook Parkway
Suite 110
Indianapolis, IN 46205
(317) 253-6166
AREA OF OPERATION: Statewide

REGION: V
Jackson Local Development Company (The)
City Hall, Eighth Floor
161 West Michigan
Jackson, MI 49201
(517) 788-4187
AREA OF OPERATION: Jackson County

REGION: V
Kalamazoo Small Business Development Corporation
241 West South Street

Kalamazoo, MI 49007
(616) 385-8050
AREA OF OPERATION: Within City of Kalamazoo

REGION: V
Kenosha Area Development Corporation
812-56th Street
Kenosha, WI 53140
(414) 654-7134
AREA OF OPERATION: Countywide

REGION: V
Lake County Economic Development Corporation
18 North County Street
Waukegan, IL 60085
(312) 360-6350
AREA OF OPERATION: Lake, County, IL

Lake County Small Business Corporation
Camelot Building
Lakeland Community College
Mentor, OH 44060
(216) 951-2769
AREA OF OPERATION: Lake County

REGION: V
Lapeer Development Corporation
449 McCormick Drive
Lapeer, MI 48446
(313) 667-0080
AREA OF OPERATION: Lapeer County

REGION: V
Lawndale Local Development
1111 South Homan Avenue
Suite 204
Chicago, IL 60624
(312) 265-8500
AREA OF OPERATION: Bound by (S) 22nd Street, (N) Harrison Ave., (E)
    Western Ave., (W) City Limits

REGION: V
Lawrence Avenue Development Corporation
4745 North Kedzie Avenue
Chicago, IL 60625
(312) 478-0202
AREA OF OPERATION: Albany Park (Area of Chicago)

REGION: V Loran 503 Development Corporation
200 W. Erie Avenue
Lorain, OH 44052
(216)
AREA OF OPERATION: City of Lorain

REGION: V
Lorain County Certified Development Corporation
226 Middle Avenue
Elyria, OH 44035
(216) 322-6341
AREA OF OPERATION: Lorain County

REGION: V
MSP 503 Development Corporation
8th Floor, One Cascade Plaza
Akron, OH 44308
(216) 376-5550
AREA OF OPERATION: Summit, Portage and Medina Counties

REGION: V
Madison Development Corporation
102 State Street
Madison, WI 53703
(608) 256-2799
AREA OF OPERATION: City of Madison

REGION: V
Mahoning Valley Economic Development Corporation
3200 Belmont Avenue
Youngstown, OH 44505
(216) 759-3668
AREA OF OPERATION: Mahoning, Columbiana, and Trumbull Counties

REGION: V
Marathon County Certified Development Company, Inc.
407 Grant Street
Wausau, WI 54401
(715) 675-3311
AREA OF OPERATION: Marathon County

REGION: V
Mentor Economic Assistance Corporation
8500 Civi Center Boulevard
Mentor, OH 44060
(216) 255-1100
AREA OF OPERATION: City of Mentor

REGION: V
Metro Small Business Assistance Corporation
Old Post Office Place—#208
100 N.W. Second Street
Evansville, IN 47708
(812) 425-0922
AREA OF OPERATION: Posey, Gibson, and Vanderburgh Counties

REGION: V
Metropolitan Growth & Development Corporation
28777 Six Mile Road, #200
Livonia, MI 48152-2660
(313) 591-3450
AREA OF OPERATION: Wayne County

REGION: V
Metropolitan Milwaukee Enterprise Corporation
809 North Broadway
P.O. Box 324
Milwaukee, WI 53201
(414) 223-5812
AREA OF OPERATION: Milwaukee, Ozaukee, Washington and Waukesha Counties

REGION: V
Michigan Certified Development Corporation
P.O. Box 30234
Lansing, MI 48909
(517) 373-6378
AREA OF OPERATION: Statewide

REGION: V
Mid City Pioneer Corporation
c/o Indianapolis Growth Project
48 Monument Circle
Indianapolis, IN 46204
(317) 236-6241
AREA OF OPERATION: Marion County

REGION: V
Minneapolis Economic Development Company
c/o Minn. Comm. Dev. Agency
331 2nd Avenue, South, Room 900
Minneapolis, MN 55405
(612) 342-1378
AREA OF OPERATION: City of Minneapolis

REGION: V
Mohican Investment Corporation
211 South Market Street
P.O. Box 894
Wooster, OH 44691
(216) 669-2977
AREA OF OPERATION: Ashland, Holmes, and Wayne Counties


REGION: V
Montgomery County Business Development Corporation
1700 Miami Valley Tower
40 West 4th Street
Dayton, OH 45402
(513) 225-6328
AREA OF OPERATION: Montgomery County, Ohio


REGION: V
Northeast Michigan Development Company
P.O. Box 457
114 North Court Avenue
Gaylord, MI 49735
(517) 732-2451
AREA OF OPERATION: Alcona, Alpena, Cheboygan, Crawford, Montmorency,
   Oscoda, Otsego, and Presque Isle Counties


REGION: V
Oakland County Local Development Company
1200 North Telegraph Road
Pontiac, MI 48053
(313) 858-0732
AREA OF OPERATION: Oakland County


REGION: V
Ohio Statewide Development Corporation
P.O. Box 1001
30 East Broad Street
Columbus, OH 43215
(614) 466-5043
AREA OF OPERATION: Statewide


REGION: V
Opportunities Minnesota Incorporated
150 E. Kellogg Boulevard
Room 900
St. Paul, MN 55101

(612) 296-0582
AREA OF OPERATION: Statewide

REGION: V
Oshkosh Commercial Development Corporation
P.O. Box 280
120 Jackson Street
Oshkosh, WI 54902
(414) 236-5260
AREA OF OPERATION: Winnebago County

REGION: V
Ottawa County Development Company, Inc.
414 Washington Street
Grand River, MI 49417
AREA OF OPERATION: Ottawa County, Michigan

REGION: V
Peoria Economic Development Association
331 Fulton Street
Suite 407
Peoria, IL 61602
(309) 674-5800
AREA OF OPERATION: Citywide in Peoria, Counties of Peoria, Tazewell and
   Woodford

REGION: V
Prairieland Economic Development Corporation
2524 Broadway Avenue
P.O. Box 265
Slayton, MN 56172
(507) 836-8549
AREA OF OPERATION: Cottonwood, Jackson, Lincoln, Lyon, Murray, Nobles,
   Pipestone, Redwood, and Rock Counties

REGION: V
Racine County Business Development Corporation
5802 Washington Avenue
Suite 201
Racine, WI 53406
(414) 636-3118
AREA OF OPERATION: Racine County

REGION: V
Red Cedar Certified Development Corporation
P.O. Box 6672

East Lansing, MI 48823
(517) 351-6566
AREA OF OPERATION: East Lansing/Meridian Township

REGION: V
Region Eight Development Corporation d/b/a/ REDCO Dev.
2 Fountain Place
Suite 240
Grand Rapids, IN 49503
(616) 458-7287
AREA OF OPERATION: Allegan, Ionia, Kent, Lake, Mason, Mecosta, Montcalm,
   Newaygo and Osceola Counties

REGION: V
Region Nine Development Corporation
410 S. Fifth Street
P.O. Box 3367
Mankato, MN 56001
(507) 387-5646
AREA OF OPERATION: Blue Earth, Brown, Faribault, LeSueur, Martin, Nicollet,
   Sibley, Waseca and Watonwan Counties

REGION: V
Richland County 503 Corporation
30 North Diamond Street
Manfield, OH 44902
(419) 526-2600
AREA OF OPERATION: County of Richland

REGION: V
Rockford Local Development Corporation
515 N. Court Street
Rockford, IL 61103
(815) 987-8127
AREA OF OPERATION: CIty of Rockford

REGION: V
SAMCOR Development Corporation
4 North Cicero Avenue, Room 38
Chicago, IL 60644
(312) 626-6295
AREA OF OPERATION: North Ave., Roosevelt Road, Hamlin and Austin Boulevard

REGION: V
Saint Paul 503 Development Company
25 West Fourth Street

St. Paul, MN 55102
(612) 292-6155
AREA OF OPERATION: City of St. Paul

REGION: V
Scioto Economic Development Corporation, Inc.
Scioto County Courthouse
P.O. Drawer 1606
Portsmouth, OH 45662
(614) 354-7779
AREA OF OPERATION: Scioto, Adams, Pike, Jackson and Lawrence Counties

REGION: V
Small Business Assistance Corporation
316 N. Michigan Ave.
Suite 700
Toledo, OH 43624
(419) 255-6077
AREA OF OPERATION: City of Toledo

REGION: V
South Central IL Regional Planning & Dev. Commission
Marion County Public Service Building
Salem, IL 62881
(618) 548-4234
AREA OF OPERATION: Counties of Effingham, Fayette and Marion; also Cities
   of Centralia and Wamac

REGION: V
South Towns Business Growth Corporation
1154 Ridge Road
Suite 100
Homewood, IL 60430
(312) 957-6970
AREA OF OPERATION: South Suburban Cook County and Eastern Will County

REGION: V
Southeastern IL Regional Planning & Dev. Commission
Harrisburg National Bank Building
Harrisburg, IL 62946
(618) 252-7463
AREA OF OPERATION: Gallatin, Hamilton, Hardin, Pope and Salin Counties

REGION: V
Southwestern Michigan Development Company, Inc.
2907 Division Street

St. Joseph, MI 49085
(616) 983-1529
AREA OF OPERATION: Berrien, Cass, Van Buren, St. Joseph, and Allegan
  Counties

REGION: V
Springfield Certified Development Company
204 Municipal Building
Springfield, IL 62701
(217) 787-3686
AREA OF OPERATION: Sangamon County, Illinois

REGION: V
St. Joseph County Certified Development Corporation
228 W. Jefferson Road
c/o McGinty & Assoc.
South Bend, IN 46601
(219) 237-0452
AREA OF OPERATION: St. Joseph County

REGION: V
Stark County Certified Development Corporation
501 E. Tuscarawas Street
Canton, OH 44702
(216)
AREA OF OPERATION: City of Canton

REGION: V
Stark Development Board Finance Corporation
200 West Tuscarawas Street
County Administration Building
Canton, OH 44702
(216) 438-0916
AREA OF OPERATION: Stark County

REGION: V
The Small Business Finance Alliance
203 West Main Street
Collinsville, IL 62234
(618) 344-4080
AREA OF OPERATION: Bond, Clinton, Madison, Monroe, St. Clair, Randolph
  and Washington Counties

REGION: V
Traverse City Area Industrial Fund, Inc.
P.O. Box 387

Traverse City, MI 49684
(616) 946-1551
AREA OF OPERATION: Antrim, Kalkska, Grand Traverse and Leelanau Counties

REGION: V
Warren Redevelopment and Planning Corporation
106 E. Market Street—#814
Warren, OH 44481-1103
(216) 841-2566
AREA OF OPERATION: City of Warren and Trumbull County

REGION: V
Warrick County Local Development Corporation
301 West Main Street
Boonville, IN 47601
(812) 897-1506
AREA OF OPERATION: Warrick County, Indiana

REGION: V
Western Illinois Development Corporation
223 South Randolph Street
Macomb, IL 61455
(309) 837-2942
AREA OF OPERATION: Fulton, Hancock, Henderson, Knox, McDonough, and
   Warren Counties

REGION: V
Western Upper Peninsula Development Company, Inc.
326 Shelden Avenue
P.O. Box 365
Houghton, MI 49931
(906) 482-7206
AREA OF OPERATION: Gogebic, Ontonagon, Iron, Houghton, and Baraga Coun-
   ties

REGION: V
Western Wisconsin Development Corporation
Route 2, Box 8
Turtle Lake, WI 54889
(415) 986-4310
AREA OF OPERATION: Barron, Bayfield, Burnett, Chippewa, Dunne, Polk,
   Rusk, Sawyer and Washburn

REGION: V
Will County Local Development Company
302 North Chicago Avenue

Joliet, IL 60433
(815) 727-8768
AREA OF OPERATION: Will County

REGION: V
Wisconsin Business Development Finance Corporation
217 South Hamilton Street
Madison, WI 53703
(608) 258-8830
AREA OF OPERATION: Statewide

REGION: V
Xenia-Greene County Small Business Dev. Company, Inc.
50 South Detroit Street
Xenia, OH 45385
(513) 372-0444
AREA OF OPERATION: Green County

REGION: VI
Ark-La-Tex Investment & Development Corporation
P.O. Box 37005
Shreveport, LA 71133
(318) 226-7557
AREA OF OPERATION: Parishes of Bienville, Bossier, Caddo, Claiborne,
  DeSoto, Lincoln, Natchitoches, Red River, Sabine & Webster

REGION: VI
Ark-Tex Regional Development Company, Inc.
911 Loop 151, Suite 200
Texarkana, TX 75501
(214) 832-7542
AREA OF OPERATION: Bowie, Cass, Delta, Franklin, Hopkins, Red River,
  Lamar, Morris, and Titus Counties in Texas; also Miller County in Arkansas

REGION: VI
Association of South Central Governments Econ. Dev. Corp.
802 Main
P.O. Box 1647
Duncan, OK 73533
(405) 252-0595
AREA OF OPERATION: McClain, Grady, Caddo, Comanche, Cotton, Tillman,
  Stephens, and Jefferson Counties

REGION: VI
Beaumont Economic Development Foundation

450 Bowie
P.O. Box 3150
Beaumont, TX 77704
(713) 838-6581
AREA OF OPERATION: Jefferson and Orange Counties

REGION: VI
Big Country Development Corporation
1025 East North 10th Street
P.O. Box 3195
Abilene, TX 79604
(915) 672-8544
AREA OF OPERATION: Planning Service Region #7

REGION: VI
Big Spring Area Development Company
1106 Big Spring Industrial Park
Box 391
Big Spring, TX 79720
(915) 267-2531
AREA OF OPERATION: Howard County

REGION: VI
Brenham Industrial Foundation, Inc.
314 S. Austin
Brenham, TX 77833
(409) 836-3695
AREA OF OPERATION: City of Brenham and 2 miles beyond city limits

REGION: VI
Brownsville Local Development Company, Inc.
P.O. Box 911
Brownsville, TX 78520
(512) 541-8691
AREA OF OPERATION: Citywide Brownsville and its environs

REGION: VI
Business and Industry Development Corporation
#1 State Capitol Mall
Room 4C-300
Little Rock, AR 72201
(501) 371-5187
AREA OF OPERATION: Statewide

REGION: VI
CLD Development Corporation

131 West Second
Roswell, NM 88201
(505) 623-5909
AREA OF OPERATION: Chaves, De Baca and Lincoln Counties


REGION: VI
Capital Economic Development District Council, Inc.
4864 Constitution Avenue
Suite 2A
Baton Rouge, LA 70808
(504) 926-4371
AREA OF OPERATION: Ascension, E. Baton Rouge, El Feliciana, Iberville, Liv-
ingston, Pointe Coupee, St. Helena, St. Tammany, Tangipahoe, Washington, W.
Baton Rouge, W. Felicinan


REGION: VI
Caprock Local Development Company
P.O. Box 3730
1328 58th Street
Lubbock, TX 79452-3730
AREA OF OPERATION: Baily, Cochran, Crosby, Dickens, Floyd, Garza, Hale,
Hockley, King, Lamb, Lubbuck, Lynn, Motley, Terry & Yoakum


REGION: VI
Central Arkansas Certified Development Corporation
112 N.E. Front Street
P.O. Box 187
Lonoke, AR 72086
(501) 374-6976
AREA OF OPERATION: Saline, Faulkner, Pulaski, Lonoke, Prairie and Monroe
Counties


REGION: VI
Central Texas Certified Development Company
c/o Central Texas Econ.
P.O. Box 4408
Waco, TX 76705
(817) 799-0259
AREA OF OPERATION: Bell, Bowque, Coryell, Falls, Hamilton, Hill, Freestone,
Limestone, McLennan, Milam, Navarro, Somervell, & Robertson Counties


REGION: VI
College Station Certified Development Corporation
1300 Jersey Street
College Station, TX 77840

(409) 696-8989
AREA OF OPERATION: Brazos County

REGION: VI
Dallas Small Business Corporation
Room 6-D N., City Hall
1500 Marilla
Dallas, TX 75201
(214) 670-3068
AREA OF OPERATION: City of Dallas

REGION: VI
Deep East Texas Regional Cert. Development Corporation
118 East Hospital Street
Nacogdoches, TX 75961
(409) 569-0328
AREA OF OPERATION: Angelina, Houston, Jasper, Nacogdoches, Newton, Polk,
  Sabine, San Augustine, San Jacinto, Shelby, Trinity and Tyler

REGION: VI
Development Authority of New Mexico, Inc.
P.O. Box 5115
Santa Fe, NM 87502
(505) 827-8934
AREA OF OPERATION: Cibola, Colfax, Harding, Los Alamos, Mora, McKinley,
  Rio Arriba, Sandoval, San Juan, San Miguel, Santa Fe, Taos, Union, Valencia

REGION: VI
East Arkansas Planning & Development District
1801 Stadium Boulevard
P.O. Box 1403
Jonesboro, AR 72401
AREA OF OPERATION: Counties of Clay, Craighead, Crittenden, Cross, Greene,
  Lawrance, Lee, Mississippi, Phillips, Roinsette, Randolph, St. Francis

REGION: VI
East Texas Regional Development Company, Inc.
3800 Stone Road
Kilgore, TX 75662
(214) 984-3989
AREA OF OPERATION: Anderson, Camp, Cherokee, Gregg, Harrison, Henderson, Marion, Panola, Rains, Rusk, Smith, Upshur, Van Zandt and Wood Counties

REGION: VI
Fort Worth Economic Development Corporation

2914 East Rosedale, Suite 204
Fort Worth, TX 76105
(817) 535-2167
AREA OF OPERATION: City of Fort Worth, Tarrant, Wise, Parker and Johnson
  Counties

REGION: VI
Garland Local Development Corporation, Inc.
3960 Broadway
Suite 200
Garland, TX 75043
(214) 271-9993
AREA OF OPERATION: Within city limits of Garland, Texas

REGION: VI
Houston-Galveston Area Local Development Corporation
3555 Timmons Lane
Suite 500
Houston, TX 77027
(713) 627-3200
AREA OF OPERATION: 13 Counties of Gulf Coast State Planning Region

REGION: VI
Imperial Calcasieu Regional Certified Development, Inc.
New City Hall, 326 Pujo Street
4th Floor
Lake Charles, LA 70601
(318) 433-1771
AREA OF OPERATION: Parishes of Allen, Beauregard, Calcasieu, Cameron, and
  Jefferson Davis

REGION: VI
Industrial Development Corporation of Lea County
Broadmoor Building
P.O. Box 1376
Hobbs, NM 88240
(505) 397-2039
AREA OF OPERATION: Lea County, New Mexico

REGION: VI
Kisatchie-Delta Reg. Planning & Development District, Inc.
5212 Rue Verdun
P.O. Box 8076
Alexandria, LA 71306
(318) 487-5454

AREA OF OPERATION: Parishes of Avoyelles, Catahoula, Concordia, Grant, La
Salle, Rapides, Vernon and Winn

REGION: VI
Lafayette Centre Certified Development Company, Inc.
705 W. University Avenue
P.O. Box 4017-C
Lafayette, LA 70502
(318) 261-8408
AREA OF OPERATION: Lafayette Parish

REGION: VI
Louisiana First Certified Development Corporation
150 Ridge Road
P.O. Box 31978
Lafayette, LA 70503
(318) 837-3410
AREA OF OPERATION: Statewide

REGION: VI
Lower Rio Grand Valley Cert. Development Corporation (The)
Texas Commerce Bank Building
Suite 207
McAllen, TX 78501
(512) 682-1109
AREA OF OPERATION: Cameron, Hidalgo, and Willacy Counties

REGION: VI
Metro Area Development Corporation
116 Dean McGee Avenue
Oklahoma City, OK 73102
(405) 232-5181
AREA OF OPERATION: Canadian, Cleveland and Oklahoma Counties

REGION: VI
Mora San Miguel Guadalupe Development Corporation
131 Bridge Street
Las Vegas, NM 87701
(505) 425-9302
AREA OF OPERATION: Mora, San Miguel, and Guadalupe Counties

REGION: VI
New Orleans Citywide Development Corporation
301 Camp Street
Suite 216
New Orleans, LA 70130

(504) 524-6172
AREA OF OPERATION: City of New Orleans

REGION: VI
North Texas Certified Development Corporation
306 N. Hamilton Street
Room 101-A
Trenton, TX 75490
(214) 989-2720
AREA OF OPERATION: Grayson, Ranes, Fannin, Hunt, Collin, Cooke, and
  Rockwall Counties

REGION: VI
North Texas Regional Development Corporation
2101 Kemp Boulevard
Wichita Falls, TX 76309
(817) 322-9392
AREA OF OPERATION: Archer, Baylor, Childress, Clay, Cottle, Foard, Harde-
  man, Jack, Montague, Wichita, Wilbarger and Young Counties

REGION: VI
Northeast Louisiana Industries, Inc.
141 DeSiard Street
Suite 100
Monroe, LA 71201
(318) 387-0787
AREA OF OPERATION: Ouachita, Union, Morehouse, Richland, Caldwell, Jack-
  son, Franklin, Tensas, East Carroll, West Carroll and Madison Parishes

REGION: VI
Northern Oklahoma Small Business Development Corp.
3201 Santa Fe Trail
Enid, OK 73703
(405) 237-4811
AREA OF OPERATION: Osage, Garfield, Pawnee, Noble, Blaine, Major, Kay,
  Kingfisher, Alfalfa and Grant Counites

REGION: VI
Northwest Arkansas Certified Development Company
1313 Highway 62–65
P.O. Box 190
Harrison, AR 72601
(501) 741-8009
AREA OF OPERATION: Benton, Carroll, Boone, Baxter, Marion, Washington,
  Madison, Newton, and Searcy Counties

REGION: VI
Pecan Valley Economic Development District
P.O. Box 1745
Brownwood, TX 76801
(915) 643-2587
AREA OF OPERATION: Coleman, Brown, Comanche, Mills, McCulloch, San
  Saba and Lampasas Counties

REGION: VI
Permian Basin Regional Development Corporation
2514 Pliska Drive
Midland, TX 79711
(915) 563-1061
AREA OF OPERATION: Andrews, Borden, Crane, Dawson, Ector, Gaines,
  Glasscock, Howard, Martin, Midland, Pecos, Reeves, Terrell, Upton, Ward and
  Winkler Counties

REGION: VI
Rural Enterprises, Inc.
10 Waldron Drive
Durant, OK 74701
(405) 924-5094
AREA OF OPERATION: 25 Counties in Southeastern Quadrant of Oklahoma

REGION: VI
S.T.E.D. Corporation
P.O. Box 2187
Laredo, TX 78041
(512) 722-3995
AREA OF OPERATION: Starr, Zapata, Jim Hogg and Webb Counties

REGION: VI
SWODA Development Corporation
P.O. Box 569
Burns Flat, OK 73624
(405) 562-4886
AREA OF OPERATION: Beckham, Custer, Greer, Harmon, Jackson, Kiowa,
  Roger Mills, and Washita Counties

REGION: VI
San Antonion Local Development Corporation
P.O. Box 9365
San Antonio, TX 78204
(512) 244-0518
AREA OF OPERATION: City of San Antonio

REGION: VI
Southeast Arkansas Economic Development District, Inc.
P.O. Box 6806
Pine Bluff, AR 71611
(501) 536-1990
AREA OF OPERATION: Grant, Jefferson, Arkansas, Cleveland, Lincoln, Desha,
    Bradley, Drew, Ashley and Chicot

REGION: VI
Southeast Louisiana Certified Development Corporation
c/o Regional Planning Comm.
333 St. Charles Ave., Suite 900
New Orleans, LA 70130
(504) 568-6641
AREA OF OPERATION: Parishes of: Assumption, Jefferson, Lafourche, Plaquem-
    ines, St. Bernard, St. Charles, St. James, and Terrebonne

REGION: VI
Southwest Arkansas Regional Development Corporation
600 Bessie Street
P.O. Box 767
Magnolia, AR 71753
(501) 234-4039
AREA OF OPERATION: Calhoun, Columbia, Dallas, Hempstead, Howard, Lafay-
    ette, Little River, Miller, Nevada, Quachita, Sevier and Union Counites

REGION: VI
Texas Certified Development Company, Inc.
13740 Research Blvd.
Austin, TX 78750-1834
(512) 258-8312
AREA OF OPERATION: Area under jurisdiction of SBA's San Antonio and Har-
    lingen District Officer, including the Corpus Christi Branch Office

REGION: VI
Texas Panhandle Regional Development Corporation
2736 West Tenth Avenue
Amarillo, TX 79102-1120
(806) 372-3381
AREA OF OPERATION: 25 Counties in Panhandle area

REGION: VI
Trinity Development Corporation
P.O. Box 549
Trinity, TX 75862

(713) 594-3856
AREA OF OPERATION: Trinity County

REGION: VI
Tulsa Economic Development Corporation
130 N. Greenwood
Tulsa, OK 74120
(918) 585-8332
AREA OF OPERATION: Citywide Tulsa

REGION: VI
Upper Rio Grande Development Company
Two Civic Center Plaza
El Paso, TX 79999
(915) 541-4068
AREA OF OPERATION: El Paso, Hudspeth, Culberson, Jeff David, Presidio and
   Brewster Counties

REGION: VI
Verd-Ark-Ca Development Corporation
800 West Okmulgee
Suite C
Mudkogee, OK 74401
(918) 683-4634
AREA OF OPERATION: Adair, Cherokee, McIntosh, Muskogee, Okmulgee,
   Wagoner, Rogers, Mayes, Haskell, Sequoyah, Nowata, LeFlore, Craig, Wash-
   ington, Ottawa, Delaware

REGION: VI
West Central Arkansas Planning & Dev. District Incorporated
ABT Towers, Suite 502
P.O. Box 1558
Hot Springs, AR 71901
(501) 624-1036
AREA OF OPERATION: Johnson, Pope, Conway, Yell, Perry, Montgomery, Gar-
   land, Hot Springs, Pike and Clark Counties

REGION: VI
Western Arkansas Planning and Development District, Inc.
P.O. Box 2067
Fort Smith, AR 72902
(501) 785-2651
AREA OF OPERATION: Crawford, Franklin, Sebastian, Logan, Scott and Polk
   Counties

REGION: VI
White River Planning & Development District, Inc.

Highway 25 North
P.O. Box 2396
Batesville, AR 72501
(501) 793-5233
AREA OF OPERATION: Cleburne, Fulton, Independence, Izard, Jackson, Sharp,
Stone, Van Buren, White and Woodruff Counties

REGION: VII
Avenue Area Incporated
8th and State Ave., Suite 395
Newbrotherhood Building
Kansas City, KS 66101
(913) 371-0065
AREA OF OPERATION: Downtown Area of Kansas City, Kansas; Wyandotte,
County, Kansas

REGION: VII
Bi-State Business Finance Corporation
1504 Third Avenue
Rock Island, IL 61201
(309) 793-1181
AREA OF OPERATION: Scott and Muscatine Counties in Iowa; Henry, Mercer
and Rock Island Counties in Illinois

REGION: VII
Big Lakes Certified Development Company
104 South Fourth
Manhattan, KS 66502
(913) 776-0417
AREA OF OPERATION: Clay, Geary, Marshall, Pottawatomie and Riley Counties

REGION: VII
Black Hawk County Economic Development Committee, Inc.
209 West Fifth Street, Suite N
Waterloo, IA 50701
(319) 235-0311
AREA OF OPERATION: Blackhawk County

REGION: VII
Business Development Corporation of Nebraska (The)
139 South 52nd Street
Lincoln, NE 68501
(402) 483-0382
AREA OF OPERATION: Statewide

REGION: VII
Central Ozarks Development, Inc.
Lake of the Ozarks Council of Local Governments
P.O. Box 786
Camdenton, MO 65020
(314) 346-5692
AREA OF OPERATION: Phelps, Gasconade, Crawford, Washington, Dent,
    Maries, Camden, Laclede, Pulaski, Miller and Morgan Counites

REGION: VII
Citywide Development Corp. of Kansas City, Kansas, Inc.
701 North 7th Street, 7th Floor
Kansas City, KS 66101
(913) 321-4406
AREA OF OPERATION: Kansas City, Kansas

REGION: VII
Clay County Development Corporation
2900 Rockcreek Parkway
Suite 510
North Kansas City, MO 64117
(816) 472-5775
AREA OF OPERATION: Clay County

REGION: VII
Corporation for Economic Dev. in Des Moines (The)
The Armory Building
East 1st & Des Moines Str.
Des Moines, IA 50307
(515) 283-4161
AREA OF OPERATION: Citywide Des Moines

REGION: VII
Crawford County Industrial Development Corporation
109 North 14th Street
Denison, IA 51442
(712) 263-5621
AREA OF OPERATION: Crawford County

REGION: VII
Crossroads Economic Dev. Corp. of St. Charles County, Inc.
207 N. 5th Street
P.O. Box 1454
St. Charles, MO 63301
(314) 946-4377
AREA OF OPERATION: St. Charles, Warren, Franklin, and Lincoln Counties

REGION: VII
E.C.I.A. Business Growth, Inc.
P.O. Box 1140
Fischer Building, Suite 22B
Dubuque, IA 52001
(319) 556-4166
AREA OF OPERATION: Cedar, Clinton, Delaware, Dubuque, and Jackson Counties as well as the Cities located therein

REGION: VII
Economic Development Corp. of Jefferson County, MO (The)
P.O. Box 623
Hillsboro, MO 63050
(314) 789-4594
AREA OF OPERATION: Jefferson County, Missouri

REGION: VII
Enterprise Development Corporation
1015 East Broadway, Suite 210
P.O. Box 566
Columbia, MO 65201
(314) 875-8117
AREA OF OPERATION: Audrain, Boone, Callaway, Cole, Cooper, Montgomery and Randolpha Counties

REGION: VII
Four Rivers Development, Inc.
119 North Hersey Street
Beloit, KS 67420
(913) 738-2210
AREA OF OPERATION: Jewell, Republic, Washington, Mitchell, Cloud, Lincoln, Ottawa, Ellsworth, Dickinson, and Saline Counties

REGION: VII
Great Plains Development, Inc.
100 Military Plaza—Suite 214
P.O. Box 1116
Dodge City, KS 67801
(316) 227-6406
AREA OF OPERATION: 28 Counties in Southwest Kansas

REGION: VII
Green Hills Rural Development, Inc.
815 Main Street
Trenton, MO 64683
(314) 359-5086

AREA OF OPERATION: Nine Counties of Caldwell, Daviess, Grundy, Harrison, Linn, Livingston, Mercer, Putnam and Sullivan

REGION: VII
Iowa Business Growth Company
901 Insurance Exchange Building
Des Moines, IA 50309
(515) 282-2164
AREA OF OPERATION: Statewide

REGION: VII
Kansas City Corporation for Industrial Development
920 Main Street
Suite 1212
Kansas City, MO 64105
(816) 474-3560
AREA OF OPERATION: Kansas City

REGION: VII
Leavenworth Area Economic Development Corporation
518 Shawnee
P.O. Box 151
Leavenworth, KS 66048
(913) 682-6579
AREA OF OPERATION: Leavenworth County

REGION: VII
Lee's Summit Economic Development Council (The)
600 Miller Street
P.O. Box 710
Lee's Summit, MO 64063
(816) 525-6617
AREA OF OPERATION: City of Lee's Summit, Missouri

REGION: VII
Lenexa Development Company, Inc.
P.O. Box 14244
Lenexa, KS 66215
(913) 888-3624
AREA OF OPERATION: City of Lenexa

REGION: VII
McPherson County Small Business Development Association
P.O. Box 1032
McPherson, KS 67460
(316) 241-0431
AREA OF OPERATION: McPherson County

REGION: VII
Mid-America, Inc.
1701 S. Broadway
Pittsburg, KS 66762
(316) 231-8267
AREA OF OPERATION: Allen, Anderson, Bourbon, Cherokee, Crawford, Labette, Neosho, Montgomery, Wilson and Woodson Counties

REGION: VII
Mo-Kan Development, Inc.
1302 Faraon Street
St. Joseph, MO 64501
(816) 233-8485
AREA OF OPERATION: Missouri Counties of Andrew, Buchanan, Clinton and Dekalb; Kansas Counties of Atchison, Brown and Doniphan

REGION: VII
NEOSHO Basin Development Company, Inc.
Cremer Hall—ESU Campus, Rm. 208
1200 Commercial—Box 46
Emporia, KS 66801
(316) 343-1200
AREA OF OPERATION: Chase, Coffey, Franklin, Lyon, Morris, Osage, and Wabaunsee Counites

REGION: VII
North Platte Development Corporation
512 North Bailey
P.O. Box 968
North Platte, NE 69101
(308) 532-4966
AREA OF OPERATION: Lincoln County

REGION: VII
Northeast Missouri Certified Development Company
Adair County Courthouse
P.O. Box 965
Kirksville, MO 63501
(816) 665-0202
AREA OF OPERATION: Adair, Clark, Knox, Schuyler and Scotland Counties

REGION: VII
Pioneer Country Development, Inc.
414 N. West Street
Box 248
Hill City, KS 67642
(913) 674-3488

AREA OF OPERATION: Cheyenne, Decatur, Ellis, Gove, Graham, Logan, Norton, Osborne, Phillips, Rawlins, Rooks, Russell, Sherman, Sheridan, Smith, Thomas, Trego and Wallace

REGION: VII
Platte County Industrial Development Commission
10920 Ambassador Drive
Room 531
Kansas City, MO 64153
(816) 891-9480
AREA OF OPERATION: Platte County, Missouri

REGION: VII
Rural Missouri, Inc.
1014 Northeast Drive
Jefferson City, MO 65101
(314) 635-0136
AREA OF OPERATION: Statewide

REGION: VII
Siouxland Economic Development Corporation
400 Orpheum Electric Building
Sioux City, IA 51101
(712) 279-6430
AREA OF OPERATION: Woodbury, Plymouth, Cherokee, Ida and Monona Counties in Iowa; Dakota, Nebraska and Union Counties in South Dakota

REGION: VII
South Central Kansas Economic Development District, Inc.
River Park Place, Suite 580
727 North Waco
Wichita, KS 67203
(316) 262-5246
AREA OF OPERATION: Butler, Chautauqua, Cowley, Elk, Greenwood, Harper, Harvey, Kingman, Marion, McPherson, Reno, Rice, Sedgwick and Sumners Counites

REGION: VII
St. Louis County Local Development Company (The)
130 S. Bemiston
Clayton, MO 63105
(314) 721-0900
AREA OF OPERATION: Throughout St. Louis County

REGION: VII
St. Louis Local Development Company (The)
1300 Convention Plaza

3rd Floor
St. Louis, MO 63103
(314) 231-3500
AREA OF OPERATION: City of St. Louis

REGION: VII
Topeka/Shawnee County Development Corporation, Inc.
820 Quincy, Room 501
Topeka, KS 66612
(913) 234-0076
AREA OF OPERATION: Shawnee County

REGION: VII
Wakarusa Valley Development, Inc.
901 Kentucky, #206
P.O. Box 1743
Lawrence, KS 66044
(913) 841-7120
AREA OF OPERATION: Douglas County

REGION: VII
Wichita Area Development, Inc.
350 West Douglas
Wichita, KS 67202
(316) 265-7771
AREA OF OPERATION: Sedgwick County

REGION: VIII
Areawide Business Council, Inc.
P.O. Box 687
Yankton, SD 57078
(605) 665-4409
AREA OF OPERATION: Aurora, Bon Homme, Brule, Charles Mix, Hanson Davi-
  son, Douglas, Gregory, Hutchinson, Jerauld, Sanborn, and Yankton Counties

REGION: VIII
Central Utah Certified Development Company
152 West Center Street
P.O. Box 1849
Provo, UT 84603
(801) 374-1025
AREA OF OPERATION: City of Provo and Utah County

REGION: VIII
Community Economic Development Company of Colorado

1801 California
Suite 2840
Denver, CO 80202
(303) 344-5257
AREA OF OPERATION: Statewide

REGION: VIII
Denver Urban Economic Development Corporation
303 W. Colfax Avenue
Suite 1025
Denver, CO 80204
(303) 575-5540
AREA OF OPERATION: Countywide Denver

REGION: VIII
Fargo-Cass Economic Development Corporation
321 N. 4th Street
P.O. Box 2443
Fargo, ND 58108
(701) 237-6132
AREA OF OPERATION: Fargo-Cass County

REGION: VIII
First District Development Company
124 First Avenue, N.W.
P.O. Box 1207
Watertown, SD 57201
(605) 886-7225
AREA OF OPERATION: Brookings, Clark, Codington, Deuel, Grant, Hamlin,
   Kingsbury, Lake, Miner and Moody Counites

REGION: VIII
Greater Salt Lake Business District DBA Deseret Cert. Dev. Company
4885 South 900 East
Suite 304
Salt Lake City, UT 84117
(801) 266-0443
AREA OF OPERATION: Statewide

REGION: VIII
Historic 25th Street Development Company (The)
252 25th Street
Ogden, UT 84401
(801) 399-8241
AREA OF OPERATION: Weber County

REGION: VIII
Montana Community Finance Corporation
P.O. Box 916
555 Fuller Avenue
Helena, MT 59624
(406) 442-3850
AREA OF OPERATION: Statewide

REGION: VIII
Northern Hills Community Development, Inc.
P.O. Box 677
722 Main Street
Spearfish, SD 57783
(605) 642-7106
AREA OF OPERATION: Butte, Lawrence, Meade and Pennington Counties

REGION: VIII
Old Colorado City Development Company
1112 West Colorado Avenue
Colorado Springs, CO 80904
(303) 578-6962
AREA OF OPERATION: El Paso County, Colorado

REGION: VIII
SCEDD Development Company
720 North Main
Suite 444
Peublo, CO 81002
(304) 545-8680
AREA OF OPERATION: 19 Southern Colorado Counties

REGION: VIII
Small Business Development Corp. for Wyoming, Inc.
145 S. Durbin Street
Suite 201
Casper, WY 82601
(307) 234-5352
AREA OF OPERATION: Statewide

REGION: VIII
South Dakota Development Corporation (The)
221 South Central
Pierre, SD 57501
(605) 773-5032
AREA OF OPERATION: Statewide

438 DIRECTORY OF CAPITAL SOURCES

REGION: VIII
Southern Colorado Development Corporation
108 E. Pitkin Avenue
Pueblo, CO 81004
(303) 544-7133
AREA OF OPERATION: Pueblo County, Colorado


REGION: IX
Amador Economic Development Corporation
P.O. Box 596
Jackson, CA 95642
AREA OF OPERATION: County of Amador

REGION: IX
Antelope Valley Local Development Corporation
104 East Avenue K-4
Suite A
Lancaster, CA 93535
(805) 945-2741
AREA OF OPERATION: Antelope Valley Area—Northern Los Angeles County,
    Communities of Lancaster and Palmdale

REGION: IX
Arcata Economic Development Corporation
630 Ninth Street
P.O. Box 4168
Arcata, CA 95521
(707) 822-4616
AREA OF OPERATION: Humboldt and Del Norte Counties

REGION: IX
Arizona Enterprise Development Corporation
1700 West Washington, 4th Floor
Phoenix, AZ 85007
(602) 255-1782
AREA OF OPERATION: Statewide

Arvin Development Corporation
200 Campus Drive
Box 546
Arvin, CA 93203
AREA OF OPERATION: Kern County

REGION: IX
Bay Area Business Development Company

717 Market Street
Suite 204
San Francisco, CA 94107
(415) 541-0694
AREA OF OPERATION: San Francisco, Marin, Sonoma, Napa, Solano, Contra
  Costa, Alameda, Santa Clara and San Mateo Counties

REGION: IX
Bay Area Employment Development Company
251 Lafayette Circle
Suite 200
Lafayette, CA 94549
(415) 283-3760
AREA OF OPERATION: San Francisco, San Mateo, Santa Clara, Alameda, Con-
  tra Costa, Solano, Napa, Sonoma and Marin

REGION: IX
Butte County Overall Economic Development Corporation
1001 Willow Street
P.O. Box 6250
Chico, CA 95927
(916) 893-8732
AREA OF OPERATION: Butte County

REGION: IX
Calexico Industrial Development Corporation
747 Imperial Avenue
Calexico, CA 92231
(619) 357-6455
AREA OF OPERATION: Imperial County

REGION: IX
Central California Certified Development Corporation
2300 Tulare Street
Suite 210
Fresno, CA 93721
(209) 488-4503
AREA OF OPERATION: Fresno County

REGION: IX
Central Coast Development Corporation
100 Civic Center Plaza
Lompoc, CA 93438
(805) 736-1445
AREA OF OPERATION: Counties of San Louis Obispo, Santa Barbara, and Ventura

REGION: IX
Commercial Industrial Development Company, Inc.
1275 Main Street
P.O. Box 2343
El Centro, CA 92244
(619) 352-6241
AREA OF OPERATION: City of El Centro

REGION: IX
Crown Development Corporation of Kings County
1222 West Lacey Boulevard
Suite 101
Hansford, CA 93230
(209) 582-4326
AREA OF OPERATION: Kings County

REGION: IX
Economic Development Foundation of Sacramento, Inc.
7509 Madison Avenue
Suite 111
Citrus Heights, CA 95610
(916) 962-3669
AREA OF OPERATION: Sacramento, Yuba, Sutter, Yolo, Contra Costa, San
   Joaquin, El Dorado, Place, Alameda, Napa, Sonama, Solano, Marin, San Fran-
   cisco, Santa Clara, San Mateo, Mendino, Santa Cruz, San Benito, Nevado,
   Sierra, Fresno

REGION: IX
Economic Development Corporation of Shasta County
737 Auditorium Drive
Suite D
Redding, CA 96001
(916) 225-5300
AREA OF OPERATION: Shasta, Trinity, Siskiyou and Modoc Counties

REGION: IX
Economic Development Corp. of Los Angeles County
550 S. Vermont Avenue
3rd Floor
Los Angeles, CA 90017
(213) 387-0322
AREA OF OPERATION: Los Angeles County

REGION: IX
Economic Development Corporation of Monterey County, Inc. (The)
3 Howard Street

P.O. Box 634
Salinas, CA 93902
(408) 424-0154
AREA OF OPERATION: Monterey County

REGION: IX
Gold Country Certified Development Company, Inc.
55 Stockton Street
Suite C
Sonora, CA 95370
(209) 532-6404
AREA OF OPERATION: Tuolumne, Alpine, Mariposa, and Calaveras Counties

REGION: IX
Greater Sacramento Certified Development Corporation
917 7th Street
P.O. Box 1017
Sacramento, CA 95805
(916) 446-8019
AREA OF OPERATION: Sacramento, El Dorado, Place and Yolo Counties

REGION: IX
HEDCO Local Development Corporation
222 S. Vineyard St. PH-1302
Honolulu, HI 96813-2445
(808) 521-6502
AREA OF OPERATION: Statewide and American Samoa

REGION: IX
Hawaii Certified Development Corporation
1150 South King Street
Rm. 203-A
Honolulu, HI 96814
(808) 531-7502
AREA OF OPERATION: City and County of Honolulu (Island of Oahu)

REGION: IX
Ingelwood Development Corporation
One Manchester Boulevard
3rd Floor, City Hall
Inglewood, CA 90301
(213) 412-5290
AREA OF OPERATION: City of Inglewood

REGION: IX
La Habra Local Development Company, Inc.

Civic Center
P.O. Box 337
La Habra, CA 90633-0337
(213) 905-9714
AREA OF OPERATION: Orange and Los Angeles Counties

REGION: IX
Little Lake Development Corporation
390 South Main Street
Willits, CA 95490
(707) 459-3505
AREA OF OPERATION: Mendocino County

REGION: IX
Long Beach Local Development Corporation
333 West Ocean Boulevard
3rd Floor
Long Beach, CA 90802
(213) 590-6847
AREA OF OPERATION: City of Long Beach and Signal Hill

REGION: IX
Los Angeles LDC, Inc.
200 North Spring Street
Suite 2008
Los Angeles, CA 90012
(213) 624-6753
AREA OF OPERATION: Citywide Los Angeles

REGION: IX
Los Medanos Fund, A Local Development Company
501 Railroad Avenue
Pittsburg, CA 94565
(415) 439-1056
AREA OF OPERATION: City of Pittsburg, Humboldt, Contra Costra, Solano,
    Sonoma, Napa, San Francisco, San Mateo, Santa Clara, Alameda, Marin Coun-
    ties

REGION: IX
Mid State Development Corporation
515 Truxton Avenue
Bakersfield, CA 93301
(805) 326-3765
AREA OF OPERATION: The County of Kern

REGION: IX
Nevada State Development Corporation

350 South Center
Suite 310
Reno, NV 89501
(702) 323-3625
AREA OF OPERATION: Statewide

REGION: IX
New Ventures Capital Development Company
716 South Sixth Street
Las Vegas, NV 89101
(702) 384-3293
AREA OF OPERATION: Clark County

REGION: IX
Oakland Certified Development Corporation
Dufwin Towers—519 17th Street
Suite 111
Oakland, CA 94612
(415) 763-4297
AREA OF OPERATION: City of Oakland

REGION: IX
Pasadena Development Corporation
586 North Lake Avenue
Pasadena, CA 91101
(818) 792-5764
AREA OF OPERATION: City of Pasadena

REGION: IX
Phoenix Local Development Corporation of Phoenix, AZ
1 North First Street, 7th Floor
Suite D
Phoenix AZ 85004
(602) 262-6004
AREA OF OPERATION: Citywide Phoenix

REGION: IX
Riverside County Economic Development Corporation
3499 Tenth Street
P.O. Box 1180
Riverside, CA 92501
(714) 787-9770
AREA OF OPERATION: Riverside County

REGION: IX
San Diego County Local Development Corporation
1100–22nd Street

P.O. Box 8128
San Diego, CA 92102
(619) 234-8811
AREA OF OPERATION: County of San Diego

REGION: IX
San Francisco Business Local Development Corporation
987 Valencia Street
San Francisco, CA 94110
(415) 282-8444
AREA OF OPERATION: Marin, Alameda, San Mateo, Santa Clara, and San Francisco Counties

REGION: IX
San Francisco Industrial Development Fund
100 Larking Street
San Francisco, CA 94102
(415) 558-5383
AREA OF OPERATION: City & County of San Francisco

REGION: IX
Santa Ana City Economic Development Corporation
20 Civic Center Plaza
Suite 624
Santa Ana, CA 92701
(714) 647-6971
AREA OF OPERATION: City of Santa Ana

REGION: IX
Six Rivers Local Development Corporation
1213 Fifth Street
Eureka, CA 95501
(707) 445-9561
AREA OF OPERATION: Humboldt County

REGION: IX
Small Business Development Corporation
Suite 204, Calvo Insurance Bldg.
115 Chalan Santo Papa
Agana, GU 96910
(   ) 472-8083
AREA OF OPERATION: Territory of Guam

REGION: IX
Southern Nevada Certified Development Corporation
2770 South Maryland Parkway #216
Las Vegas, NV 89106

(702) 732-3998
AREA OF OPERATION: Mineral, Emseralda, Nye, Lincoln, Lyon, Douglas, White Pine and Clark Counties

REGION: IX
Stanislaus County Economic Development Corporation
621 14th Street
Suite B
Modesto, CA 95354
(209) 521-9333
AREA OF OPERATION: Stanislaus County

REGION: IX
Tracy/San Joaquin County Certified Development Corp.
803 Central Avenue
P.O. Box 891
Tracy, CA 95376
(209) 468-3500
AREA OF OPERATION: San Joaquin County

REGION: IX
Tucson Local Development Corporation
250 W. Alameda
P.O. Box 27210
Tucson, AZ 85726-7210
(602) 791-4444
AREA OF OPERATION: Pima County, except the Indian Reservation

REGION: IX
Tulare County Economic Development Corporation
2380 West Whitendale Avenue
P.O. Box 5033
Visalia, CA 93278
(209) 627-0766
AREA OF OPERATION: Tulare County

REGION: IX
West Valley Certified Development Company
9650 Business Center Drive
Rancho Cucamong, CA 91762
(714) 989-1485
AREA OF OPERATION: San Bernardino County

REGION: X
C.C.D. Business Development Corporation

744 S. E. Rose Street
Roseburg, OR 97470
(503) 672-6728
AREA OF OPERATION: State of Oregon, except Wallowa County

REGION: X
Cascades West Financial Services, Inc.
155 S.W. Madison, #5
Corvallis, OR 97333
(503) 737-6854
AREA OF OPERATION: 7 County area (Benten, Lane, Lincoln, Linn, Marion, Polk and Yamhill)

REGION: X
Clearwater Economic Development Association
P.O. Box 9183
Moscow, ID 83843
(208) 882-3470
AREA OF OPERATION: Counties of Clearwater, Idaho, Latah, Lewis and Nez Perce in Idaho; Asotin, Garfield and Whitman in Washington

REGION: X
Columbia River Development Association
100 Columbia Way
Vancouver, WA 98661
(206) 694-5006
AREA OF OPERATION: Clark, Cowlitz, Lewis, Pacific, Wahkiakum, Skamania & Klicktat Counites of WA; Clatsop, Columbia, Tillamook, Multnomah Counties of OR

REGION: X
East-Central Idaho Development Company
12 North Central Street
P.O. Box 330
Rexburg, ID 83440
(208) 356-4524
AREA OF OPERATION: Bonneville, Butte, Clark, Custer, Fremont, Jefferson, Lemhi, Madison, and Teton Counties

REGION: X
Evergreen Community Development Association
2122 Smith Tower
Seattle, WA 98104
(206) 622-3731
AREA OF OPERATION: State of Washington except Garfield County

REGION: X
FPS Development Association
121 Astor Street
Box 214
Colville, WA 99114
(509) 684-4571
AREA OF OPERATION: Ferry, Pend, Oreille and Steven Counties

REGION: X
Greater Eastern Oregon Development Corporation
17 S.W. Frazer, Suite 20
P.O. Box 1041
Pendleton, OR 97801
(503) 276-6745
AREA OF OPERATION: Gilliam, Grant, Morrow, Umatilla, Wheller, Union,
  Baker, and Wallowa Counties

REGION: X
Greater Pocatello Development Corporation
427 North Main, Suite A
P.O. Box 626
Pocatello, ID 83201
(208) 234-7541
AREA OF OPERATION: Bannock, Power, Bear Lake, Bingham, Caribou, Frank-
  lin and Oneida Counties

REGION: X
Greater Spokane Business Development Association
W. 808 Spokane Fall Blvd.
Spokane, WA 99201
(509) 456-4380
AREA OF OPERATION: State of Washington except Pacific County

REGION: X
Lewis Clark Economic Development Corporation
P.O. Box 1989
Bollinger Plaza, Suite 303
Lewiston, ID 83501
(208) 743-1321
AREA OF OPERATION: Nez Perce County, Idaho; Asotin County, Washington,
  and the Whitman Port Area, Washington

REGION: X
Oregon Certified Business Development Corporation
1135 W. Highland

P.O. Box 575
Redmond, OR 97756
(503) 548-8163
AREA OF OPERATION: Crook, Deschutes, Harney, Jefferson, Klamath, Lake and
   Malheur Counties

REGION: X
Oregon Economic Development Corporation
595 Cottage Street, N.E.
Salem, OR 97310
(503) 373-7364
AREA OF OPERATION: Statewide

REGION: X
Panhandle Area Council, Inc.
11100 Airport Drive
Hayden, ID 83835
(208) 772-0584
AREA OF OPERATION: 5 Northern Counties of Idaho—Benewah, Bonner, Boundary, Kootenai, Shoshone

REGION: X
Railbelt Community Development Corporation
2805 Dawson Street
Anchorage, AK 99503
(907) 561-5226
AREA OF OPERATION: State of Alaska except First Judicial District (Southeast
   Alaska)

REGION: X
Regional IV Development Corporation
1300 Kimberly Road
P.O. Box 1844
Twin Falls, ID 83301
(208) 734-6387
AREA OF OPERATION: Blaine, Camas, Cassia, Gooding, Jerome, Lincoln, Mini-
   doka, and Twin Falls Counties

REGION: X
River East Progress, Inc.
3802 N.E. Union Avenue, #203
Portland, OR 97212
(503) 284-7440
AREA OF OPERATION: Multnomah, Clackamas and Washington Counites

REGION: X
Southeastern Washington Development Association

901 N. Colorado Street
Kennewick, WA 99336
(509) 735-6222
AREA OF OPERATION: Benton, Franklin, Grant, Adams, Yakima and Walla
   Walla Counties

REGION: X
Treasure Valley Certified Development Corporation
7243 Potomac
Boise, ID 83704
(208) 375-4651
AREA OF OPERATION: Idaho counties of Ada, Adams, Boise, Canyon, Elmore,
   Gem, Owyhee, Payette, Valley and Washington; Oregon counties of Harney and
   Malheur

## VENTURE CAPITAL NETWORKS

Below is a list of not-for-profit venture capital networks that bring
entrepreneurs and funding outlets together. They generally charge a small
fee for their services. These networks are funding facilitators that act only
as clearninghouses. They do not have their own capital for investment purposes, nor will they negotiate deals.

Venture Capital Network, Inc.
P.O. Box 882
Durham, N.H. 03824
(603) 862-3556

Indiana Seed Capital Network
Institute of New Business Ventures, Inc.
One North Capital, Suite 420
Indianapolis, Ind. 46204
(317) 634-8418

Venture Capital Network of New York, Inc.
TAC
State University College of Arts
   and Sciences
Plattsburgh, NY 12901
(518) 564-2214

Midwest Venture Capital Network
P.O. Box 4659
St. Louis, MO 63108
(314) 534-7204

Venture Capital Network of Atlanta, Inc.
230 Peachtree St. N.E., Suite 1810
Atlanta, GA 30303
(404) 658-7000

The Computerized Ontarior Investment
  Network (COIN)
Ontario Chamber of Commerce
2323 Yonge Street
Toronto, Ontario
Canada M4P 2C9
(416) 482-5222

Upper Peninsula Venture Capital
  Network, Inc.
206 Cohodas Administration Center
Northern Michigan University
Marquette, MI 49855
(906) 227-2406

Investment Contact Network
Institute for the Study of
  Private Enterprise
University of North Carolina
The Kenan Center 498A
Chapel Hill, NC 27514

Heartland Venture Capital Network
Evanston Business Investment Corporation
1710 Orrington Avenue
Evanston, IL 60201
(312) 864-7970

Mississippi Venture Capital Clearinghouse
Mississippi Research and Development Center
3825 Ridgewood Road
Jackson, Miss. 39211
(601) 982-6425

Casper College
Small Business Development Center
125 College Drive
Casper, WY 82601
(307) 235-4825

University of South Carolina at Aiken
171 University Parkway

Aiken, SC 29801
(803) 648-6851


## VENTURE CAPITAL CLUBS

Below is a list of venture capital clubs. They are membership organizations that operate as informal funding facilitators. They bring entrepreneur and investor together in group meetings. The entrepreneur will pitch his/her deal in front of the funding outlets. These clubs do not have their own capital for investment purposes, nor will they negotiate deals.

Venture capital clubs are noted for assisting firms in the seed and/or start-up phase of financing.

*Alabama*
Birmingham Venture Club
P.O. Box 10127
Birmingham, AL 35202
(205) 323-5461
Patricia Tucker Fox

Montgomery Venture Group
P.O. Box 1013
Montgomery, AL 36192
(205) 834-5100

*California*
Sacramento Valley
Venture Capital Forum
P.O. Box 1975
Davis, CA 95617
(916) 756-6430
Richard C. Dorf

Orange Coast Venture Group
P.O. Box 7282
Newport Beach, CA 92658
(714) 261-0130
Linder C. Hobbs

San Diego Venture Group
Suite 1900
701 B. Street
San Diego, CA 92101

(619) 457-2797
Robert Weaver

Channel Islands Venture Association
1157 Westridge Drive
Ventura, CA 93003
Mark B. Shappee
(805) 644-5335

*Colorado*
Colorado Venture Group
7353 S. Alton Way, Penthouse
Englewood, CO 80112
(303) 850-7611
John Fitzgerald

*Connecticut*
Connecticut Venture Group
P.O. Box 1333
Stamford, CT 06904
(203) 323-3143
Ginger M. More, President
Elizabeth McAuliffe, Executive
  Director

*Florida*
Gold Coast Venture Capital Club
110 E. Atlantic Ave., Suite 208 E
Del Ray Beach, FL 33444
(305) 272-1040      Oscar Ziemba

West Florida Venture Club
302 N. Barcelona Street
Pensacola, FL 32501
(904) 433-5619
Dan Horvath

*Illinois*
Chicago Venture Capital Network
32 W. Randolph Street
Suite 1450
Chicago, IL 60601
(312) 236-3623
Tim Eckerman

Southern Illinois
Venture Capital Group
2120 Richview Road
Mount Vernon, IL 62864
Thomas M. Green

*Kansas*
Kansas City Venture Group
35 Corporate Woods
9101 W. 110th Street
Overland Park, KS 66210
(913) 451-0026
Peter C. Brown

*Kentucky*
Central Kentucky
Venture Capital Club
P.O. Box 508
Elizabeth Town, KY 42701
(502) 769-1410
Ralph M. Mobley

*Maryland*
Baltimore-Washington Venture Group
P.O. Box 965
Bowie, MD 20715

*Michigan*
New Enterprise Forum
912 North Main Street

Ann Arbor, MI 48104
(313) 662-0550
Thomas S. Porter

Southeastern Michigan Venture Group
Rennaissance Center Station
P.O. Box 43181
Detroit, MI 48243
(313) 446-7169
Ben Jozefowicz

*Missouri*
Missouri Venture Forum, Inc.
8000 Maryland Ave. Suite 1540
St. Louis, MO 63105
(314) 862-5475
Lary R. Kirchenbauer

*Montana*
Economic Growth Council of
    Great Falls
P.O. Box 1273
Great Falls, MT 59403
(406) 761-5036
Gayle Keith

*Nebraska*
Nebraska Venture Group
Neb. Business Devel. Center
University of Nebraska
1313 Farnham-on-the-Mall
Omaha, NE 68182-0248
(402) 554-8381
Mary L. Woita

*New Jersey*
Southern New Jersey
Venture Capital Club
1200 Campus Drive RD#1
Mount Holly, NJ 08060
(609) 261-6000
Robert R. Little

Bergen County Venture Club

East 210 Route 4
Paramus, NJ 07652
(201) 843-0430
John R. Lieberman

*New Mexico*
Venture Capital Club of New Mexico
538 Camino del Monte Sol
Santa Fe, NM 87501
(505) 984-2905
Bill Royal

*New York*
Long Island Venture Group
Business Research Institute
Hofstra University
Hempstead, NY 11550
(516) 560-5175
George O. Goldner, Chairman
Russell M. Moore, Secretary-Contact

Hudson Valley Venture Group
P.O. Box 488
Washingtonville, NY 10992
(212) 249-0412
Scott Saland

Westchester Venture Capital Network
c/o County Chamber of Commerce
222 Mamaroneck Avenue
White Plains, NY 10605
(914) 948-2110
Harold E. Vogt

*Ohio*
Columbus Investment Int. Group
37 North High Street
Columbus, OH 43215
(614) 221-1321
Sue Erwin

*Oregon*
Southern Willamette Invest. Forum
2865 Taylor Street

Eugene, OR 97405
(503) 686-2688
Stephen Robinson

Venture Capital Group of Portland
P.O. Box 3983
Portland, OR 97208
(503) 665-2336
Michael B. Heller

*Tennessee*
Midsouth Venture Capital Assoc.
5475 Crestview Suite 100
Memphis, TN 38134
(901) 388-3050
Carla J. Marcrum

Tennessee Venture Group
Tennessee Manufacturers & Taxpayers
   Association
226 Capitol Blvd. Suite 800
Nashville, TN 37219
(615) 256-5141
Sharon Bell

*Texas*
East Texas Venture Capital Group
P.O. Box 2763
Beaumont, TX 77704
(409) 898-0227
George Weller

*Utah*
Mountain West Venture Group
P.O. Box 210
Salt Lake City, UT 84144
(801) 533-0777
Roy Jesperson

*Virginia*
Richmond Venture Capital Club
Ronald R. Eagle
Bank of Virginia
P.O. Box 25339
Richmond, VA 23260

*Washington*
Northwest Venture Group
P.O. Box 3293
Kirkland, WA 98033
(206) 746-1973
Keith Oppenneer

*Wisconsin*
Wisconsin Venture Network
611 N. Broadway Suite 333
Milwaukee, WI 53202
(414) 271-8252
Kenneth Burgess

*Canada*
Venture Capital Committee
Edmonton Chamber of Commerce
600 10123 99th Street
Edmonton, Alberta, Canada T5J 3G9
(403) 426-4620
Wayne L. Millar, Chairman

Toronto Venture Capital Club
Suite 207
825 Eglinton Ave. W.
Toronto, Ontario, Canada M5N 1E7
(416) 789-2654
Jerry Steiner

Venture Capital/Entrepreneurship
  Club of Montreal Inc.
3420 St-Hubert Suite 12
Montreal P.Q., Canada H2L 3Z7
(514) 288-5125
Claude Belanger

*Puerto Rico*
Puerto Rico Venture Capital Club
P.O. Box 2284
Hato Rey, Puerto Rico 00919
(809) 787-9040
Antonio Vázquez

*South Africa*
Johannesburg Venture Capital Club
c/o Arthur Andersen & Co.
37th Floor, Commissioner Street
Carlton Centre, Johannesburg
South Africa 2000
G.R. Rosenthal

# APPENDICES

## APPENDIX A

Dun & Bradstreet
99 Church Street
New York, New York 10007

KEY BUSINESS RATIOS

*Retailing*
Auto and home supplies
Children's and infants' wear stores
Clothing and furnishings, men's and boys'
Department stores
Discount stores
Discount stores, leased departments
Family clothing stores
Furniture stores
Gasoline service stations
Grocery stores
Hardware stores
Household appliance stores
Jewelry stores
Lumber and other building materials dealers
Miscellaneous general merchandise stores
Motor vehicle dealers
Paint, glass and wallpaper stores
Radio and television stores
Retail nurseries, lawn and garden supply dealers
Shoe stores
Variety stores
Women's ready-to-wear stores

*Wholesaling*
Air conditioning and refrigeration equipment and supplies
Automotive equipment
Beer, wine and alcoholic beverages

Chemicals and allied products
Clothing and accessories, women's and children's
Clothing and furnishings, men's and boys'
Commercial machines and equipment
Confectionery
Dairy products
Drugs, drug proprietaries, and sundries
Electrical appliances, TV and radio sets
Electrical apparatus and equipment
Electronic parts and equipment
Farm machinery and equipment
Footwear
Fresh fruits and vegetables
Furniture and home furnishings
Groceries, general line
Hardware
Industrial machinery and equipment
Lumber and construction materials
Meats and meat products
Metals and minerals
Paints, varnishes, and supplies
Paper and its products
Petroleum and petroleum products
Piece goods
Plumbing and heating equipment and supplies
Poultry and poultry products
Scrap and waste materials
Tires and tubes
Tobacco and its products

*Manufacturing and Construction*
Agricultural chemicals
Airplane parts and accessories
Bakery products
Blast furnaces, steel works, and rolling mills
Blouses and waists
Books, publishing and printing
Broad woven fabrics, cotton
Canned and preserved fruits and vegetables
Commercial printing except lithographic
Communication equipment
Concrete, gypsum and plaster products
Confectionery and related products
Construction, mining and handling machinery and equipment
Converted paper and paperboard products
Cutlery, hand tools and general hardware
Dairy products
Dresses

Drugs
Electric lighting and wiring equipment
Electric transmission and distribution equipment
Electrical industrial apparatus
Electrical work
Electronic components and accessories
Engineering, laboratory and scientific instruments
Fabricated structural metal products
Farm machinery and equipment
Footwear
Fur goods
General building contractors
General industrial machinery and equipment
Grain mill products
Heating and plumbing equipment
Heavy construction, except highway and street
Hosiery
Household appliances
Industrial

## Cost of Doing Business

*Retailing*
Apparel and accessories
Automotive dealers
Building materials, hardware, and farm equipment
Drug and proprietary stores
Eating and drinking places
Food stores
Furniture and home furnishings
Gasoline service stations
General merchandise
Liquor stores

*Wholesaling*
Alcoholic beverages
Drugs
Dry goods
Electrical goods
Farm products
Groceries
Hardware, plumbing and heating equipment
Lumber and construction materials
Machinery
Metals and minerals
Motor vehicles
Paper and its products
Petroleum and its products

*Manufacturing*
Apparel
Chemicals and allied products
Electrical supplies and equipment
Fabricated metal products
Food products (bakery products, beverage industries, canned goods, dairy
    products, grain mill products, meats, and sugar)
Furniture and fixtures
Leather and its products
Lumber and wood products
Machinery
Motor vehicles and equipment
Ordnance. except guided missiles
Paper and allied products
Petroleum refining
Primary metal industries
Printing and publishing
Rubber and miscellaneous plastics products
Scientific industries
Stone, clay, and glass products
Textile mill products
Tobacco
Transportation equipment

*Services, Transportation and Communications*
Advertising
Air transportation
Automobile parking, repair and service
Business services
Electrical companies and systems
Hotels
Medical services
Motion picture production
Motion picture theaters
Personal services
Pipeline transportation
Radio and television broadcasting
Railroad transportation
Repair services
Telephone and telegraph services
Trucking and warehousing
Water supply and other sanitary services
Water transportation

*Finance, Insurance, and Real Estate*

*Agriculture and Mining*

Robert Morris Associates
Philadelphia National Bank Building
Philadelphia, Pennsylvania 19107

*Manufacturing*
Advertising displays and devices
Apparel and other finished fabric products:
   Canvas products
   Children's clothing
   Curtains and draperies
   Men's, youths' and boys' suits, coats and overcoats
   Women's dresses
   Women's suits, skirts, sportswear and coats
   Women's undergarments and sleepwear
Beverages:
   Flavoring extracts and syrups
   Malt liquors
   Wines, distilled liquor and liqueurs
Caskets and burial supplies
Chemicals and allied products:
   Drugs and medicines
   Fertilizers
   Industrial chemicals
   Paint, varnish and lacquer
   Perfumes, cosmetics and other toilet preparations
   Plastic materials and synthetic resins
   Soap, detergents and cleaning preparations
Food and kindred products:
   Bread and other bakery products
   Candy and dried fruits and vegetables
   Dairy products
   Flour and other grain mill products
   Frozen fruits, fruit juices, vegetables, and specialties
   Meat packing
   Prepared feeds for animals and poultry
   Vegetable oils
Furniture and fixtures:
   Mattresses and bedsprings
   Metal household furniture
   Store, office, bar and restaurant fixtures
   Wood furniture—except upholstered
   Wood furniture—upholstered

Jewelry, precious metals
House furnishings
Leather and leather products:
  Footwear
  Furs
  Hats
  Men's and boys' sport clothing
  Men's work clothing
  Men's, youths' and boys' separate trousers
  Men's, youths' and boys' shirts, collars and nightwear
  Luggage and special leather products
Tanning, currying, and finishing
Lumber and wood products:
  Millwork
  Prefabricated wooden buildings and structural members
  Sawmills and planing mills
  Veneer, plywood, and hardwood
  Wooden boxes and containers
Machinery, equipment and supplies—electrical:
  Air conditioning
  Electronic components and accessories
  Equipment for public utilities and industrial use
Machinery, except electrical equipment:
  Ball and roller bearings
  Construction and mining machinery and equipment
  Farm machinery and equipment
  General industrial machinery and equipment
  Industrial and commercial refrigeration equipment and complete air conditioning units
  Machine shops—jobbing and repair
  Machine tools and metal working equipment
  Measuring, analyzing, and controlling instruments
  Oil field machinery and equipment
  Special dies and tools, die sets, jigs and fixtures
  Special industry machinery
Metal industries—primary:
  Iron and steel forgings
  Iron and steel foundries
  Non-ferrous foundries
Metal products—fabricated (except ordnance, machinery, and transportation equipment):
  Coating, engraving and allied services
  Cutlery, hand tools and general hardware
  Enameled iron, metal sanitary ware and plumbing supplies
  Fabricated plate ware
  Fabricated structural steel
  Heating equipment, except electric

Metal cans
Metal doors, sash, frames, molding and trim
Metal stampings
Miscellaneous fabricated wire products
Miscellaneous non-ferrous fabricated products
Screw machine products, bolts, nuts, screws, rivets and washers
Sheet metal work
Valves and pipe fittings, except plumbers' brass goods
Paper and allied products:
Envelopes, stationery and paper bags
Paperboard containers and boxes
Pulp, paper and paperboard
Printing, publishing and allied industries:
Book printing
Bookbinding and miscellaneous related work
Books: publishing
Commercial printing, lithographic
Newspapers: publishing and printing
Periodicals
Typesetting
Rubber and miscellaneous plastics products:
Miscellaneous plastics products
Rubber footwear and fabricated rubber products
Stone, clay and glass products:
Brick and structural clay tile
Concrete brick, block and other products
Minerals and earths, ground or otherwise treated
Pressed and blown glass and glassware
Ready-mixed concrete
Textile mill products:
Broad woven fabric—cotton, silk and synthetic
Broad woven fabric—woolens and worsteds
Dyeing and finishing
Hosiery—anklets—children's, men's and boys'
Hosiery—women's—full fashioned and seamless
Knitting—cloth, outerwear and underwear
Narrow fabrics and other smallwares
Yarn—cotton, silk and synthetic
Toys, amusement, sporting and athletic goods:
Games and toys, except dolls and children's vehicles
Sporting and athletic goods
Transportation equipment:
Aircraft parts (except electric)
Motor vehicle parts and accessories
Motor vehicles
Ship and boat building and repairing

*Wholesaling*
Automotive equipment and supplies:
   Automobiles and other motor vehicles
   Automotive equipment
   Tire and tubes
Beauty and barber supplies and equipment
Drugs, drug proprietaries and druggists' sundries
Electrical equipment:
   Electrical supplies and apparatus
   Electronic parts and supplies
   Radios, refrigerators and electrical appliances
Flowers and florists' supplies
Food, beverages and tobacco:
   Coffee, tea and spices
   Confectionery
   Dairy products and poultry
   Fish and sea foods
   Frozen foods
   Fruits and vegetables
   General groceries
   Grains
   Meats and meat products
   Tobacco and tobacco products
   Tobacco leaf
   Wine, liquor and beer
Furniture and home furnishings:
   Floor coverings
   Furniture
General merchandise
Iron, steel, hardware and related products:
   Air conditioning and refrigeration equipment and supplies
   Hardware and paints
   Metal products
   Metal scrap
   Plumbing and heating equipment and supplies
   Steel warehousing
Lumber, building materials and coal:
   Building materials
   Coal and coke
   Lumber and millwork
Machinery and equipment:
   Agricultural equipment
   Heavy commercial and industrial machinery and equipment
   Laundry and dry cleaning equipment and supplies
   Mill supplies
   Professional equipment and supplies
   Restaurant and hotel supplies, fixtures and equipment
   Transportation equipment and supplies, except motor vehicles

Paper and paper products:
  Printing and writing paper
  Wrapping or coarse paper and products
Petroleum products:
  Fuel oil
  Petroleum products
Scrap and waste materials:
  Textile waste
Sporting goods and toys
Textile products and apparel:
  Dry goods
  Footwear
  Furs
  Men's and boys' clothing
  Women's and children's clothing
  Wool

*Retailing*
Aircraft
Apparel and accessories:
  Family clothing stores
  Furs
  Infants' clothing
  Men's and boys' clothing
  Shoes
  Women's ready-to-wear
Boat dealers
Books and office supplies:
  Books and stationery
  Office supplies and equipment
Building materials and hardware:
  Building materials
  Hardware stores
  Heating and plumbing equipment dealers
  Lumber
  Paint, glass and wallpaper stores
Cameras and photographic supplies
Department stores and general merchandise:
  Department stores
  Dry goods and general merchandise
Drugs
Farm and garden equipment and supplies:
  Cut flowers and growing plants
  Farm equipment
  Feed and seed—farm and garden supply
Food and beverages:
  Dairy products and milk dealers
  Groceries and meats
  Restaurants

Fuel and ice dealers:
  Fuel, except fuel oil
  Fuel oil dealers
Furniture, home furnishings and equipment:
  Floor coverings
  Furniture
  Household appliances
  Radio, TV, and record players
Jewelry
Liquor
Luggage and gifts
Motor vehicle dealers:
  Autos—new and used
  Gasoline service stations
  Mobile homes
  Motorcycles
  Tires, batteries, and accessories
  Trucks—new and used
Musical instruments and supplies
Road machinery equipment
Sporting goods
Vending machine operators, merchandise

*Services*
Advertising agencies
Auto repair shops
Auto and truck rental and leasing
Bowling alleys
Cable television
Car washing
Commercial research and development laboratories
Data processing
Direct mail advertising
Engineering and architectural services
Farm products warehousing
Funeral directors
Insurance agents and brokers
Intercity bus lines
Janitorial services
Laundries and dry cleaners
Linen supply
Local trucking
Local trucking—without storage
Long distance trucking
Motels, hotels, and tourist courts
Nursing homes
Outdoor advertising
Photographic studios

Radio broadcasting
Real estate holding companies
Refrigerated warehousing, except food lockers
Refuse systems
Telephone communications
Transportation on rivers and canals
Travel agencies
Television stations
Water utility companies

*Contractors*

*Not Elsewhere Classified*
Beef cattle raisers
Bituminous coal mining
Bottlers—soft drinks
Commercial feed lots
Construction, sand and gravel
Crude petroleum and natural gas mining
Horticultural services
Poultry, except broiler chickens
Seed companies (vegetable and garden)

Accounting Corporation of America
Research Department
1929 First Avenue
San Diego, California 92101

Apparel, children's and infants
Apparel, men's specialty
Apparel, men's and women's
Apparel, women's specialty
Appliance stores
Auto parts and accessories
Bakeries
Beauty shops
Cocktail lounges
Confectionery stores
Contractors—building
Contractors—specialty
Dairies
Dentists
Doctors of medicine
Dry cleaning shops
Drug stores
Feed and seed stores
Florists
Food stores—combination

Food stores—specialty
Furniture stores
Garages
Gift and novelty stores
Hardware stores
Jewelry stores
Laundromats and hand laundries
Laundries, plant
Liquor stores
Lumber and building material
Machine shops
Meat markets
Motels
Music stores
New car dealers
Nursery and garden supplies
Paint, glass and wallpaper
Photographic supply stores
Plumbing and heating equipment
Printing shops

Professional—others
Repair services
Restaurants
Service stations
Shoe stores
Sporting goods stores

Taverns
TV radio sales and service
Transportation
Used car dealers
Variety stores

## National Cash Register Company

Apparel stores
Appliance and radio-TV dealers
Automobile dealers
Auto parts dealers
Beauty shops
Book stores
Building material dealers
Cocktail lounges
Department stores
Dry cleaners
Feed stores
Florists
Food stores
Furniture stores
Garages
Gift, novelty and souvenir stores
Hardware stores
Hotels
Jewelry stores
Laundries

Liquor stores
Mass merchandising stores
Meat markets
Men's wear stores
Motels and motor inns
Music stores
Novelty stores
Nursery and garden supply stores
Photographic studio and supply
   stores
Professional services
Repair services
Restaurants
Service Stations
Shoe stores (family)
Sporting goods stores
Supermarkets
Transportation and service
Variety stores

## TRADE ASSOCIATIONS

Associations which have published
ratio studies in the past include the following:

American Camping Association
5000 State Road, 67 North
Martinsville, IN
46151
317-342-8456

American Jewelry Distributors Association
1900 Arch Street
Philadelphia, PA
19103
215-564-3484

American Association
   of Advertising Agencies
666 Third Avenue
New York, NY
10017
212-682-2500

American Meat Institute
P.O. Box 3556
Washington, DC
20001
202-841-2400

American Paper Institute
260 Madison Avenue
New York, NY
10016
212-340-0600

American Society of Association Executives
1575 Eye Street NW
Washington, DC
20005
202-626-2723

American Supply Association
20 N. Wacker Drive, Suite 2260
Chicago, IL
60600
312-236-4082

Bowling Proprietors Association
   of America
Box 5802
Arlington, TX
76011
817-460-2121

Building Owners and Managers Assoc.,
   International
1250 Eye Street NW, Suite 200
Washington, DC
20005
202-289-7000

Door and Hardware Institute
7711 Old Springhouse Road
McLean, VA
22102
703-556-3990

Florists Transworld Delivery Assoc.,
   Interflora
29200 Northwestern Highway
Southfield, MI
48076
313-355-9300

Food Marketing Institute
Suite 700, 1750 K Street, NW

Washington, DC
20006
202-452-8444

Foodservice Equipment Distributors
   Association
332 South Michigan Avenue
Chicago, IL
60604
312-427-9605

Independant Insurance Agents of America
100 Church Street
New York, NY
10007
212-285-4250

Laundry and Cleaners Allied Trade
   Association
543 Valley Road
Upper Montclair, NJ
07043
201-744-0090

Material Handling Equipment Distributors
   Assoc.
201 Route 45
Vernon Hills, IL
60061
312-680-3500

Mechanical Contractors Association
   of America
5410 Grosvenor Lane, Suite 120
Bethesda, MD
20814
301-897-0770

Menswear Retailers of America
Suite 600, 2011 Eye Street, NW
Washington, DC
20006
202-347-1932

Motor and Equipment Manufacturers
   Association
300 Sylvan Avenue

Englewood Cliffs, NJ
07632
201-568-9500

Nat'l Assoc. of Textile and Apparel
  Wholesalers
P.O. Box 759
Mamaroneck, NY
10543
914-381-5660

Nat'l Lumber and Building Material
  Dealers Assoc.
40 Ivy Street S.E.
Washington, DC
20036
202-547-2230

National American Wholesale Grocers
  Association
201 Park Washington Court
Falls Church, VA
20046
703-532-9400

National Art Materials Trade Association
178 Lakeview Drive, Box 739
Clifton, NJ
07015
201-546-6400

National Association of Accountants
Ten Paragon Drive
Montvale, NJ
07645
201-573-9000

National Association
  of Electrical Distributors
28 Cross Street
Norwalk, CT
06851
203-846-6800

National Association
  of Furniture Manufacturers

P.O. Box HP-7
High Point, NC
27261
919-884-5000

National Association
  of Music Merchants, Inc.
5140 Avenida Encinas
Carlsbad, CA
92008
619-438-8001

National Association
  of Plastics Distributors
5001 College Blvd., Suite 201
Leawood, KS
66211
913-431-4698

National Association
  of Retail Dealers of America
Ten East 22nd St.
Lombard, IL
60148
312-953-8950

National Association
  of Tobacco Distributors
1199 N. Fairfax Street, Suite 701
Alexandria, VA
22314
703-683-8336

National Beer Wholesalers Association
  of America
5205 Leesburg Pike, Suite 505
Falls Church, VA
22041
703-578-4300

National Confectioners Association
  of the U.S.
645 Michigan Avenue, Suite 1006
Chicago, IL
60611
312-280-1460

National Consumer Finance Association
4th Floor, 1101 14th Street
Washington, DC
20005
202-289-0400

National Decorating Products Association
1050 North Lindbergh Blvd.
St. Louis, MO
63132
314-991-3470

National Electrical Contractors Association,
   Inc.
7315 Wisconsin Avenue, 13th Fl.
Bethesda, MD
20814
301-657-3110

National Electrical Manufacturers Association
2101 L. Street, NW
Washington, DC
20037
202-457-8400

National Farm
   and Power Equipment Dealers Assoc.
10877 Watson Road
St. Louis, MO
63127
314-821-7220

National Grocers Association
Suite 820, 1825 Samuel Morse Drive
Reston, VA
22090
703-437-5300

National Home Furnishings Association
405 Merchants Mart Plaza
Chicago, IL
60654
312-836-0777

National Kitchen Cabinet Association
P.O. Box 6830
Falls Church, VA

22046
703-237-7580

National Machine Tool Builders
   Association
7901 Westpark Drive
McLean, VA
22102
703-893-2900

National Office Products Association
301 North Fairfax Street
Alexandria, VA
22314
703-549-9040

National Oil Jobbers Council
1120 Vermont Avenue, NW, Suite 1130
Washington, DC
20005
202-331-1198

National Paint and Coatings Association
1500 Rhode Island Avenue NW
Washington, DC
20005
202-462-6272

National Paper Box and Packing Association
231 Kings Highway East
Haddonfield, NJ
08033
609-429-7377

National Paper Trade Association
111 Great Neck Road
Great Neck, NY
11021
516-829-3070

National Parking Association
1112 16th Street NW, Suite 2000
Washington, DC
20036
202-296-4336

National Restaurant Association

311 First Street, NW
Washington, DC
20001
202-638-6100

National Retail Hardware Association
770 North High School Road
Indianapolis, IN
46224
317-248-1261

National Retail Merchants Association
100 West 31st Street
New York, NY
10016
212-244-8780

National Shoe Retailers Association
1414 Sixth Avenue
New York, NY
10019
212-752-2555

National Soft Drink Association
1101 16th Street, NW
Washington, DC
20036
202-436-6732

National Sporting Goods Association
1699 Wall Street
Mt. Prospect, IL
60056
312-439-4000

National Tire Dealers and Retailers
1250 Eye Street, NW, Suite 400
Washington, DC
20005
202-789-2300

National Wholesale Druggists Assoc.
105 Oronoco Street
Alexandria, VA
22314
703-684-6400

National Wholesale Hardware Association
1900 Arch Street
Philadelphia, PA
19103
215-564-3484

North American Heating
  and Air Conditioning Wholesales Assoc.
P.O. Box 16790
Columbus, OH
43216
614-488-1835

North American Wholesale Lumbers Association
Suite 680, 2340 South Arlington Heights Road
Arlington Heights, IL
60005
312-981-8630

Northeastern Retail Lumbermans Association
339 East Avenue
Rochester, NY
14604
716-325-1626

Optical Laboratories Association
P.O. Box 2000
Merrifield, VA
22116
703-849-8550

Painting and Decorating Contractors
  of America
7223 Lee Highway
Falls Church, VA
22406
703-534-1201

Petroleum Equipment Institute
Box 2380
Tulsa, OK
74101
918-743-9941

Printing Industries of America, Inc.
1730 North Lynn Street

Arlington, VA
22209
703-841-8100

Scientific Apparatus Makers of America
1101 Sixteenth Street, Suite 300, NW
Washington, DC
20036
202-223-1360

Shoe Service Institute of America
154 West Hubbart Street
Chicago, IL
60610
312-670-3732

Textile Care Allied Trades Association
543 Valley Road
Upper Montclair, NJ
07043
201-744-0090

The Society of the Plastics Industry, Inc.
1025 Connecticut Avenue, NW, Suite 409
Washington, DC
20036
202-822-6700

United Fresh Fruits
  and Vegetables Association
727 N. Washington Street
Alexandria, VA
22314
703-836-3410

Urban Land Institute
Suite 300, 1090 Vermont Avenue, NW
Washington, DC
20005
202-289-8500

Wine and Spirit Wholesalers
  of America
2033 M. Street, NW, Suite 400
Washington, DC
20026
202-293-9220

472

# APPENDIX B

## SMALL BUSINESS DEVELOPMENT CENTERS

University of Alabama
Small Business Development Center
Birmingham, AL 35294
(205) 934-6760

University of Arkansas
Small Business Development Center
Little Rock, AR 77203
(501) 371-5381

University of Connecticut
Small Business Development Center
School of Business Administration
Storrs, CT 06268
(203) 486-4135

Howard University
Small Business Development Center
Washington, D.C. 20059
(202) 636-7187

University of West Florida
Small Business Development Center
School of Business Administration
Pensacola, FL 32504
(904) 476-9500, Ext. 2908

University of Georgia
Small Business Development Center
Athens, GA 30602
(404) 542-5760

Iowa State University
Small Business Development Center
Center for Industrial Research and
  Service
Ames, IA 50011
(515) 294-3420

University of Kentucky
Small Business Development Center
Lexington, KY 40506
(606) 257-1751

University of Massachusetts
Small Business Development Center
School of Business Administration
Amherst, MA 01003
(413) 549-4930, Ext. 304

University of Southern Maine
Small Business Development Center
Portland ME 04102
(207) 780-4432

St. Thomas College
Small Business Development Center
St. Paul, MN 55105
(612) 697-5840

University of Mississippi
Small Business Development Center
Jackson, MS 39211
(601) 982-6684

St. Louis University
Small Business Development Center
School of Business and Administra-
  tion
St. Louis, MO 63108
(314) 658-3826

University of Nebraska—Omaha
Small Business Development Center
Omaha, NE 68182
(402) 554-3291

Rutgers University
Small Business Development Center
Newark, NJ 07102
(201) 648-5621

University of Pennsylvania
Small Business Development Center
The Wharton School
Philadelphia, PA 19104
(215) 243-4861, Ext. 228

University of South Carolina
Small Business Development Center
Basic Service Center
College of Business Administration
Columbia, SC 29208
(803) 777-5118

University of Utah
Small Business Development Center
Graduate School of Business
Salt Lake City, UT 84112
(801) 581-7905

Small Business Development Center
  of Vermont, Inc.
Chance Mill, One Mill St.

Burlington, VT 05401
(802) 862-0200

Washington State University
Small Business Development Center
Pullman, WA 99164
(509) 335-1576

University of Charleston
Small Business Development Center
Charleston, WV 25304
(304) 346-9471

University of Wisconsin
Small Business Development Center
Madison, WI 53706
(608) 263-2221

474

# APPENDIX C

# BUSINESS DEVELOPMENT PAMPHLETS (SBA)

*Financial Management and Analysis*

___MA 1.001 The ABC's of Borrowing
___MA 1.004 Basic Budgets for Profit Planning
___MA 1.009 A Venture Capital Primer for Small Business
___MA 1.010 Accounting Services for Small Service Firms
___MA 1.011 Analyze Your Records to Reduce Costs
___MA 1.015 Budgeting in a Small Business Firm
___MA 1.016 Sound Cash Management and Borrowing
___MA 1.017 Keeping Records in Small Business
___MA 1.018 Checklist for Profit Watching
___MA 1.019 Simple Breakeven Analysis for Small Stores
___MA 4.013 A Pricing Checklist for Small Retailers


*General Management and Planning*

___MA 2.002 Locating or Relocating Your Business
___MA 2.004 Problems in Managing a Family-Owned
           Business
___MA 2.007 Business Plan for Small Manufacturers
___MA 2.008 Business Plan for Small Construction Firms
___MA 2.010 Planning and Goal Setting for Small Business
___MA 2.011 Fixing Production Mistakes
___MA 2.014 Should You Lease or Buy Equipment?
___MA 2.016 Checklist for Going Into Business
___MA 2.020 Business Plan for Retailers
___MA 2.022 Business Plan for Small Service Firms
___MA 2.025 Thinking About Going Into Business
___MA 2.026 Feasibility Checklist for Starting a Small
           Business of Your Own
___MA 2.027 How to Get Started with a Small Business
           Computer
___MA 2.028 The Business Plan for Homebased Business
___MA 3.005 Stock Control for Small Stores
___MA 3.010 Techniques for Problem Solving
___MA 5.009 Techniques for Productivity Improvement
___**MA 6.004 Selecting the Legal Structure for Your Business**
___MA 7.007 Evaluating Franchise Opportunities


*Crime Prevention*

___MA 3.006 Reducing Shoplifting Losses
___MA 5.005 Preventing Employee Pilferage


*Marketing*

___MA 4.002 Creative Selling: The Competitive Edge
___MA 4.005 Is the Independent Sales Agent for You?

—MA 4.012 Marketing Checklist for Small Retailers
—MA 4.015 Advertising Guidelines for Small Retail Firms
—MA 4.018 Plan Your Advertising Budget
—MA 4.019 Learning about Your Market
**—MA 4.023 Selling by Mail Order**
—MA 7.003 Market Overseas with U.S. Government Help

*Personnel Management*

—MA 5.001 Checklist for Developing a Training Program
—MA 5.007 Staffing Your Store
—MA 5.008 Managing Employee Benefits

*New Products/Ideas/Inventions*

—MA 2.013 Can You Make Money with Your Idea or
          Invention?
—MA 6.005 Introduction to Patents
—SBIR-T1  Proposal Preparation for Small Business
          Innovation Research

*Miscellaneous*

—SBB 2    Home Businesses*

*A *Small Business Bibliography (SBB)* includes some text,
but is mainly an in-depth bibliography on a whole range of
books, newsletters, associations, etc.

# TO ORDER

1. Check the titles that you want.

2. Figure the cost below:
   No. of Pamphlets _____ × $.50 = $_____

3. Write a check or money order to:
   **U.S. SMALL BUSINESS ADMINISTRATION**
   (NOTE: No cash, credit cards, or purchase orders)

4. Fill in your name and address on reverse page.

5. Mail order form and payment to:
   **U.S. SMALL BUSINESS ADMINISTRATION**
   **P.O. BOX 30**
   **DENVER, CO 80201-0030**

6. Please allow six weeks for delivery.

476

## APPENDIX D

## BUSINESS DEVELOPMENT BOOKLETS (SBA)

**To Order:** Complete the Order Form and check off requested publications. Send it with your check or money order to the Superintendent of Documents, Government Printing Office, Washington, D.C. 20402. Make check or money order payable to the **Superintendent of Documents.** Do not send postage stamps or cash. **These booklets are not sold by the Small Business Administration. Do not send payment for booklets to SBA.** If Business Development Pamphlets are also being ordered (Form 115A), send a **separate payment** to SBA for the pamphlets. Foreign remittances should be made by international money order payable to the Superintendent of Documents, by draft drawn in U.S. dollars on an American or Canadian bank located in the U.S. or Canada, or by UNESCO coupons. **Please note:** In accordance with U.S. Department of the Treasury regulations, checks drawn on Canadian banks for amounts of less than four U.S. dollars ($4.00) cannot be accepted. This regulation also applies to Canadian money orders. If the value of your order is less than $4.00, we suggest you charge your order to your MasterCard or VISA account. Please include your card number and date of expiration. Prices subject to change without notice.

### Small Business Management Series

The books in this series discuss specific management techniques or problems.

**No.**

9. **Cost Accounting for Small Manufacturers**
   Assists managers of small manufacturing firms establish accounting procedures that help control production and business costs.
15. **Handbook of Small Business Finance**
20. **Ratio Analysis for Small Business**
25. **Guides for Profit Planning**
   Guides for computing and using the breakeven point, the level of gross profit, and the rate of return on investment.
29. **Management Audit for Small Manufacturers**
   A questionnaire for manufacturers.
30. **Insurance and Risk Management for Small Business**
31. **Management Audit for Small Retailers**
   149 questions to review business operations.
32. **Financial Recordkeeping for Small Stores**
33. **Small Store Planning for Growth**
   Covers merchandising, advertising and display, and provides checklists to increase sales.
35. **Franchise Index/Profile**
   Presents an evaluation process that may be used to investigate franchise opportunities.
36. **Training Salesmen to Serve Industrial Markets**
37. **Financial Control by Time-Absorption Analysis**

**No.**
38. **Management Audit for Small Service Firms**
    A questionnaire for service firms.
39. **Decision Points in Developing New Products**
    Provides a path from idea to marketing plan for the small
    manufacturing or R & D firm.
41. **Purchasing Management and Inventory Control for Small
    Business**
42. **Managing the Small Service Firm for Growth and Profit**
43. **Credit and Collections for Small Stores**
44. **Financial Management: How to Make a Go of Your Business**


## Starting and Managing Series

This series is designed to help the small
entrepreneur "to look before leaping" into a
business.

**No.**
  1. **Starting and Managing a Small Business of Your Own**
101. **Starting and Managing a Small Service Business**
102. **Starting and Managing a Small Business from Your Home**
103. **Small Business Incubator Handbook: A Guide for Start-up
     and Management**


## Nonseries Publications

**A Basic Guide to Exporting**
003-009-00349-1 (Commerce Dept.)
**U.S. Government Purchasing and Sales Directory**
A directory for businesses interested in selling to the U.S.
Government. Lists the purchasing needs of various Agencies.
045-000-00226-8
**Managing for Profits**
Discusses the various management functions.
045-000-00206-3
**Buying and Selling a Small Business**
045-000-00164-4
**Women Business Owners: Selling to the Federal Government**
045-000-00229-2


## Business Basics

Each of the 23 self-study booklets in this series
contains text, questions, and exercises that teach a
specific aspect of small business management.

**No.**
1001  The Profit Plan
1002  Capital Planning
1003  Understanding Money Sources

## Business Basics (continued)

1004  Evaluating Money Sources
1005  Asset Management
1006  Managing Fixed Assets
1007  Understanding Costs
1008  Cost Control
1009  Marketing Strategy
1010  Retail Buying Function
1011  Inventory Management—Wholesale/Retail
1012  Retail Merchandise Management
1013  Consumer Credit
1014  Credit and Collections: Policy and Procedures
1015  Purchasing for Manufacturing Firms
1016  Inventory Management—Manufacturing/Service
1017  Inventory and Scheduling Techniques
1018  Risk Management and Insurance
1019  Managing Retail Salespeople
1020  Job Analysis, Job Specifications, and Job Descriptions
1021  Recruiting and Selecting Employees
1022  Training and Developing Employees
1023  Employee Relations and Personnel Policies

## Order Form Check List
## Small Business Management Series

| No. | Stock No. | Price |
|---|---|---|
| 9. _____ | 045-000-00162-8 | $6.00 |
| 15. _____ | 045-000-00208-0 | 4.50 |
| 20. _____ | 045-000-00150-4 | 4.50 |
| 25. _____ | 045-000-00137-7 | 4.50 |
| 29. _____ | 045-000-00151-2 | 4.25 |
| 30. _____ | 045-000-00209-8 | 5.00 |
| 31. _____ | 045-000-00149-1 | 4.50 |
| 32. _____ | 045-000-00142-3 | 5.50 |
| 33. _____ | 045-000-00152-1 | 5.50 |
| 35. _____ | 045-000-00125-3 | 4.50 |
| 36. _____ | 045-000-00133-4 | 2.50 |
| 37. _____ | 045-000-00134-2 | 5.50 |
| 38. _____ | 045-000-00203-9 | 4.50 |
| 39. _____ | 045-000-00146-6 | 4.25 |
| 41. _____ | 045-000-00167-9 | 4.50 |
| 42. _____ | 045-000-00165-2 | 4.25 |
| 43. _____ | 045-000-00169-5 | 5.00 |
| 44. _____ | 045-000-00233-1 | 2.50 |

## Starting and Managing Series

| No. | Stock No. | Price |
|---|---|---|
| 1. _____ | 045-000-00212-8 | $4.75 |
| 101. _____ | 045-000-00207-1 | 4.50 |
| 102. _____ | 045-000-00232-2 | 1.75 |
| 103. _____ | 045-000-00237-3 | 8.50 |

## Nonseries Publications

| Stock No. | Price |
|---|---|
| _____ 003-009-00349-1 | $6.50 |
| _____ 045-000-00226-8 | 5.50 |
| _____ 045-000-00206-3 | 5.50 |
| _____ 045-000-00164-4 | 5.00 |
| _____ 045-000-00229-2 | 2.75 |

## Business Basics

| No. | Stock No. | Price |
|---|---|---|
| 1001. | _____ 045-000-00192-0 | $4.50 |
| 1002. | _____ 045-000-00193-8 | 4.50 |
| 1003. | _____ 045-000-00194-6 | 4.75 |
| 1004. | _____ 045-000-00174-1 | 5.00 |
| 1005. | _____ 045-000-00175-0 | 2.75 |
| 1006. | _____ 045-000-00176-8 | 4.75 |
| 1007. | _____ 045-000-00195-4 | 3.25 |
| 1008. | _____ 045-000-00187-3 | 4.75 |
| 1009. | _____ 045-000-00188-1 | 4.75 |
| 1010. | _____ 045-000-00177-6 | 4.50 |
| 1011. | _____ 045-000-00190-3 | 4.50 |
| 1012. | _____ 045-000-00178-4 | 4.75 |
| 1013. | _____ 045-000-00179-2 | 4.50 |
| 1014. | _____ 045-000-00180-6 | 4.75 |
| 1015. | _____ 045-000-00181-4 | 4.75 |
| 1016. | _____ 045-000-00182-2 | 4.75 |
| 1017. | _____ 045-000-00183-1 | 4.75 |
| 1018. | _____ 045-000-00184-9 | 4.50 |
| 1019. | _____ 045-000-00189-0 | 4.75 |
| 1020. | _____ 045-000-00185-7 | 4.50 |
| 1021. | _____ 045-000-00186-5 | 4.50 |
| 1022. | _____ 045-000-00191-1 | 4.50 |
| 1023. | _____ 045-000-00196-2 | 4.50 |

## APPENDIX E
### SMALL BUSINESS ADMINISTRATION DISTRICTS

*Alabama*
2121 8th Avenue North
Suite 200
Birmingham, AL 35203-2398
205/731-1344

*Alaska*
Room 1068, Module G
8th & C Street
Anchorage, AK 99513
907/271-4022

*Arizona*
2205 North Central Avenue
5th Floor
Phoenix, AZ 95004
602/261-3732

*Arkansas*
320 W. Capitol Avenue
Suite 601
Little Rock, AR 72201
501/378-5871

*California*
2202 Monterey Street
Suite 108
Fresno, CA 93721
209/487-5189

350 S. Figueroa Street
Sixth Floor
Los Angeles, CA 90071
213/894/2956

880 Front Street
Suite 4-S-29
San Diego, CA 92188
619/293-7272

211 Main Street
4th Floor
San Francisco, CA 94105
415/974-0642

*Colorado*
721—19th Street
Denver, CO 80202-2599
303/844-2607

*Connecticut*
440 Main Street
2nd Floor
Hartford, CT 06106
203/240-4700

*Delaware*
Branch Office
844 King Street, Room 5207
Lockbox 16
Wilmington, DE 19801
302/573-6294

*District of Columbia*
1111—18th Street, N.W.
Sixth Floor
Washington, DC 20036
202/634-4950

*Florida*
1320 S. Dixie Highway
Suite 501
Coral Gables, FL 33146
305/536-5521

400 West Bay Street
Room 261
Jacksonville, FL 32202

*Georgia*
1720 Peachtree Road, N.W.
6th Floor
Atlanta, GA 30309
404/347-4749

*Hawaii*
300 Ala Moana
Room 2213
Honolulu, HI 96850
808/541-2990

*Idaho*
1020 Main Street
Suite 290
Boise, ID 83702
208/334-1696

*Illinois*
219 South Dearborn St.
Room 437
Chicago, IL 60604
312/353-4528

*Indiana*
575 N. Pennsylvania Street
Room 578
Indianapolis, IN 46204-1584
317/269-7272

*Iowa*
373 Collins Road, N.E.
Room 100
Cedar Rapids, IA 52404
319/399-2571

210 Walnut Street
Room 749
Des Moines, IA 50309
515/284-4422

*Kansas*
Main Place Building
110 East Waterman Street
Wichita, KS 67202
316/269-6571

*Kentucky*
Federal Office Building
600 Federal Place
Room 188
Louisville, KY 40202
502/582-5976

*Louisiana*
Ford-Fisk Building
1661 Canal St.—2nd Floor
New Orleans, LA 70112
504/589-6685

*Maine*
40 Western Avenue
Room 512
Augusta, ME 04330
207/622-8378

*Maryland*
20 N. Calvert Street
3rd Floor
Baltimore, MD 21202
301/962-4392

*Massachusetts*
10 Causeway Street
Room 265
Boston, MA 02222-1093
617/565-5590

*Michigan*
McNamara Building
477 Michigan Avenue
Room 515
Detroit, MI 48226
313/226-6075

*Minnesota*
100 North 6th Street
Room 610
Minneapolis, MN 55403
612/349-3550

*Mississippi*
Dr. A.H. McCoy Federal Building
100 West Capitol Street
Suite 322
Jackson, MS 39269
601/965-4378

*Missouri*
1103 Grand Avenue
6th Floor
Kansas City, MO 64106
816/374-3419

815 Olive Street
Room 242

St. Louis, MO 53101
314/425-6600

*Montana*
301 South Park Avenue
Room 528
Helena, MT 59626
406/449-5381

*Nebraska*
11145 Mill Valley Road
Omaha, NE 68154
402/221-4691

*Nevada*
Box 7527—Downtown St.
301 E. Stewart
Las Vegas, NV 89125
702/388-6611

*New Hampshire*
55 Pleasant Street
Room 210
P.O. Box 1257
Concord, NH 03301
603/225-1400, Ext. 4402

*New Jersey*
60 Park Place
4th Floor
Newark, NJ 07102
201/645-3683

*New Mexico*
Patio Plaza Building, Suite 320
5000 Marble Avenue, N.E.
Albuquerque, NM 87110
505/262-6171

*New York*
26 Federal Plaza
Room 3100
New York, NY 10278
212/264-1318

Federal Building, Room 1071
100 South Clinton Street

Syracuse, NY 13260
315/423-5383

*North Carolina*
222 South Church Street
Room 300
Charlotte, NC 28202
704/371-6563

*North Dakota*
Federal Building
657 Second Avenue, North
Room 218
Fargo, ND 58102
701/237-5771

*Ohio*
AJC Federal Bldg., Room 317
1240 East 9th Street
Cleveland, OH 44199
216/522-4180

Federal Building, U.S. Courthouse
85 Marconi Blvd., Rm 512
Columbus, OH 43215-2887
614/469-6860

*Oklahoma*
200 N.W. 5th Street
Suite 670
Oklahoma City, OK 73102
405/231-4301

*Oregon*
Federal Building, Room 676
1220 S.W. Third Avenue
Portland, OR 97204-2882
503/294-5221

*Pennsylvania*
231 St. Asaphs Road
Suite 400 East
Bala Cynwyd, PA 19004
215/596-5801

960 Penn Avenue
5th Floor

Pittsburgh, PA 15222
412/644-2780

*Puerto Rico/Virgin Islands*
Federico Degatau Federal Building
Room 691
Carlos Chardon Avenue
Hato Rey, PR 00918
809/753-4002

*Rhode Island*
380 Westminster Mall
Providence, RI 02903
401/528-4586

*South Carolina*
1835 Assembly Street
Room 358
Columbia, SC 29202
803/765-5376

*South Dakota*
101 South Main Avenue
Suite 101, Security Building
Sioux Falls, SD 57102-0577
605/336-2980

*Tennessee*
404 James Robertson Pkwy.
Suite 1012, Parkway Towers
Nashville, TN 37219
615/736-5881

*Texas*
1100 Commerce Street
Room 3036
Dallas, TX 75242
214/767-0605

10737 Gateway West
Suite 320
El Paso, TX 79935
915/541-7586

222 E. Van Buren St.
Suite 500

Harlingen, TX 78550
512/427-8533

2525 Murworth
Suite 112
Houston, TX 77054
713/660-4401

1611 10th Street
Suite 100
Lubbock, TX 79401

Federal Bldg., Room A-513
727 East Durango Street
San Antonio, TX 78206
512/229-6250

*Utah*
125 South State Street
Room 2237
Salt Lake City, UT 84138-1195
801/524-5800

*Vermont*
87 State Street
Room 205
Montpelier, VT 05602
802/828-4474

*Virginia*
400 North 8th Street
Room 3015
P.O. Box 10126
Richmond, VA 23240
804/771-2617

*Washington*
915 Second Avenue
Room 1792
Seattle, WA 98174
206/442-5534

W. 920 Riverside Avenue
Room 651
Spokane, WA 99210
509/456-3783

*West Virginia*
168 West Main Street
5th Floor
Clarksburg, WV 26301
304/623-5631

*Wisconsin*
212 E. Washington Avenue

Room 213
Madison, WI 53703

*Wyoming*
100 East B Street
Federal Bldg., Room 4001
P.O. Box 2839
Casper, WY 82602-2839
307/261-5761

485

# APPENDIX F

SMALL BUSINESS ADMINISTRATION

## REQUEST FOR COUNSELING

Print

| Name of Company | Name of Inquirer | Telephone # |
|---|---|---|

| Street | City | State | County | Zip |
|---|---|---|---|---|

| Employer ID # | Social Security Number | Veteran | Viet Era Veteran |
|---|---|---|---|
| | | Yes ☐  No ☐ | Yes ☐  No ☐  Discharged: |

Are you presently:
- In Business? Yes ☐ No ☐
- Starting a Business? Yes ☐ No ☐
- SBA Borrower? Yes ☐ No ☐

Can you furnish a recent:
- Balance Sheet? Yes ☐ No ☐
- Profit & Loss Statement? Yes ☐ No ☐

Kind of business/services (Please specify)
- Retail (Selling) _____
- Service (Kind) _____
- Manufacturing (Product) _____
- Construction _____
- Wholesale (Selling) _____
- Other (Specify) _____

Check the problem areas for which you seek assistance.
- ☐ 1. Starting a New Business
- ☐ 2. Sources of Credit and Financing
- ☐ 3. Increasing Sales
- ☐ 4. Advertising & Sales Promotion
- ☐ 5. Market Research
- ☐ 6. Selling to the Government
- ☐ 7. Bidding and Estimating
- ☐ 8. International Trade
- ☐ 9. Recordkeeping and Accounting
- ☐ 10. Financial Statements
- ☐ 11. Office or Plant Management
- ☐ 12. Personnel
- ☐ 13. Engineering and Research
- ☐ 14. Inventory Control
- ☐ 15. Purchasing
- ☐ 16. Credit & Collections

Please describe how SBA may be of assistance.

I request management assistance from the Small Business Administration. I understand that this assistance is free of charge. I agree to cooperate should I be selected to participate in surveys designed to evaluate SBA assistance services. I authorize SBA to furnish relevant information to the assigned management counselor although I expect that information to be held in strict confidence by him/her.

I further understand that any counselor has agreed not to: (1) recommend goods or services from sources in which he/she has an interest and (2) accept fees or commissions developing from this counseling relationship. In consideration of SBA's furnishing management or technical assistance, I waive all claims against SBA personnel or counselors arising from this assistance.

| Signature and Title of Requestor | Date |
|---|---|

SBA Form 641 (9-85)  Use 4-84 Edition Until Exhausted

* U.S GPO 1986 – 623-252

# APPENDIX G

## U.S. DEPARTMENT OF COMMERCE FIELD OFFICES

*Alabama*
Room 302
2015 2nd Avenue, North
3rd Floor, Berry Bldg.
Birmingham, AL 35203
(205) 731-1331

*Alaska*
701 C Street
P.O. Box 32
Anchorage, AK 99513
(907) 271-5041

*Arizona*
Federal Bldg. & U.S. Courthouse
230 North 1st Avenue, Rm 3412
Phoenix, AZ 85025
(602) 261-3285

*Arkansas*
Suite 811
Savers Federal Building
320 W. Capitol Avenue
Little Rock, AK 72201
(501) 378-5794

*California*
Room 800
11777 San Vicente Boulevard
Los Angeles, CA 99049
(213) 209-6705

116-A W. 4th Street
Suite #1
Santa Ana, CA 92701
(714) 836-2461

6363 Greenwich Drive
San Diego, CA 92122
(619) 293-5395

Federal Building
Box 36013
450 Golden Gate Avenue
San Francisco, CA 94102
(415) 556-5860

*Colorado*
Room 119
U.S. Customhouse
721–19th Street
Denver, CO 80202
(303) 844-3246

*Connecticut*
Room 610-B
Federal Office Building
450 Main Street
Hartford, CT 06103
(203) 240-3530

*Delaware*
Serviced by Philadelphia District Office

*District of Columbia*
Room 1066 HCHB
Department of Commerce
14th and Constitution Ave., N.W.
Washington, DC 20230
(202) 377-3181

*Florida*
Suite 224
Federal Building
51 S.W. First Avenue
Miami, FL 33130
(305) 536-5267

128 North Osceola Avenue
Clearwater, FL 33515
(813) 461-0011

Independence Square
Suite 3205C
Jacksonville, FL 32202
(904) 791-2796

75 East Ivanhoe Boulevard
Orlando, FL 32802
(305) 425-1234

Collins Building, Rm 401
107 W. Gaines Street

Tallahassee, FL 32304
(904) 488-6469

*Georgia*
Suite 504
1365 Peachtree Street, N.E.
Atlanta, GA 30309
(404) 347-7000

*Hawaii*
4106 Federal Building
P.O. Box 50026
300 Ala Moana Boulevard
Honolulu, HI 96850
(808) 541-1782

*Idaho*
Statehouse
Room 113
Boise, ID 83720
(208) 334-2740

*Illinois*
1406 Mid Continental Plaza Building
55 East Monroe Street
Chicago, IL 60603
(312) 353-4450

W. R. Harper College
Algonquin & Roselle Rd.
Palatine, IL 60067
(312) 397-3000, Ext. 532

515 North Court Street
P.O. Box 1747
Rockford, IL 61110-0247
(815) 987-8123

*Indiana*
357 U.S. Courthouse
    & Federal Office Bldg.
46 East Ohio Street
Indianapolis, IN 46204
(317) 269-6214

*Iowa*
817 Federal Building

210 Walnut Street
Des Moines, IA 50309
(515) 284-4222

*Kansas*
River Park Place
Suite 565
727 North Waco
Wichita, KS 67203
(316) 269-6160

*Kentucky*
Room 636B
Gene Snyder Courthouse
    & Customhouse Bldg.
601 W. Broadway
Louisville, KY 40202
(502) 582-5006

*Louisiana*
432 World Trade Center
No. 2 Canal Street
New Orleans, LA 70130
(504) 589-6546

*Maine*
77 Sewell Street
Augusta, ME 04330
(207) 622-8249

*Maryland*
415 U.S. Customhouse
Gay and Lombard Streets
Baltimore, MD 21202
(301) 962-3560

*Massachusetts*
World Trade Center
Suite 307
Commonwealth Pier Area
Boston, MA 02210
(617) 565-8563

*Michigan*
1140 McNamara Bldg.
477 Michigan Avenue

Detroit, MI 48226
(313) 226-3650

300 Monroe N.W.
Room 409
Grand Rapids, MI 49503
(616) 456-2411

*Minnesota*
108 Federal Building
110 S. Fourth Street
Minneapolis, MN 55401
(612) 348-1638

*Mississippi*
328 Jackson Mall Office Center
400 Woodrow Wilson Boulevard
Jackson, MS 39213
(601) 965-4388

*Missouri*
7911 Forsyth Boulevard
Suite 610
St. Louis, MO 63105
(314) 425-3302-4

Room 635
601 East 12th Street
Kansas City, MO 64106
(816) 374-3141

*Montana*
Serviced by Denver District Office

*Nebraska*
1113 "O" Street
Omaha, NE 68137
(402) 221-3664

*Nevada*
1755 E. Plumb Lane, #152
Reno, NV 89502
(702) 784-5203

*New Hampshire*
Serviced by Boston District Office

*New Jersey*
3131 Princeton Pike
Building 4D
Suite 211
Trenton, NJ 08648
(609) 989-2100

*New Mexico*
517 Gold, S.W.
Suite 4303
Albuquerque, NM 87102
(505) 766-2386

*New York*
1312 Federal Building
111 West Huron Street
Buffalo, NY 14202
(716) 846-4191

121 East Avenue
Rochester, NY 14604
(716) 263-6480

Federal Office Building
26 Federal Plaza
Foley Square
New York, NY 10278
(212) 264-0634

*North Carolina*
324 West Market Street
P.O. Box 1950
Greensboro, NC 27402
(919) 333-5345

*North Dakota*
Serviced by Omaha District Office

*Ohio*
9504 Federal Office Building
550 Main Street
Cincinnati, OH 45202
(513) 684-2944

Room 668
666 Euclid Avenue

Cleveland, OH 44114
(216) 522-4750

*Oklahoma*
5 Broadway
Executive Park Suite 200
6601 Broadway Extension
Oklahoma City, OK 73116
(405) 231-5302

440 Houston Street
Tulsa, OK 74127
(918) 581-7650

*Oregon*
Room 618
1220 S.W. 3rd Avenue
Portland, OR 97204
(503) 221-3001

*Pennsylvania*
9448 Federal Building
600 Arch Street
Philadelphia, PA 19106
(215) 597-2850

2002 Federal Building
1000 Liberty Avenue
Pittsburgh, PA 15222
(412) 644-2850

*Puerto Rico*
Room 659
Federal Building
San Juan, PR 00918
(809) 753-4555, Ext. 555

*Rhode Island*
7 Jackson Walkway
Providence, RI 02903
(401) 528-5104, Ext. 22

*South Carolina*
Strom Thurmond Federal Bldg.
Suite 172
1835 Assembly Street

Columbia, SC 29201
(803) 765-5345

17 Lockwood Drive
Charleston, SC 29401
(803) 724-4361

*South Dakota*
Serviced by Omaha District Office

*Tennessee*
Suite 1114
Parkway Towers
404 James Robertson Parkway
Nashville, TN 38013-1505
(615) 736-5161

555 Beale Street
Memphis, TN 38103
(901) 521-4137

*Texas*
Room 7A5
1100 Commerce Street
Dallas, TX 75242
(214) 767-0542

410 East 5th St.
Room 304
Austin, TX 78711
(512) 472-5059

2625 Federal Courthouse
515 Rusk Street
Houston, TX 77002
(713) 229-2578

*Utah*
Room 340
U.S. Courthouse
350 S. Main Street
Salt Lake City, UT 84101
(801) 524-5116

*Vermont*
Serviced by Boston District Office

490

*Virginia*
8010 Federal Building
400 North 8th Street
Richmond, VA 23240
(804) 771-2246

*Washington*
3131 Elliott Avenue
Suite 290
Seattle, WA 98121
(206) 442-5616

West 808 Spokane Falls Boulevard
Room 623
Spokane, WA 99201
(509) 456-4557

*West Virginia*
3402 New Federal Building
500 Quarrier Street
Charleston, WV 26301
(304) 347-5123

*Wisconsin*
Federal Building
U.S. Courthouse
517 E. Wisconsin Avenue
Milwaukee, WI 53202
(414) 291-3473

*Wyoming*
Serviced by Denver District Office

# APPENDIX H
## MINORITY BUSINESS DEVELOPMENT AGENCY (MBDA)
### REGIONAL OFFICES

SAN FRANCISCO REGIONAL
OFFICE
211 Main Street, 12th Floor
San Francisco, CA 94105
415-974-9597
FTS-454-9597
Alaska, American Samoa, Arizona, California, Hawaii, Idaho, Nevada, Oregon, Washington

WASHINGTON REGIONAL OFFICE
14th & Constitution Avenue, N.W.
Room 6711
Washington, D.C. 20230
202-377-8275
FTS-377-8275
Delaware, Maryland, Pennsylvania, Virginia, Washington, D.C., West Virginia

ATLANTA REGIONAL OFFICE
1371 Peachtree Street, N.E.
Suite 505
Atlanta, GA 30309
404-347-4091
FTS-257-4091
Alabama, Florida, Georgia, Kentucky, Mississippi, No. Carolina, So. Carolina, Tennessee

CHICAGO REGIONAL OFFICE
55 East Monroe Street
Suite 1440
Chicago, IL 60603
312-353-0182
FTS-353-0182
Illinois, Indiana, Iowa, Kansas, Michigan, Minnesota, Missouri, Nebraska, Ohio, Wisconsin

NEW YORK REGIONAL OFFICE
26 Federal Plaza, Room 3720
New York, NY 10278
212-264-3262
FTS-264-3262
Connecticut, Maine, Massachusetts, New Hampshire, New Jersey, Puerto Rico, Rhode Island, Vermont, The Virgin Islands

DALLAS REGIONAL OFFICE
1100 Commerce Street
Room 7B19
Dallas TX 75242
214-767-8001
FTS-729-8001
Arkansas, Colorado, Louisiana, Montana, New Mexico, No. Dakota, So. Dakota, Oklahoma, Texas, Utah, Wyoming

### DISTRICT OFFICES

2500 Wilshire Blvd., Suite 908
Los Angeles, CA 90057
213-688-7157
FTS-798-7157

Federal Office Bldg., Room 930
51 SW 1st Avenue
Miami, FL 33130
305-350-5054
FTS-350-5054

10 Causeway Street, Room 418
Boston, MA 02222-1041
617-565-6850
FTS-835-6850

Federal Office Bldg., Rm. 9436
600 Arch Street
Philadelphia, PA 19106
215-597-9236
FTS-597-9236

MINORITY BUSINESS DEVELOPMENT CENTERS (MBDC)

ALASKA MBDC
1011 East Tudor Rd., Suite 210
Anchorage, AK 99503
907-562-2322

BIRMINGHAM MBDC
2000 First Avenue North, Ste. 722
Birmingham, AL 35203
205-252-3682

MOBILE MBDC
4321 Downtowner Loop North
Suite D
Mobile, AL 36609
205-344-9650

MONTGOMERY MBDC
503 South Court Street, Suite 400
Montgomery, AL 36104
205-263-0818

LITTLE ROCK MBDC
One Riverfront Place, Suite 415
North Little Rock, AR 72114
501-372-7312

PHOENIX MBDC
5050 North 19th Avenue
Suite 405
Phoenix, AZ 85015
602-433-0153

AMERICAN INDIAN
  CONSULTANTS MBDC
2070 East Southern Avenue
Tempe, AZ 85282
602-945-2635

ARIZONA INDIAN MBDC
2111 East Baseline Rd., Ste. F-8
Tempe, AZ 85283
602-831-7524

TUCSON MBDC
181 West Broadway

Tucson, AZ 85701
602-629-9744

ANAHEIM MBDC
2700 North Main St., Suite 810
Santa Ana, CA 92701
714-667-8200

BAKERSFIELD MBDC
1308 Chester Avenue
Bakersfield, CA 93301
805-328-1111

CALIFORNIA INDIAN MBDC
9650 Flair Drive, Suite 303
El Monte, CA 91731-3008
818-442-3701

FRESNO MBDC
NEDA San Joaquin Valley
2010 North Fine, Suite 103
Fresno, CA 93727
209-252-7551

LOS ANGELES NORTH MBDC
3460 Wilshire Blvd., Suite 1006
Los Angeles, CA 90010
213-382-5032

LOS ANGELES SOUTH MBDC
3807 Wilshire Blvd., Suite 700
Los Angeles, CA 90010-3108
213-380-9541

OXNARD MBDC
451 West 5th Street
Oxnard, CA 93030
805-483-1123

RIVERSIDE MBDC
3601 University Avenue, Suite 200
Riverside, CA 92501
714-788-9777

SACRAMENTO MBDC
530 Bercut Drive, Suite C
Sacramento, CA 95814
916-443-0700

SALINAS MBDC
137 Central Avenue, Suite 1
Salinas, CA 93901
408-422-3701

SAN DIEGO MBDC
6363 Alvarado Court, Room 225
San Diego, CA 92120
619-265-3684

SAN FRANCISCO/OAKLAND
  MBDC
One California Street, Suite 2100
San Francisco, CA 94111
415-989-2920

SANTA BARBARA MBDC
829 De La Vina, Suite 300
Santa Barbara, CA 93101
505-564-2414

SAN JOSE MBDC
4701 Patrick Henry Drive, Bldg. 9
Santa Clara, CA 95054
408-980-0371

STOCKTON MBDC
37th West Yokuts, Suite C-4
Stockton, CA 95207
209-957-5721

DENVER/COLORADO SPRINGS
  MBDC
428 East 11th Avenue
Denver, CO 80203
303-832-2228

CONNECTICUT MBDC
410 Asylum Street, Suite 243
Hartford, CT 06103
203-246-5371

JACKSONVILLE MBDC
333 North Laura Street, Suite 465
Jacksonville, FL 32202-3508
904-353-3826

MIAMI/FT. LAUDERDALE MBDC
7925 N.W. 12th Street, Suite 117
Miami, FL 33126
305-591-7355

ORLANDO MBDC
132 East Colonial Dr., Suite 211
Orlando, FL 32801
305-422-6234

TAMPA MBDC
5020 West Cypress Street
Sun Bank Building, Suite 617
Tampa, FL 33607
813-875-1711

WEST PALM BEACH MBDC
1675 Palm Beach Lakes Blvd.
Tower, A, Suite 1002
West Palm Beach, FL 33401
305-683-4400

ATLANTA MBDC
75 Piedmont Avenue, N.E., Suite 256
Atlantic, GA 30303
404-586-0973

AUGUSTA MBDC
1208 Laney Walker Blvd.
P.O. Box 1283
Augusta, GA 30901
404-722-0994

COLUMBUS MBDC
1214 First Avenue, Suite 430
P.O. Box 1696
Columbus, GA 31902-1696
404-324-4253

SAVANNAH MBDC
31 West Congress St., Suite 201

Savannah, GA 31401
912-236-6708

HONOLULU MBDC
1001 Bishop Street, Room 1340
Honolulu, HI 96813
808-533-4401

CHICAGO SOUTH MBDC (1)
35 East Wacker Drive, Suite 790
Chicago, IL 60601
312-977-9190

CHICAGO NORTH MBDC (2)
600 Prudential Plaza 6th Floor
130 East Randolph
Chicago, IL 60601
312-565-4710

GARY MBDC
567 Broadway, P.O. Box 9007
Suite 4
Gary, IN 46402
219-883-5802

INDIANAPOLIS MBDC
1201 Merchants Plaza
101 West Washington Street
Indianapolis, IN 46204
317-636-5592

LOUISVILLE MBDC
835 West Jefferson St., Suite 103
Louisville, KY 40202
502-589-7401

BATON ROUGE MBDC
2036 Wooddale Blvd., Suite D
Baton Rouge, LA 70806
504-924-0186

NEW ORLEANS MBDC
1440 Canal Street, Suite 1619
New Orleans, LA 70112
504-529-5157

SHREVEPORT MBDC
4050 Linwood Avenue, Suite 206
Shreveport, LA 71108-2430
318-636-6969

BOSTON MBDC
Twin City Office Plaza
264 Msgr. O'Brien Highway
Cambridge, MA 02141
617-776-8980

BALTIMORE MBDC
2901 Druid Park Drive, Suite 203
Baltimore, MD 21215
301-462-3700

DETROIT MBDC
65 Cadillac Square, Suite 2215
Detroit, MI 48226-2822
313-961-2100

MINNESOTA CHIPPEWA TRIBE
  MBDC
Route 2, Facility Center
P.O. Box 217
Cass Lake, MN 56633
218-335-2252

MINNEAPOLIS/ST. PAUL MBDC
950 East Hennepin Avenue
Minneapolis, MN 55414
612-623-3977

KANSAS CITY MBDC
Commerce Bank Building, Suite 1000
1000 Walnut Street
Kansas City, MO 64106
816-221-6500

ST. LOUIS MBDC
500 Washington Avenue, Suite 1200
St. Louis, MO 63101
314-621-6232

JACKSON MBDC
1350 Livingston Lane, Suite A

Jackson, MS 39213
601-362-1631

CHARLOTTE MBDC
230 So. Tryon Street, Suite 810
Charlotte, NC 28202
704-334-7522

CHEROKEE MBDC
Qualla Boundary, P.O. Box 1200
Cherokee, NC 28719
704-497-9335

FAYETTEVILLE MBDC
114½ Anderson Street
P.O. Box 1387
Fayetteville, NC 28302
919-483-7513

RALEIGH/DURHAM MBDC
114 West Parrish Street
P.O. Box 1008
Durham, NC 27702
919-683-1047

BISMARCK IBDC
3315 University Drive
Bismarck, ND 58501
701-255-3285

NEW BRUNSWICK MBDC
134 New Street, Room 102
New Brunswick, NJ 08901
201-247-2000

NEWARK MBDC
60 Park Place, Suite 1604
Newark, NJ 07102
201-623-7710

ALBUQUERQUE MBDC
718 Central Street, S.W.
Albuquerque, NM 87102
505-843-7114

NEW MEXICO INDIAN MBDC
1015 Indian School Road, N.W.
P.O. Box 6507, Station B
Albuquerque, NM 87197-6507
505-242-4774

LAS VEGAS MBDC
701 East Bridger, Suite 701
Las Vegas, NV 89101
702-384-3293

BRONX MBDC
349 East 149th Street, Suite 702
Bronx, NY 10451
212-665-8583

BROOKLYN MBDC
50 Court Street, Suite 304
Brooklyn, NY 11201
718-797-9224

OPPORTUNITY DEVELOPMENT
  ASSO. MBDC
12 Heyward Street
Brooklyn, NY 11211
718-522-5620

BUFFALO MBDC
523 Delaware Avenue
Buffalo, NY 14202
716-885-0336

QUEENS MBDC
110–29 Horace Harding Expressway
Corona, NY 11368
718-699-2400

NASSAU/SUFFOLK MBDC
555 Broadhollow Road, Suite 230
Melville, NY 11747
516-420-4090

MANHATTAN MBDC
551 Fifth Avenue, Suite 320

New York, NY 10176
212-661-8044

ROCHESTER MBDC
One Marine Midland Plaza, Suite 1400
Rochester, NY 14604
716-454-1644

CINCINNATI/DAYTON MBDC
113 West Fourth Street, Suite 600
Cincinnati, OH 45202
513-381-4770

CLEVELAND MBDC
601 Lakeside Avenue, Room 335
Cleveland, OH 44114
216-664-4150

COLUMBUS MBDC
815 E. Mound Street, 2nd Floor
Columbus, OH 43205
614-252-0197

OKLAHOMA CITY MBDC
1500 NE 4th Street, Suite 101
Oklahoma City, OK 73117
405-235-0430

OKLAHOMA INDIAN MBDC
1600 19th Street, S.E. Suite 501
Edmond, OK 73013
405-341-5047

TULSA MBDC
240 East Apache Street
Tulsa, OK 74106
918-584-0001

PORTLAND MBDC
8959 SW Barbur Blvd., Suite 102
Portland, OR 97219
503-245-9253

PHILADELPHIA MBDC
30 South 15th, 1 Penn Square
14th Floor

Philadelphia, PA 19102
215-561-7300

PITTSBURGH MBDC
1040 Fifth Avenue
Pittsburgh, PA 15219
412-261-3073

MAYAGUEZ MBDC
P.O. Box 3146, Marina Station
Mayaguez, PR 00709
809-833-7783

PONCE MBDC
19 Salud Street
Ponce, PR 00731
809-840-8100

SAN JUAN MBDC
207 O'Neill Street
GPO Box 3631
San Juan, PR 00936
809-753-8484

CHARLESTON MBDC
701 East Bay Street, Suite I-539
Box 1413
Charleston, SC 29403-5033
803-724-3477

COLUMBIA MBDC
2700 Middleburg Drive, Suite 208
P.O. Box 5915
Columbia, SC 29250
803-256-0528

GREENVILLE/SPARTANBURG
  MBDC
300 University Ridge, Suite 210
Greenville, SC 29601
803-271-8753

MEMPHIS MBDC
Five North Third Street, 2nd Floor
Memphis, TN 38103
901-527-2298

NASHVILLE MBDC
404 James Robertson Parkway
Suite 1920
Nashville, TN 37219
615-255-0432

AUSTIN MBDC
2009 B East Riverside Drive
Austin, TX 78741
512-448-4101

BEAUMONT MBDC
3155 Executive Blvd., Suite 210
Beaumont, TX 77705
409-842-1958

BROWNSVILLE MBDC
855 West Price Road, Suite 6
Brownsville, TX 78520
512-544-7173

CORPUS CHRISTI MBDC
3649 Leopard Street, Suite 514
Corpus Christi, TX 78408
512-887-7961

DALLAS/FT. WORTH/WACO
  MBDC
800 Allied Bank Tower
Dallas, TX 75202
214-855-7373

EL PASO MBDC
3707 Admiral, Suite A
El Paso, TX 79925
915-592-2020

HOUSTON MBDC
2870 Citicorp Center
1200 Smith Street
Houston, TX 77002
713-650-3831

LAREDO MBDC
800 East Mann Road, Suite 101

Laredo, TX 78041
512-742-8305

McALLEN MBDC
4307 North 10th Street, Suite F
McAllen, TX 78501
512-687-8336

LUBBOCK/MIDLAND-ODESSA
  MBDC
1301 Keith Street
Midland, TX 79701
915-683-6152

SAN ANTONIO MBDC
Business Development Center
College of Business Administration
University of Texas at San Antonio
San Antonio, TX 78285
512-224-1945

SALT LAKE CITY MBDC
350 East 500 South, No 101
Salt Lake City, UT 84111
801-328-8181

NEWPORT NEWS MBDC
2600 Washington Avenue, Suite 502
Newport News, VA 23607
804-928-2222

NORFOLK MBDC
One Main Plaza, Suite 801
Norfolk, VA 23510
804-627-5254

RICHMOND MBDC
Heritage Building
1001 East Main Street, Suite 525
Richmond, VA 23219
804-648-0200

U.S. VIRGIN ISLAND MBDC
P.O. Box 838

St. Thomas, VI 00801
809-774-7215

SEATTLE MBDC
North Gate Executive Center One
155 N.E. 100th, Suite 401
Seattle, WA 98125
206-525-5617

MILWAUKEE MBDC
135 West Wells Street, Suite 428
Milwaukee, WI 53203
414-272-8300

## STATE AND LOCAL OFFICES

STATE OF ALASKA
Alaska Department of Commerce
 & Economic Development
Office of Enterprise
P.O. Box D
Juneau, AK 99801
907-465-2018

CITY OF PHOENIX
Equal Opportunity Department
251 West Washington, 3rd Floor
Phoenix, AZ 85003-2299
602-262-7716

CITY OF SAN DIEGO
202 C Street, M.S.9A
San Diego, CA 92101
619-236-6945

CITY OF SAN FRANCISCO
 S & L GOV'T
City Hall, Room 284
San Francisco, CA 94102
415-554-6748

CITY OF HARTFORD S & L GOV'T
Finance Department
550 Main Street
Hartford, CT 06103
203-722-6608

CITY OF WILMINGTON
City County Building
800 French Street, 5th Floor
Wilmington, DE 19801
302-571-4323

IOWA STATE UNIVERSITY
205 Engineering Annex
Ames, IA 50011
515-294-3420

STATE OF ILLINOIS
Small Business Assistance Bureau
100 West Randolph Street, Suite 3-400
Chicago, IL 60601
312-917-3263

KANSAS DEPARTMENT
 OF ECONOMIC DEVELOPMENT
Capitol Towers
400 West 8th Street, 5th Floor
Topeka, KS 66603-3957
913-296-3583

PRINCE GEORGE'S COUNTY GOV'T
County Administration Building
Room L-22
Upper Marlboro, MD 20772
301-952-4413

STATE OF MISSOURI/MBDO
Truman State Office Building
301 West High Street
P.O. Box 809
Jefferson City, MO 65102
314-751-2249

CITY OF JACKSON
Human & Cultural Services
201 South President Street
P.O. Box 17
Jackson, MS 39205          601-960-1594

CITY OF ATLANTIC CITY
City Hall, Room 706
Atlantic City, NJ 08401
609-347-6483

OKLAHOMA STATE MBDA
Oklahoma Department of Commerce
6601 Broadway Extension
Oklahoma City, OK 73116
405-521-2401

CITY OF HARRISBURG
10 North Market Square
Harrisburg, PA 17101
717-255-3027

MUNICIPALITY OF PONCE
City Hall Box 1709
Ponce, PR 00731
809-840-4141

MUNICIPALITY OF SAN JUAN
Call Box 857
Hato Rey, PR 00919
809-756-5080

MARYLAND MINORITY
  CONTRACTORS' ASSOCIATION, Inc.
540 North Milton Street, 2nd Floor
P.O. Box 1677
Baltimore, MD 21203
301-675-2149

UNITED STATES HISPANIC CHAMBER
  OF COMMERCE
Board of Trade Center
4900 Main, Suite 700
Kansas City, MO 64112
816-531-6363

ALBUQUERQUE HISPANO
  CHAMBER OF COMMERCE
1520 Central S.E.
Albuquerque, NM 87106
505-842-9003

NEDCO, INC.
701 East Bridger, Suite 701
Las Vegas, NV 89101
702-384-3293

BRONX VENTURE CORPORATION
2804 Third Avenue, 7th Floor
Bronx, NY 10454
212-665-7170

ASIAN PACIFIC & MBD
  ADVOCACY PROJECT
Chinatown Neighborhood Local
  Development Corporation
456 Broadway, 3rd Floor
New York, NY 10013
212-219-1661

NATIONAL MINORITY SUPPLIER
  DEVELOPMENT COUNCIL
1412 Broadway, 11th Floor
New York, NY 10018
212-944-2430

SPANISH MERCHANTS ASSOCIATION
  OF PHILADELPHIA, INC.
2825 North 5th Street
Philadelphia, PA 19133
215-739-2915

CHAMBER OF COMMERCE OF PONCE
Franchise Ownership Development Program
10 Salud Street, Suite 512
Ponce, PR 00731
809-844-4400

CHAMBER OF COMMERCE
  OF PUERTO RICO
100 Tetuan Street
San Juan, PR 00904
809-721-6060

CARIBBEAN MARKETING OVERSEAS
  CORP.
P.O. Box 6338, Loiza Street Station

Santurce, PR 00914
809-728-1240

TEXAS ASSOCIATION OF MEXICAN
   AMERICAN CHAMBERS OF
   COMMERCE
P.O. Box 3628
2211 South IH35, Suite 103
Austin, TX 78741
512-447-9821

SOUTH TEXAS PRIVATE INDUSTRY
   COUNCIL, INC.
P.O. Box 1757
4217 North Bartlett Avenue

Laredo, TX 78044-1757
512-722-3973

LOWER RIO GRANDE VALLEY
   CONFERENCE OF MAYORS
1401 West Polk Street
P.O. Box 744
Pharr, TX 78577
512-783-0711

UNIVERSITY OF TEXAS AT
   SAN ANTONIO CENTER
   FOR ECONOMIC DEVELOPMENT
University of Texas at San Antonio
San Antonio, TX 78285-0660
512-224-1945

# APPENDIX I

The enclosed company profile is ☐ a new listing or ☐ an updated listing.
## PROCUREMENT AUTOMATED SOURCE SYSTEM (PASS) — COMPANY PROFILE

**IDENTIFICATION** PASS is designed only for small businesses organized for profit and independently owned and operated.

COMPANY NAME _____

MAILING ADDRESS _____

CITY _____ STATE _____ ZIP _____

PHONE _____
Area Code        Number

EMPLOYER IDENTIFICATION NO. (if avail.) _____

DUNS NO. (if available) _____

TOTAL SALES LAST FISCAL YEAR _____

YEAR BUSINESS ESTABLISHED _____

NAME OF CONTACT _____

NUMBER OF EMPLOYEES _____

**BUSINESS TYPES:** PASS is divided into 4 types of businesses. Please estimate the percentage of your business allocated to the following (total must equal 100%) and complete the appropriate Section(s).

| **MANUFACTURING/SUPPLIES** | % | **CONSTRUCTION** | % |
|---|---|---|---|

CHECK APPLICABLE BOX(ES)

☐ Manufacturer   ☐ Dealer   ☐ Wholesale Distributor

MANUFACTURING FACILITY SIZE _____ SQ. FT.

MAXIMUM CURRENT BONDING LEVEL $_____ if avail.

MAXIMUM OPERATING RADIUS_____ Miles
Anywhere in U.S., Enter 3999 Above
Anywhere in the World, Enter 9999 Above

| **RESEARCH & DEVELOPMENT** | % | **SERVICES** | % |
|---|---|---|---|

No. of Engineers & Scientists _____

Expertise of key personnel _____

MAXIMUM CURRENT BONDING LEVEL $ _____ if avail.

MAXIMUM OPERATING RADIUS_____ Miles
Anywhere in U.S., Enter 3999 Above
Anywhere in the World, Enter 9999 Above

**CAPABILITIES (Limit 32 words; avoid abbreviations)**

List products, services, special capabilities, and important categories under which you want your business listed. The system searches businesses based on the capabilities you list in this section. _____

**CODES (if not available, leave blank)**

Standard Industrial Classification (SIC) Code(s):

Federal Supply Classification/Commodity/Product Service Code(s):

**DO YOU HAVE A FORMAL QUALITY ASSURANCE SYSTEM?**

YES ☐   NO ☐   INDICATE TYPE OR SOURCE OF
APPROVAL: _____

**EXPORTS (check one box ✓ )**

☐ ACTIVE EXPORTER
☐ INTERESTED IN EXPORTS
☐ NOT INTERESTED IN EXPORTS

**OWNERSHIP (check all applicable boxes) ✓**

Company is at least 51%
OWNED, CONTROLLED and
ACTIVELY MANAGED BY:

☐ VETERAN(S)
☐ CHECK IF ANY SERVICE WAS IN THE VIETNAM ERA (1964-1975)
☐ WOMAN/WOMEN
☐ MINORITY PERSON(S)

**IF MINORITY OWNER, check ✓**

☐ BLACK AMERICAN   ☐ HISPANIC AMERICAN
☐ NATIVE AMERICAN (includes American Indian, Eskimo, Aleut & Native Hawaiian)
☐ ASIAN/INDIAN AMERICAN (includes India, Pakistan, Bangladesh)
☐ ASIAN/PACIFIC AMERICAN (includes Asia, Indian Sub continent & Pacific Islands & Orientals)

**SIGNATURE Important! Signature is required!**

**CERTIFICATION** — I certify that information supplied herein (including all pages attached) is correct and that neither the applicant nor any person (or concern) in any connection with the applicant as a principal or officer, so far as is known, is now debarred or otherwise declared ineligible by any agency of the Federal Government from making offers for furnishing materials, supplies, or services to the Government or any agency thereof.

**Information Contained In This Profile May Be Disclosed At The Discretion Of The Small Business Administration.**

PLEASE SIGN HERE ➡
_____   _____   _____
Signature of Company Officer        Title        Date

502

**APPENDIX J**

STATE SMALL BUSINESS ASSISTANCE OFFICES

*Alabama*
Alabama Development Office
State Capitol
Montgomery, AL 36130
(205) 263-0048

Office of Minority Business Enterprise
135 South Union Street
Montgomery, AL 36130
(205) 263-0048

*Alaska*
Office of Enterprise
Department of Commerce and
   Economic Development
Post Office Box D
Juneau, AK 99811
(907) 465-2017

Department of Commerce and
   Economic Development
Office of Enterprise
3601 C Street, Suite 722
Anchorage, AK 99503
(907) 563-2165

Minority Business Development Center
1011 East Tudor Road, Suite 210
Anchorage, AK 99503
(907) 562-2322

*Arizona*
Arizona Department of Commerce
1700 West Washington Street
Phoenix, AZ 85007
(602) 255-5374

*Arkansas*
Minority Business Development
Arkansas Industrial Development
   Commission

Number One Capitol Mall
Little Rock, AR 72201
(501) 371-1060

Small Business Development Center
University of Arkansas-Little Rock
2801 South University
Library, Room 512
Little Rock, AR 72204
(501) 371-5381

*California*
Office of Small Business
Department of Commerce
1121 L Street, Suite 600
Sacramento, CA 95814
(916) 445-6545

Office of Small and Minority Business
Department of General Services
1808 14th Street, Room 100
Sacramento, CA 95814
(916) 322-5060

*Colorado*
Office of Regulatory Reform
1525 Sherman Street, Room 110
Denver, CO 80203
(303) 866-3933

Colorado Minority Business
   Development Agency
1525 Sherman Street, Room 701
Denver, CO 80203
(303) 866-2077

*Connecticut*
Office of Small Business Services
Connecticut Department of Economic
   Development
210 Washington Street

Hartford, CT 06106
(203) 566-4051

*Delaware*
Delaware Development Office
99 Kings Highway
P.O. Box 1401
Dover, DE 19903
(302) 736-4271

*District of Columbia*
Office of Business
  & Economic Development
1111 E Street, N.W., Suite 700
Washington, D.C. 20004
(202) 727-6600

Minority Business Opportunity
  Commission
2000 14th Street, N.W., Room 324
Washington, D.C. 20009
(202) 939-8780

*Florida*
Bureau of Business Assistance
Florida Department of Commerce
G-26 Collins Building
Tallahassee, FL 32301-8132
(904) 488-9357

Department of General Services
G-9 Bloxham Building
Tallahassee, FL 32301
(904) 487-0915

*Georgia*
State Office
Small Business Development Center
Chicopee Building
The University of Georgia
Athens, GA 30602
(404) 542-1721

Office of the Governor
State Capitol, Room 245
Atlanta, GA 30334     (404) 656-1794

*Hawaii*
Small Business Information Service
Department of Planning and Economic
  Development
P.O. Box 2359
Honolulu, HI 96804
(808) 548-7645 and (808) 548-4608

*Idaho*
Economic Development and Data
Department of Commerce
Statehouse, Room 108
Boise, ID 83720
(208) 334-4719

*Illinois*
Small Business Assistance Bureau
620 East Adams
Springfield, IL 62701
(217) 782-7500

Small Business Assistance Bureau
Department of Commerce
  and Community Affairs
100 West Randolph, Suite 3-400
Chicago, IL 60601
(312) 917-7179

*Indiana*
Indiana Department of Commerce
Office of Business Regulatory
  Ombudsman
One North Capitol Avenue, Suite 700
Indianapolis, IN 46204
(317) 232-8798

Minority and Women Business
  Development Division
Indiana Department of Commerce
One North Capitol Avenue, Suite 700
Indianapolis, IN 46204
(317) 232-8820

*Iowa*
Iowa Department of Economic
  Development

Bureau of Business Promotion
& Development
200 East Grand Avenue
Des Moines, IA 50309
(515) 281-8310 or 8324

*Kansas*
Small Business Office
Kansas Department of Commerce
400 West 8th, Suite 500
Topeka, KS 66603-3450
(913) 296-5298

Kansas Department of State Economic
Development
Office of Minority Business
400 West 8th Street, Suite 500
Topeka, KS 66603-39507
(913) 296-3583

*Kentucky*
Department of Economic Development
Small Business Division
Capital Plaza Tower, 22nd Floor
Frankfort, KY 40601
(502) 564-4252

Minority Business Division
Department of Economic Development
22nd Floor
Capital Plaza Tower
Frankfort, KY 40601
(502) 564-2064

*Louisana*
Office of Commerce and Industry
Louisiana Department of Commerce
P.O. Box 94185
Baton Rouge, LA 70804-9185
(504) 342-5366

Governor's Office for Minority
Business Enterprises
P.O. Box 94094
Baton Rouge, LA 70804-9095
(504) 342-6491

*Maine*
Business Assistance Division
State Development Office
State House Station 59
Augusta, ME 04333
(207) 289-5700

*Maryland*
Maryland Business Assistance Center
Department of Economic and
Community Development
45 Calvert Street
Annapolis, MD 21401
(301) 269-3514
Toll-free Hotline: 1-800 OK-GREEN

Office of Minority Affairs
1123 North Utah Street, Room 723
Baltimore, MD 21201
(301) 383-5555

*Massachusetts*
Small Business Assistance Division
Massachusetts Department of Commerce
100 Cambridge Street, 13th Floor
Boston, MA 02202
(617) 727-4005 or 727-6875

State Office of Minority Business
Assistance
Department of Commerce
100 Cambridge Street, 13th Floor
Boston, MA 02202
(617) 727-8692

*Michigan*
Local Development Services
Department of Commerce
P.O. Box 30225
Lansing, MI 48909
(517) 373-9642

*Minnesota*
Minnesota Small Business
Assistance Office
900 American Center Building

150 East Kellogg Boulevard
St. Paul, MN 55101
(612) 296-3871

*Mississippi*
Mississippi Small Business
  Clearinghouse
3825 Ridgewood Road
Jackson, MS 39211
Toll-free 1-(800) 521-7258

Mississippi Minority Supplier
  Development Council
510 George Street, Suite 232
Jackson, MS 39202
(601) 353-6865

*Missouri*
Missouri Department of
  Economic Development
Truman State Office Building
P.O. Box 1157
Jefferson City, MO 65102
(314) 751-4962

*Montana*
Business Assistance Division
Department of Commerce
1424 Ninth Avenue
Helena, MT 59620
(406) 444-3923

Minority Business Enterprise Office
Montana Department of Highways
Capitol Station
2701 Prospect Avenue
Helena, MT 59620
(406) 449-4723

*Nebraska*
Small Business Division
Nebraska Department of Economic
  Development
P.O. Box 94666
301 Centennial Mall South

Lincoln, NE 68509
(402) 471-3742

*Nevada*
Commission on Economic Development
Capitol Complex
Carson City, NV 89710
(702) 885-4325 or (800) 336-1600

*New Hampshire*
Office of Industrial Development
Department of Resources and
  Economic Development
P.O. Box 856
Concord, NH 03301
(603) 271-2591

*New Jersey*
Office of Small Business Assistance
Department of Commerce and
  Economic Development
One West State Street, CN 823
Trenton, NJ 08625
(609) 984-4442

Office of Minority Business Enterprise
New Jersey Department of Commerce
  and Economic Development
One West State Street
Trenton, NJ 08625
(609) 292-0500

*New Mexico*
Economic Development and
  Tourism Department
State of New Mexico
Joseph M. Montoya Building
1100 Sant Francis Drive
Santa Fe, NM 87503
(505) 827-0325

Minority Business Development
  Program
State Purchasing Division
General Services Department

1100 St. Francis Drive
Santa Fe, NM 87503
(505) 827-0425

*New York*
The Division for Small Business
New York State Department
  of Commerce
230 Park Avenue, Room 834
New York, NY 10169
(212) 309-0460

*North Carolina*
Small Business Development Division
North Carolina Department of Commerce
Dobbs Building, Room 2019
430 North Salisbury Street
Raleigh, NC 27611
(919) 733-7980

Minority Business Development Agency
430 North Salisbury Street
Raleigh, NC 27611
(919) 733-2712

*North Dakota*
North Dakota Economic Development
  Commission
Liberty Memorial Building
Bismarck, ND 58501
(701) 224-2810

*Ohio*
Small and Development Business
Ohio Department of Development
P.O. Box 1001
Columbus, OH 43266-0101
(614) 466-4945 or
(800) 282-1085 (in state)

Women's Business Resource Program
Ohio Department of Development
P.O. Box 1001
Columbus, OH 43266-0101
(614) 466-4945

*Oklahoma*
Small Business Center
Southwestern State University
100 Campus Drive
Weatherford, OK 73096
(405) 772-6611, Ext. 3050

Small Business Center
East Central State University
1036 East 10th
Ada, OK 74820
(406) 436-3190

Small Business Center
Northeastern State University
Tahlequah, OK 74464
(918) 456-5511, Ext. 3086

Small Business Center
Northwestern State University
Alva, OK 73717
(405) 327-1700, Ext. 318

Small Business Center
Southeastern State University
517 West University
Durant, OK 74701
(405) 924-0277

*Oregon*
Business Development Division
Economic Development Department
595 Cottage Street, N.E.
Salem, OR 97310
(503) 373-1225

Financial Services Division
Economic Development Department
595 Cottage Street, N.E.
Salem, OR 97310
(503) 378-6359

*Pennsylvania*
Office of Small Business
Pennsylvania Department of Commerce

435 Forum Building
Harrisburg, PA 17120
(717) 787-2565

Pennsylvania Minority Business
  Development Authority
Department of Commerce
486 Forum Building
Harrisburg, PA 17120
(717) 783-1127

*Puerto Rico*
Department of Commerce
P.O. Box 4275
San Juan, PR 00905
(809) 724-0542

*Rhode Island*
Small Business Development Division
Rhode Island Department of
  Economic Development
7 Jackson Walkway
Providence, RI 02903
(401) 277-2601

Minority Business Affairs
Department of Economic Development
7 Jackson Walkway
Providence, RI 02903
(401) 277-2601

*South Carolina*
Industry-Business
  & Community Services
South Carolina State Development
  Board
North Carolina National Bank
Post Office Box 927
Columbia, SC 29202
(803) 734-1400

Small and Minority Business Assistance
Edgar A. Brown Building
1205 Pendleton Street, Room 305
Columbia, SC 29201     (803) 734-0562

*South Dakota*
Department of State Development
711 Wells Avenue
Pierre, SD 57501
Toll-free (800) 843-800 (out of state)
        (800) 952-3625 (in state)

*Tennessee*
Small Business Office
Department of Economic and
  Community Development
7th Floor, Rachel Jackson Building
Nashville, TN 37219-5308
(615) 741-2626; (in state)
(800) 872-7201 (toll free)

Director of Minority Business
  Enterprise
7th Floor, Rachel Jackson Building
Nashville, TN 37219-5308

*Texas*
Small and Minority Business
  Development Division
Texas Economic Development
  Commission
P.O. Box 12728, Capitol Station
410 East Fifth Street
Austin, TX 78711
(512) 472-5059

Office of Small and Minority
  Business Advocacy
Texas Economic Development
  Commission
Box 12728 Capitol Station
Austin, TX 78711
(512) 472-5059

*Utah*
Division of Business
  and Economic Development
State Office Building
Salt Lake City, UT 84114
(801) 533-5325

*Vermont*
Economic Development Department
109 State Street
Montpelier, VT 05602
(802) 828-3221

*Virginia*
Virginia Department of Economic
  Development
Office of Small Business and Financial
  Services
1000 Washington Building
Richmond, VA 23219
(804) 786-3791

Office of Minority Business Enterprise
200–202 North Ninth Street, 11th Floor
Richmond, VA 23219
(804) 786-5560

*Virgin Islands*
Small Business Development Agency
P.O. Box 2058
St. Thomas, U.S. Virgin Islands 00801
(809) 774-8784

Minority Business Development Center
P.O. Box 878
St. Thomas, U.S. Virgin Islands 00801
(809) 774-7215

*Washington*
Department of Trade and Economic
  Development
101 General Administration Building,
  AX-13
Olympia, WA 98504
(206) 753-5634

Office of Minority and Women's
  Business Enterprise
406 South Water
Olympia, WA 98504-4611
(206) 753-9693

*West Virginia*
Small Business Development Center
  Division
Governor's Office of Community and
  Industrial Development
State Capitol
Charleston, WV 25305
(304) 348-2960
(800) 225-5982

*Wisconsin*
Small Business Ombudsman
Wisconsin Department of Development
123 West Washington Avenue
P.O. Box 7970
Madison, WI 53707
(608) 266-0562

Bureau of Minority Business
  Development
Wisconsin Department of Development
123 West Washington Avenue
P.O. Box 7970
Madison, WI 53707
(608) 266-8380

*Wyoming*
Small Business Development Center
944 East 2nd Street
Casper, NY 86201
(307) 235-4835

# APPENDIX K

## IRS Publications

Accounting Periods and Methods, Publication 538.
Business Expenses, Publication 535.
Basis of Assets, Publication 551.
Tax Information on Corporations, Publication 542.
Depreciation, Publication 534.
Employment Taxes, Publication 539.
Employer's Tax Guide (Circular E), Publication 15.
Your Federal Income Tax, Publication 17.
Tax Guide for Small Business, Publication 334.
Tax Calendars for 1983, Publication 509.
Investment Credit, Publication 572.
Net Operating Losses and the At-Risk Limits, Publication 536.
Tax Information on Partnerships, Publication 541.
Self-Employment Tax, Publication 533.

## APPENDIX L

### PROFESSIONAL ASSOCIATIONS REPRESENTING SMALL BUSINESSES

Active Corps of Executives
c/o Small Business Administration
1129 20th Street, N.W.
Suite 410
Washington, DC 20416
(202) 652-6279

American Association of Small
  Research Companies
1200 Lincoln
Suite 5
Prospect, PA 19076
(215) 522-1500

American Business Women's Association
P.O. Box 8728
9100 Ward Parkway
Kansas City, MO 64114
(816) 361-6621

American Federation of Small Business
407 S. Dearborn Street
Chicago, IL 60605
(312) 427-0207

Association for Small Business
  Advancement
7507 Standish Place
Rockville, MO 20855
(302) 770-6610

Center for Family Business
P.O. Box 24268
Cleveland, OH 44124
(216) 442-0800

Conference of American Small Business
  Organizations
407 S. Dearborn Street
Chicago, IL 60605
(312) 427-0207

Continental Association of Resolute
  Employers
511 C. Street, N.E.

Washington, DC 20002
(202) 546-4609

International Council for Small Business
3642 Lindell Blvd.
St. Louis University
St. Louis, MO 63108

International Entrepreneurs Association
2311 Pontius Avenue
Los Angeles, CA 90064
(213) 478-0437

National Alliance of Homebased
  Businesswomen
P.O. Box 306
Midland Park, NJ 07432
(201) 423-9131

National Association for the College
  Industry
P.O. Box 14460
Chicago, IL 60614
(312) 472-8116

National Association of Women
  Business Owners
600 S. Federal Street
Suite 400
Chicago, IL 60605
(312) 346-2330

National Association
  of the Self Employed
2324 Gravel Road
Ft. Worth, TX 76118
(817) 589-2475

National Business League
4324 George Avenue, N.W.
Washington, DC 20011
(202) 829-5900

National Family Business Council
60 Revere Drive          Suite 500

Northbrook, IL 60062
(312) 480-9080

National Federation of Independent
  Business
150 W. 20th Avenue
San Mateo, CA 94403
(415) 341-7441

National Small Business Association
1155 15th Street, N.W.
7th Floor
Washington, DC 20005
(202) 293-8830

Service Corps of Retired Executives
  Association
c/o Small Business Administration
1129 20 Street, N.W.
Suite 410
Washington, DC 20416
(202) 653-6279

Smaller Business Association
  of New England
Small Business United
69 Hickory Drive
Waltham, MA 02154
(617) 890-9070

Small Business Foundation of America
20 Park Plaza
Boston, MA 02116
(617) 350-5096

Small Business Legislative Council
1025 Vermont Avenue, N.W.
Suite 1201
Washington, DC 20006
(202) 293-8830

Support Service Alliance, Inc.
20 Old Turnpike Road
Nanuet, NY 10036
(914) 623-8665

United States Chamber of Commerce
1615 H. Street, N.W.
Washington, DC 20062
(202) 659-6000

Women Entrepreneurs
2030 Union Street
Suite 310
San Francisco, CA 94123
(415) 929-0129

Small Business Report
203 Calle del Oaks
Monterey, CA 93940

Venture Magazine
521 Fifth Avenue
New York, NY 10175

National Venture Capital Association
1655 N. Fort Myer Dr., Ste. 700
Arlington, VA 22209
(202) 528-4370

National Association of Small Business
  Investment Companies
1156 15th St., N.W., Ste. 1101
Washington, DC 20005
(202) 833-8230

American Association of Minority
  Enterprise Small Business
Investment Companies
915 15th St., N.W., Ste. 700
Washington, DC 20005
(202) 347-8600

National Commercial Finance
  Conference
225 W. 34th St.
New York, NY 10001
(212) 594-3490

## APPENDIX M

The Small Business Reporter
Department 3120
P.O. Box 37000
San Francisco, California

Apparel Stores
Auto Parts
Bars
Bicycle Stores
Book Stores
Building Maintenance Services
Independent Camera Stores
Proprietary Day Care Centers
Independent Drug Stores
Coin Operated Dry Cleaning Stores
Business Equipment Rental
Convenience Food Stores
The Handicraft Business
Health Food Stores

Home Furnishing Stores
Independent Liquor Stores
Mail Order Enterprises
Mobile Home and Recreation Dealers
Independent Pet Shops
Plant Shops
Small Job Printing Shops
Repair Services
Restaurants and Food Services
Service Stations
Sewing and Needlecraft Shops
Shoe Stores
Independent Sporting Goods
Toy and Hobby Craft Stores

## APPENDIX N

PUBLICATIONS EMPHASIZING SMALL BUSINESS TOPICS

Barter News
P.O. Box 3024
Mission Viejo, CA 92690

The Business Owner
383 South Broadway
Hicksville, NY 11801

Entrepreneur Magazine
2311 Pontius Avenue
Los Angeles, CA 90064

Entrepreneurial Manager's Newsletter
311 Main Street
Worcester, MA 01608

Inc. Magazine
38 Commercial Wharf
Boston, MA 02110

Journal of Applied Management
1700 Ygnacio Valley Road, Suite 222
Walnut Creek, CA 94598

Journal of Small Business Management
Bureau of Business Research
West Virginia University
Morgantown, West Virginia 26506

Managing, the Entrepreneur's Guide to Success
757 Third Avenue
New York, NY 10017

Small Business Report
497 Lighthouse Avenue
Monterey, CA 93940

Venture Magazine
35 W. 45th Street
New York, NY 10037


# APPENDIX O

## ASSOCIATIONS REPRESENTING VENTURE CAPITAL FIRMS

National Venture Capital Association
1225 19th Street, N.W. Suite 750
Washington, D.C. 20036
(202) 659-5756

Western Association of Venture Capitalists
3000 Sand Hill Road
Building 2, Suite 260
Menlo Park, California 94025
(415) 854-1322

New York Venture Capital Forum
c/o AMEV Capital Corporation
2 World Trade Center, Suite 9766
New York, New York 10048
(212) 755-1912

Connecticut Venture Group
P.O. Box 2451
Darien, Connecticut 06820
(203) 323-3143

APPENDIX P

New England Venture Capital Association
183 Essex Street
Boston, Massachusetts 02111
(617) 423-4355

Venture Capital Club of New Mexico
524 Camino del Monte Sol
Santa Fe, New Mexico 87501
(505) 983-1769

# APPENDIX P

ASSOCIATIONS REPRESENTING SMALL BUSINESS INVESTMENT COMPANIES

National Association of Small Business Investment Companies
618 Washington Building, N.W.
Washington, D.C. 20005
(202) 638-3411

American Association of Minority Enterprise Small Business Investment
Companies
915 15th Street, N.W.
Washington, D.C. 20005
(202) 347-8600

# APPENDIX Q

National Commercial Finance Conference
One Penn Plaza
New York, New York 10001
(212) 594-3490

American Association of Equipment Lessors
1700 North Moore Street
Suite 1930
Arlington, Virginia 22209

# APPENDIX R*

OUTLINE OF AN INVESTMENT AGREEMENT

What follows is a detailed outline of the contents of a venture investment agreement. The main sections of a typical agreement are briefly described and many of the terms that might appear in each section are noted. However, not all of the terms listed will appear in an investment agreement. Venture capital investors select terms from among those listed (and some not listed) to best serve their needs in a particular venture-investment situation.

## 1. Description of the Investment

This section of the agreement defines the basic terms of the investment. It includes descriptions of the:

a. Amount and type of investment.
b. Securities to be issued.
c. Guarantees, collateral subordination and payment schedules associated with any notes.
d. Conditions of closing: time, place, method of payment.

When investment instruments are involved that carry warrants, or debt conversion privileges, the agreement will completely describe them. This description will include the:

a. Time limits on the exercise of the warrant or conversion of the debt.
b. Price and any price changes that vary with the time of exercise.
c. Transferability of the instruments.
d. Registration rights on stock acquired by the investor.
e. Dilution resulting from exercise of warrants or debt conversion.
f. Rights and protections surviving after conversion, exercise, or redemption.

## 2. Preconditions to Closing

This section covers what the venture must do or what ancillary agreements and documents must be submitted to the investor before the investment can be closed. These agreements and documents may include:

a. Corporate documents; e.g., by-laws, articles of incorporation, resolutions authorizing sale of securities, tax status certificates, list of stockholders, and directors.
b. Audited financial statements

*Reprinted with the permission of Jeffry A. Timmons and Paul T. Babson, from their book entitled, *New Venture Creation* (pp. 599-602), published by Richard D. Irwin, Inc., Homewood, Illinois. © copyright 1977.

*c.* Any agreements for simulataneous additional financing from another source or for lines of credit.

*d.* Ancillary agreements; e.g., employment contracts, stock option agreements, key man insurance policies, stock repurchase agreements.

*e.* Copies of any leases or supply contracts.

## 3. Representations and Warranties by the Venture

This section contains legally binding statements made by the venture's officers that describe its condition on or before the closing date of the investment agreement. The venture's management will warrant:

*a.* That it is a duly organized corporation in good standing.

*b.* That its action in entering into an agreement is authorized by its directors, allowed by its by-laws and charter, legally binding upon the corporation and not in breach of any other agreements.

*c.* If a private placement, that the securities being issued are exempt from registration under the Securities Act of 1933 as amended, under state securities law, and that registration is not required under the Securities Exchange Act of 1934.

*d.* That the capitalization, shares, options, directors, and shareholders of the company are as described (either in the agreement or an exhibit).

*e.* That no trade secrets or patents will be used in the business that are not owned free and clear or if rights to use them have not been acquired.

*f.* That no conflicts of interest exist in their entering the agreement.

*g.* That all material facts and representations in the agreement and exhibits are true as of the date of closing (includes accuracy of business plan and financials).

*h.* That the venture will fulfill its part of the agreement so long as all conditions are met.

*i.* That any patents, trademarks, or copyrights owned and/or used by the company are as described.

*j.* That the principal assets and liabilities of the company are as described in attached exhibits.

*k.* That there are no undisclosed obligations, litigations or agreements of the venture of a material nature not already known to all parties.

*l.* That any prior year income statements and balance sheets are accurate as presented and have been audited. And that there have been no adverse changes since the last audited statements.

*m.* That the venture is current on all tax payments and returns.

## 4. Representations and Warranties by the Investor

This section contains any legally binding representations made by the investor. They are much smaller in number than those made by the company. The investor may warrant:

*a.* If a corporation, that it is duly organized and in good standing.

*b.* If a corporation, that its action in entering into an agreement with the venture is authorized by its directors, allowed by its by-laws and charter, legally binding upon the corporation, and not in breach of any existing agreements.

*c.* If a private placement, that the stock being acquired is for investment and not with a view to or for sale in connection with any distribution.

*d.* The performance of his or her part of the contract if all conditions are met.

## 5. Affirmative Covenants

In addition to the above representations and warranties, the company in which the investor invests usually has a list of affirmative covenants with which it must comply. These could include agreeing to:

*a.* Pay taxes, fees, duties, and other assessments promptly.

*b.* File all appropriate government or agency reports.

*c.* Pay debt principal and interest.

*d.* Maintain corporate existence.

*e.* Maintain appropriate books of accounts and keep a specified auditing firm on retainer.

*f.* Allow access to these records to all directors and representatives of the investor.

*g.* Provide the investor with periodic income statements and balance sheets.

*h.* Preserve and provide for the investor's stock registration rights as described in the agreement.

*i.* Maintain appropriate insurance, including key man life insurance with the company named as beneficiary.

*j.* Maintain minimum net worth, working capital, or net assets levels.

*k.* Maintain the number of investor board seats prescribed in the agreement.

*l.* Hold prescribed number of directors' meetings.

*m.* Comply with all applicable laws.

*n.* Maintain corporate properties in good condition.

*o.* Notify the investor of any events of default of the investment agreement within a prescribed period of time.

*p.* Use the investment proceeds substantially in accordance with a business plan that is an exhibit to the agreement.

## 6. Negative Covenants

These covenants define what a venture must not do, or must not do without prior investor approval; such approval not to be unreasonably withheld. A venture usually agrees not to do such things as:

*a.* Merge, consolidate with, acquire, or invest in any form of organization.

*b.* Amend or violate the venture's charter or by-laws.

*c.* Distribute, sell, redeem, or divide stock except as provided for in the agreement.

*d.* Sell, lease, or dispose of assets whose value exceeds a specified amount.

*e.* Purchase assets whose value exceeds specified amount.

*f.* Pay dividends.

*g.* Violate any working capital or net worth restrictions described in the investment agreement.

*h.* Advance to, loan to, or invest in individuals, organizations, or firms except as described in the investment agreement.

*i.* Create subsidiaries.

*j.* Liquidate the corporation.

*k.* Institute bankruptcy proceedings.

*l.* Pay compensation to its management other than as provided for in the agreement.

*m.* Change the basic nature of the business for which the firm was organized.

*n.* Borrow money except as provided for in the agreement.

*o.* Dilute the investors without giving them the right of first refusal on new issues of stock.

## 7. Conditions of Default

This section describes those events that constitute a breach of the investment agreement if not corrected within a specified time and under which an investor can exercise specific remedies. Events that constitute default may include:

*a.* Failure to comply with the affirmative or negative covenants of the agreement.

*b.* Falsification of representations and warranties made in the investment agreement.

*c.* Insolvency or reorganization of the venture.

*d.* Failure to pay interest or principal due on debentures.

## 8. Remedies

This section describes the actions available to an investor in the event a condition of default occurs. Remedies depend on the form an investment takes. For a common stock investment the remedies could be:

*a.* Forfeiture to the investor of any stock of the venture's principals that was held in escrow.

*b.* The investor receiving voting control through a right to vote some or all of the stock of the venture's principals.

*c.* the right of the investor to "put" his stock to the company at a predetermined price.

For a debenture, the remedies might be:

*a.* The full amount of the note becoming due and payable on demand.

*b.* Forfeiture of any collateral used to secure the debt.

In the case of a preferred stock investment, the remedy can be special voting rights (e.g., the right to vote the entrepreneurs' stock) to obtain control of the Board of Directors.

## 9. Other Conditions

A number of other clauses that cover a diverse group of issues often appear in investment agreements. Some of the more common issues covered are:

*a.* Who will bear the costs of closing the agreement; this is often borne by the company.
*b.* Who will bear the costs of registration of the investors' stock; again, the investors like this to be borne by the company for the first such registration.
*c.* Right of first refusal for the investor on subsequent company financings.

# APPENDIX S

Form Approved
OMB No. 3245-0016

U.S. Small Business Administration

## APPLICATION FOR BUSINESS LOAN

**I. Applicant**

| 30 | |
|---|---|

Trade Name of Borrower

| 32 | |
|---|---|

Street Address

| 34 | |
|---|---|

| City | County | State | Zip | Tel. No. (Inc. A/C) |
|---|---|---|---|---|
| 36 | | 37 | 39 | |

| Employers ID Number | Date of Application | Date Application Received by SBA | Number of Employees (including subsidiaries and affiliates) |
|---|---|---|---|
| 33 | | 5 | |

Type of Business | Date Business Established

☐ Existing Business — At Time of Application _____
☐ New Business
☐ Purchase Existing Business — If Loan is Approved _____

Bank of Business Account

**II. Management** (Proprietor, partners, officers, directors and stockholders owning 20% or more of outstanding stock)

| Name | Address | % Owned | Annual Comp. | Military Service | | *Race | *Sex |
|---|---|---|---|---|---|---|---|
| | | | | From | To | | |
| | | | $ | | | | |
| | | | $ | | | | |
| | | | $ | | | | |
| | | | $ | | | | |

*This data is collected for statistical purposes only. It has no bearing on the credit decision to approve or decline this application.

| III. Use of Proceeds: (Enter Gross Dollar Amounts Rounded to Nearest Hundreds) | Loan Requested | SBA USE ONLY Approved | | | | |
|---|---|---|---|---|---|---|
| ⑤ Land Acquisition | $ | | | ② | SBA Office Code | ① ① SBA Loan Number |
| ⑥ New Plant or Building Construction | | | | | | |
| ⑦ Building Expansion or Repair | | | | | | |

**IV. Summary of Collateral:**

If your collateral consists of (A) Land and Building, (D) Accounts Receivable and/or (E) Inventory, fill in the appropriate blanks. If you are pledging (B) Machinery and Equipment, (C) Furniture and Fixtures, and/or (F) Other, please provide an itemized list (labeled Exhibit A) that

| 12a | Payoff SBA Loan | | B. | Machinery & Equipment | | | |
| 12b | Payoff Bank Loan (Non SBA Associated) | | C. | Furniture & Fixtures | | | |
| 12c | Other Debt Payment (Non SBA Associated) | | D. | Accounts Receivable | | | |
| 13 | All Other | | E. | Inventory | | | |
| 14 | Total Loan Requested $ | | F. | Other | | | |
| | Term of Loan | | | Total Collateral $ | | $ | $ |

V. Previous Government Financing: If you or any principals or affiliates have ever requested Government Financing (including SBA), complete the following :

| Name of Agency | Amount | Date of Request | Approved or Declined | Balance | Status |
|---|---|---|---|---|---|
| | $ | | | $ | |
| | $ | | | $ | |
| | $ | | | $ | |

3) Previous SBA Financing (Check One)  ☐ (1) No  ☐ (2) Repaid/Other  ☐ (3) Present Borrower    4) Loan Number of 1st SBA Loan

VI. Indebtedness: Furnish the following information on all installment debts, contracts, notes, and mortgages payable. Indicate by an asterisk (*) items to be paid by loan proceeds and reason for paying same (present balance should agree with latest balance sheet submitted).

| To Whom Payable | Original Amount | Original Date | Present Balance | Rate of Interest | Maturity Date | Monthly Payment | Security | Current or Delinquent |
|---|---|---|---|---|---|---|---|---|
| | $ | | $ | | | $ | | |
| | $ | | $ | | | $ | | |
| | $ | | $ | | | $ | | |
| | $ | | $ | | | $ | | |

SBA Form 4 (11—82) REF SOP 50 10          PREVIOUS EDITIONS ARE OBSOLETE          (OVER)

All Exhibits must be signed and dated by person signing this form.

1. Submit SBA Form 912 (Personal History Statement) for each person e.g. owners, partners, directors, major stockholders, etc; the instructions are on SBA Form 912.

2. Furnish a signed current personal balance sheet (SBA Form 413 may be used for this purpose) for each stockholder (with 20% or greater ownership), partner, officer, and owner. Social Security number should be included on personal financial statement. Label this Exhibit B.

3. Include the statements listed below: 1, 2, 3 for the last three years; also 1, 2, 3, 4 dated within 90 days of filing the application; and statement 5, if applicable. This is Exhibit C (SBA has Management Aids that help in the preparation of financial statements.)

1. Balance Sheet      2. Profit and Loss Statement
3. Reconciliation of Net Worth
4. Aging of Accounts Receivable and Payable
5. Earnings projections for at least one year where financial statements for the last three years are unavailable or where requested by District Office.

(If Profit and Loss Statement is not available, explain why and substitute Federal Income Tax Forms.)

4. Provide a brief history of your company and a paragraph describing the expected benefits it will receive from the loan. Label it Exhibit D.

5. Provide a brief description of the educational, technical and business background for all the people listed in Section II under Management. Please mark it Exhibit E.

6. Do you have any co-signers and/or guarantors for this loan? If so, please submit their names, addresses and personal balance sheet(s) as Exhibit F.

7. Are you buying machinery or equipment with your loan money? If so, you must include a list of the equipment and the

## AGREEMENTS AND CERTIFICATIONS

Agreement of Nonemployment of SBA Personnel: I/We agree that if SBA approves this loan application I/We will not, for at least two years, hire as an employee or consultant anyone that was employed by the SBA during the one year period prior to the disbursement of the loan.

Certification: I/We certify:  (a) I/We have not paid anyone connected with the Federal Government for help in getting this loan. I/We also agree to report to the SBA Office of Security and Investigations, 1441 L Street N.W., Washington, D.C., 20416 any Federal Government employee who offers, in return for any type of compensation, to help get this loan approved.

(b) All information in this application and the Exhibits is true and complete to the best of my/our knowledge and is submitted to SBA so SBA can decide whether to grant a loan or participate with a lending institution in a loan to me/us. I/We agree to pay for or reimburse SBA for the cost of any surveys, title or mortgage examinations, appraisals etc., performed by non-SBA personnel provided I/We have given my/our consent.

(c) I/We give the assurance that we will comply with sections 112 and 113 of Title 13 of the Code of Federal Regulations. These Code sections prohibit discrimination on the grounds of race, color, sex, religion, marital status, handicap, age, or national origin by recipients of Federal financial assistance and require appropriate reports and access to books and records. These requirements are applicable to anyone who buys or takes control of the business. I/We realize that if I/We do not comply with these nondiscrimination requirements SBA can call, terminate, or accelerate repayment of my/our loan. As consideration for any Management and Technical Assistance that may be provided, I/We waive all claims against SBA and its consultants.

I/We understand that I/We need not pay anybody to deal with SBA. I/We have read and understand Form 394 which explains SBA policy on representatives and their fees.

For Guaranty Loans please provide an original and one copy

10. Do you or your spouse or any member of your household, or anyone who owns, manages, or directs your business or their spouses or members of their households work for the Small Business Administration, Small Business Advisory Council, SCORE or ACE, any Federal Agency, or the participating lender? If so, please provide the name and address of the person and the office where employed. Label this Exhibit J. If none, check here ☐

11. Does your business have any subsidiaries or affiliates? If yes, please provide their names and the relationship with your company along with a current balance sheet and operating statement for each. This should be Exhibit K.

12. Do you buy from, sell to, or use the services of any concern in which someone in your company has a significant financial interest? If yes, provide details on a separate sheet of paper labeled Exhibit L.

13. If your business is a franchise, include a copy of the franchise agreement and a copy of the FTC disclosure statement supplied to you by the Franchisor. Please include it as Exhibit M.

CONSTRUCTION LOANS ONLY

14. Include in a separate exhibit (Exhibit N) the estimated cost of the project and a statement of the source of any additional funds.

15. File all the necessary compliance documents (SBA Form-Series 601). The loan officer will advise which forms are necessary.

16. Provide copies of preliminary construction plans and specifications. Include them as Exhibit O. Final plans will be required prior to disbursement.

DIRECT LOANS ONLY

17. Include two bank declination letters with your application. These letters should include the name and telephone number of the persons contacted at the banks, the amount and terms of the loan, the reason for decline and whether or not the bank will participate with SBA. In cities with 200,000 people or less, one letter will be sufficient.

SBA Form 4 (11-82)

persons rendering assistance in preparation of this form. Check here if none: ☐

| Name and Occupation | Total Fees Paid |
| --- | --- |
| Address | Fees Due |
| Name and Occupation | Total Fees Paid |
| Address | Fees Due |

If you make a statement that you know to be false or if you over value a security in order to help obtain a loan under the provisions of the Small Business Act, you can be fined up to $5,000 or be put in jail for up to two years, or both.

_____
Signature of Preparer if Other Than Applicant

_____
Print or Type Name of Preparer

_____
Address of Preparer

If Applicant is a proprietor or general partner, sign below:

By: _____ Date _____

If Applicant is a corporation, sign below:

Corporate Seal

By: _____ Date _____
       Signature of President

Attested by: _____
       Signature of Corporate Secretary

U.S. GOVERNMENT PRINTING OFFICE : 1982   O—394-355

Return Executed Copies 1, 2, and 3 to SBA

**United States of America**

**SMALL BUSINESS ADMINISTRATION**

**STATEMENT OF PERSONAL HISTORY**

**Please Read Carefully - Print or Type**

Each member of the small business concern requesting assistance or the development company must submit this form in TRIPLICATE for filing with the SBA application. This form must be filled out and submitted:

1. If a sole proprietorship, by the proprietor;
2. If a partnership, by each partner;
3. If a corporation or a development company, by each officer, director, and additionally, by each holder of 20% or more of the voting stock;
4. Any other person, including a hired manager, who has authority to speak for and commit the borrower in the management of the business.

| Name and Address of Applicant (Firm Name)(Street, City, State and ZIP Code) | SBA District Office and City |
| --- | --- |
| | Amount Applied for: |

1. Personal Statement of: (State name in full, if no middle name, state (NMN), or if initial only, indicate initial). List all former names used, and dates each name was used. Use separate sheet if necessary.

First          Middle          Last

2. Date of Birth:   (Month, day and year)

3. Place of Birth: (City & State or Foreign Country)

U.S. Citizen? ☐ yes   ☐ no

If no, give alien registration number:
#

4. Give the percentage of ownership or stock owned or to be owned in the small business concern or the Development Company.

Social Security No.

5. Present residence address

From          To          Address          City          State

Home Telephone No. (Include A/C)          Business Telephone No. (Include A/C)

Immediate past residence address

From          To          Address

**BE SURE TO ANSWER THE NEXT 3 QUESTIONS CORRECTLY BECAUSE THEY ARE IMPORTANT.**

**THE FACT THAT YOU HAVE AN ARREST OR CONVICTION RECORD WILL NOT NECESSARILY DISQUALIFY YOU.**

7. Have you ever been charged with or arrested for any criminal offense other than a minor motor vehicle violation?

☐ Yes  ☐ No    If yes, furnish details in a separate exhibit. List name(s) under which charged, if applicable.

8. Have you ever been convicted of any criminal offense other than a minor motor vehicle violation?

☐ Yes  ☐ No    If yes, furnish details in a separate exhibit. List name(s) under which convicted, if applicable.

9. Name and address of participating bank

The information on this form will be used in connection with an investigation of your character. Any information you wish to submit, that you feel will expedite this investigation should be set forth.

Whoever makes any statement knowing it to be false, for the purpose of obtaining for himself or for any applicant, any loan, or loan extension by renewal, deferment or otherwise, or for the purpose of obtaining, or influencing SBA toward, anything of value under the Small Business Act, as amended, shall be punished under Section 16(a) of that Act, by a fine of not more than $5000, or by imprisonment for not more than 2 years, or both.

| Signature | Title | Date |
| --- | --- | --- |
|  |  |  |

It is against SBA's policy to provide assistance to persons not of good character and therefore consideration is given to the qualities and personality traits of a person, favorable and unfavorable, relating thereto, including behavior, integrity, candor and disposition toward criminal actions. It is also against SBA's policy to provide assistance not in the best interests of the United States, for example, if there is reason to believe that the effect of such assistance will be so encourage or support, directly or indirectly, activities inimical to the Security of the United States. Anyone concerned with the collection of this information, as to its voluntariness, disclosure or routine uses may contact the FOIA Office, 1441 "L" Street, N.W., and a copy of §9 "Agency Collection of Information" from SOP 40 04 will be provided.

SBA FORM 912 (1-81) SOP 50 10 1 EDITION OF 3-79 WILL BE USED UNTIL STOCK IS EXHAUSTED

Form Approved
OMB No. 3245–0017

## PERSONAL FINANCIAL STATEMENT

As of _____, 19 ___.

**Return to:**

Small Business Administration

**For SBA Use Only**

SBA Loan No. _____

Complete this form if 1) a sole proprietorship by the proprietor; 2) a partnership by each partner; 3) a corporation by each officer and each stockholder with 20% or more ownership; 4) any other person or entity providing a guaranty on the loan.

**Name and Address, Including ZIP Code** *(of person and spouse submitting Statement)*

This statement is submitted in connection with S.B.A. loan requested or granted to the individual or firm, whose name appears below:

**Name and Address of Applicant or Borrower, Including ZIP Code**

SOCIAL SECURITY NO. _____

Business *(of person submitting Statement)*

**Please answer all questions using "No" or "None" where necessary**

| ASSETS | | LIABILITIES | |
|---|---|---|---|
| Cash on Hand & In Banks . . . . . . . . . . . $ | | Accounts Payable . . . . . . . . . . . . . . . . . $ | |
| Savings Account in Banks . . . . . . . . . . . | | Notes Payable to Banks . . . . . . . . . . . . . | |
| U. S. Government Bonds . . . . . . . . . . . . | | *(Describe below - Section 2)* | |
| Accounts & Notes Receivable . . . . . . . . . | | Notes Payable to Others . . . . . . . . . . . . . | |
| Life Insurance-Cash Surrender Value Only . . | | *(Describe below - Section 2)* | |
| Other Stocks and Bonds . . . . . . . . . . . . | | Installment Account (Auto) . . . . . . . . . . . | |
| *(Describe - reverse side - Section 3)* | | Monthly Payments $ | |
| Real Estate . . . . . . . . . . . . . . . . . . . | | Installment Accounts (Other) . . . . . . . . . . | |
| *(Describe - reverse side - Section 4)* | | Monthly Payments $ | |
| Automobile - Present Value . . . . . . . . . . | | Loans on Life Insurance . . . . . . . . . . . . . | |
| Other Personal Property . . . . . . . . . . . . | | Mortgages on Real Estate . . . . . . . . . . . . | |
| *(Describe - reverse side - Section 5)* | | *(Describe - reverse side - Section 4)* | |
| Other Assets . . . . . . . . . . . . . . . . . . | | Unpaid Taxes . . . . . . . . . . . . . . . . . . . | |
| *(Describe - reverse side - Section 6)* | | *(Describe - reverse side - Section 7)* | |
| | | Other Liabilities . . . . . . . . . . . . . . . . . | |
| | | *(Describe - reverse side - Section 8)* | |
| | | Total Liabilities . . . . . . . . . . . . . . . . . | |
| | | Net Worth . . . . . . . . . . . . . . . . . . . . . | |

Salary . . . . . . . . . . . . . . . . . . . . . . . . $

Net Investment Income . . . . . . . . . . . . . . .

Real Estate Income . . . . . . . . . . . . . . . . . . . .

Other Income *(Describe)* . . . . . . . . . . . . . . .

As Endorser or Co-Maker . . . . . . . . . . . . . . . . $

Legal Claims and Judgments . . . . . . . . . . . .

Provision for Federal Income Tax . . . . . . . . .

Other Special Debt . . . . . . . . . . . . . . .

Description of items listed in Section I

*Not necessary to disclose alimony or child support payments in "Other Income" unless it is desired to have such payments counted toward total income.

Life Insurance Held *(Give face amount of policies - name of company and beneficiaries)*

## SUPPLEMENTARY SCHEDULES

### Section 2. Notes Payable to Banks and Others

| Name and Address of Holder of Note | Amount of Loan | | Terms of Repayments | Maturity of Loan | How Endorsed, Guaranteed, or Secured |
|---|---|---|---|---|---|
| | Original Bal. | Present Bal. | | | |
| | $ | $ | $ | | |
| | | | | | |
| | | | | | |
| | | | | | |

SBA FORM 413 (12-78)  REF: SOP 50 50      Edition of 8-67 May Be Used Until Stock Is Exhausted

**Section 3.  Other Stocks and Bonds:**  Give listed and unlisted Stocks and Bonds  *(Use separate sheet if necessary)*

| No. of Shares | Names of Securities | Cost | Market Value Statement Date | |
|---|---|---|---|---|
| | | | Quotation | Amount |
| | | | | |
| | | | | |
| | | | | |

**Section 4.  Real Estate Owned.**  *(List each parcel separately.  Use supplemental sheets if necessary.  Each sheet must be identified as a supplement to this statement and signed).  (Also advises whether property is covered by title insurance, abstract of title, or both).*

Title is in name of _____    Type of property _____

Address of property (City and State)

Original Cost to (me) (us) $ _____
Date Purchased _____
Present Market Value $ _____
Tax Assessment Value $ _____

Name and Address of Holder of Mortgage (City and State)

Date of Mortgage _____
Original Amount $ _____
Balance $ _____
Maturity _____
Terms of Payment _____

Status of Mortgage, i.e., current or delinquent.  If delinquent describe delinquencies

**Section 5.  Other Personal Property.**  *(Describe and if any is mortgaged, state name and address of mortgage holder and amount of mortgage. terms of payment and if delinquent, describe delinquency.)*

**Section 7. Unpaid Taxes.** *(Describe in detail, as to type, to whom payable, when due, amount, and what, if any, property a tax lien, if any, attaches)*

**Section 8. Other Liabilities.** *(Describe in detail)*

(I) or (We) certify the above and the statements contained in the schedules herein is a true and accurate statement of (my) or (our) financial condition as of the date stated herein. This statement is given for the purpose of: *(Check one of the following)*

☐ Inducing S.B.A. to grant a loan as requested in application, of the individual or firm whose name appears herein, in connection with which this statement is submitted.

☐ Furnishing a statement of (my) or (our) financial condition, pursuant to the terms of the guaranty executed by (me) or (us) at the time S.B.A. granted a loan to the individual or firm, whose name appears herein.

| Signature | | Date |
|---|---|---|
| Signature | | |

SBA FORM 413 (12-78) REF: SOP 50 50

Page 2

GPO : 1982 O—392—391

# INDEX